Power and Protest in American Life

Power and Protest in American Life

ALEC BARBROOK
Director, School of Continuing Education
University of Kent at Canterbury

CHRISTINE BOLT
Reader in American History
University of Kent at Canterbury

ST. MARTIN'S PRESS NEW YORK

St. Martin's Press, Inc., 175 Fifth Avenue, New York, NY 10010
Printed in the United States of America
First published in the United States of America in 1980

ISBN 0-312-63369-6

Library of Congress Cataloging in Publication Data

Barbrook, Alec.
Power and protest in American life.

Bibliography: p.
Includes index.
1. Radicalism—United States. 2 Social movements
—United States. 3. Power (Social sciences)
4. Ethnic groups. 5. Civil rights—United States.
I. Bolt, Christine, joint author. II. Title.
HN90.R3B34 303.4'84 80-17116
ISBN 0-312-63369-6

7/83

for Margaret
for Ian

Contents

Preface

Writing on American pressure groups is not so extensive that one needs to excuse a new text in this field. The amount of easily accessible material on the range of groups analysed in this book is small enough to justify both our coverage of the most prominent of them and our examination of the origins of the styles of pressure-politics that they represent.

Our objective has been to trace some of the newer or underrated trends in American pressure-group activity and their roots in American history. In the process we have tried to show that the findings of history and political science can be fed into one study to make it more effective than it would be if tackled from the standpoint of either discipline alone.

Since World War II, but especially during the last fifteen years, the variety of pressure groups operating on the American political scene has increased and the long-established domination of the major economic pressure groups has consequently been challenged. New groups have been particularly active on behalf of women and ethnic minorities and in the 'public interest' area, as defined by associations such as Common Cause and the Ralph Nader 'Network'. It is our contention that these developments are firmly rooted in American history, that they are a natural outcome of deep-seated social and political tendencies culminating in the last few decades. The organizational categories identified above are examined in the context of group theory, which has often been used by political scientists in the United States as apologia for the proliferation of pressure groups, and against the intellectual traditions and social structure that have shaped dissent in America from colonial times. Case-study material is combined with theoretical and narrative discussion, and each category is described in terms of its historical development and current practice. Thus, for example, such contemporary ethnic pressure groups as PUSH and AIM are looked at in the light of a preceding account of a whole range of nineteenth- and twentieth-century ethnic movements, while the more recent women's associations are related to the women's suffrage campaign and other feminist causes of the nineteenth and early twentieth centuries. A contrast is also drawn between the relative success of the groups studied here, with the exception of urban community organizations among the poor, and the relative failure of post-war radical movements, especially among students, which quickly abated after their brief period of prominence in the 1960s.

Despite some contemporary resurgence in the power of economic pressure groups in Washington and elsewhere, it is suggested that most of these newer or once neglected categories are likely to remain prominent in American politics for the foreseeable future. Whether or not our arguments about their significance and current contribution to the health of the American political system are valid will only be demonstrated with the passage of time, but that they will leave a definite mark seems undisputed. Some evaluation of their ideas and tactics, their problems and achievements, would therefore appear to be very timely.

Writing a book in tandem is no easy task and each of us must pay tribute to the patience of the other in preparing the final manuscript, as well as to the exertions of the secretarial staff of the University of Kent. Both of us have been greatly helped by grants which financed research and field work in the United States. The generosity of the Nuffield Foundation and the American Council of Learned Societies facilitated the investigation of the modern women's and public-interest groups, and much of the field work could not have been undertaken without the assistance of many Americans, including the representatives of the contemporary organizations reviewed in these pages. Their courtesy and patience in answering questions was considerable and we hope that they feel that we have done justice to their aspirations and to those of the associations for which they spoke. Work on Western American pressure groups, including the woman's suffrage organizations in California, and on Indian and other ethnic groups was undertaken with the help of a Fellowship and Huntington–Haynes Foundation grant from the Henry E. Huntington Library in San Marino, California, and of a British Academy–Newberry Library Fellowship for study in Chicago, and tribute must be made to the generosity of these bodies and the kind advice of their library and other expert staff. We are also most indebted to colleagues who have tendered advice and have read all or part of the manuscript; in particular, Dr Philip Haffenden, Professor Duane Lockard and Professor Maldwyn Jones. Ours is the responsibility, of course, for any errors or infelicities which may remain.

ALEC BARBROOK
CHRISTINE BOLT
University of Kent at Canterbury
March 1979

Abbreviated Titles of Pressure Groups

AAL	Afro-American League of the United States
AIM	American Indian Movement
ANB	Alaska Native Brotherhoods
BIA	Bureau of Indian Affairs
CC	Common Cause
CCNY	City Club of New York
CFA	Consumers Federation of America
CHWO	Clearing-House of Women's Organizations
CMAA	Council of Mexican American Affairs
CORE	Congress of Racial Equality
Critical Mass	Citizen's Movement for Safe and Efficient Energy
CSO	Community Service Organization
GGA	Good Government Association
IRA	Indian Rights Association
ISS	Intercollegiate Socialist Society
IWW	Industrial Workers of the World
JACL	Japanese American Citizen's League
LULAC	League of United American Citizens
LWV	League of Women Voters
Mohonk	Lake Mohonk Conference of Friends of the Indian
NAACP	National Association for the Advancement of Coloured People
NACW	National Association of Coloured Women
NAIA	National Association on Indian Affairs
NAWSA	National American Woman Suffrage Association
NWSA	National Woman Suffrage Association
NIYC	National Indian Youth Council
NNLU	National Negro Labour Union
NOW	National Organization for Women
NWP	National Woman's Party
NWPC	National Women's Political Caucus
PASSO	Texas Political Association of Spanish-Speaking Organizations
PEL	Political Equality League of California

PIRG	Public Interest Research Group
PL	Progressive Labour (a faction inside SDS)
PUSH	People United to Save Humanity
RYM	Revolutionary Movement (a faction inside SDS)
SAI	Society of American Indians
SCLC	Southern Christian Leadership Conference
SDS	Students for a Democratic Society
SLID	League for Industrial Democracy (student wing)
SNCC	Student Non-Violent Co-ordinating Committee
UNIA	Universal Negro Improvement Association
Urban League	National League on Urban Conditions Among Negroes
WEAL	Women's Equity Action League
WCTU	Woman's Christian Temperance Union
WNIA	Women's National Indian Association of Philadelphia
YIP	Youth International Party

Power and Protest in American Life

CHAPTER 1

A Nation of Groups

Whatever generalizations one can make about American society, surely one of the most valid is that patterns of change can be rapid without undermining its essential fabric. During the twentieth century, many basic characteristics of that society, for example the essentially centrist nature of party politics, have altered but little, yet some of the other features of American political and social life that were believed to be almost immutable have altered considerably in comparatively brief periods of time, the attitudes of American student bodies in the 1960s being a good case in point. Our argument in these pages will be that, in the comparatively narrow area of organized-group pressures on the American political system, certain patterns of change have been cumulative *and* rapid, such as the emergence of the concept of the 'public interest' in group activity. In other words, one can detect the beginnings of this development early in the century, and it is vital to acknowledge trends which have become much more noticeable in recent years, when an acceleration has increased their influence on American life.

It must be admitted at the outset that an examination of phenomena which appear to have become more important at a near-contemporary period contains one basic danger and that is the temptation to overrate a transitory trend. It may be that the importance of a certain style of American pressure-group activity is already waning and that it will soon be seen as short-lived, the traditional dominance of pressure-group activity by economic groups having reasserted itself. Clearly, a movement which has been encouraged by the relative affluence of American society in the 1960s is highly likely to have been affected by the downturn in economic activity that has taken place in the mid-seventies. Observers are already noticing this: 'Public-interest groups—supporting a range of causes from women's rights to better television programmes—have come upon hard times'.[1*] Although there has been little contraction of the pattern as yet, its development has certainly been brought to an abrupt halt. It will take some time to see whether the tendency for public-interest pressure groups to increase in importance in the American polity will fade away; it may only be a temporary check that we are witnessing at the present time. In particular, an upturn in economic activity, the end of the recent American recession, may well give a new fillip to those pressure groups whose main motivation does not depend on the economic interests of their members. If this happens, our study will assume an increased importance, and even if the powerful trilogy of American pressure-group life—business, labour, farm—resumes its stranglehold over the spectrum, we will still have noted an important phase in recent American history.

It may seem to curious to emphasize the importance of the group in American life when one thinks of the lip-service that is paid to the individualistic nature of the 'American dream', that concept of society in which the individual, by his own efforts, can move quickly from rags to riches (the ghost of Samuel Smiles and the dogma of self-help survive more clearly in the USA than in present-day Britain). Yet what is usually known as 'group theory' has been a consistent theme of the interpretation of the motivations of American society, especially as analysed by social scientists. If one goes back to the formative years of the Republic and that key set of newspaper articles now hallowed under the title of the '*Federalist* Papers', one finds early fears of the dangers of group excess, or 'faction' as it was termed. Hamilton, Jay and Madison were, at various times, the 'Publius' of the papers but it was Madison especially who produced what was perhaps the earliest critique of the darker side of the pressure group in Paper No. 10, one of the best-known of the set: 'By faction I understand a number of citizens, whether amounting to a majority of the whole, who

* Notes for each chapter are to be found at the back of the book.

are united and actuated by some common impulse of passion, or of interest, adverse to the rights of other citizens, or to the permanent and aggregate interests of the community.'[2] This is still an effective definition of the special-interest group and an implicit defence of the public interest—if that can be ascertained! Madison recognized that the 'nature of man' and the nature of society made faction, or the expression of interest, inevitable. Like many commentators since, he emphasized the power of economic interest in dividing society: 'A landed interest, a manufacturing interest, a mercantile interest, a moneyed interest, with many lesser interests, grow up of necessity in civilized nations, and divide them into different classes, actuated by different sentiments and views.'[3] A republic, governed by the wiser heads in society, was Madison's remedy for the evils of the special interest; perhaps it was an over-optimistic look ahead to the later years.

If one moves on half a century, to the major French observer of American life and American politics before the Civil War period, it is only to find that Tocqueville emphasizes the nineteenth-century American's special delight in combining with his fellow-men to propagate some cause or press a common viewpoint:

> Americans of all ages, all stations in life, and all types of disposition are for ever forming associations. There are not only commercial and industrial associations in which all take part, but others of a thousand different types—religious, moral, serious, futile, very general and very limited, immensely large and very minute. . . .[4]

On again to Bryce, another half-century later, and much the same comment is found:

> Associations are created, extended, and worked in the United States more quickly and effectively than in any other country. In nothing does the executive talent of the people better shine than in the promptitude wherewith the idea for a common object is taken up, in the instinctive discipline that makes every one who joins in starting it fall into his place, in the practical business-like turn which the discussions forthwith take.[5]

It is not surprising that commentators on the developing American political system find some dependence on the technique of collective action supplementing the creed of rugged individualism (and in our next chapter the evolution of this technique from colonial times will be traced). Even in those periods of American history and in those places in which individualism was supposed to be paramount it was often found necessary to band together to produce a desired action; the Westerner, product of the individualistic myth supreme, needed the support of a posse for rough justice or the townsfolk to build the schoolhouse! During the twentieth century the concept of the 'group' has become almost the equivalent of an American ideology, especially among a generation of American political scientists infected with what is usually described as the 'behaviouralist' approach. Early in the century a barely noticed text on government set up the group concept as the supreme interpretation of politics and suggested that its comprehension would bring instant understanding of the inner nature of the science:

> The great task in the study of any form of social life is the analysis of these groups. It is much more than classification, as that term is ordinarily used. When the groups are adequately stated, everything is stated. When I say everything I mean everything. The complete description will mean the complete science, in the study of social phenomena, as in any other field.[6]

Arthur Fisher Bentley, the author of the above quotation, may well have exaggerated a little, in that one would want to add other dimensions to a general model of the political system apart from the group; it is unreasonable to ignore the place of individuals, and even that of ideas, in the patterns of social and political life. Yet he did emphasize a most important aspect of modern society, the influence of group behaviour as a dynamic force in social change.

However, it was not until the 1950s that the pervasive nature of what was becoming known as 'group theory' became evident. It can be seen in the sort of democratic theory developed by Robert Dahl, who contrasted his view of American society (one which depended on an interpretation of American politics compounded of minorities, groups which provided a shifting series of coalitions able to support majority decisions) with those of interpreters of American society such as C. Wright Mills and Floyd Hunter, who detected the influence of a 'power elite' at every turn. Dahl's belief in the power of the electoral process to regulate this 'pluralistic' pattern by producing governing coalitions is often criticized but it does provide one of the most intriguing explanations of the decision-making process in the USA and those 'liberal democracies' that resemble it:

> Elections and political competition do not make for government by majorities in any very significant way, but they vastly increase the size, number and variety of minorities whose preference must be taken into account by leaders in making policy choices. I am inclined to think that it is in this characteristic of election—not minority rule but minorities rule—that we must look for some of the essential differences between dictatorships and democracies.[7]

Dahl's conceptualization is essentially a societal view of the United States, one which attempts to explain the balance of power inside the political system. A slightly different emphasis, although complementary to some extent, is provided by those theorists who regard actual pressure-group activity as the major motivating force in the system. David Truman (even earlier than Dahl) and Earl Latham are perhaps the most prominent pair of writers tending in this direction. They built quite deliberately on Bentley, with a certain degree of genuflection towards the work of Pendleton Herring and Peter Odegard; the latter's study of the Anti-Saloon League (published in 1928) and the former's study of Washington pressure groups (1929) were especially influential ingredients in the development of group theory and the definition of the place of pressure groups in the American political system.[8]

The basic argument put forward by writers such as Truman and Latham is that the American political system is peculiarly suited to influence by organized groups. Truman has summarized this view in the introduction to the second edition of his variant of the Bentley theme; the book was first published in 1951 and even its title—*The Governmental Process*—owes something to Bentley: 'It is no accident that interest or 'pressure' groups entered the literature of American political science long before reference was made to them in the analyses of the politics of other countries . . . the system of government in the United States makes such groups highly visible, even to the relatively casual observer.'[9] Truman's theory is that the political process is naturally carried on via groups, that any of these groups can generate an interest and that the most evident type of interest group is the kind usually described as 'associational'—that is, a group in which individuals band together because they perceive that they can further a common aim, one which they have selected relatively freely. It might be suggested that the most common type of interest group, that based on 'association' (the 'economic' pressure group as represented by trade unions and employers' groups, for example) embraces individuals who have little opportunity to choose membership of the group in question, but when one compares the associational with the non-associational group, in the way that Gabriel Almond has used the terms, it can be seen that there is an element of free choice in the entry to an associational group.[10] One is born, or at least socialized, into a non-associational interest group, family, ethnic bloc and the like, whereas the trade unionist or the employer can often transfer to another organization which will claim to represent his interest, or even into another economic field in which a new range of organizations represent associational interests. It will be argued that many workers are trapped to some degree within the associational group that represents their interests, especially where the closed shop operates and where it is not feasible to transfer to another occupation, but if the motivation is great enough, change is at least a possibility; no man can change his racial origin, however, nor do many want to transform, say, their religious faith, if it is deeply held. Even in 1951 Truman noted that, in the United States and other industrialized societies, the proliferation and diversification of interest groups was taking place:

> The causes of this growth lie in the increased complexity of techniques for dealing with the environment, in the specializations that these involve, and in associated disturbances of the manifold expectations that guide individual behaviour in a complex and interdependent society. Complexity of technique, broadly conceived is inseparable from complexity of social structure. This linkage we observe in industrialized societies the world over.[11]

Such a statement accords to some degree with the assertion made at the beginning of this chapter, but it does not necessarily follow that one would in turn support Truman when he maintains, as Bentley does—and even in rather similar phraseology—that the interest group is that feature of the political process around which the remaining pieces of the political system revolve.

Truman was not the only political scientist of note to base his image of the motivation of the political system firmly on the theory of the group. Earl Latham, for example, was as fervent an exponent of the 'group basis of politics' as was Truman and the article which the former published under that title in 1952 is still used as a definitive description of group theory and as support for 'the view that the group is the basic political form'.[12] Latham refers to the work carried out in a variety of disciplines which tried to defuse the 'mystique' of idealistic and legalistic approaches to human behaviour and builds a construct which pictures political outcomes as dependent on competing group pressures; there is even some acknowledgment of Galbraith's concept of 'countervailing power' as a parallel in the economic field. The individual as such gets short shrift; only where he can move large groups to action or to support of his actions is he regarded as important. As with Truman and Bentley, one can admire Latham's isolation of the profoundly important place that group motivation plays in the activation of the political system, without being quite convinced that all is explained when the group is explained! In addition, one would tend today to be sceptical about the degree to which countervailing power operates in the political arena. Sometimes it does but often it does not, a fact which is frequently illustrated by reference to the way in which a producer–consumer antithesis has been built up in modern industrial society without the countervailing or balancing pressure said to exist between capital and labour in the industrial world itself. This tends to push one on to the question (to be dealt with later) of whether there can be such a thing as a consumer—or possibly even 'public' interest in contemporary industrial society (see Chapter 7).

Not all political scientists who specialize in the study of pressure groups try to define the complete driving force of the political system in terms of these groups. Many writers on this topic are careful to balance the undoubted power of the pressure group in Western politics with the other forces that contribute to political decision-making and the general exercise of 'power'. Harmon Zeigler has cast a cooler eye on the power of pressure groups than some of his contemporaries have done: 'In the process whereby rewards are distributed, organized groups may, under certain conditions be major actors; but in other situations they may be no more than peripheral and ineffective participants.'[13] In other words, despite his obvious admiration for Bentley and Truman, Zeigler tends to present the pressure group as one—but not the sole—major actor in the political process. Zeigler reviews two criticisms of group theory, namely, the claim that it downgrades institutional and environmental factors to an absurd degree and the argument that its failure to account for a 'public interest' is contrary to the values of democratic society. This second plank is of special interest to our thesis and it is perhaps a pity that Zeigler shrugs it off with the remark that groups do defend the democratic ethos, for 'it is the position of the group theorists that opposing conceptions of the national welfare constitute the very heart of the political process'.[14] This seems rather like a throwback to the concept of countervailing power and does not entirely solve the problem of overweening power held by certain groups, despite both relatively small memberships and views about the political process which would fail to win majority acceptance if put to the test.

It is unlikely that many contemporary students of the political system would accept an interpretation which was based entirely on the interaction of groups for the motivated production of outcomes and although the pressure group, as a specific 'associational' type of group is almost invariably incorporated in any systemic interpretation of politics, dependence on it alone as the impetus of the system has been downgraded in recent years. The questioning of group theory has been especially associated with criticisms of purely 'transactional' theories of politics. As W. J. M. Mackenzie has put it: 'A weakness of the pressure group scheme of things was that it never shook off the notion that there is always a government, that government has a stock of goodies, and the people in general have no political role but to demand things from governments by threats and promises.'[15] Professor Mackenzie, attempting to sketch a more complex explanation of the political system seems to tend towards self-balancing models, despite the fact that it is much more tempting to drop these aspects and concentrate on the political system as an ongoing process. Over the years David Easton, Karl Deutsch and, in particular, Gabriel Almond have given flesh to the model of the political system as a continuous process, altering, adapting, facing and overcoming crisis, subject to pressures and feeling its way towards outcomes which, by the 'feedback' mechanism, will relieve the stress on the system.[16] Perhaps the most sophisticated attempt to consolidate this work in the last few years is the series of studies by Gabriel Almond and his colleagues which takes the political crisis, or 'systems development problem', as a focus for showing how choice and decision-making occur and recur at all critical times in the developmental process.[17] It is reasonable, they argue, to see the focus of the political process as the taking of significant decisions not often concerned with crisis, though these will be the most significant ones; crisis, stress, general damage to the system are in fact usually avoided through the regular pattern of decision-making that governments tend to adopt. In this process the pressure group strives to modify outcomes in a special way. Unlike political parties (admittedly, another type of 'group', if one does want to use the term in its wider sense), the pressure groups stand to one side in the final act of decision-making; as Duverger commented on pressure groups, 'they act to influence power while remaining apart from it'.[18]

All models of the political system are merely tools, designed to reduce complex patterns of human behaviour to discernible shapes and thus to make possible some understanding of reality. What has been suggested above is that pressure groups are best appreciated as part of a general dynamic model of the political system and best examined as major contributors to the ongoing sets of outcomes that are a feature of all modern political systems. In effect, pressure groups that persist over time as pressure groups (for there are many groups that exercise power over political outcomes only very occasionally) must be ranked to a considerable extent according to the degree to which they are effective in influencing decision-making in those areas that concern them. Much of the writing on pressure-group activity in the United States tries to do just this. The tendency is towards classification in the first place, followed by some assessment of the power of different types of pressure groups to affect outcomes. One can see this exemplified in the work of the late V. O. Key, one of the most highly respected of American political scientists who died in 1963. Several of Key's books became accepted as standard texts in their particular fields, a whole generation of undergraduate students in the United States must have derived their principal knowledge of American parties and pressure groups from his volume on these two vital inputs to the political system. Where Key was especially influential—though hardly innovative—was in his classification of American pressure groups, first as mainly economic—only a relatively small minority of the important ones were 'non-economic' in content—and, secondly, as associated with agrarianism, workers or business. He uses the *Federalist* Papers to support his view: 'The most common basis for group action is economic. As the authors of "The Federalist" long ago concluded, "the most common and durable source of faction has been the various and unequal distribution of property".'[19] Yet, Key accepted not only this strain in the *Federalist* Papers which we noted earlier but also accepted another, which admitted that 'when all else is lacking, "the most frivolous and fanciful distinctions" are sufficient to excite "the most violent conflicts"' (the internal quotations here are from the *Federalist*, No. 10).[20] When Key comes to deal with his residual category of 'other interest groups' he asserts that the only prerequisite for a group that intends to try to affect public policy is a shared attitude or set of attitudes among its members which will provide some reason for an interaction between the group and the policymakers. Key claims to draw on Truman for this rationale, though in fact he seems less inclined to the overall group interpretation of political life than Truman. He admits that his residual category is a 'miscellany'—and indeed it encompasses veterans' organizations, religious organizations and the professions, among others. In supporting the 'shared attitude' interpretation of pressure-group activity, Key particularly repudiates crude economic determinism as an interpretation of this pattern of political activity, and his emphasis on the predominance of economic motivation in the spectrum of pressure-group activity is obviously based on observation and research. For the time at which Key was writing, it was a reasonable assessment of the balance between economic and non-economic pressures brought by organized groups; we would argue, however, that the balance has shifted in the thirty years or so since Key's book first appeared, largely because of changes in the overall cultural pattern in this period.

Most writing on American pressure groups that is at all contemporaneous with that of Key follows a line similar to his, either explicitly or implicitly. Textbooks such as that by Harmon Zeigler and collections of papers and excerpts such as that by Mahood all tend to accentuate the farm/business/worker trilogy and, as we mentioned earlier, Zeigler seems to go along with the general repudiation of the concept of a public (or, as he terms it, a 'national') interest. The evidence of the last ten to fifteen years has begun to call these two contentions to account; there is some debate over whether pressure-group activity in the United States is absolutely dominated by economic power considerations and whether the public interest cannot be identified in itself. As early as 1958 Samuel Eldersveld listed a range of ways in which pressure groups were adapting to changes in American political life as a consequence of 'the growing complexity and fluidity of American society' and he suggests, for example, that: 'The trend towards social and economic equality has directed groups into setting goals concerned with the development of a "social politics", preoccupation with issues such as social equality and issues with a secondary economic importance.'[21]

Theodore Lowi, some twelve years later, while stressing that 'trade associations' (that is, economic groups) are a basic feature of the pressure group universe, admits that 'there are multitudes of non-economic groups' and suggests that both economic and non-economic groups are oligarchical because they 'are run by the few on behalf of the many'.[22] It is true that this latter contention is applicable to most interest groups and it is difficult to see how it could be otherwise in many instances.

The reason for joining pressure groups, notably those that profess 'causes', is based on an initial identification of interest with the group and a desire for the group to press this viewpoint in interventions in the public arena. In effect, the 'few' perform a service on behalf of the 'many' in return for the dues on which most pressure groups depend for their continuance. Yet, as we shall see, many of the newer pressure groups, especially those seeking to encompass a wide range of 'public' interests, do attempt to ascertain the views of their members on issues by canvassing them from time to time.

The modifications that one detects in the range of pressure groups active in the American political system stem from two main developments, namely, the decline in the domination of the pressure group universe by economic groups and the emergence of broadly based groups claiming to support what is termed the 'public interest'. Of course, it is often the case that those professing the 'public interest' tend to promote issues that are, to a great extent, economic. As noted earlier, it is sometimes argued that the division of the business and industrial world, as far as countervailing power between capital and labour is concerned, is now outdated and that a third force should be reckoned with—the consumer. Truman maintained that consumers will always fail to organize as effectively as producers, a contention that seems to be shared by a number of social scientists, including Anthony Downs, who has discerned that 'producers are much more likely to become influencers than consumers'.[23] The thread of the argument is that consumers are too widespread in their interests to influence any one area, whereas producers, with their livelihoods at stake, tend to focus very readily on the need to provide detailed information to government to defend specific interests and to bear the cost of this action. For all these objections, it is quite clear that organizations have appeared which claim to support the consumer as against the producer, or to protect the public against the actions of government or those with 'special interests'—that is, any group which seems to act against some agreed definition of the 'public interest', the actual definition of the public interest being the kernel of the problem here.

The newer and wider patterns of pressure-group activity that we are trying to delineate may tend to modify the older view of pressure groups as, at best, a necessary evil. This view was based on the assumption that pressure groups operating on legislatures and other centres of authoritative decision-making inevitably employed dubious practices, occasionally even outright bribery, in trying to bend decisions to their preferences. In Washington, despite the occasional well-publicized case, it is recognized that comparatively little outright bribery goes on. Lester Milbrath has argued this point, though he admits that a great deal of virtually purposeless entertaining is provided by lobbyists—purposeless because legislators are wined and dined quite liberally at government expense. Milbrath quotes one lobbyist: 'I have never met a member of Congress whom I felt I could bribe with any amount of money. I do know of a member I can get so drunk that he can't appear on the Hill the next day.'[24] However, it is often suggested that other parts of the American body politic are less incorruptible than Congress and indeed one of Mibrath's respondents suggested that state legislatures, for example, are a 'horse of another colour'.[25] A well-known study of (four) state legislatures and their attendant lobbyists did try to refute the belief that pressure groups were an insidious force in state politics and encouraged corruption. One of the four states was Massachusetts, where our research in the mid-1960s encouraged acceptance of the widely held view that corruption had played some part in state politics in the previous decade or so.[26] Nevertheless, Zeigler and Baer are emphatically of the opinion that 'it is highly probable that even in Massachusetts bribery and other forms of corruption are not characteristic of the entire population of legislators and lobbyists. Our data indicates less bribery in Massachusetts than the other states.'[27]

Such findings notwithstanding, it would be naïve to try to argue that pressure groups do not contribute to political corruption. The fact that this happens more frequently in state and local politics in the USA than in Washington is perhaps obvious to some extent; out of fifty state political systems, for instance, it is hardly surprising that a scandal touches one or two at any one time. A more systemic reason for their vulnerability is the closer proximity in time of many state polities to the 'machine age' of American politics. It was especially true that states with large populations of the 'newer immigrants' were forced to keep a 'private-regarding' or brokerage style of politics after it had been largely discarded elsewhere. Immigration patterns are not the only cause of the persistence of machine habits though, as can be seen by their retention in many Southern states where—among the whites—Anglo-Saxon stock often dominated. The explanation may lie in the access offered to groups within the local political system; where ethnic and working-class voters form the main clientele of the majority party, 'business and commercial elites' endeavour to break through to the point of decision-making by corrupt means and pressures will accordingly be accompanied by suggestions of bribery and other dubious practices.[28] These do occur in the United States but may be declining as part of the overall governmental morality, a process encouraged by greater public awareness, by education and by rising living standards. It may seem optimistic to predict an ongoing improvement in the ethics of government but it did seem in the mid-seventies, in the wake of the Watergate crisis, that public pressure would intensify the trend. The tendency of some of the newer pressure groups to attempt to cleave to the 'public interest', combining with this a trend towards greater ethical accountability in government, is likely to affect the pressure group universe to such an extent that the 'evil' aspects of group pressure will become muted and less evident.

If the pressure group universe is changing as distinctly as we are suggesting it has done in the last decade or so, why is this change occurring now? It is unlikely to be fortuitous and is probably linked with changes in the larger social structure of the country. One possible explanation can be found by looking at the model of an emerging society framed by writers such as Daniel Bell, who believe that the essential factor of this new society is that it can be considered 'post-industrial', although many subsidiary terms—such as the 'knowledge society'[29]—are also used to try to describe the world into which the United States and some other Western societies are now moving. Bell has defined the post-industrial society by specifying 'dimensions' to indicate the pattern of change which is typical of a society entering the post-industrial phase:

1. Economic sector: the change from a goods-producing to a service economy;
2. Occupational distribution: the pre-eminence of the professional and technical class;
3. Axial principle: the centrality of theoretical knowledge as the source of innovation and policy formulation for the society;

4. Future orientation: the control of technology and technological assessment;
5. Decision-making; the creation of a new 'intellectual technology'.[30]

As has been occasionally suggested, there is possibly something Utopian about the ideal type of post-industrial society as put forward by Bell, though it is an idea that has its followers even among European neo-Marxists such as Alain Touraine.[31] It is perhaps no more than a tendency as yet, one which may be more of a reality in the twenty-first rather than the twentieth century, but this tendency is obviously making some impact on American society already and therefore it is reasonable to note those changes in society that appear to take place in the advanced phase of industrialism. Technical innovation, the increasing numerical weight of an educated, professional middle class, an array of technological and educational institutions in which the dissemination of knowledge is pursued with intensity if not always with enthusiasm—these aspects of society are not new even in the United States but they are becoming increasingly important and, taken together, they may point the way towards an infrastructure which could demand new responses from and provide new supports for the political system. Bell sees the post-industrial society framing a new conception of the political system:

> The political ethos of an emerging post-industrial society is communal, insofar as social goals and priorities are defined by and national policy is directed to the realization of these goals. It is sociologizing rather than economic insofar as the criteria of individual utility and profit maximization become subordinated to broader conceptions of social welfare and community interest—particularly as the ancillary effects of ecological devastation multiply social costs and threaten the amenities of life.[32]

He admits that the 'communal ethos' required for the post-industrial society will only be developed with difficulty; yet in fact it is just this sort of ethos that many groups inside the United States are trying to press on the public consciousness, although it must go almost without saying that a new ethos takes time to develop and cannot be instilled merely by the agitation of a few.

However, the value of participatory movements seems to be evident to observers at many points along the political spectrum. Touraine who, as a French neo-Marxist, is several removes from Bell in ideological terms, also advocates a type of community power as a counterbalance in the political system, though there is little doubt that their respective views of how the community should operate would be rather different in practice! According to Touraine, 'The worker-consumer is more and more led to combat technocratic and statist pretensions by reinforcing community organizations, whether regional, local, or professional, because only by concrete social and cultural membership in them can the individual be defended.'[33] Of course, the fear of the individual and the community being metaphorically crushed by interests notable for their size and power is far from new and tends to stretch across the political spectrum from radical right to anarchist, bypassing the traditional, liberal centre of political power. With the increasing complexity of the technocratic and bureaucratic state, this fear cannot reasonably be said to have abated even if the liberal democratic state, for example, ostensibly restricts choice or harms the environment for the very best of reasons. In fact, the pressures in the liberal democracy for more egalitarianism and ever higher standards of living without any deterioration in the 'quality of life' can have their own (often unforeseen) consequences. A simple alternative, such as cheaper and more plentiful fuel on the one hand, or the preservation of scenic beauty in rural areas or on the coastline on the other, illustrates the essential dilemma and, not surprisingly, this dilemma has become important to certain pressure groups active in environmental issues.

One of the features of the 'post-industrial' model of society is the pre-eminence accorded to knowledge, in the form of education, research, technological expertise, acting as a catalyst bringing about the change from the older pattern of society to the new. It is among the highly literate, well-educated groups that tend to be in the vanguard of the American variant of post-industrialism that one finds the main support for the public-interest pressure groups, some of which will be reviewed in these pages. They tend to be, in Edward Banfield's phrase, 'public-regarding' rather than 'private-regarding'; in other words, the gains and losses involved in the exercise of power relate to values that transcend the actor's private circle rather than to those revolving around his own immediate wellbeing and that of his family and friends.[34] Although Banfield is a little cynical of the power exercised by civic associations and other 'public interest' lobbies emerging in the Chicago of the late fifties, he recognizes that there is an aspect of decision-making on which the influence of 'public values' is genuinely brought to bear. Against this, he is inclined to give primacy to 'market forces', and the 'mixed decision–choice' model favoured in the Chicago study seems to bear more than a passing resemblance to the pluralist model put forward by Dahl and others.

What is perhaps more relevant to the main point of this argument about post-industrial society, as far as we are concerned, is the conclusion reached a few years later by Banfield and his colleague James Q. Wilson that certain 'subcultures' are highly prone to employ public-regarding principles in that area of decision-making where actual voting for one candidate rather than another emphasizes that an overall choice in the public sector is being made.[35] Banfield and Wilson showed that public-regarding principles tended to go hand in hand with higher rather than lower income and with certain ethnic groupings—Anglo-Saxon, Jewish or black rather than, say, Polish or Irish. Apart from the black voter—a special case in some ways because of his lower economic status—the picture of the public-regarding voter is a consistent one, for he is on the whole the educated suburbanite, a type heavily worked over by American research in sociology and political science. Writers such as Robert Lane, Lester Milbrath and Robert Wood have picked out the correlation between education, suburban living and levels of political participation, a connection which, for example, emphasizes the importance of educational opportunity in the suburbs. In Wood's words: 'Since education is of such unparalleled importance in making money, in the achievement of success, and especially in the wellbeing of a democratic society, it is a "unique" function. If it is unique, it has priority above all other governmental responsibilities.'[36] Much of this kind of writing dates from the 1950s and early 1960s but, if anything, the suburban ethos seems subsequently to have intensified; only the party differential has had to be changed since those days to allow for the lowering of the Republican vote, following an increase in

Democratic and independent registration. It is tempting to overrate the effects of the expanding suburban dweller as an educated and highly discerning participant in political life. Many are anything but this and intolerance, snobbishness, class prejudice and similar faults are typical of much of suburban living. Nevertheless, it is the suburbs which have produced something of the lifestyle that may mark the beginnings of the post-industrial era. The suburbanites who are highly educated and conscious of the major issues of the day tend to be the backbone of many of the newer pressure groups concerned with issues such as the environment and governmental reform. As a study of one Pennsylvania township concludes: 'Radnor and other suburbs of this type exhibit a very strong commitment to the goals of popular democracy, both in theory and practice. Here you have the highest achievement of the fundamental idea of citizen participation.'[37]

This 'fundamental idea' brings one back almost full circle to the concept of collective action which some of the early commentators saw as typical of the political process in the United States. If the United States is a 'nation of groups', then it can be argued that the majority of them are encouraged to participate in the political process most of the time, although not all groups achieve equal opportunity to penetrate the decision-making centre of the process or do so to anything like the same degree. Dahl himself recognized this in his original outline of the pluralist thesis, making the question basically a test of the 'legitimacy' of the groups involved:

> By 'legitimate', I mean those whose activity is accepted as right and proper by a preponderant portion of the active. In the South, Negroes were not recently an active group. Evidently, Communists are not now a legitimate group. As compared with what one would expect from the normal system, Negroes were relatively defenceless in the past, just as the Communists are now.[38]

Black groups are now accepted as a legitimate avenue of pressure on the political system but even today self-professed communists would find it much more difficult to make their voices heard than most other political groups.

The fact that black groups constitute a vastly stronger political force than they did a generation or so ago may seem, on the face of it, a strange link with the emergence of post-industrial society, but it seems to be a fact that not only is black consciousness and determination to be heard a feature of contemporary American society but that ethnic consciousness of all types is also on the increase. Alongside the features that we have described as typical of the educated middle-class suburbanite, each group now seems more conscious of its racial origins than in that recent past when the accent was on the concept of the 'melting pot'.[39] It is a way for the white ethnic groups to counterbalance the growing homogenization of American society to some extent, although with groups such as the blacks, the Indians and the Chicanos the main motivation is obviously that of redressing the discrimination and relative lack of opportunity that they have suffered over decades (in some cases, centuries) of inferior status. A growing tolerance in American society and the necessity for minority groups to develop the newer skills required in a mature industrial society mean that class and ethnic divisions are less and less likely to run parallel, as they once did. Therefore, the expression of ethnic pride is a viable group feeling in contemporary America, one with deep historical roots and which will concern us vitally later in these pages.

It may be argued that the pressures from ethnic groups are neither especially altruistic nor particularly in the 'public interest'. It is true that such groups press for advantages that are confined in the main to their own interests but these are held (by them) to redress imbalances in the society that have existed for long periods and are therefore intended to bring about a more equitable society. Much the same argument could be used about the long maturing women's movements which culminated in the more vocal and radical voices heard over the last few years; an equal place for women may be an essential part of a just society. 'Public interest', in fact, is a term which, though difficult to define, is central to our argument. Glendon Schubert has argued that 'there is no public-interest theory worthy of the name' in his review of the many attempts that have been made to identify and define it.[40] However, it is difficult to see what other linking concept could be said to exist between the growing number of groups that further other interests than those of rigidly defined sections of the American people, whether framed in economic or even, in many cases, in non-economic terms. Bell and Kristol, in inaugurating the first issue of the journal which bears the title *The Public Interest*, admitted that 'as much mischief has been perpetrated upon the human race in the name of "the public interest" as in the name of anything else.'[41] But they defended its use on the ground that it did exist as a real force in society and that many organizations (they cited the American Political Science Association as an example!) exist mainly to further not selfish ends but interests which seem to benefit the mass of the public. In fact, the authors support a definition used by Walter Lippmann some years ago: 'The public interest may be presumed to be what men would choose if they saw clearly, thought rationally, acted disinterestedly and benevolently.'[42] The likelihood of the bulk of voters acting on Lippmann's dictum at any one time seems remote! For the purpose of this introduction, it might be preferable to sidestep the considerable debate that has gone on over the last few years about the nature of the 'public interest' and whether, for example, it can be distinguished from the majority interest at any one time.[43]

Our aim is to study, among other things, the nature of those organized groups in American political life that claim and have claimed to be motivated by concerns other than pure self-interest, economic or otherwise. The counterclaim made by these groups—consumer-oriented and 'good government' groups, for example—is that they exist to further some concept of the public good (although there will inevitably be a debate about the exact nature of that 'good'). For our needs, it should be sufficient to lay down a few guidelines to suggest why one believes that certain groups act in what it is conventional to term the 'public interest'. This concept would appear to be relevant when:

(i) the group applies pressure for the adoption of policies which are not of direct or exclusive benefit to its members;
(ii) the group belief is that the policies for which it presses are of general benefit to a universe which it conceives to be the public at large;
(iii) the policies concerned appear to be more in the public interest than 'what are taken to be the available alternatives'.[44]

As far as the 'public-interest' dimension of our thesis is concerned, it is evident that much of its significance lies in the intent and beliefs of the members of the groups purporting to act in this manner. Indeed, all of the groups that we are examining would claim to be acting in a manner which placed their actions on a higher plane than that of any crude model of economic self-interest. Whether this is true in every instance is a question that we shall have to consider but this pattern of intent is a linking device and a *raison d'être* for the preparation of this study. At a time when American life seems to be uncertain of its overall direction, or even whether the prevailing ethos is a liberal or a new conservative one, it appears useful to look at the 'participatory group' as a variable in the American political system and especially at the way in which what were relatively minor forms of the pressure group are now emerging as important factors in the formation of public policy in the United States.

CHAPTER 2

The Historical Background: Protest Movements and Intellectual Dissent from the Eighteenth to the Early Twentieth Century

If it is now plainly acknowledged that the 'American societal and political order is interest-based', this was by no means the case in the eighteenth century, when organized pressure groups exerted little influence, and when political leaders as well as political and economic doctrine emphasized the importance of the autonomous individual, exaggerating his power, playing down the effect of his social environment, and largely denying the existence of class conflict. Such groups clearly have a long history on both sides of the Atlantic, however, and the notion of bringing 'pressure from without' on the political system was firmly established by the time the expression 'pressure group' came into currency in the 1930s.

In assessing the factors which have contributed to the present power and diversity of such groups, and to their development from colonial times, some guiding definitions, objectives and difficulties have been borne in mind. Existing singly or in coalitions, pressure groups have commonly been divided into those which are based on interest, concerned to obtain or protect material—often economic—resources, and the cause crusades, their members united by shared attitudes and with an orientation towards more symbolic or intangible ends. To qualify for the title, in recent times, the group or groups have normally had to possess a distinctive ideology and a definite organization over a period of years, and have had to be involved in the pursuit of specified, though not necessarily unchanging, goals. To achieve these they have had to work, at least partly, for legislative change, by bringing pressure to bear on governments (but without directly promoting candidates for office).[1]

The presence in important past alliances of some but not all of these elements is, of course, apparent. Organization alone does not constitute a group interest, any more than lobbying or other forms of 'interest articulation', while many associations have existed without formal organization or programme, yet operating to an extent as pressure groups. This was particularly the case during the eighteenth century, before the development of modern political parties, when various sectional interests were active in politics within as well as outside the legislatures, acting as pressure groups on occasion but neither operating exclusively as such nor maintaining a consistent identity. With the rise of parties the need for many of these factions vanished. Charitable bodies working for the underprivileged and interest groups united by class, kinship, ethnic or religious ties might equally take on the guise of pressure groups intermittently, if legislation—or the lack of it—appeared to threaten their welfare, scope and efficiency. Obviously interests and organizations of this kind cannot be ignored in any study of the growth of modern pressure politics.

The quest for a single unifying theme running through the activities of the groups chosen, though attractive, has been avoided. Such missions tend to obliterate the sense of what is distinctive about the experience of succeeding generations, with a view to proving the deep roots of American radicalism, expansionism, or some other factor. Yet a number of questions have been asked about all the organizations under review, from which continuities have emerged. Certain problems have faced all embryonic pressure groups, no matter when they have appeared. It has, for example, proved consistently difficult to keep in touch with, and then control, the membership of an association, and to retain original objectives in the face of changing circumstances or hard experience.

Some social scientists have seen a clear distinction between pressure groups and social movements, the latter aiming at fundamental change in the social order through organized effort, the former comprising merely limited alliances—usually special interests—formed for the pursuit of a particular goal and seeking to create a favourable public opinion and to impose their demands on one or more of the political parties.[2] But in practice this distinction is difficult to maintain, not least because contemporaries have frequently perceived a graver threat in the operations of protest groups than have later commentators, who have been more influenced by the moderate impact of their objectives, once established.

The main purpose of the historical portion of the present study is to seek from the past some illumination of the debate over group theory; in the process it will try to trace the ideological and social framework in which certain important associations have developed, and specifically to analyse their motives, composition, techniques and ideas. It will also seek the components of their success as well as the ways in which this may be judged, acknowledging the organizational and other difficulties they have faced. Attention will be focused on the ethnic and so-called 'ideological' struggle groups, rather than on the economic alliances which have preoccupied social scientists (for reasons already explained), but notice will be taken throughout of the economic environment vitally shaping even the non-economic pressure groups. Since the primary objective will be to trace, assess, and account for the changing shape of protest activity, investigating along the way a large number of hitherto neglected or unrelated organizations, there will be no comparably detailed reference to the parties and other centres of political power with which these organizations must interact and to which they are often subordinated. Yet despite this focus, the groups studied are not in any sense credited with an independent power; they obviously possess no such thing in the American setting, a point which is particularly stressed with reference to many of the ethnic, youth and urban community associations among the poor.[3]

On the whole it may be said that the factors contributing to the success of any group are predictable and constant. The first asset is a membership drawn from high-ranking social or economic strata; and since political participation generally increases with both, then the chances are that working-class pressure groups—the trade unions being a notable and important exception—will not be numerous. Money, the adoption of goals in harmony with society's values, and acceptance by those in a position to make authoritative decisions, perhaps as a result of their personal involvement in the group, are also vital. Size may be, but is not automatically, a key factor. Associations with simple or even negative objectives, such as the repeal of a piece of legislation, would seem to have both the best chance of keeping their original purpose to the forefront and the best prospects of success, although groups like the Ku Klux Klan, whose anxieties can only be appeased by turning back the clock, may thrive indefinitely without complete success, finding some comfort simply in the association and activities of their members. It is, however, extremely difficult to determine the degree of credit due to any organization, once its demands have been taken up by the political parties or a branch of government.

The Colonial and Revolutionary Background to Pressure-Politics

In the early colonial period innumerable environmental factors inhibited the effective development of protest movements or pressure groups. Until the nineteenth century there were always more tasks and opportunities in the New World than settlers to grasp them. As a result immigration had to be deliberately augmented through the 'head-right' system (the colonies offered individuals land grants for each labourer brought over), the recruitment of indentured servants, and large importations of slaves. The newcomers encountered a great variety of Indian tribes, whose numbers have been estimated at 600,000–800,000 and who were especially concentrated along the coasts and waterways where Europeans first congregated. Persistent attempts were made to enslave the natives, from the time of the earliest Spanish explorations in the sixteenth century, but because of Indian resistance the solution to the labour needs of the white population lay elsewhere. Nonetheless, after the end of the seventeenth century, as a result of both a high birth rate and large-scale immigration, white numbers were increasing rapidly; in fact, approximately doubling every twenty-five years. In addition to the Negroes, and the English elements dominating New England and the South, the settlers included Scots, Scotch-Irish, Germans, French, Irish and Dutch. And if, by the 1780s, the French observer Crèvecoeur could suggest that in America 'the poor of Europe have by some means met together' and 'individuals of all nations are melted into a new [breed] of men',[4] the process of adjustment and amalgamation did not take place without tension, which was often increased by fears of Indian or Negro violence.

In this racial and ethnic variety, reinforcing the geographical differences between the colonies, lay the foundations of many future protest groups, yet their very number often militated against the formation of larger social movements and, as Crèvecoeur's comment makes plain, a commitment to the merging together of different ethnic groups had established itself at an early date, implying in particular the desirability of preserving a central Anglo-American culture. Indeed, faith in the ultimate Americanization of the newcomers was essential in keeping the antipathies of established citizens in check, however misplaced such faith might have been, and in subordinating local group allegiances to patriotic loyalty, a hard task until after the Civil War.

The attention of most early Americans, from whatever background, was in fact focused on all the engrossing tasks of settling a new country; few men enjoyed the leisure for politics or philanthropy and the majority were obliged to adapt themselves to a wide variety of tasks, simply to survive. The size alone of their terrain made concerted activity difficult before the establishment of effective means of communication. Colonial governments during the seventeenth century provided for the laying out of roads, but their laws were largely honoured in the breach, and travellers overland made slow progress by horse or on foot. Real improvements did not come until the next century, with the introduction of freight-wagon and stagecoach passenger services, as well as an imperial postal system. Although the dirt and plank roads frequently became impassable, by 1770 the main coastal towns were connected by decent highways, as were communities up to forty or fifty miles inland. River traffic was similarly slow before the development of steam in the nineteenth century, and the vast number of keelboats which plied American waters were at the mercy of winds, currents and all manner of natural hazards. The nationwide campaigns undertaken by later reformers were consequently a physical impossibility, though conditions did not deter the more limited activities of itinerant Protestant revivalists in back-country regions.

Rudimentary educational facilities, widespread land ownership, and the limited role of governments in men's lives also militated against the formation of enduring pressure groups. In the early years education was primarily a family responsibility outside New England, and illiteracy, though less common than in England, was still high. If a lower class of slaves, servants, apprentices, labourers, tenant farmers and seamen developed in the colonies, no large landless proletariat existed until the nineteenth century; only about 20 per cent of white men did not own land in the Revolutionary period, with the result that the franchise was widely enjoyed. Other New World resources were equally abundant, and American wages exceeded those of Europe. Consequently, the economic motives which are generally thought to be the most common basis for group action were comparatively muted in the New World until the nineteenth century.[5] Even the complaints about English fiscal and political measures after the Seven Years War chiefly demonstrate the lax enforcement of mercantilist restrictions before the 1760s and the resentment of any attempts to delay progress towards colonial self-government, already well advanced. By 1763 all the colonies had elective assemblies, which raised taxes, made appropriations, initiated legislation and were turning increasingly to charter provisions, local precedents and the traditional rights of Englishmen to justify and enlarge their powers. But just as successive English administrations struggled to extract revenue from their American subjects, so the colonial legislatures and governors found it difficult to secure enough money for defence, to settle differences with neighbours, to regulate settlement or to keep the peace. Taxes were hard to gather, though light by English standards.

All this is not, of course, to deny the existence in America of pronounced, if sometimes inchoate, class and sectional conflict of a kind which would later manifest itself in modern pressure politics. Indeed, the very environmental factors sketched above, while making group organization difficult, positively encouraged competing local factions, and freedom of speech and the press gave their grievances essential publicity. Thus rich resources, a heterogeneous population (particularly in the middle colonies), geographical diversity and inadequate government fostered both a high degree of economic development in the colonial period and the emergence of opposing economic 'interests'—a term also common in England by the eighteenth century. Merchants and planters were often at odds with farmers and workers, landowners with proprietors, and the inhabitants of the eastern seaboard with those of the interior. Yet although the powerful economic interests profoundly influenced colonial politics, of the economic protest groups which had appeared by the time of the Revolution, most were alliances of the 'underprivileged'; none had an organization worthy of the name; and their members tended to become rebels or rioters rather than campaigners. For as New York scholar and later governor, Cadwallader Colden, wrote in 1734, great changes in society were effected by the rich and powerful; 'any other commotions generally produced only some short lived disorders and confusions'.[6] Nonetheless, they did make an impact on politics and class attitudes, if only in terms of reinforcing prevailing prejudices or intensifying the debate about the kind of society that should be growing in America.

Discontented interior farmers in Virginia, for example, who resorted to force during the 1670s in an unsuccessful attempt to extract concessions from the aristocracy regarding local government, taxation and debtor relief, at least obtained protection for the frontier settlements against Indian attack and the dismissal of an obnoxious governor, although the colony's social structure remained unaltered. There were a number of other late seventeenth-century rebellions against colonial government—in Massachusetts, Maryland and, most notably, New York—where aspiring religious and economic interests were pitted against entrenched local elites. In New York city, however, and in other middle colonies, ethnic considerations were also of crucial importance, and Jacob Leisler represented, as Thomas Archdeacon reminds us, the old Dutch elite displaced by 'the new English order'. This elite was able to appeal to and sustain a considerable popular following among the Dutch settlers, thereby helping in a singular fashion to establish a political tradition in which 'voting became an expression of choice rather than a ratification of authority.'[7] Over seventy years after Leisler's defeat, back-country dissidents in North Carolina, agitating against high lawyers' fees, corrupt officials, excessive taxes and high prices for land, and for more representative government, courts and clergy, formed an association of Regulators which sought satisfaction through the assembly and courts. They eventually resorted to direct action when these efforts failed, intimidating enemies and freeing their imprisoned leaders from gaol.

In the end, like the Virginia farmers, the Regulators became ineffective rebels, though their activities may have paved the way for the adoption of a 'democratic' constitution once Independence was secured, despite the Loyalist sympathies of many of their number. (Since they were not adversely affected by British economic policies and since the planter-merchant aristocracy was mainly in the patriot camp, such sympathies are not surprising.) The forceful tactics of the Regulators nevertheless lost them support even among radical elements in the colony, notwithstanding the fact that the radical press elsewhere was inclined to present them as martyrs who had vainly struggled for legal redress.[8] In Pennsylvania, New York and Massachusetts comparable protests were expressed during the later part of the eighteenth century. But while there was some accommodation of the discontented in the first Pennsylvania state constitution, generally the problems of debtors, the differences between inland and coastal regions and the reluctance of established groups to yield their power continued to plague American politics after 1783, eventually strengthening conservative anxiety to set up a strong national government.

The determined articulation of grievances and the use of

violence in the last resort were obviously encouraged by the events of the Revolution. If, as Pauline Maier points out, Revolutionary leaders urged resistance to illegitimate government though opposing indiscriminate rioting—liberty without licence—the colonists had a long tradition of debate and participation in public affairs, within and outside the assemblies. The Sons of Liberty, extra-legal bodies in the movement for American independence which sprang up during the Stamp Act crisis, frequently grew out of existing social, civic or religious organizations. The same personnel were often subsequently involved in non-importation associations. Both groups aimed to build a wide base of support, circulated petitions, intimidated British officials and opponents, promoted a network of correspondence between radical colonists as well as social activities and rallies, and publicized their efforts and those of foreign radicals, with a view to persuading the British government to revoke unacceptable legislation, particularly the Stamp Act and the Townshend Duties.[9]

Although the boycott of British goods collapsed in 1770, the initial success of these activities, a new spate of unwise laws and the failure of British sympathizers to intervene or fully to grasp American fears resulted in fresh colonial attempts at economic coercion of the mother country. Yet now the movement won still wider support and was taken up by the Continental Congress. In other words, the aims of the Revolutionary pressure groups, ultimately opposed by statesmen in Britain, were accepted by many colonists, and while contributing to the rejection of British ties and authority, they also helped to broaden the political debate and to prepare the ground for important political changes within the colonies. Naturally, the influence of the Sons of Liberty and non-importation organizations was not uniform but depended in any area, as A. G. Olson has shown, on the size of the urban working class, the extent of the franchise and the strength of the local oligarchy. Equally important was the standing of the governor, the persuasiveness of the opposition leaders and their relations with the mass of assemblymen, the threat they posed to the assembly itself, and the strategic advantages to be gained for particular factions from opposition to legislation by king and Parliament. They were, moreover, greatly assisted by the absence of effective British pressures on the assemblies: local Tory parties were not assisted during the crisis, any more than colonial merchants' associations or royal officials.[10] And by the 1770s, as a result of the competition of new social and economic elites in the colonies, religious toleration had been strengthened and ancient legal privileges and land laws undermined, together with respect for traditional political institutions.

The religious impetus to change and reform before the Revolution was as influential as the political and economic pressures. By the early eighteenth century the diversity of immigration had created a multiplicity of sects, especially in the middle colonies. Comparative freedom of conscience accounts for the absence of a Dissenting interest on the English model, but objections grew to religious tests for office and to the paying of taxes which supported the established Churches—Congregational or Anglican—notably in democratic frontier regions where such Churches were not to be found. Reinforcing these pressures was a cyclical revivalist tradition, arising from the struggle among religious groups to preserve both religious liberty and purity in the face of bigotry, scepticism or apathy. The Great Awakening of the 1730s and 1740s had particularly important social ramifications in the encouragement it gave to religious and intellectual freedom and educational improvement. Although by placing a fresh emphasis upon personal grace and inner religion the Awakening reaffirmed the Puritan belief in man's total depravity and dependence on God, its exponents also adopted a fundamentally optimistic approach to the problems of man and his destiny in America. This approach would be reflected in the outlook of later revivalist preachers who were more directly involved in social reform. In the meantime the Awakening may have increased (the still slight) religious indictments of slavery, and inspired missionary work among the Indians as well as humanitarian endeavours among whites. Under its impact habits of deference in religious matters were eroded, while the denominations supported by the lower class—the Methodists and the Baptists—were strengthened, as was the representation of this class in the two Calvinist sects, the Presbyterians and the Congregationalists.

If the social significance of the Revolution has sometimes been exaggerated and the extent of earlier social and political changes underestimated, its impact on religious practice was considerable and progressive. Accordingly, the Anglican Church was disestablished, and a number of states conferred religious freedom and equal rights on all Christians, albeit the Congregationalists retained certain of their privileges in New England and many Jews and Catholics continued to suffer disabilities. But the conflict with Britain clearly involved more than just a discussion of the scope of metropolitan jurisdiction in the colonies. Revolutionary writers, whose views were disseminated through pamphlets and newspapers that circulated widely, increasingly concerned themselves with a broader evaluation of the nature of government and the liberties and destiny of colonial society, even though, as Staughton Lynd has pointed out, the statesmen of the Revolution failed to resolve the conflict posed by moderate and radical theorists of the eighteenth century between the inalienable rights of conscience and the more respectable rights of property.[11] 'America', wrote John Adams, 'was designed by Providence for the theatre on which man was to make his true figure, on which science, virtue, liberty, happiness, and glory were to exist in peace.'[12] Denunciations of political 'slavery' made many reflective Americans demand not only religious freedom but also the emancipation of Negro slaves. Service by blacks in the Revolutionary war strengthened the more theoretical (often religious) appeals for equality, and the North's economic commitment to slavery did not seem irrevocable. From the 1780s judicial and constitutional action against the institution was taken by the Northern and Middle states, and legislation to end the slave trade passed by all except South Carolina and Georgia. The Constitution drafted in 1787 restricted Congressional power to interfere with the trade for twenty years, but it was then outlawed by the second Jefferson administration. Reformers were optimistic. Unfortunately, slavery received a fillip from the expansion of the cotton plantation and of demand for its product, while the early anti-slavery societies were moderate and usually opposed to working with black abolitionists. In addition, a few individuals—primarily Quakers—crusaded for prison and penal reform, better treatment for the insane, and for peace and temperance. The colonial landed aristocracy was ostensibly undermined by the expropriation of proprietary and loyalist estates and the abolition of quitrents, entails and primogeniture, though such devices were no longer widespread on the eve of the Revolution. However, much of the confiscated land went to wealthy speculators and extensive patriot holdings remained intact.

Although conservative forces were by no means routed or their opponents united, the former colonies managed to fashion new constitutions and to agree to the first federal Constitution. At the state level there was concern to protect those 'rights of men' so fiercely defended in the debate with Britain—to uphold at least the basic assertion that governments derived their authority from the people and should be responsive to popular will. Specifically, this involved limiting the powers of the executive and enlarging those of the legislature, without destroying the separation of powers, as urged by radical elements. It required the enactment of bills of rights guaranteeing, among other things, the freedom of speech, press and conscience which were widely exercised. Provision was made for frequent elections, ease of constitutional amendment, and sometimes for a reduction of office-holding and suffrage restrictions, as well as for the reapportioning of legislative seats. Yet the claims of the rich and well born to dominate office were not exploded; though no single leadership class existed, the value of the wide franchise was accordingly reduced. Equal representation of all districts in proportion to population and the sovereignty of the popular house of the legislature were not established. Local government continued to enjoy only limited autonomy, and the social responsibilities of state governments—for instance, in the fields of education and penal reform—were not enlarged as some radicals would have wished. The firm belief persisted in many quarters that factions which formed to express peaceful resistance to established authority—however crucial to the colonial victory—were seditious: the people were expected to respect their new government as once they had obeyed the Crown. Finally, if the Articles of Confederation, ratified in 1781, represented a victory for those who wished to keep government as limited and as localized as possible, by 1789 the Articles had been replaced by a federal Constitution which was a triumph for nationalist forces. Ironically, however, in providing a balanced government strong enough to protect liberty and property at home and abroad, despite parochial pressures, the Founding Fathers also brought representatives of diverse interests together under one jurisdiction, thereby both intensifying awareness of group differences and local loyalties, and increasing the need for the political parties which were still so much mistrusted.[13]

The successful Revolution not only furthered long-maturing changes in colonial society; it also confirmed the old Puritan conviction that Americans were a chosen people with a unique destiny, and strengthened the egalitarian aspects of the colonial system of values: the belief in civic responsibility, experimentalism, individual opportunity and achievement. But as we have seen, men of conservative temper had been defeated ideologically, rather than physically destroyed, and the Revolution failed to meet the aspirations of the politically radical or materially distressed. Political considerations and the tensions produced by the war scare of 1798 led to the temporary persecution of 'subversive' elements in the population under the Alien and Sedition Acts (passed in 1798 and repealed or allowed to expire between 1800 and 1802). And even with the defeat of the conservative Federalist party in the national elections of 1800, 'the people', the body from whom government derived authority, was not subsequently an all-inclusive term; for Jeffersonians it meant mainly farmers and planters and for the Jacksonian Democrats, planters, farmers, mechanics and labourers. The lot of slaves freed by Northern decree or Southern masters in their wills was bondage without chains; the position of women and indentured servants remained unchanged, while urban working men continued to be regarded with distaste and their problems ignored by most of the leading politicians of the early republican period, notwithstanding the promotion by state and local governments of a host of economic ventures. The poor, who protested violently against British revenue measures, impressment and troops during the Revolution, continued their protests after it was over, their efforts possessing both ideological content and political purpose, though supplemented and overshadowed by the activities of middle-class reformers.[14]

In seeking to bring society more closely into line with the ideals expressed in the Declaration of Independence or with some other view of a perfectible society, pressure groups in the young republic had to overcome the suspicion that they were merely demanding, in undemocratic fashion, special privileges for minorities—minorities, moreover, which coveted the influence of the entrenched interests against which they campaigned. If political leaders found their justification—not least for failing to gratify all the demands made upon them—in the concept of the national interest, their critics evolved a similar moral language, claiming authority by reason of a 'higher law' or the public interest, though the last concept did not find its fullest expression until comparatively recently.[15] In contrast, reformers from earliest times have been haunted by the problems of appearing to deny the efficacy of individual action by resort to group activity and of fostering enlarged government power to meet their requests. Similarly, the tendency of American pluralist society to encourage diversity and change has been constant, with the corollary that 'extremists' who oppose such tendencies, out of conviction or because they are adversely affected by them, have generally displayed—more than other dissidents—an obsession with history combined, unhappily, with a lack of historical understanding. This obsession has been accompanied by assumptions of moral superiority, a consequent tendency to view opponents as illegitimate conspirators, and an unwillingness to participate wholeheartedly in democratic politics.[16] Such inclinations have set these 'extremists' apart from the majority of pressure groups, though the latter, too, may be prepared to condone violent tactics if everything else fails.

Bearing all these factors in mind, it is possible to identify two main phases of protest activity in the nineteenth century, which developed in the context of a relatively unchanging set of basic national values but within a society and an economy in flux, with roots in the eighteenth century and consequences that were apparent as late as the 1920s.

The Era of Humanitarian Reform

During the years after Independence, fundamental changes in the economy and political culture transformed the prospects and influenced the range of pressure groups in the United States. The rapid economic growth and social diversification of the colonies in the eighteenth century had helped, of course, both to cause the conflict with Britain and to ensure its success but, as we have seen, the size of the country and a shortage of manpower, capital and crucial skills had inhibited the forces of modernization, however grandiose the vision of America's prospects entertained by some of its citizens. After the war of 1812 the transitional period of adjustment to Independence and its problems was over, and the economy, though still geared to British trade and dependent on British capital, was beginning to gratify the 'almost *universal ambition to get forward*'.[17] A 'revolution' in transportation, which rendered the vastness of the republic less a difficulty than an opportunity, was accompanied by the enlargement and diversification of the population, a great expansion in the volume of available goods, and major alterations in the methods of production and relations between employers and labour. Trade, manufacturing, and cities increased dramatically in importance and, economically at least, the New World became more like the Old. Fresh fortunes were made, while the prosperity of the Mid-West and North-East was much enhanced. In view of the early antipathies towards industrialization and its effects, and the importance of the farmers, farming regions and their values, these developments predictably produced anxieties as well as enthusiasm—anxieties in no way allayed by the fact that the democratization of American politics had kept pace with the progress of the American economy.

If the depression following the panic of 1819 drove debtors throughout the country, but particularly in the South and West, to look for relief to the state legislatures, interest in politics thus aroused was sustained for a number of reasons. Opportunities for personal and group advancement were enhanced, following the decline of the first party system, as a result of the Republicans' eventual complacency and factionalism combined with the Federalists' organizational weakness and failure to adapt their ideology to alterations in society. By the 1820s white manhood suffrage had been achieved in most states because of popular demand and the realization among conservatives that tax-paying qualifications frequently fostered fraud at elections. The emergence of a mass electorate and a new party system able to mobilize it was as divisive as it was significant, and in time such political changes, like those in the economy, stimulated the formation of new interest and 'attitude' groups.

During the first half of the nineteenth century, by reason of numerical strength and generous political representation, American farmers generally managed to achieve their objectives regarding land law, Indian 'control', fiscal matters and territorial acquisition and were able to block unwelcome policy proposals from opposing interests, although the demands of merchants, transport developers, bankers and manufacturers did not go entirely unanswered. Most of these activities were either short-lived or loosely organized or both. Indeed, it is clear that governmental intervention was initially prompted as much by an awareness of the weakness of certain economic enterprises, and a consequent desire to encourage them, as by the need to respond to sectional pressures.[18]

However, with the appearance of employers' associations and craft unions from the end of the eighteenth century came the development by each side of more enduring defensive techniques—prosecutions under conspiracy laws ranged against boycotts, strikes and the closed shop. It was in this period that the major 'potential' economic interest groups became a reality, as a result of the greater self-awareness and sense of divergent objectives induced by the rise of American capitalism; of the resentment produced by deteriorating working conditions; and of a comparison by working men of their status and prospects with those of other elements in society or with their own position in times past. Economic groups organized to fulfil their functions in the productive sphere were better placed than 'attitude' groups to mobilize their members for political action and to keep them united over any length of time.[19] Nonetheless, neither employers nor labour achieved more than rudimentary organization until the late nineteenth century. Factory and home workers, as well as unskilled labourers, for example, remained outside the early union movement, the membership of which dwindled alarmingly during years of depression.

Even so, by the 1820s and 1830s many local unions and city trades assemblies were being formed and alliances of craft unions effected, concerned chiefly with improving wages and working conditions.[20] Encouraged by the further progress of America towards political democracy, North-Eastern labour leaders also turned to politics to realize cherished goals, including the ten-hour day, free tax-supported schools, the abolition of prison contract labour and imprisonment for debt and limitations on the power of monopolies. The result was partly a campaign within the existing major parties, leading to the establishment of a radical 'Locofoco' wing inside the Democratic parties of New York and other states, and partly a recourse to the formation of working men's parties, most of which disappeared within five years of their birth, often being absorbed by the Democrats. The explanations for the failure of these parties are much the same as those for the collapse of independent pressure groups: doctrinal quarrels, lack of experienced leadership, shortage of funds and the opposition of the two main parties, the Democrats and the Whigs.[21]

It is difficult to estimate the precise impact of such dissidents upon the politics of their day. Led by middle-class reformers and intellectuals, they were scarcely representative of urban working men, among whom they polled rather badly. Nevertheless, they advocated programmes more extreme than those of the Whigs or the Democrats, and their amalgamation with the latter undoubtedly enhanced Democracy's somewhat undeserved reputation for radicalism. For there was a considerable contrast between that party's actions and its rhetoric. Although pressure for the ten-hour day, later sustained by the craft unions, eventually paid off at both state and federal level, and the replacement of the Bank of the United States by the Independent Treasury scheme might be seen as a gesture to labour, which had been badly hit by the 1837 depression, there were few other causes for rejoicing. (The Independent Treasury involved the holding of federal monies in sub-treasuries under government control. While government was thus taken out of the banking business, it did not result in hard-money policies or produce a sound currency, as supporters had hoped.) The working-class vote was frequently spread between Whigs and Democrats, both of which were coalitions of competing interests, divided as much by ethnic or religious as by economic factors. After the failure of the working men's parties, the unions devoted themselves increasingly to traditional objectives, and with the decline of the union movement from the end of the decade until the 1850s the battle for their wider goals was taken up by other protest groups.

All this is not to deny the attractions of Democratic ideology. But the Jacksonian majority, as its legislative record shows, had a negative concept of the powers of government, particularly in economic matters, albeit combined with a most positive appreciation of the value of modern political organization. The most important changes of the era—such as the adoption of the convention system, the trend towards the popular choice of governors, electors and other state officials, and rotation in office—while they were initiated by earlier aspiring politicians at the state level rather than by the Democrats, were skilfully used by the latter to build up a formidable party structure. However, the party leaders, though assiduously addressing themselves to the voters and not just to other politicians, were restrained by the very complexities of the popular electoral system and still operated under a constitutional structure which prevented responsible party rule: three separate branches of government, different terms and modes of election for Congressmen, Senators and the President and the division of authority between the states and the federal government. Moreover, eighteenth-century suspicion of parties as instruments of power had not been dissipated even by the age of Jackson, despite appeals for popular support. Indeed, the functional Democratic system, because of its novelty and political success, was a cause for intense dismay among conservatives, notwithstanding the development of certain organizational, ideological and membership similarities between the two dominant parties by the 1840s, or the greater willingness of the largely unsuccessful Whigs to take a positive view of the responsibilities of government at whatever level. With the emergence of the second party system, the terms 'lobby', 'lobby agent' and 'lobby member' came into popular usage; and if they did not arouse the distaste in the United States that they did in Britain, even late in the nineteenth century, the terms were associated sufficiently closely with corruption or backstairs activity to make many American reformers hesitate over employing a lobbyist, at least one by such a name.[22]

This cautious public attitude to the immediate framers of legislation reflects a wider ambivalence towards the law itself in the United States. If the Constitution had established a system of federal courts and a government of laws shaped by the representatives of the people, many Americans in rural or frontier areas long retained a hostility to the law and its practitioners, regarding them as imposing cynical constraints upon their natural intelligence and freedom. English Common Law, transferred across the Atlantic, lost its mystique but not its importance; the meaning of the Constitution became a matter which brought political parties into dispute with an ostensibly independent judiciary, and the state governments into conflict with federal authority. Yet the need for a legal profession in a growing country was speedily established, together with its reputation for erudition and its popularity as an avenue for personal advancement. Furthermore, the relish of Americans for suing each other in the courts was widely remarked, although in the first forty or so years of the new republic the federal courts seemed to associate themselves with an often unwelcome restraint of economic progress and innovation.[23]

The deficiencies of the Democratic party, though it favoured both expansion and experiment, not only blocked the early political demands of American labour but also encouraged the formation of a host of non-economic pressure groups. In fact, the classic economic interests were greatly outnumbered before the Civil War by cause crusades, whose members may have been activated in part by the social and economic ferment of these years, yet did not have any vested material interests in the causes they embraced. And if attitudes to parties had not been fully modernized, so that expectations of what would follow from appealing to them therefore remained comparatively low by modern standards, the adoption of new organizational forms was further stimulated by the significant intellectual developments of the period. In particular, there was a widespread repudiation of eighteenth-century economic and psychological determinism, epitomized by the writings of Locke and enshrined in the political theory and experiments of the Founding Fathers. The most important secular and religious reform movements were united instead by their search for a more perfect society and sustained in it by a belief in human perfectibility. Perfectionism had its antecedents in the ideas of the Awakening and the Enlightenment, in their confidence in the goodness of man and his capacity for growth through the application of reason and the influence of Christ. But a new emphasis was now placed on the immediate prospects of communion with God and earthly progress. Both the meaning of the American experiment and the duties of the individual citizen were at stake. The religious revivals which swept the country during the first half of the nineteenth century, influencing especially the Baptist, Methodist and Presbyterian sects, and the emergence in New England of such faiths as Unitarianism, Transcendentalism and Universalism, alike bear witness to the further decline of traditional Calvinist doctrine. Rather than considering themselves to be members of an elite which had been saved and set apart, the active adherents of a more liberal Arminian Protestantism were exhorted to ensure their salvation through good works and social reform. Revivalism might also be justified as a vital unifying thread in the midst of unprecedented religious diversity. Neither the recent past nor the heritage left behind in Europe, it was claimed, should be allowed to inhibit present endeavour for, as the popular poet and journalist, Walt Whitman, put it, 'All that we enjoy of freedom was in the beginning but an experiment.'[24]

Much of this religious activity reflected the desire of its leaders to see Church membership keep pace with an expanding land and population—a vain quest since at least the eighteenth century. If the numerical strength of the Protestant denominations was still unchallenged, none enjoyed any special advantage other than those conferred by a long history in the United States. They were obliged to compete for members and their rivalry led inevitably to a reduction of the Puritan emphasis upon a complex doctrine and an educated clergy in favour of a greater stress upon individual morality. Moreover, one of the traditional means of self-assertion for the socially or economically oppressed in America has been the formation of new religious sects or communities.[25] Clearly, this is not a tendency which has been viewed with equanimity, and the response of the established Churches has often been to adapt their own dogma and organization to the changed situation, in order to retain their influence.

Emancipation from extreme Puritan fears of sin and judgement, first heralded by the diversification of the New England economy, seemed appropriate in the face of nineteenth-century prosperity, which both confirmed American individual and collective merit and released considerable surplus capital for philanthropic ventures. The absence of a major external threat to national security and the conquest of the Indians, the chief internal enemies of an earlier era, gave a further boost to feelings of optimism about the future, and despite hostility to mass immigration in some quarters, national confidence spelled death to parochialism. Before the Civil War reform was a more cosmopolitan affair than it would be again until after World War II, and there was a notable Anglo-American connection in this field, the two nations being held together by ties of blood, commerce and religion.[26] In such a climate flourished intrepid New England activists who could see no absurdity in a Club for the Study and Diffusion of Ideas and Tendencies Proper to the Nineteenth Century or an alliance of Friends of Universal Reform.

Yet the very freedom and opportunities provided by the United States, as well as its lack of fixed social distinctions, migh foster anxieties among men and women of conservative inclinations in all classes: among those whose power and prosperity were directly threatened by progress, or who were temperamentally opposed to the advance of democracy, Arminianism, industrialization and territorial expansion. Concern about the scope and rapidity of the changes taking place in America by the 1830s is shown in the writings of labour leaders, educators, artists, evangelists, small producers and politicians from all parties.[27] And though each element had its own particular grievances, there was a common preoccupation with the decline of traditional values and the impact on the individual of impersonal economic forces, developments which seemed peculiarly disturbing at a time when political and religious doctrine was extolling the individual's rationality and capabilities. The results of the defensive instincts thus aroused, in organizational terms, range from craft unions to such benevolent alliances as the Bible Society, the Sunday School Union, the Educational Society and the Home Missionary Society, interdenominational Protestant associations designed to foster proper political and social conduct as well as to win souls.[28] Although the leaders of these societies were generally prosperous businessmen and professionals, supporters of the Whig party and its commitment to elitist and positive government and hostile to the Democratic party's association with secularism, free thinking and majority rule, it has been argued that many of the larger reform agencies attracted the backing of those whose social or regional importance was declining. It is understandably true that the early temperance, anti-slavery, free public education and peace movements drew heavily—though by no means exclusively—upon the services of New Englanders perturbed by the lawless urban masses and the growth of the godless West; but it remains to be proved that the influence of those individuals was seriously threatened in their own communities, or that status anxieties at all explain their involvement in philanthropy.[29] For although, as Bertram Wyatt-Brown has pointed out, the evangelical reformers in Jacksonian America were frequently denounced as puritanical snobs, the leaders of the anti-clerical masses might equally well be Democratic 'aristocrats' annoyed 'with the competitiveness and tone of moral superiority' involved in evangelicalism.[30]

The aim, then, of most reformers, whether they were socially successful or insecure, conservative or progressive, was to perfect a world manifestly imperfect but possessing unique potential. Reform seemed both possible on the evidence of past experience and necessary in view of present disturbing developments; it began with moral regeneration of the individual through conversion and education. Since the days of the first settlements, leaders had valued instruction for its own sake and for a host of practical reasons: to ensure a literate clergy, as a means of inculcating patriotism while fitting settlers for the duties of citizenship, and as an aid to help them earn a livelihood in the exacting conditions of the New World. After personal purification came the improvement of society at large—indeed, the two processes could hardly be separated. The evils of a society impinged upon all individuals who remained within its bounds; indifference perpetuated them and was therefore just as much a sin as deliberate personal wickedness.

A number of modern scholars have maintained that there is a useful distinction to be made between moral and social reform and have stressed the extreme individualism of some reformers, their refusal to compromise and work through existing institutions.[31] While it is apparent that the federal system has made it difficult to achieve national political reforms (whereas the British parliamentary system has facilitated them), the nineteenth-century British experience does not suggest that other strong national institutions would have provided dissidents with alternative means of access to the sources of power. Such institutions—an established Church, the army, the national universities—did not serve in this capacity during the Victorian period, not least because they were never dominated by the middle classes from which philanthropists were largely drawn. And in many cases the institutional inadequacies of ante-bellum America were more a cause than a consequence of reformer reliance on the well-motivated individual—the limitations of the major political parties, for example, have already been discussed. Yet despite these deficiencies, a wide range of cause groups looked to the state and national legislatures for redress, and the federal system allowed initial experiments to be made at the state level with little risk, before they were launched on a national scale. Among the reformers who pressed for government action were campaigners for better prisons, hospitals, orphanages and asylums; nativists in favour of delaying or limiting civil rights for immigrants; advocates of stricter Sabbath laws, the distribution of religious tracts in schools, compulsory arbitration of foreign policy disputes and the prohibition of the manufacture and sale of liquor. A gradualist wing of the anti-slavery movement exhorted Congress to make full use of its power to suppress the external and internal slave trade, to prohibit slavery in the territories and in the District of Columbia, and to refuse admission to new slave states. Since women were denied opportunities for advancement and control over their lives by discriminatory laws and exclusion from the franchise, it was natural that they should persistently seek better laws and a voice in making them, no matter how strong the political opposition to their demands. Equally clearly, the desire of reformers to see a literate populace could only be satisfied, in the face of family pressures upon the young to start earning and conservative fears about educating individuals above their station, by tax support for schools and compulsory attendance laws: in other words, through political action.

Of course, there were zealots in every crusade to whom political compromise was anathema, as well as those among the moderate abolitionists and disciples of temperance who were eventually driven in exasperation to advocate the founding of third parties to achieve their objectives, despite the traditional reluctance of Americans to waste their votes on minority parties. (They have usually been doomed to failure in a country where political activity is highly expensive and a host of technical factors, including the election of single executives, the single-member electoral district, the electoral college and the absence of proportional representation, contribute to the preservation of the two-party system.) New communities built upon socialist or religious principles provided a more radical escape route for the discontented, an alternative to the institutions of a competitive, industrializing nation. Some intellectuals, disillusioned with their experiences as members of such Utopias and unfitted by temperament or attainments to enjoy co-operative labours—though concerned, in a distinctively American fashion, not to become merely decorative commentators upon the national scene—may have agreed with the poet and essayist Ralph Waldo Emerson that man's 'solitude is more prevalent and beneficient than the concert of crowds'.[32] And disgusted perfectionists in the anti-slavery movement advocated 'coming out' of all existing institutions corrupted by their support for human bondage. Yet between them they constituted a small minority of the total reform spectrum. Appeals to a higher law than the Constitution or those promulgated by Congress were part of the conventional language of protest and were only rarely used to justify civil disobedience.

An analysis of pressure-group methods during the antebellum era also suggests that an initial impression of eccentricity, created by focusing unduly on the Utopias, is quite misleading. Agitators took great pains to stress the practical as well as the moral benefits that would follow from their proposals—the more efficient labour force that would emerge from the abolition of slavery or prohibition, for instance. And they strove to reach as wide an audience as possible. Conservative evangelicals and radical abolitionists alike approved the mobilization and direction of public opinion through regular meetings and the distribution of literature of all kinds. Aided by increasing prosperity, improved transport and education, especially in the North, where only 5 per cent of the adult white population was illiterate in 1860, major movements were able to support full-time organizers, writers and preachers, to evolve a network of societies sustained by the small initiation fees and subsequent subscriptions of non-active members, and to establish national offices, usually in Boston, Philadelphia or New York. The great days of the professional lobbyist would not come until the late nineteenth century, but contacts with state and national legislators were carefully cultivated and deputations sent to the White House, while the right of petition guaranteed by the First Amendment to the Constitution and contested by defenders of slavery, was staunchly vindicated. Indeed, it became part of a general argument, astutely cultivated by pressure groups, that their activities, far from involving the coercion of the majority by minorities, were intended to protect freedom of speech, voluntary association and other basic democratic rights.

Judgements about the membership, scope and success of these groups present some difficulties. However conspicuous the spokesmen for change may have been, they and their followers remained a small part of American political life. More people were unaffected by religious revivals than were impelled to join the newer sects and, through their conversion, to take up social reform; more people remained apathetic—if not hostile—to abolitionism, pacifism or feminism than were convinced of their validity. The largest social movements were those concerned with temperance, anti-slavery in its various forms and the control of immigration. Between 1826 (when it was founded in Boston) and 1834, the membership of the American Society for the Promotion of Temperance rose from sixteen to 1,000,000, with some 5000 branches; that of the Washington Temperance Society allegedly climbed from 6 to over 500,000 between 1840 and 1843. At the height of its strength in the 1830s, the American Anti-Slavery Society claimed about 2000 societies with 200,000 members. The nativists did not manage to develop a coherent organization—their activities ranged from anti-Catholic societies to anti-immigrant gangs in Eastern cities—but their eventual resort to third-party politics from the local to the national level was unusually successful in New England, the South and the border states during the disturbed political conditions of the 1840s and 1850s.[33] All three movements also won some backing from the Whigs and later the Republicans.[34] However, none of them tapped more than a fraction of the potential support available in a population which grew from 5.3 million in 1800 to more than 31 million by 1860, of whom about 26.9 million were whites; and we still know little about the motives of the rank and file supporters of reform or of how they related to the leaders of their respective organizations.

Numbers, to be sure, provide no automatic guide to influence. The peace crusade never had more than a few thousand members concentrated in the North-Eastern states, despite its employment of the full range of pressure-group tactics, yet proposals for an international court of arbitration would eventually bear fruit at the beginning of the twentieth century, and the movement in one guise or another has survived alongside the folly and waste which have been its inspiration.[35] Individual drive sustained many campaigns to improve conditions for the deviant and afflicted; it does no injustice to their co-workers or sympathetic legislators to emphasize the efforts of Thomas Gallaudet and Samuel Howe, who sought to provide education for deaf-mutes and the blind, and those of Dorothea Dix, who strove for better insane asylums in Massachusetts, Rhode Island, New Jersey, Pennsylvania and many other states.

Nor does the nature of the leadership of ante-bellum pressure groups offer a key to the understanding of their different levels of achievement, since all groups were dominated by individuals from the middle class and all had their share of the ambitious, narrow and neurotic as well as the apparently disinterested and humane. After the anti-slavery crusade had drawn women on to the public platform and had stimulated an independent feminist campaign in the process, women were actively involved in most good causes, finding in them appealing alternatives to domestic sacrifice or employment as servants, factory workers and teachers.[36] The economic depressions of the 1830s and 1850s were impartially damaging to appeals for public generosity, and the large number of philanthropic concerns competing for funds and attention deprived any of complete victory. Financial setbacks sharpened the disruptive differences in most movements between 'conservatives' who favoured gradual reform, combined with direct involvement in politics, and 'radicals' anxious for immediate change but neglectful of contemporary political realities and the arguments of their opponents. It was the acceptability to the public of the reformers' basic aims, however, not their tactics, which determined success or failure.[37]

Research into the functioning of modern interest groups suggests that although leaders exaggerate the gulf separating them from the group, they tend to be more active and liberal, better educated and connected, and more upwardly mobile.[38] They may therefore be in constant danger of losing touch with their actual and potential followers. Among those who did so before the Civil War we may include the Utopians. While these experimental communities have recently attracted favourable comment, due to current interest in 'primitive' societies which renounce the pursuit of unfettered individualism and material progress, most of them survived for only a few years. Urging a complete reformation of contemporary society, they relied for recruits on the force of example and publicity. But it was difficult to make many converts to the common ownership of property, a principle upon which the settlements rested, in a country where land was so abundant and its ownership so much respected, and where the lure of the cities was already apparent. The prevalence of saloons or the influx of Catholics were tangible problems and widely recognized; the increase of class conflict in an industrial order not yet fully established, though acknowledged by some prominent Democrats, was more usually ignored by the fearful or the ignorant.[39] Rejection by Utopians of conventional religious teaching, marriage, the family and the rigid sexual division of labour also aroused dismay among their conservative neighbours. Of the groups which resorted to conventional pressure politics, the feminists found it particularly hard to forge a permanent organization or to win much sympathy for crucial objectives such as the vote.

Nonetheless, the regular occurrence of mob violence in ante-bellum America, often directed against recent immigrants and blacks, suggests that some of the white victims of the new industrial order had their own ideas about the best way of advertising its evils. Recent scholarship indicates that these disturbances were far from being spontaneous outbursts among an apolitical rabble, as was once supposed, and even won the support of substantial citizens, equally alarmed though differently affected by economic change.[40] Unfortunately, violent protest, while effective as a means of controlling 'threatening' elements in society, did nothing positive to enhance the bargaining power of the working class as a whole.

In the end success, as always, depended on the viewpoint of the judge. Perfectionists were permanently thwarted, whereas moderate man could take satisfaction in an efficient membership drive, a single legislative victory, the consciousness of having helped another individual. Whigs and Democrats favoured different reforms; no one movement could allay all fears or give full expression to the varied manifestations of contemporary self-confidence; and few organizations were genuinely national in scope. By the 1830s the anti-slavery crusade, like so many others, was concentrated in parts of the North-East and West, although racialism and a belief that the movement encouraged foreign criticism as well as domestic disturbances provoked much hostility towards abolitionists in these areas. Such anxieties were only to be overcome during the 1850s when, as a result of the political crisis of the decade, it seemed to the supporters of the new Republican party that the threat to the Union, the Constitution and the right of states to govern their own affairs posed by the allegedly expansionist Southern slave power was greater than the danger abolitionists had once seemed to constitute.[41] Yet if the South could not be reconciled to anti-slavery agitators, feminism or pressures for economic democracy, its citizens warmed to benevolent societies, temperance and efforts to improve the treatment of the afflicted.

Laws that defied social custom or opposed vigorous social trends might be repealed or flouted within a short time of their passage, as the fate of much local-option temperance legislation and restrictions on immigrants makes plain. However, in each case, later campaigners found in these abortive achievements part of the encouragement they needed to keep going. Improvements like those in prison conditions or education, which seemed the epitome of progress in their own time, were destined to appear dated within a generation, and their chief value lay perhaps in building the foundation for subsequent reforms. In recent times pressure groups formed to achieve a specific end have shown a reluctance to disband, after once developing a successful leadership and organization. During the nineteenth century the Civil War, coming in the wake of a depression, disrupted a number of apparently well-established movements, notably the women's rights campaign and the temperance cause.[42] Even so, many individual reformers proved to be not only catholic in their philanthropic interests but also ready to find new ones in the aftermath of victory or defeat. Thus for much of the 1860s former abolitionists involved themselves in freedmen's aid societies and then went on to labour for a variety of Indian aid associations. By doing so they helped to compensate for the violent and disruptive conflict through which their first objective had been achieved, a conflict made inevitable less by their agitation than by the refusal of the master class in the South to yield its power.

Nonetheless, under the impact of war, with its emphasis upon discipline, co-operation, organization and governmental direction, perfectionism could no longer provide a major inspiration for reform. Accepting the changed circumstances, many abolitionists abandoned their old suspicion of working with politicians and, in fact, of any course which did not aim at converting the masses to a belief in racial equality.[43] Although the defenders of freedmen's aid presented it as 'a reconstructive movement' designed to 'remodel public opinion in regard to the black man' by helping him to acquire Christian instruction, relief and then employment, so fitting him for the responsible exercise of civil rights, critics rightly pointed out that blacks wanted justice, not charity.[44] For moderates, however, citizenship did not necessarily require the suffrage and they showed no understanding of the difficulties involved in imparting the values of middle-class white society to a community of ex-slaves. Moreover, the organizations in which reformers now placed so much faith—the United States Sanitary Commission, the Freedmen's Aid Bureau, the Freedmen's Savings Bank and the various freedmen's aid associations—though managed by whites, never enjoyed realistic financial backing from Congress or the general public.[45] We see in their activities the reassertion of that conservative tradition in philanthropy epitomized by the ante-bellum benevolent societies, and strengthened not only by the war but by the conviction that, as industrialization and westward expansion continued apace, the last opportunity for elite control of American society might now be at hand.

If it is a truism that warfare means welfare, enthusiasm for the latter seldom continues long after the end of hostilities, because considerations of economy, peace and the future soon overshadow the claims of past victims and crusades. The Republican party drew back from its drive to establish legislative supremacy during the 1860s and its leaders, though heirs to Whig faith in positive government, baulked at taking over the policy-making role in politics from the executive on a permanent basis. Having pushed through a series of economic reforms in the interests of an acquisitive middle class—homestead legislation, aid to railroads, stabilization of the currency and a national banking system—the Republicans had achieved many of their original objectives, and the extension of civil rights to the black population was as much as most Northern politicians and voters wished to see in the field of race relations. Disturbed by public disapproval and internal feuds, and acting ostensibly out of its concern for national unity, the party abandoned such experiments as the Freedmen's Bureau, leaving behind no institutional monuments to

Reconstruction.[46] But American history, more than most, is the history of reform. Although the great Utopian and humanitarian crusades were over and future protest movements would find in politics their most visible expression, the problems produced by the economic growth and political and value systems of the United States still awaited solution, and the solutions offered would often seem far from novel.

The Era of Political and Economic Protest

The pressure groups of this period, like those of the antebellum era, arose in response to a distinctive material environment, as well as to changing social and political theories which at last acknowledged the importance of group activity in American life. This did not mean an abrupt abandonment of the historic national commitment to self-help and selective *laissez-faire*, strengthened at first—during the disillusioned aftermath of Reconstruction—by the supposedly scientific laws of Social Darwinism, which discovered a pattern in economic chaos while providing a justification for the existing social order and an indictment of the coercive state.[47] Instead, the growing complexity of the economic system, a belated awareness that the natural resources of the country were not limitless, and uneasiness about the widening gulf between different classes and ethnic groups brought a gradual appreciation of the power of environmental influences to circumscribe the freedom of even the best-intentioned individual, and a subsequent attempt to reshape old commitments in the light of current needs.

The organization of the great economic interests, foreshadowed in the early nineteenth century, followed inevitably from the increase in commercial farming and American dependence on world markets for commodities, the proliferation of huge industrial cities, the development of a national banking and transport system (with as many deficiencies as it had advantages, from the users' point of view) and the consolidation of giant corporations in such key enterprises as steel, oil, railroads and banking. Technological change, which Americans have been so ready to advocate and accept, was as usual proceeding faster than the modernization of government institutions or social values.

Farmers might understandably have resented the politically subordinate position they came to occupy in an industrial nation, at odds with both their continuing importance as export producers and the traditional folklore which had accorded them moral and civic superiority over all other classes. Until the galvanizing hardship of the 1930s, however, they were unable to devise any effective organization among the tenants, sharecroppers and labourers rendered so vulnerable by the increasing mechanization of American farms. Nor were they able to recover overall economic parity with other groups in society, their objective from the late nineteenth century onwards, because the associations which influenced federal policy after World War I primarily represented farm owners, even more than the militant Populist party had done some thirty years before. After the failure of Populism attempts to build strength through a farmer–labour alliance enjoyed only limited success in such states as Minnesota, Montana and the Dakotas, due to internal conflicts of interest and the conservative opposition aroused by so unusual a combination. Nonetheless, until the early 1920s, third parties appeared to be the best alternative to farm co-operatives, whose narrow scope precluded them from exerting pressure on the major parties for that enlarged federal assistance which farmers now desired but which proved so difficult to win, despite the persistent over-representation of rural areas in Congress and the state legislatures. It was an international crisis, the Depression, which ultimately persuaded industrial countries of the need to subsidize agriculture.[48]

Of all the major economic interests, business was the most successful in its political activities by the late nineteenth century. As we have seen, the precedent of granting favours to the underdeveloped parts of the economy had been set in the early days of the republic. Once the infant industries had become established, had organized themselves for their own protection, and had established their pre-eminence over agriculture, corporations proved both willing and able to supply campaign funds, fees and investment opportunities to legislators who could influence currency, tariff and transport policies in their favour.[49] And although the Republican party (to which they largely turned in national politics) commanded the support of rural regions in the Mid-West and in New England, while there was no unanimity on economic matters within its ranks, the inducements of the corporations, unmatched by other interests, proved irresistible. Even during the retreat from racial democracy beginning in the 1870s, however, the Republicans included a fair number of civil service reformers and labour sympathizers, while by the end of the century they were responding to the demands of smaller businessmen, who felt that unless irresponsible industrial growth were restrained, class conflict and social insecurity would dangerously increase.[50] This disaffected element found itself in a curious Progressive reform alliance with discontented farmers and labour spokesmen of a kind ineffectively attempted by the Populists and destined to modify the attitudes towards government power first of the Republican party and then of the Democrats.[51]

But for the most part, labour and industry remained locked in their traditional contest, with each side now nationally organized—businessmen through the National Association of Manufacturers (1895) and the Chamber of Commerce (1912), the craft unions from 1886 through the American Federation of Labour.[52] Torn between demands for the regulation of corporate practices and the improvement of conditions for working men, governments and courts inclined to the conservative business sector, which not only enjoyed the power that accompanies great wealth but the advantage of appealing to an ancient conviction that individual freedom and responsibility were the foundations of civic virtue and economic prosperity.

Pre-war perfectionists such as Walt Whitman and Wendell Phillips had deplored the weakness of American political parties, resulting in their control by professional politicians and selfish economic interests, but they had not been able to show how the popular will could be brought to bear against evil without the use of mediating institutions.[53] After Reconstruction the inclination of the two main parties was to modify the disruptive sectional ideologies dominant since the 1850s, to woo the expanding electorate, and to preserve their traditional areas of strength. Despite the apparent Republican ascendancy, they competed on roughly equal terms, as neither party was able to control the presidency and both Houses of Congress simultaneously; both suffered from a scarcity of distinguished candidates until the turn of the century and produced little positive legislation. These deficiencies, as well as the Republican subservience to business pressure, helped to stimulate the upsurge of reform demands known as Progressivism.

In an era of large-scale economic organization it seemed more important than ever to direct popular disapproval against social injustice, political graft and unregulated capitalism and, however much they might deplore group conflict, few reformers now feared collective effort. Numerous private civic associations were founded to stimulate and channel protest, among them the National Consumers' League, the National Child Labour Committee, the National Municipal League and the National Conference of Social Work. Political changes long advocated—the secret ballot, direct primaries, the popular election of Senators, the initiative, referendum and recall—were adopted ostensibly to restore the power of the voter, though it is doubtful whether this ever amounted to much. Through the concerted efforts of concerned citizens, it was further and perhaps more realistically argued, the political machines could be curbed. Special interests might then be driven out and permanently excluded by devices ranging from new forms of city government to laws limiting campaign expenses and lobbying activities, now extensive and frequently corrupt. Once purified and democratized, the functions of governments at every level might safely be expanded, so that they could scientifically set about the elimination of waste and misery by controlling the trusts, reforming the banking and railroad systems, improving public utilities and tackling such pressing social problems as slum housing, long working hours in poor conditions and without insurance, child labour, antiquated prisons and inadequate schools.[54]

The Progressive alliance, much wider in its aims and support than the Populist crusade, embraced journalists, clergymen and politicians of every type, professionals, social workers and intellectuals, as well as economic interests. Concerned in part to reassert the importance of declining social units and old values, and touched by an urban version of the revivalist tradition, they lacked the soaring religious faith and supreme confidence of the ante-bellum reformers, and their belief in the people was distinctly paternalistic.[55] Nonetheless, a section of the Progressives evolved an optimistic ideology which rejected determinism and stressed the value of applied reason and the experimental method, of beneficent change through the agency of the state and an enlightened educational policy, which would produce not only responsible citizens but also the experts necessary for the administration of a complex society. Unlike the old Utopians, who had rejected the city and had no counterpart in the early twentieth century, these men and women often found employment—and invariably their inspiration—in the urban world. Although sharing the national nostalgia for frontier America, they bore witness to that dramatic shift of wealth and power from the country to the town which would make the United States officially an urban nation by the 1920s.

In time the customary gap developed between the intellectuals and the practical reformers. The former placed far more emphasis than the latter on the transformation of culture and sexual relations as a prerequisite to fundamental changes in society, scorning the middle-class morality of most Progressives and their excessive reliance upon legislative programmes. For their part, many conservatives and Democratic Progressives mistrusted theorists of the kind who wrote for the liberal journal, the *New Republic*. These writers, they felt, were alarmingly willing to dispense with the checks and balances of the old political system, to condone encroachments upon individual liberties and to welcome economic concentration when accompanied by labour unionization, on the assumption that only mass production could ensure a steadily rising standard of living for the masses.[56]

No group of reformers has ever captured a major political party, except briefly for a limited objective such as prohibition, and although the different versions of Progressivism provoked a genuine ideological debate during the national elections of 1912, as well as the establishment of an independent Progressive party, dissidents had to be content with the adoption of sections of their programme, according to the circumstances and inclinations of those in office. Regulation of business was officially achieved, but while the legal technicalities involved were immense, the agencies appointed for the purpose exercised limited powers and soon deferred to the corporations. The political machines might be corrupt, but they survived clean-up campaigns both by co-operating with municipal reformers and by providing immediate personal benefits for the urban working class which were available from no other source. Despite all the political reforms designed to renew democracy, American cities were still hampered by governments and revenues inadequate to their needs, and Congress remained ill-equipped to handle the increasing demands made upon it. Voluntary associations, however elaborate their bureaucracies and far-reaching their propaganda, could achieve little beyond the partial amelioration of suffering when the basic political and economic institutions of the nation remained—with their approval—fundamentally unchanged. Yet the moderation of most Progressives was the key to their considerable legislative success.

After World War I a general repression of dissent followed in the wake of labour militancy, economic depression, terrorist incidents and the foundation of the American Communist Party. This period of reaction, although it did not destroy the Progressive movement, reduced it to conflicting fragments, only a few of which would be associated with the next great phase of economic and governmental reform in the 1930s.[57]

During the eighteenth century the development of pressure groups was hindered by poor communications and rich individual opportunities, by a vast terrain and an ideology which emphasized individual effort while deploring selfish political factions; conversely, they were encouraged by the variety of the new country, the diversity of its population and the inequalities of condition which were quickly apparent, in defiance of its egalitarian philosophy and settler expectations alike. But because these differences did not become intolerable until well into the nineteenth century and the unwanted political parties which emerged thought it wise to devise a rhetoric which minimized class conflict, the first really striking wave of protest organizations were concerned with moral, not economic, reform and displayed a damaging ambivalence towards political involvement, albeit combined with a shrewd appreciation of the power of an aroused public opinion. Clearly, however, the ante-bellum pressure groups were as much a response to industrialization as a rejection of it or an evasion of its implications. Economic depression also adversely affected their operations, as it did those of the early unions, just as wars disrupted and redirected reformer endeavours (even if the impact of the Civil War, though profound, may have been exaggerated).

Many continuities may be detected, despite the existence of distinct phases of protest activity. Thus if the appalling effects of the industrial revolution were dominating reformer thinking by the beginning of the twentieth century and had produced a new willingness to work collectively for political remedies, and if a new respectability had been acquired by the interest groups, among which the big employers' alliances had become particularly effective, the poor remained ill organized and voluntary associations paternalistic and conservative. Moreover nostalgia for the old America could still be found in the emphasis of some Progressives upon the need to restore competition, encourage experimentalism, and reduce the power of corrupt 'interests' over government. And while racial attitudes had obviously been transformed in certain ways since the Revolution, under the impact of Darwinism and with the decline of environmentalist arguments, the ethnic organizations had always found that segregation, inadequate educational facilities, and legal or *de facto* discrimination had dictated moderate demands and methods, on pain of futility or worse.

CHAPTER 3

The Problems of the Melting Pot: Ethnic Movements from the Nineteenth Century to World War I

Early Responses to Ethnic Diversity

In the last few years scholars and politicians alike have proclaimed the continuing importance of ethnicity in American life, engaging in a spirited debate about the desirability and utility of ethnic 'survivals' and reopening the old argument over the difference between the experiences of white ethnics and racial minorities. Whether such developments are seen as a side-effect of the persecution and response of racial minorities, or as part of a larger protest against ineffectual liberalism and individual insecurity in mass society, they cannot be ignored, and there is a strong case for studying the history of racial and ethnic groups in conjunction.

Skin colour can make a crucial difference to one's options in society, as can the economic or political opportunities available at particular times or in particular places, but the line drawn between race and ethnicity is easily obliterated. (Nathan Glazer suggests the fine difference when he states: '*Race* tends to refer to the biological aspect of group difference, *ethnic* to a combination of the cultural aspect plus a putative biological element because of the assumption of common descent.' For convenience, unless otherwise indicated in the text, the term ethnic is used in Chapters 3 and 4 to embrace white and non-white groups, of which the latter will be our primary concern.)[1] Moreover, in an urban environment especially, the problems faced by the mass of the poor are extremely similar, although there will be very different responses to these problems even among non-white groups, the voluntary associations of black Americans, for instance, asserting an influence quite unlike that of the organizations existing in Oriental communities, which depend upon unavoidable regional, clan and extended family allegiances.[2] It is also unfortunate for a whole range of ethnic protest groups in the United States that so many have yet to perfect their techniques, just when the complexity of modern society may be rendering obsolete the notion of the democratic politician acting as a broker between competing interests. The current emphasis on social planning and forecasting, the growing importance of educated technicians of all kinds in government and of the executive within governments and the decay of old-style political parties all make it more difficult than hitherto for pressures to be exerted directly on the political system from without.[3] Yet having looked to politics to redress economic injustice often rooted in racial discrimination, and having achieved some progress by this means, ethnic minorities are unlikely to modify such hopes for advancement. Far more probable is a continuing determination to uphold anachronistic but responsive political machines, though this may be supplemented by an increasing resort to militant action, litigation and divisive propaganda.[4]

The current heated debate over 'reverse discrimination' in university admission policies is a good example of the fears of the disadvantaged about the consequences of a meritocratic educational system and of the more fortunate about the destruction of educational excellence.[5] On the legal front the suits brought by a number of eastern Indian tribes to recover land which they claim was taken from them illegally some two hundred years ago are opening up immense possibilities of redress for the survivors at the expense of local whites, a nice irony but one which is not likely to improve race relations in the states concerned.[6]

As a result of their formative experiences in North America, however, it seems clear that the racial minorities lacked most of the essentials for success in pressure-group activity even before the changes in society noted above. If race, like sex, held members of the oppressed group together with a strong and inescapable tie, in the larger society the aversion to changing institutional and economic arrangements which were buttressed by prevailing racial or sexual theories was still stronger.

It is commonly argued that the essential elements of the national creed were agreed upon comparatively early in American history, and that among these a cherished place was held by the concept of the melting pot—of America as the land of freedom, democracy and opportunity in which people of all races, creeds and colours were accepted on equal terms.[7] A belief in the harmonious assimilation of huge numbers of immigrants, fostered by advantageous social circumstances and Christian faith in the brotherhood of men, is perhaps the most crucial element in this concept and had its exponents as early as the eighteenth century.[8] Indeed, throughout American history civic leaders at every level of public life have extolled the twin ideals of ethnic assimilation and the American Dream embodied in the melting pot, in order to strengthen the bonds of unity in a diverse and growing democracy. Even immigrant leaders analysed assimilation as if it were 'a one-way process by which America completely transformed its new peoples'. In that process they, like most other commentators, tended to see the immigrant as being cleansed and uplifted, though some Progressives emphasized the often valuable cultural accretions resulting from immigration, rather than the necessity of racial blending to make it acceptable.[9]

The justifications for such sanguine expectations could be either environmental or racist: hence their potency. That is to say, both the American conditions of freedom, plenty and opportunity and the ability of the allegedly superior Anglo-Saxon race to absorb and subordinate newcomers of other races helped to create the melting pot. Thus in the years before the Civil War native antipathies towards immigrants were held in check by economic prosperity and geographical expansion, while in the period before World War I the national confidence of imperialists combined with the selfishness of businessmen short of labour in an expanding economy to the same effect. For alongside the idea of the melting pot, either in its original form as a vision of America's 'cosmopolitan nationality' or in its later less attractive varieties, there had grown up a pronounced vein of hostility towards immigrants as Catholics, Jews, radicals or job stealers, which had strengthened existing racial prejudices among whites against Indians and blacks, institutionalized as early as colonial times by laws permitting the enslavement of both, limiting racial intermarriage and curtailing the rights of free persons of colour.[10]

If the New World in some respects fashioned new men, settlers facing an acute labour shortage and boundless resources did not shed any unfavourable opinions of Africans and Indians they might have formed in the Old World; rather, such opinions were reinforced.[11] After the adoption and expansion of slavery as a 'necessary evil' came its eventual defence as a means of controlling or elevating racial 'inferiors'. Although the Revolutionary leaders who feared political slavery imposed by Britain saw the inconsistency of supporting chattel slavery in their midst, they dreaded still more the colonial disunity and economic disruption which might follow from attacking the institution, and in debating its validity they tragically strengthened existing prejudices.[12] As a result, the best opportunity of abolishing black bondage was lost, albeit the institution was abandoned in the North, where it had not become essential.[13] Indian slavery, which once operated in all the colonies, prompted by the scarcity of agricultural labour and justified as the reward of victorious wars against the heathen, ultimately proved difficult to maintain and was abandoned, though ironically tribes like the Choctaws, the Chickasaws, the Cherokees, the Creeks and the Seminoles enslaved blacks until the general emancipation of 1865.[14]

White prejudices hardened as the balance of power on the American continent tipped heavily in the settlers' favour, even though such antipathies, as is customary, received their most violent expression in areas where non-whites were concentrated and the 'superior' race felt threatened.[15] Once it seemed practical to claim this vast region as a white man's country, the temptation to do so proved overwhelming. Yet the hostility expressed towards native Americans was different in character from that directed towards American blacks, however similar the consequences, and despite the fact that in framing public policies towards both minorities the objectives of whites rather than non-whites, politicians rather than humanitarians, prevailed. This was only to be expected, since the two oppressed races had little in common as far as their original culture, numbers and appearance were concerned. Whereas initially Indians had the negotiating assets of territory, military prowess and local knowledge, in the circumstances of the international slave trade the Negro qualities of strength and adaptability could be exploited without even the pretence of consulting their wishes. While both were enslaved, the resistance of the Indians and the wars they fought, as well as their unsuitability for heavy plantation labour, prevented the cynical attribution to them of slave-like qualities until the tribes were demoralized by defeat, liquor and disease; in a violent frontier society the peaceful resistance practised by many members of the black community was generally despised, although the recurrent fears of slave revolt suggest that the militant black minority was not totally discounted. If the native Americans, like the Africans, were described as savages, by the nineteenth century—when much was known about the customs of the former but little about the latter—whites were willing to accord some nobility, even beauty, to the ancient inhabitants of their New World, and early men of science apparently confirmed that in the 'fixed' hierarchy of races Indians ranked above blacks though below Caucasians. The marriage tie might allegedly be regarded lightly by each race, yet at least Indian (unlike Negro) men were not pictured as permanently lusting after white women, in retaliation for slavery or as a means of social climbing. The rather more complex reactions of whites towards the Indian population help to explain the perpetuation of that special legal status and relationship with the federal government fashioned for the tribes, despite the impatience of many army and Western spokesmen about the observation of legal niceties between 'savage' and civilized powers.[16]

It would, however, be unwise to assume that opposing pronouncements on the two largest minority groups meant that either was ever regarded as other than inferior, or encouraged consistently contrasting policies regarding Indians and blacks. For there has been no unchanging commitment to Indian separation, while from earliest times the ostensible ambition of assimilating the Negroes (without miscegenation) has coexisted with the practice of stringent segregation. White ambitions and fears of an alliance between the racially oppressed nonetheless dictated different treatment for Indians and blacks on the 'divide and rule' principle, with red men being employed as slave catchers to offset the dangerous example of tribes like the Seminoles, who welcomed Negro runaways and allowed those they kept in bondage a freer existence than was possible in the Southern states.[17]

Neither has the plight of non-whites in American society attracted a uniform practical response from white reformers. Anti-slavery sentiment was aroused on behalf of red and black men alike, but until well on into the nineteenth century there was no great transatlantic humanitarian community able to mobilize political activity on behalf of aboriginal peoples throughout the world such as existed to agitate over the questions of slavery and the slave trade. Although censorious European visitors might complain of Indian removal by acquisitive whites to territory west of the Mississippi,[18] the European powers were using arguments akin to the notion of Manifest Destiny to take the lands of native peoples in the Pacific, Africa and the East.[19]

Before the Civil War the early optimistic faith of some humane commentators that the red and white races could live together in harmony had been shaken by the slow process of acculturation and the continuation of tribal warfare, while the devising of humane policies towards the native Americans still seemed properly the concern of 'experts', whether these were missionaries or administrators. Reformers seeking to enlarge their constituency support are always reluctant to complicate their message, and though individuals like William Lloyd Garrison, Lydia Maria Child, Wendell Phillips, the Motts and the Grimkés were concerned about the plight of Indians as well as Southern slaves, they gave priority to what they regarded as the most pressing evil. In view of reformer inclinations and the belief that Indian problems could be practically shelved by Indian removal, whereas black colonization schemes were a signal failure, it should not be too surprising that black Americans attracted more attention. Moreover, 'the very optimistic faith in the American progress which sustained so many of the moral reformers worked against those whose ideas were held to be perversely static, and resistant to the great liberating forces of Christianity and education'.[20] Free blacks might be drawn into the anti-slavery movement and share some of the aims of the white reformers with whom they co-operated, but Indian spokesmen generally found it difficult to work with humanitarians whose encroachment upon their cultural integrity they regarded as no less dangerous than settler encroachment upon their lands. And of course the multiplicity and great diversity of Indian groups would have presented problems even to white negotiators anxious to understand native organizations, supposing such men could have been found.

The Origins of Ethnic Pressure Groups

Black Organization up to the Civil War

The majority of the early black protest movements emerged, predictably, in the urbanized Northern states. Cities traditionally provide their inhabitants with greater opportunities for developing a diverse economic and leadership structure than are available in a rural setting, and by the beginning of the nineteenth century most of the 60,000 or so free Negroes lived in the urban centres of the North, Maryland and Delaware.[21] Particularly important were the black conventions, which after 1830 sent numerous petitions to the federal and state governments demanding equal suffrage, legal and educational rights and an end to segregation, building on a petition tradition already well-established by the end of the eighteenth century. Such demands were also expressed in black newspapers, which began appearing from the late 1820s and of which seventeen were published before the Civil War, while independent Churches and fraternal or benevolent organizations, developing in the black communities during the eighteenth century, fostered racial solidarity and provided a training ground for black leaders.[22] By 1849 in Philadelphia alone there were more than a hundred Negro mutual aid societies.[23] There has been a general feeling in America, where Church and state have generally been separated since the early nineteenth century, that religious groups should keep out of politics except to protest discrimination, which has been marked only when sects—Catholics, Jews, Mormons, Jehovah's Witnesses and Christian Scientists at various times—have seemed to be at odds with American values or a threat to American institutions. But the Negro Church, one of the few institutions within which blacks have been free to manage their own affairs, has proved an exception to this rule, consistently producing spokesmen for the race.[24]

There was every possible cause for organized agitation among the country's free blacks. In the South they were feared as a danger to the institution of slavery, were liable to be reduced to bondage and were increasingly subjected to segregation as well as to severe restrictions on their civil rights and economic opportunities. In the North free people of colour were generally poor, unwelcome if they went there from the South, excluded from the unions and in competition for jobs with the growing numbers of immigrants. Yet despite the oppressive discrimination which affected all aspects of their lives and prevented them from moving to the newer states of the West, free blacks throughout the nation intensified their protests against inequality in the two decades before the Civil War.[25] By 1840 blacks had been disfranchised in the South, as well as in New Jersey, Pennsylvania and Connecticut, where they had once enjoyed the vote, and exercised political rights only in New York (providing they could meet property and residence requirements), Massachusetts, New Hampshire, Vermont and Maine. Nonetheless, many had accumulated considerable political experience and determination and resented the fact that black exclusion from the polls was taking place just when the white working-class vote was being expanded. Accordingly, by the 1840s some Negro spokesmen were eager to take advantage of the disturbed political conditions which produced first the Liberty and then the Free Soil Party.[26]

It would be wrong, however, to expect greater unity from

members of a minority group than is usual among the dominant groups in any society and unwise to forget that black leaders at this time were conditioned by white values and institutions, while black voters responded to the usual dictates of habit, local circumstances, and economic and ethnocultural factors. Thus if 'most blacks revealed a desire and willingness to use voting and the political system for effecting their elevation', both to improve the lot of the freemen and to eradicate slavery, a restraining influence was exerted on some black leaders by their own conservative convictions or by white abolitionist colleagues, who similarly opposed political affiliations of any kind (and even shrank from political equality between the races). Negroes divided over the wisdom of supporting the anti-slavery parties, sometimes fearing to alienate the established parties, sometimes doubting the commitment of the new groups to black suffrage.[27]

Debates took place about the best methods of expressing black views. Just as the first black institutions had seemed 'but a weak image of those of white society' in style and structure,[28] so the black conventions spent time discussing the 'accepted patterns of self-improvement' and produced statements of their general views which might have been put out by any white reform association of the day, emphasizing their reliance upon God, their admiration for the Declaration of Independence, their gratitude for having been born in a bountiful land, and their faith in 'the spirit of American liberty'.[29] Even so, blacks in time developed a number of independent positions on contemporary questions, being the first, for example, to oppose the gradualism of the American Colonization Society.[30] Disliking confinement within exclusively Negro organizations, not all influential blacks were drawn into the conventions, and although such meetings gained invaluable publicity for the cause, it was difficult (as the women's movement discovered at the same time)[31] to ensure that action would follow upon the agreed resolutions. Ongoing political associations were clearly needed.[32]

The white anti-slavery societies, which were interested in a great variety of reforms and concerned to alleviate the lot of Northern Negroes as well as that of Southern slaves, should have provided an ideal platform for black activists, who were often involved in the contemporary crusades for temperance, prison reform, peace, women's suffrage and educational improvement.[33] But this proved to be far from the case. Although the Negro workers certainly enhanced the reputation of the abolitionists as dangerous radicals at odds with the prevailing values of American society (notwithstanding their appeals to Revolutionary ideals), black abolitionists frequently charged their white brethren with consigning them to inferior positions in the anti-slavery organizations, patronizing or shunning them socially, pursuing abstract principles rather than practical projects, especially for the free Negro, and suppressing dissent.[34]

By the 1850s, after years of apparently fruitless activity —activity which confounds the judgement of Ray Stannard Baker, who much later asserted: 'In the ante-bellum slavery agitation Negroes played no consequential part; they were an inert lump of humanity possessing no power of inner direction'—black abolitionists were in fact increasingly questioning the achievements of white civilization and turning towards more radical solutions to the *impasse*.[35] These included emigration,[36] slave revolts, civil disobedience directed by state Negro leagues, even proposals for the overthrow of the government.[37] There was considerable black opposition, during the first half of the nineteenth century, to schemes for repatriating free Negroes in Africa, partly because of hostility towards the racist Colonization Society, partly because emigration to countries like Canada was thought to promise more and partly because many blacks considered themselves to be American, not African. Nonetheless, as peaceful coexistence and equality between the races continued to elude them, some black leaders' interest in emigration projects increased. In organizational terms, the result of white abolitionist prejudice was often the establishment of segregated local auxiliaries, notwithstanding official denunciations of this practice; and though most black spokesmen initially opposed such separation, in time some came to believe that they should speak and act for themselves: 'If we act with our white friends, the words we utter will be considered theirs, or their echo.' R. C. Dick suggests that black attitudes fluctuated on the question of separating the races in other spheres, however, with leaders expressing doubts about the segregated churches they had once accepted, for fear of seeming to uphold the rightfulness of segregation, but willing to accept segregated schools, which they had opposed in principle, as a first step towards meeting the educational needs of blacks.[38]

Despite these disappointments and frustrations, blacks played a vital role in the anti-slavery movement, aiding some of their race to escape from the South, providing vital speakers and publicists and generally keeping it in touch with reality. The abolitionist crusade stimulated the black press, gave black leaders a wider audience than they would otherwise have enjoyed, helped to strengthen their determination to fight for their rights, and provoked independent thinking within the black community about the larger society and the ways in which it might be changed. It is, of course, impossible to judge the impact of these black activists upon either the black or the white population as a whole, but it seems probable that if the mass of Northerners inclined to some sort of anti-slavery view, this owed more to economic and political considerations than to anything else. Even the evidence of courage, eloquence and accomplishment among Negro abolitionists could not persuade many of their white co-workers to acknowledge black equality, however much they might empathize with the slave.

As far as their own people were concerned, although the motives of black reformers were not so frequently called into question as those of middle-class whites, the circumscribed lives of most freemen meant that their leaders—especially if at all fêted by the dominant society—might even more quickly lose touch with the masses, might more keenly fear returning to the poverty from which they had so often emerged. No black leader in the ante-bellum period enjoyed a vast following, though individuals did claim to speak for blacks at large, an ambitious claim which other ethnic leaders were less prone to advance. Blacks, like other sectors of the community, were divided on class, religious, political and regional lines, and those with light skins were inevitably tempted to 'pass' or model themselves on white neighbours or colleagues.[39] Such divisions, since they have always helped the ruling group to retain its hegemony, have been unduly emphasized by whites, who have additionally flattered themselves that every able

Negro has some white blood, and the major ideological efforts of nationalist movements have accordingly been directed towards the creation or reaffirmation of group pride and unity.

Indian Problems in the Ante-Bellum Period

Similar divisions existed among those Indian tribes who were in close contact with white civilization in the ante-bellum years and had an interest in influencing government decisions in their favour. For their own convenience whites designated the tribes independent nations whose representatives could negotiate with the United States, thus providing useful ammunition for twentieth-centry Indian nationalists but assisting their forebears very little. Formal treaties with the Indians gave government land deals with them the appearance of legality, though some white critics thought such treaties were no longer necessary by the nineteenth century, in view of white strength, while others condemned them as a cynical farce.[40] The government-organized visits of Indian chiefs to the East, intended to acquaint them with the wonders of white civilization, frequently failed to impress the visitors with anything but the superiority of native cultures, and Indians did not stay in Washington long enough to affect white policies.[41] In any case, the emphasis placed by successive presidents on the need for Indians to adopt white customs and agricultural methods could only be disagreeable when accompanied by unrelenting efforts to relieve the tribes of their 'surplus' land, however much American statesmen might try to persuade themselves otherwise, or however willing Indians proved, from the time of their earliest contacts with Europeans, to borrow from the invaders what they found attractive, from trade goods to less tangible items.[42] Moreover, the spokesmen for Indian peoples were even more unrepresentative of mass opinion than black leaders, for to a still greater extent they were chosen by whites, were in many cases of mixed blood or had intermarried with whites (though some mulattos were also prominent in black causes) and might stand to gain from the negotiations in which they were involved.[43] They were, in fact, both used and abused by the Americans with whom they had dealings, the latter being contemptuous of Indian 'parochialism' and unwillingness to 'differentiate power into religious, political, or economic categories' but only too happy to benefit from the resulting scarcity of secure, hierarchical leaders enjoying influence throughout an entire tribe.[44]

Even when tribal spokesmen acted in good faith, they could be misled by grandiose white promises and their failure to appreciate the white commitment to individual land ownership. As the great Sauk and Fox war chief Black Hawk recalled in his autobiography, in connection with a fateful council in St Louis, at which he treated for peace with the Americans, but without full awareness of what he was agreeing to:[45]

> Here for the first time I touched the goose quill to sign the treaty, not knowing, however, that by the act I consented to give away my village. Had that been explained to me I should have opposed it and never would have signed their treaty, as my recent conduct will clearly prove. What do we know of the manners, the laws, and the customs of the white people? They might buy our bodies for dissection, and we would touch the goose quill to confirm it and not know what we were doing. This was the case with me and my people in touching the goose quill the first time.

Where power rivalries existed within tribes, encouraged by the European powers in North America—as witness the conflict between the pro-British Black Hawk and pro-American Keokuk of the Sauk and Fox[46]—their unity and the ability of old leaders to control young warriors and dissidents was further eroded, while traditional animosities, buttressed by great cultural differences, prevented the concerted resistance of Indians to white encroachment through the linking or enlargement of tribal 'confederacies', such as those, at different times, of Powhatan, King Philip, the Iroquois and Tecumseh.[47]

The opposition to Indian removal, which policy was pushed with vigour after 1830, came from tribes already weakened and able to be individually coerced. In 1835 a removal treaty was signed with the Cherokees, some of whom lived in a manner indistinguishable from that of their white neighbours, after negotiations which involved less than 500 delegates out of a population of some 17,000, and those delegates showing themselves deeply divided. Appeals to the Supreme Court by Chief Ross and a missionary ally, the Reverend Samuel A.

Worcester, brought favourable decisions but no practical protection against determined state action; petitions to the Senate were equally ineffectual, and emigration was enforced by the United States army.[48] A similarly acculturated Southern tribe, the Creeks, split into 'progressive' and 'conservative' factions as a result of white incursions, were subjected to a series of controversial treaties culminating in an agreement to cede all remaining lands east of the Mississippi in 1832, signed by a group of seven Creeks who seemed unaware that their territory was now permanently alienated; removal followed, after an appalling period of fraud and disorder.[49] Other tribes east of the Mississippi fared little better, even where they offered no resistance, and the divisive tactics deliberately employed by white authorities paid a double dividend, not only facilitating the initial removal legislation but also creating new feuds which would undermine the political effectiveness of the displaced Indians for decades to come, and which, like tribal factionalism generally, have been comparatively little studied by scholars.[50]

It was indeed disastrous, given the linguistic and cultural gulf separating the tribes from their white opponents, that they could neither join forces with any other oppressed group nor win the protection of a sizeable section of whites. Although blacks fought alongside Indians in the Seminole wars they merely increased their own chances of emancipation and helped to delay removal; the extensive red–black alliance Southerners so dreaded in colonial times had been prevented by the exercise of vigilant control over the slaves and the numerical superiority of the settlers. Before the Civil War the missionaries, Indian service personnel and white reformers who cared about the native Americans were unfortunately divided in their counsels; some argued against removal, whereas others, bearing in mind the greed and corrupting influence of frontier whites, welcomed it as the best means of ensuring the survival of the red men. Furthermore, friends and enemies of the Indians alike took the view that the native title to land depended on their farming in a 'civilized' fashion.[51]

Conditions for the Indians and other non-whites did not improve further west. The migrating tribes clashed regularly with those already beyond the Mississippi and the federal government failed to provide its promised protection and aid for the migrants. White-settler pressure on the natural resources of the Great Plains, as well as transmission of epidemic diseases, antagonized the occupying tribes, and those in the former Mexican territories of Upper California and Mexico, forcibly acquired by the United States between 1846 and 1848, were little known and frequently unwilling to accept an altered way of life as a result of a change in jurisdiction they scarcely comprehended.[52] Growing hostility among the mobile Western Indians was not contained either by an ill-guided, over-extended army of indifferent calibre or by an Indian service which paid poorly in an era of limited government and was poorly served in return; while prejudices which travelled with the pioneers, strengthened by economic hardship and either personal knowledge of the cruelties of Indian warfare or hearsay, also guaranteed the persistence of that friction and misunderstanding between the two races which had prevented the development of a civilized political dialogue between them in the East.

Racial Conflict in the West

White arrogance was further encouraged by the series of victories over the earlier Spanish-speaking occupants of North America, which reached a peak in 1848. These victories were sufficiently hard-won to create dislike for the Mexicans and were aggravated by Indian involvement as well as fears of black slaves absconding into Mexico, but the struggle had not been demanding enough to engender respect for an alien culture and language. As those of the Indian population had been, the rights of the Mexicans were guaranteed by treaty in that year, due to pressure from the defeated power. Contemporary debate before the Mexican cession, however, had already made it clear that to Americans the Mexicans were Indians or men of mixed blood, incompetent to govern themselves and unfit to be placed 'on an equality with the people of the United States'. The racial 'inferiority' of their opponents, Mexican misgovernment and the failure to exploit economic opportunities justified annexation to avaricious whites, just as they excused Indian removal.[53] Once annexation had been achieved, bitter memories of the war on both sides, continuing border incidents, the failure of the American government to control the South-Western tribes,[54] and the discovery of gold in California in 1848 served to intensify ill-feeling between the races.

As long as the Mexicans remained in a majority, they stood a chance of decent treatment by the Anglos; but after the first year of the Gold Rush, when miners from all parts of the United States and the world flocked into the new territory, Mexicans in northern California were outnumbered three to one. Since many of the Mexicans knew how to work the gold and spent their earnings to the benefit of local trade, they were not unacceptable to the business community; nevertheless, they became the main victims of the Foreign Miners Tax (1850–1) and of many violent incidents in the mining camps. California already had a dismal history of discrimination against minority groups. Originally settled by large numbers of Southerners, it had outlawed slavery but sympathized with the prejudices upon which the institution rested. Indian 'peonage', persisting under Mexican rule of the province from 1822, served as a precedent for the unequal treatment of free Negroes and deterred their entry; both served to disadvantage the Chinese labourers who were leaving their own country for the West Coast in growing numbers by the late 1840s, impelled by economic distress at home and the hope of sharing the gold-fed prosperity in America. By 1850 about a quarter of California's population was foreign-born; some ten years later the proportion was approximately 40 per cent. Culturally separated as they were from the dark-skinned natives and Oriental newcomers alike, and fearing them as job competitors, white working men added clamour for discrimination against the Chinese to their persecution of the Mexicans, while politicians from the West and South joined forces in the national Congress to limit Chinese and Negro rights. Indeed, the close balance of the political parties in the West made it necessary for them to pander to local racists, just as this competitive situation eventually assisted the strong women's movement in states like California.[55]

As the largest 'minority', however, despite the huge rush of people into California which made it a state in 1850, the

Mexicans continued to attract intense hostility. Race relations were particularly strained by the economic depression of the 1850s, the confusion of land grants dating from before 1848 and the breakdown of law and order in which discontented Mexicans played no small part. Expensive legal battles and squatter challenges, combined with bad times, resulted in the dispossession of many Mexican land-owners, and white demands—reinforced by vigilante action—led to the *de facto* segregation of Mexicans by towns and states in economic and social life, housing and schools. If conditions in New Mexico, which did not seek to suppress the Spanish language, were not as severe as in California, with its more diverse population and strong working-class movement, or Texas, with its long commitment to slavery and historic struggle against Mexican rule, by the Civil War the promises of 1848 had everywhere been clearly broken.[56] Shocked by a decade of adversity, the leaders of the Mexican communities of the South-West proved unable to cope, and even before the influx of new waves of immigrants from Mexico, which came regardless of the chilly welcome they were accorded, there had never been any unity between ranchers and landless labourers, between town and country dwellers, between *mestizos* and people of Spanish descent. After political rights had been lost, Mexican Americans did slowly develop a range of defensive organizations comparable with those found among immigrant groups, but the task of recreating an interest in politics and co-operative endeavour became a Herculean one.

In terms of their retention of group solidarity, though not of their acceptance by white Americans, the Chinese immigrants initially fared rather better. From the first they aroused controversy, arriving suddenly in large numbers (among whom men predominated), clustering together and working very hard for very little. To the host society, as the historian Hubert Bancroft disagreeably explained:[57]

> These people were truly, in every sense, aliens. The color of their skins, the repulsiveness of their features, their under-size of figure, their incomprehensible language, strange customs, and heathen religion . . . conspired to set them apart had they not themselves exhibited a disposition to hold aloof from the white race.

Although whites may have believed that Asiatics were unassimilable on account of their race, newcomers—like the original occupants of the continent—were generally expected to accommodate themselves to American civilization. Those who failed to do so were suspected of undue clannishness or a desire to exploit its riches without any permanent commitment to stay, and suffered accordingly. In this category, later in the century, we may include the Mexican and Filipino immigrants, the first settlers from southern and eastern Europe and those from Japan; at this time the Chinese were the most exclusive of the immigrant groups. Essentially, during the 1850s they set about recreating in the United States their traditional social organizations, including the clans which existed for people of the same family or surname, and district associations representing those from the same locality in southern China. Clan officials, operating rather like the *padroni*, or labour bosses, who would eventually work among the Italian immigrants, found places for the new arrivals to stay and helped them to obtain work, food and protection. As well as providing advice about how to survive in the New World, the district and surname associations also strengthened the original family and community ties of the immigrants, and since membership was obligatory, though not necessarily active, they enjoyed an immense advantage over the competing voluntary associations struggling for existence in the black and other ethnic communities.[58]

These organizations in turn co-operated with a larger confederation founded in the same decade and christened the Chinese Six Companies by Americans in 1862, but subsequently officially designated the Chinese Consolidated Benevolent Association. The companies, which were soon to be found in any city with a considerable Chinese population, engaged in the usual clan activities, as well as assisting with the traditional shipment of the ashes of the dead back to China, the settlement of disputes, the collection of debts and help for the sick. However beneficial they might have been in this role, their alleged political influence was in time to make them the centre of a most heated controversy about the proper behaviour of immigrants in the United States.[59]

Ethnics and Immigrants

If contacts among different groups of non-whites were curtailed by white intervention and the geographical distance that came to separate native Americans from the rest of the nation, sympathetic relations between oppressed racial and immigrant minorities also failed to materialize. Having deliberately abandoned their countries of origin for the United States, white settlers were in many respects anxious to conform to the prevailing assimilationist doctrine, learning English and adapting their dress, behaviour and values to those established in the New World. An acceptable cultural tradition and appearance, together with the chronic labour shortage in America for much of the nineteenth century, ensured that white newcomers received a less hostile reception—especially by employers—than was afforded to non-whites; except, that is, in times of economic depression, or in urban areas whose resources could not cope with the influx, or when Catholic immigrants threatened to outnumber those of the predominant Protestant faith.

But though the first and second generation immigrants were concerned to adapt and conform, the complete erosion of group consciousness was impeded by their different origins and concentrated settlements, as well as by the feeling among old-established Americans that the first arrivals had somehow been the best, with an Anglo-Saxon 'core culture' against which late arrivals might be measured. Indeed, the maintenance of supportive institutions—albeit changing with the passage of time—was essential for the emotional wellbeing of immigrants whose assimilation, despite their own exertions, was essentially political rather than cultural.[60] Of course, the prompt extension of citizenship rights to free white aliens who had lived for two years in the United States, had satisfied the courts of their good character and had taken an oath to support the Constitution gave them an identification with the political system no racial minority possessed and removed at the outset the most basic stimulus to pressure-group activity, though neither element had more than a limited appreciation of the workings of representative government. Nonetheless, the immigrants likewise formed a host of mutual aid and fraternal associations from which their leaders emerged, and which developed a close interest in local politics and politicians.[61]

The pressures these leaders exerted, however, particularly on the urban party machines, were intended to procure not legislation but immediate favours designed to be of use to individuals rather than to advance the position of the group as a whole—specifically, assistance with jobs, housing, welfare and the law. The political parties in turn competed for the immigrant vote with promises of such favours, and the ethnic voting loyalties established in the first half of the nineteenth century proved remarkably enduring. Yet though the material foundation of this political relationship was crucial at the state and local level, in terms of national politics immigrant workers were more concerned with such issues as aid to parochial schools and the role of foreign languages in public schools, Sabbath observance, naturalization laws and temperance than they were with debates over tariffs, trusts and railroads.[62] On the question of Negro suffrage in the ante-bellum period, immigrant groups sadly tended to be even more hostile than the native-born,[63] which reflected their greater fear of black competition for jobs or land, even if immigrant attitudes to slavery were as diverse as those of Americans as a whole.[64]

Ethnic Pressure Groups from the Civil War to the Progressive Era

Black Protest through Reconstruction

Before the Civil War ethnic organizations had generally been of a defensive, benevolent kind, with recognizable pressure groups emerging only among the black population, long-established in America and resentful of continuing political impotence. In the course of the war, the emancipation of the slaves was at last achieved, the result of a fortuitous combination of military necessity, continuing abolitionist effort, presidential support, and the belief that abolition would ensure the future ascendancy of the Republican party. Unfortunately, the subsequent Reconstruction of the Southern states was undertaken against a background of phenomenal economic growth and change, while political attitudes altered slowly, if at all. Civil rights were extended to the freedmen to protect them against their former masters, to repay their wartime services to the Union and to secure their allegiance for the recently formed Republican alliance, North and South. Otherwise there was a widespread desire, in a country where the Constitution had provided one of the earliest, most prestigious bonds of union, to support the fiction that the old constitutional relationship between federal and state governments had not been disturbed. The great spate of legislation favouring industrial and commercial interests enacted during the war was made possible by the absence of Southerners from Congress; although they were excluded for a few more years, as President and Congress contested control of Reconstruction, there was to be no subsequent legislative effort to transform the social structure of the South in the interests of its black people, who were left to learn how best to use their new rights and freedoms and how to defend them when Northerners tired of this disturbing and expensive responsibility.[65] The fate of the freedmen depended very much upon existing black leadership and their numerical strength in any area or state.

With the adoption of the Fifteenth Amendment in 1870, impartial suffrage officially prevailed throughout the country. Southern blacks had already been enfranchised by Reconstruction legislation in 1867, and went on to hold public offices at the state level in addition to sending representatives to Congress. Outside South Carolina, Mississippi and Louisiana, however, they never exercised political influence in proportion to their numbers and were excluded from the key political jobs. The alliance of blacks, Southern unionists and displaced Northerners which made up the Republican party in the South was always an uneasy one; its governments were widely discredited by accusations of corruption and Southerners indulged in violence and intimidation to bring about their downfall. Thus instead of being able steadily to build up a secure vote and political leadership, the black community was again forced to resort to pressure politics from a position of weakness, protesting the indifference or monopolistic tendencies of Republican allies and the repressive activities of Democrat opponents.

Even in a state like Maryland, with a large free Negro population and leadership before the war, a high level of registration and voting during Reconstruction, and a host of other factors favourable to the participation of blacks in politics, their efforts to alter the subordinate position they were accorded in the local Republican party came to nothing, as did similar efforts elsewhere. Many pressure groups appeared during the 1870s and 1880s, but they were short-lived, usually confined to the black middle-class and to Baltimore, despite aspirations to state-wide influence, and boasting little continuity in personnel. The Republican elite largely ignored them and the Democrats shunned the black voter, so that there was no real course other than disgruntled loyalty to the party of the Great Emancipator, albeit the Equal Rights League obtained the admission of Negroes to state court juries in 1880, while the Brotherhood of Liberty played a part in securing the admission of Negroes to the state bar in 1885.[66] Without the ballot these victories would have been impossible; blacks were right to regard it as both the symbol of freedom and a practical means of obtaining better social and economic conditions, although most Reconstruction governments had no coherent economic programme. It is no accident that Democrats gave priority—particularly in states where Negroes were numerous—first to controlling black voters, then to disfranchising them slowly when circumstances permitted. Only after the full extent of this opposition to black participation in politics had been revealed did Negro leaders seriously look to other career opportunities and their followers cease to vote in remarkable numbers.[67]

Free blacks made known their hopes during Reconstruction in testimony presented to the president, sometimes personally, and to various Congressional committees investigating conditions in the South. They also sent petitions to government and employers, formulated unfortunately at unconnected conventions or meetings held throughout the country, including those of the National Negro Labour Union (NNLU). The Union bravely rejected 'discrimination as to nationality, sex, or color', hoping to evolve an organization 'capacious enough to accommodate . . . the Irish, the Negro, and the German labourer', not to mention 'the poor white native of the South', and to secure, amongst other things, legislation favourable to the interests of labour from the several states. Eventually the NNLU dissipated its strength by taking a close interest in broader issues such as education. Colonization proposals were rejected, though in a restrained tone, and petitions emphasized basic rights, not privileges, seeking equal treatment, not preferential legislation or revenge on the former slave-holders.[68] In the context of the times the pressures for the ballot, schools, land, fair wages, civil rights and protection against white violence were revolutionary and unacceptable, constituting as they did a demand for self-determination, for recognition of their rights as citizens and '*men*, children of a common Father' from those regarded by most Southerners and many Northerners as congenitally incapable of managing their own affairs. Thoroughly alarmed by black aspirations, propertied elements in the South even attempted to import Chinese labourers direct from China or via the West Coast and the West Indies as surrogate slaves, but such projects foundered on financial grounds, as well as proving unnecessary when whites recovered their former power.[69]

The options available to black spokesmen during Reconstruction were limited and their difficulties compounded by divisions within the black community. Often light-skinned and affluent, obliged to co-operate with white politicians and to adjust their aims accordingly, these leaders ran the risk of alienating the mass of Negroes. Avoiding violence, no doubt in the spirit of the Georgia preacher who warned that it would provoke 'the whole South . . . [to] come against us and kill us off, as the Indians have been killed off', and aware of the unreasoning objections to the black militias, prominent Negroes also risked leaving their race defenceless against white reactionaries who had no such scruples. Aiming at public equality and integration for the freedmen in American society, they were powerless to prevent the further growth of separate black institutions, which mirrored the separation of the two races within the ranks of the Republican party, and unable to prevent the fatal divisions which developed within that party.[70] As usual, their Churches provided Negroes with a vital avenue for advancement, many ministers going into politics during Reconstruction, but native leaders in the South were now reinforced to a remarkable degree by Northern Negroes attracted to the new opportunities opening up throughout the region. Northerners likewise initiated the Loyal Leagues, which organized black voters and were soon sustained by local enthusiasm, despite white opposition. After the Democrats recovered power in the South, however, these organizations were often transformed into more acceptable benevolent societies. In general, the solidarity of the black vote for the Republican party proved to be a disadvantage; in only a few marginal Northern states was this vote a major factor in Republican victories in the last decades of the nineteenth century. Yet there was no prospect of diversifying the voting pattern in the hope of wresting new concessions from the favoured party, as white ethnic groups were able to do, in a period when the Democrats were blaming many of the ills of the South on black enfranchisement.

Most Negroes ended Reconstruction as they had begun it; despite some real material gains, they lacked permanent organization, were economically dependent and therefore vulnerable. In the face of intensified racial prejudice which accompanied the victory of the Redeemers, blacks who rejected migration or emigration to Africa were obliged to confine themselves once more to organized economic and social activities, often Church-affiliated and modelled on those of white society, forming insurance companies, small businesses, mutual benefit societies, employment and welfare agencies, nurseries and kindergartens, fraternal orders and charitable institutions of all kinds.[71] The white humanitarians who, together with their black brethren, had pressed valiantly for equality before the law during Reconstruction were obliged to rest content with the meagrely funded and short-lived Freedmen's Bureau, an unpopular and unprecedented federal welfare agency which co-operated with the many voluntary freedmen's aid societies. And by the 1870s some of them, repairing previous neglect and recognizing the declining public interest in the freedmen, were beginning to join forces with the dedicated band of abolitionists who had long concerned themselves with Indian policy and prospects.[72]

Indian 'Reform' from the 1860s

These early white organizations founded to aid native Americans bear examination not only because they directly influenced the style and objectives of the first pan-Indian reform movements in the twentieth century but also because, successful as they were by their own standards, they illustrate many of the difficulties faced by ethnic pressure groups in the decades after Reconstruction. For much of the 1860s corruption vitiated the work of the Indian Service; Indian hostilities and partial support for the Confederacy alienated uninformed white opinion; while the westward movement which the Republicans supported involved further encroachment upon Indian lands. Those concerned about this unsatisfactory state of affairs could not agree upon the proper remedies, and bickering was particularly heated over the value of the treaty system, over whether the direction of Indian affairs should be in the hands of the army or civilians, and over the value and future of the reservations. The simple solution embodied in President Grant's so-called Peace Policy, namely, the replacing of corrupt Indian agents with virtuous churchmen—political corruption was the central preoccupation of reformers generally during Reconstruction and clean-up campaigns were to become their delight until at least World War I—had been discredited by 1876, in part because it did not affect other abuses in the Indian administration but mainly because the new personnel, however pious, were frequently as unsuitable as the old.[73] If humanitarians were unanimous in wanting to see the civilization and ultimate citizenship of the Indians, it was not clear to them how quickly they could move towards this desired end, though few doubted any more the wisdom of political activity, albeit carefully bipartisan. Despite a certain amount of pressure it had proved impossible to persuade politicians of the need to extend the benefits of the Fourteenth Amendment either to untaxed native Americans (that is, the majority) or to the female population of the United States, and the fierce opposition to its implementation where blacks were concerned was undoubtedly daunting. Moreover, if white well-wishers were sure they knew what Indians ought to want, they could not deny the need to find a more satisfactory machinery for consultation between the races and to cultivate a climate of opinion sympathetic to their endeavours.[74]

Important among the organizations formed to meet that need were the Women's National Indian Association of Philadelphia (1879), the Indian Rights Association (founded at Philadelphia in 1882) and the Lake Mohonk Conference of Friends of the Indian (originating in New York state during 1883), though there were many besides. The membership of these groups included Protestant clergymen and their wives, Quakers, missionaries, and humanitarians interested in other reform activities such as temperance, women's rights, pacifism, and freedmen's aid. Politically, Republicans were well represented, and the geographical centre of strength was the East, especially Massachusetts, Pennsylvania and New York, although there were some members from the Mid- and far-West. The societies also claimed a fair number of teachers, federal government employees, journalists and writers, educators, lawyers, businessmen and antiquarians. In other words, members of the middle class predominated, and no difficulty was experienced in gaining access to policy-makers drawn from the same stratum of society. Indeed, the Lake Mohonk Conferences, for example, which met annually until 1916 at the expense of the owner of the resort, Quaker educator Albert Smiley, were accused by some of their own members of being too much influenced after 1908 by the Bureau of Indian Affairs and the independent Board of Indian Commissioners.

The charge, notes L. E. Burgess, was unfair: Indian office men did not dominate the conference's crucial business committee, even if Indian Commissioners Jones and Leupp were involved with the committee in 1907 and 1908 respectively.[75] Some Indians appeared at these reformer gatherings, but when they did, as individuals relating the wrongs perpetrated on their people or as educated converts to white objectives—Indians of 'radical views' were not welcome at Mohonk—they were unable to make the kind of impact that more numerous black spokesmen had achieved in the anti-slavery movement.[76]

The size of the Indian reform associations is not necessarily a guide to their influence. More important in explaining success were the relationship between leaders and rank-and-file members, the resources available, the techniques employed to secure objectives and the time at which activity began—that is, after Reconstruction and the major Indian wars were over, but when the pressure of white settlers on Western lands prompted fresh attempts at resolving the future of the tribes. In the case of the Mohonk Conferences there was certainly power without numbers for a variety of reasons. Those attending were often strategically placed to influence policy decisions—for instance the chairman of the House Committee on Indian Affairs, James Sherman, and fellow member of that committee, John J. Fitzgerald.[77] The platform planks were decided unanimously each year, whereupon the Conference used its journalist members and press committee to send out news releases in a professional manner and to secure widespread publicity. And while the guest list might range from twelve in 1883 to 246 in 1914, the annual report was published in an issue of several thousands, reaching politicians, administrators, editors, colleges and other reformers, for whose ideas Mohonk also acted as a clearing-house. Delegates paid for the cost of its printing, but the remaining Conference expenses were borne by the affluent Mr Smiley.[78]

Rather different was the Indian Rights Association (IRA), which began in Philadelphia with thirty or forty members and soon developed a network of branches, though many of these languished for want of supervision or local drive. The survivors in time developed activities of their own, while continuing to contribute to the funds of the parent body and to receive visits from its important functionaries. By 1892 the total membership had climbed to 1300. Scrupulous attention was paid to the collection of dues, the soliciting of donations, the devising, monitoring or smothering of legislation and the dissemination of information (44,000 pamphlets in 1892 alone). The annual budget fluctuated between about $1700 in 1883 and $11,600 in 1916. Much of this money was spent on a corresponding secretary in Philadelphia, a full-time lobbyist in Washington (something which Mohonk avoided as too worldly and partisan) and fact-finding field trips to Indian reservations. Otherwise officers served gratuitously.[79] There seems to have been little social difference between the central and branch leadership of the IRA and the rank-and-file, which differed mainly in their degrees of activism.

The same is true of the Women's National Indian Association, which also evolved auxiliaries (fifty-six branches in twenty-seven states by 1885) and a similar financial and administrative structure. A central body provided the constitution and laid down the main lines of work through its officials and executive board, which included the chairmen of the innumerable 'departmental' committees favoured by the pressure groups of the day, each department specializing in tasks ranging from Press relations and missionary work to public meetings and memorials to government. Appeals were directed to Congress and its individual members, to

> editors, churches and societies, and . . . to the people by parlor and public meetings, and hundreds of thousands of pages of literature scattered over our land, comprising general statements of facts, appeals and representative cases collected from Government reports and other official documents, of the injust and cruel treatment of Indians.

It was estimated that in 1885 perhaps 800 to 1000 influential newspapers opened their columns to the Association, and 450 meetings had been held by its branches. Efforts were made to build up central funds by requiring each auxiliary to pay at least twenty-five cents per member to the national treasury, and a fee structure was developed which distinguished carefully between annual members, life members, male and female contributors, patrons and honorary members. Total receipts were fairly modest—$5678.60 between 1879 and the end of October 1883—but satisfactory by the standards of the day.[80]

There was a considerable overlap not only of aims but of personnel among the white reform organizations, as there is with modern pressure groups, something which did and may still produce contention. In reporting each others' operations very closely, reformers might well develop personal animosities or lose sight of their broader objectives. Factionalism was, however, a greater problem for the later associations formed by Indians themselves than for their perhaps less passionately motivated white predecessors. Great care was taken, for example, to praise the work of women anthropologists and field workers at Mohonk's male-dominated gatherings; the IRA courted the women's clubs, while the women's groups were willing to accept male associates and speakers.[81] The greatest danger of such co-operative efforts was that the converted spent their time preaching to other saints, a danger which was compounded by the scarcity of organizations and members in the West.

It is, of course, notoriously difficult to separate the techniques employed by any organization from its aims and ideas. Radical critics of liberal reformers too often pour contempt on the concern of the latter with finding new means to achieve old ends, or on their preoccupation with means as such. And yet the methods adopted may tell us a great deal about reformer ideology and may provide insights into the attitudes of the opposition. The Indian activists, if we may judge by their tactics and the disposition of their forces, were making a bid to arouse only the mass of the middle class; where substantial changes in law or administration were envisaged and a substantial section of Western, military and economic opinion presumably could not be won over, nothing was to be gained by shrill and negative denunciation of those presently in power or of any particular political party or sect. Statesmen and agents were accordingly to be presented as on the right path, if hesitant, as misinformed rather than malevolent, with petitioners pinning their hopes on a progressive future rather than drawing attention to the benighted past.[82] While such an approach might indeed win friends in high places, there was unfortunately a constant danger that the reformers would become the captives of their opponents, would convince themselves that half-measures were a success and that uniform policies could be applied to diverse cultures. This danger was aggravated by the common outlook of the humanitarians and their desire to see in the native population the characteristics they admired in white men: cleanliness, diligence, thrift, sobriety, individual conversion and salvation. In order to inculcate these virtues, all of which were presented as being in the public interest, native Americans ought, they felt, to be granted equal educational facilities, the opportunity of personal land ownership and full civil rights—the means, that is, to secure themselves against oppression and want, again something which benefited the larger society and not simply special interests. Saving the tribes from destruction was a more urgent priority in the eyes of the secular pressure groups than saving Indian souls, some reformers objecting to forcible conversion and many in the ranks of the IRA and Mohonk campaigning for years against government aid for sectarian Indian schools with a zeal quite disproportionate to the problem.[83]

The 'friends of the Indian', like the abolitionists before them, had some difficulty in evolving a consistent attitude towards contemporary social theories to which they themselves were not immune. As the abolitionists had done, they rejected arguments about the permanent inferiority of non-whites, taking comfort in environmentalism or talk about stages of evolution when taxed to explain Indian wars and ingratitude, apathy or dependence, and even looking forward to the eventual fusion of the two races.[84] But there was also a familiar ambivalence on race questions, nicely summed up by a speaker at Mohonk, who declared that 'all of us are brethren; and it is not for us to say that even the man of tinted skin is not capable of becoming manly and noble, and able to govern himself'. In their public pronouncements, although the boundless optimism of the ante-bellum era had vanished, the reformers minimized the native vices which many contemporary whites specifically identified—cruelty, immorality, unreliability, laziness and drunkenness—there being no sense in providing publicity for the opposition. Instead they preferred to emphasize the broken pledges of the United States and Indian hardships, especially health problems.[85] Nonetheless, the publications of the various organizations enshrine a number of frequently acrimonious debates. There were quarrels over the role of anthropology in the understanding of native American cultures, many philanthropists feeling that men of science were trying to preserve the tribal system they themselves wished to destroy, but both parties to the dispute recognizing that all available goodwill and expertise should be harnessed for the benefit of the Indians.[86] Similarly, disagreements developed over the permissibility of using peyote and other stimulants in a religious connection, over the practical impact of Christian mission work and the appropriate pace of change.[87]

Some whites thought that the Dawes Act of 1887 and its later additions, acts which provided for the allotment of

Indian land on an individual basis, were sufficient (building, indeed, upon the 1875 concession to Indians who left their tribes of land under the homestead legislation, whose benefits had also been reluctantly extended to Southern freedmen after 1866).[88] Others favoured the extension of American law over Indian reservations at once, without waiting for the slow process of Dawes, lest in the meantime Indians were forced to submit to arbitrary rule by the Indian Bureau and its agents. On the law issue certain reformers wanted, by way of compromise, a special interim set of courts and procedures for the reservations.[89] Nor was there unanimity about the value of the Indian Bureau. Admittedly, all agreed on the need to eliminate political placemen from the Indian service and to investigate charges against allegedly corrupt personnel. But differences surfaced—for instance, in 1916 at Lake Mohonk—as to whether some sort of independent Indian commission, responsible directly to the President, might not replace the controversial Bureau.[90]

By today's standards these objectives seem both ruthless and conventional, and the reformers' integrationist aims are particularly well illustrated in their views on education. Influenced by the leading contemporary educators and by a tradition stretching back to colonial times, they believed in something the sociology of the 1960s only began to question, namely, that schools were a crucial factor in racial advancement, that a uniform educational system was essential in a land with a diverse population, and that since its benefits worked for many, then disappointments resulted from inadequate finance or inadequate pupils, not from any faults in the system itself. Encouraged by the opportunities of a still unexhausted continent and by the experience of economic success, white philanthropists also assumed that the lives of the disadvantaged could be improved without taking anything directly from the fortunate. Education had long seemed to Americans one of the most acceptable ways of using the national wealth to provide opportunity for the poor without giving much offence to the comfortable. In the case of the Indians there should have been none at all, since the extension of educational aid was linked so satisfactorily with surrender by the tribes of their 'surplus' land. Schools had been envisaged as a way of improving the working-class, civilizing frontiersmen and of assimilating both immigrants and freedmen; small wonder that they should be regarded as the chief hope of the native Americans.

In advocating the establishment of government-supported public schools on the reservations during the 1880s, reformers were concerned to give equal opportunities for advancement to the Indians. If this meant segregated facilities, it was an accident rather than an objective, as became the case with public education in the South after Reconstruction. The inability of schools, certainly in the short term, to provide more than an avenue of advancement for exceptional individuals was seldom recognized and would have been little mourned in the last quarter of the nineteenth century. Instead progress was measured by increased government appropriations for education and in this area, according to their own judgement, the Indian pressure groups scored their greatest success. In the days when schools were still scarce, particularly in rural areas, before compulsory attendance laws had been devised and convictions about the need for scholarly attainments had penetrated many occupations, we should perhaps not ridicule a doctrine which contemporaries could defend with respect to the growing black elite, or the increasing political and other attainments of second- and third-generation immigrants. Some effort was made to meet the charges of critics who declared that the educated Indian returned to reservation life no longer suited to it and consequently discontented, perhaps even completely demoralized: a criticism reminiscent of that levied against the teachers of the freedmen, who were likewise held to be educating their charges into misfits. The answer was to break up the reservation, so often regarded as a form of prison, to make education available to all where they lived, rather than in segregated Eastern boarding schools, to emphasize vocational training, and to draw the Indians into the mainstream of American life. Philanthropists did not believe in the sanctity of the tribal relation any more than did the first, self-appointed leaders of the Indian race, and since schools have traditionally propagated the dominant values of society, their proposed solution to the problem of Indian isolation did not seem an unreasonable one.[91]

Continuing to measure achievement from a contemporary white viewpoint, by World War I the Indian organizations had considerable cause for satisfaction. Whereas in 1867 it was claimed that nobody 'pays any attention to Indian matters', although members of Congress 'understand the Negro question', by that time such groups had emerged as useful information agencies and the means had been found for 'forming and disseminating sound public opinion'. Having opposed the forcible and frequently decimating removal of Indians from their homes in order to concentrate them in uneasy proximity on Western reservations, reformers were happy to have influenced the ending of these removals, the passage of the Indian Homestead Act of 1875, the further extension of land allotments in fee simple among the tribes by the Dawes Act of 1887, and the subsequent conferral of citizenship rights on the Indians involved. Their agitation served to perpetuate the Peace Policy, to bring an end to the treaty system which had helped to preserve tribal integrity, and to terminate government support for sectarian schools, while protests had stimulated government action against corrupt individuals and the assistance of particularly distressed groups such as the Chippewa and California Indians. Limited funds meant that only a select number of 'special cases' could be taken up, though the local societies did as much as they could, and in membership as well as monetary terms the 'friends of the Indian' were never as strong as the anti-slavery movement had been.[92] In addition, humanitarians had helped to sustain civilian control over Indian policy, which in view of the callous attitudes of some army personnel engaged in Western duties was undoubtedly desirable, and had helped to bring employees among the tribes under Civil Service regulations and to 'secure the registration of family relations and the licensing and solemnisation of marriages by state and territorial laws'. Throughout their work they were inspired by the sense that such pressure-group activity confirmed 'the singular fitness for self-government which is shown by the American people'.[93]

It must be admitted, however, that the reformers made very slow headway until the 1880s and that in their major accomplishments they were assisted by an already aroused public distaste for the use of the army in politics and the political corruption which had afflicted national life during Reconstruction, as well as by the covetous greed of white settlers and developers for the 'surplus' land which the allotment policy released. Dismayed by the increased cost and scope of government after the Civil War, Congress was also ready to listen sympathetically to schemes which involved the reduction of federal responsibilities, fiscal and otherwise, for the Indians. Moreover, some desired goals were never achieved, while others, once attained, proved to have disastrous consequences. Mission work among the tribes made progress as laborious, with the assistance of the Indian aid societies, as it had always done.[94] Far worse, the Dawes Act and its successors were passed despite native opposition, particularly from the Five Civilized Tribes, who called a protest conference attended by some twenty tribes, lobbying in Washington and publicizing their objections. These and other white policies continued to aggravate that complex tribal factionalism which whites complacently regarded as merely an inevitable conflict between the forces of progress and reaction, albeit one highly convenient for humanitarians and economic interests alike.[95] Notwithstanding humanitarian concern that tribal land should be allotted with great care, in the forty-five years after this legislation approximately 90,000,000 of the Indians' 140,000,000 acres were transferred to white owners, more lands were leased to whites for mining, grazing and agricultural use, while Indians without experience of such transactions were cheated out of their territory or wasted their misconceived assets and were finally left in possession of the most arid and undesirable stretches of terrain.[96] After all the disillusioning consequences of allotment in earlier dealings with the tribes and of the 1862 Homestead Act among white Americans, a reaffirmation of their faith in the value of the family farm was the most philanthropists could devise to give economic content to their particular brand of liberalism.

The majority of Indians were still not integrated American citizens by the early twentieth century and many had become the very paupers which the reservation system had allegedly produced. Whites took comfort in the belief that a certain amount of folly and hardship must accompany profound changes of the kind embodied in Dawes or treaty termination, but that it was better for individuals to receive their inheritance at once and waste it or perish than to remain dependent on government annuities and rations.[97] Some effort was made to cushion the shock by offering 'individual opportunities of work to individual Indians' and building up 'self-supporting industries in Indian communities'—the twin objectives of the Indian Industries League, organized in 1893 in Massachusetts. The League petitioned Congress for bills to assist specified Indian groups and for the establishment of government schools to foster ancient and modern Indian crafts, opening a centre in Boston for the sale of native goods.[98] Its activities were no doubt influenced by the contemporary arts and crafts movement, but were nonetheless a welcome (if belated) recognition by whites that some aspects of the culture of the Indian peoples was worth preserving. Yet progress was inevitably slow. Most people in the East would 'not yet go much out of their way to look up' an Indian shop, while inadequate roads inhibited tourist demand on or near the Western Indian settlements. And there remained that paternalistic attitude among reformers which they ostensibly so opposed; as when an educator and member of the Board of Indian Commissioners, Warren K. Moorehead, deplored in 1910 the impact of modern technology on Indian craftsmen, urging that they should not be sent 'dyes, wools, designs and what not to bewilder their little brains, confuse their nimble fingers—and enable them to produce the atrocities we see in the curio stores'.[99]

As a result of the long assimilation crusade, the native Americans were worse off spiritually and materially than at any other time in their history. When the humanitarians ran out of inspiration the white public became convinced that there was no need for further agitation,[100] and attempts begun at Mohonk to link Indian reform with a new, white-aided effort on behalf of the black population were abandoned after a few years.[101] This is not to say, however, that white liberals avoided other movements to aid ethnic minorities which had developed by the 1890s or missed other opportunities to try and impose their values upon the main victims of the industrial era. But there were differences in the reformer approach to Indian and Negro problems at this time, just as there had been before the Civil War. Whites who took up the cause of native Americans may have been influenced by abolitionist experiences and the extension of civil rights to blacks during Reconstruction, may have feared that both 'primitive' races were destined for extinction without philanthropic intervention, in each case contrasting the benefits of civilization, the apex of social evolution, with the drawbacks of 'savagery', while finding no culture-free criteria for measuring progressive change. They also comfortably believed that there was less popular prejudice against Indians and that their small numbers made them manageable.[102]

As far as the black population was concerned, many whites were less optimistic, being convinced that only mulattos agitated against their lot, that the black masses were indifferent to 'abstract rights' and 'so-called radical movements', and that there was no unity or leadership within the black community.[103] Yet the last two decades of the nineteenth century in fact saw sporadic efforts among Negroes to organize themselves without external manipulation. Emphasizing racial pride and civil rights, activists gave warning to sympathetic whites that minorities would not progress from competition with the majority, through accommodation to assimilation, without the granting of fundamental concessions by the dominant elements in society.[104]

Black Organizations from Reconstruction to World War I

As the political and judicial interest in racial equality waned after Reconstruction and the most influential black educator, Booker T. Washington, pronounced education and economic self-help to be the ways forward for his race, Negro Equal Rights leagues in the North, undeterred by this conservative climate, petitioned state legislatures for civil rights acts, with some success. Conventions throughout the country also compiled lists of grievances in the traditional manner, memorializing Congress and the President, and sometimes producing organizations to fight for their objectives. The most important of them was the Afro-American League (AAL) of the United States. Formed in Chicago in 1890, largely through the efforts of journalist T. Thomas Fortune, the League resembled white reform organizations in its bipartisanship, dependence on Northern support and commitment to achieving 'the full privileges of citizenship' by 'the creation of healthy public opinion through the medium of the press and pulpit, public meetings and addresses'.

Its activities were to be peaceful and legal and a network of state branches was envisaged; over twenty in number, these in fact became the chief strength of the association. The significance of the League lay in its attempt to organize a national black response to injustice and to establish the utility of test cases in the courts rather than making paternalistic politicians its target, something which has become more characteristic of American interest groups than comparable alliances in other countries.[105] The AAL suffered the usual difficulties in retaining the interest of its original sponsors, in raising sufficient funds and building up mass support, and was driven to the time-honoured device of a new baptism, re-emerging in 1898 as the Afro-American Council. In both incarnations, during a depression decade marked by unprecedented white discrimination, to which organization was a direct response, it proved better able to envisage than to achieve progressive policies. Its aims included denunciations of lynching, agitation for laws to enforce the Thirteenth, Fourteenth and Fifteenth Amendments, federal aid for education, lobbyists in Washington, and a bureau to assist black migrants and to encourage commercial enterprises. In Fortune's words, uttered at the League's founding convention, it had 'undertaken a serious work which will tax and exhaust the best intelligence and energy of the race for the next century'.

Other similar groups sprang up to advance this work, particularly in the North, including the Boston Negro Suffrage League, the Equal Opportunity League of Chicago, the Negro American Political League, formed in Philadelphia (which, after various name changes, became the National Equal Rights League), the Equal Rights Council in Washington, and the Douglass Club of New York. In the South collective action tended to be confined to associations formed for social and cultural purposes, though it continued to produce black protest conventions. Aiming to secure civil rights, including the suffrage, to make whites aware of all the injustices endured by

Negroes, to meet local emergencies, challenge unfair laws, end segregation, and protest lynching as well as race riots, these organizations were ambitious, small and mainly short-lived, notwithstanding efforts to pool their leadership resources and prevent duplication of effort through the establishment of a National Federation of Coloured Organizations and Institutions in 1919.[106]

Many of those involved in the struggle for racial justice were clergymen, journalists and educators, with some white-collar workers and small businessmen—individuals drawn, that is, from the professions which dominated white philanthropy. But it was less easy for such blacks to secure their acceptance as community leaders, since the gulf which separated them from the mass of their race was larger, and they had more to lose from being associated with the characteristics of the masses, as whites understood them, through agitation on their behalf.

If moderate, they were often compromised in the eyes of real and potential followers by white patronage; if radical, they bore the brunt of white hostility. At a time when black newspapers generally had only a local circulation and the black illiteracy level was high, efforts to evolve a reply to the ideology of white supremacy involved even more extensive speaking tours by spokesmen for black associations than the size of America imposed on other pressure-group leaders seeking national remedies—hence the establishment of local societies. Although the majority of black people lived in the South, the circumstances traditionally conducive to organized protest activity, such as leisure, money, education and urbanization, were predominantly to be found in the North, so that black activists, like the white Indian reformers, were frequently speaking on behalf of those who were separated from them geographically as well as culturally.

More than most agitators in cause crusades, they tended to overestimate the inspirational effect of theorizing and preaching (because it strengthened the determination of the leadership), while underestimating the importance of class differences and swift symbolic or tangible achievements. They challenged white views of the black race and black history at meetings and in print, recognizing a duty to serve their own people, but when progress proved elusive some (and not only the considerable number of mulattos among them) were tempted to pull away from the unfortunate majority, partly conceding white indictments.[107] In addition, those who were the targets of black protest, namely, white legislators, lawyers and community spokesmen, were alienated rather than converted by the demands of Negro militants. For if ostensibly such demands did not threaten basic American values—like the suffragists, black dissidents claimed natural rights which the republic was committed to uphold—given the practical appropriation of civil rights by adult white males, groups like the AAL could accurately be described as radical by contemporaries but 'norm-orientated' by modern political scientists—in other words, 'attempting to change specific rules while accepting the value framework of society'.[108] Consequently, it was difficult before the 1960s for black activists to obtain that widespread publicity which is so necessary to the success of protest movements,[109] just as feminists found it impossible to gain a truly national coverage until World War I. Furthermore, the black population had lost political leverage within the Republican party without finding an adequate substitute, established political loyalties being notoriously difficult to change. Their leaders, as Fiona Spiers points out, evolved an ideology which concentrated on race prejudices to the exclusion of economic analysis, but it is difficult to see what this analysis would have achieved when economic self-help was frustrated by inadequate financial institutions and expertise, when craft unions dominated organized labour, opposing the admission of black workers to the crafts or confining them to segregated locals, and when white hostility excluded Negroes from the farmers' alliances, forcing the establishment of the separate Colored National Farmers' Alliance. The Populists, who took Alliance claims into politics, were defeated in part because of their courtship of Southern blacks; the Progressive party, which attracted black backing, suffered the usual fate of third parties; and the Socialists, though advanced in their racial attitudes, proved indifferent to the special problems of Negroes in American society.[110] The Churches and fraternal orders continued to exert their traditional hold upon the loyalties of the black masses; alone among voluntary associations they offered blacks opportunities for social mobility, though suffering from internal feuds, competition for members and a high mortality rate, as did the political pressure groups.[111]

This ascendency was not challenged before World War I, even by the three most widely known protest bodies, the Niagara Movement (1905), the National Association for the Advancement of Colored People (NAACP, 1909) and the National League on Urban Conditions Among Negroes (1910), generally known as the Urban League. The militants of Niagara, echoing the founders of the AAL, were resolved not to accept 'one jot or tittle less than our full manhood rights . . . political, civil and social'; they were likewise middle-class, concerned to manufacture a sympathetic public opinion, preoccupied with the South and determined to seek legal redress. But they were far more opposed to co-operation with the black accommodationists led by Washington, who was felt not only to be ideologically unsound but also to exercise an unreasonable influence with philanthropists, educators, white political leaders, employers and the Press. Washington's hostility, perhaps fuelled by feelings that his quiet work against discrimination was not sufficiently appreciated, in turn provoked the condemnation of Niagara by the black and white Press alike. Although there is evidence of considerable Negro disaffection with the Republicans during these years, the Niagara Movement's attacks on both major parties added to its radical image, as did demands for 'common school training for every child, if necessary at national expense' and higher education as well as vocational instruction. Equally alarming were demands for the suffrage and 'the denial of national representation to States who deny the rights of citizens'; for an end to discrimination in public accommodation; for freedom of speech and criticism, equal justice and the liberty to select friends, regardless of race.

In fact, in its literature the movement appealed to American methods of protest and the notion of the melting pot: 'Cannot the nation that has absorbed ten million foreigners into its political life without catastrophe absorb ten million Negro Americans into that same political life at less cost than their unjust and illegal exclusion will involve?' The establishment of a small central committee, with specialist departments and a number of state and local branches, was entirely within the bounds of respectable protest tradition, while the short life of black pressure groups should have reassured white Americans. Yet whites were not reassured, because the tone of the infrequent Niagara meetings, their invocation of race pride, co-operation and the spirit of John Brown, and their rejection of the proposition that 'the oppressor should be the sole authority as to the rights of the oppressed' suggested a new militancy among the black elite.[112]

With a maximum membership of around 400 and paltry funds, the movement had foundered by 1909. After that date, however, the emphasis by the Afro-American Council and Niagara upon legal work was sustained by the NAACP, to which many black militants transferred their allegiance. Significantly, they were now able to attract the support of a number of white progressives to counteract the endorsement of Washington by conservative whites. Although bi-racial reform coalitions have aroused much controversy among black leaders, at the beginning of the twentieth century, when the mass of Negroes expected little from pressure activities, even those connected with family and livelihood, the working involvement of sympathetic outsiders in black affairs was essential, not least for the improved finances it brought. By 1914 the New York-based NAACP, with a central executive committee and departments dominated by middle-class white reformers, could claim a largely black, similarly elitist membership of approximately 6000, in fifty branches concentrated in the North-East and Mid-West. Its journal, *The Crisis*, which enjoyed a circulation of over 31,000 and eventually became self-sufficient, was the 'leading publication devoted to the Negro . . . for well over a quarter of a century'. The objectives of the Association were:

> To promote equality of rights and eradicate caste or race prejudice among the citizens of the United States; to advance the interest of colored citizens; to secure for them impartial suffrage; and to increase their opportunities for securing justice in the courts, education for their children, employment according to their ability, and complete equality before the law.

The methods adopted included the now familiar ones of encouraging racial solidarity and repudiating doctrines of white superiority, publicizing racial injustice, lobbying, and concentrating on legal redress. Like its forerunners, and also the contemporary feminist movement, the NAACP maintained that although Negroes demanded full citizenship both as a natural right and because America claimed to be a democracy, they would make themselves worthy of such rights—opportunity, not charity, was wanted and self-help was to continue.

The Association, in contrast with some pioneering black pressure groups, was not indifferent to economic issues, and while officially non-partisan in politics, it contained a number of Socialists and Socialist sympathizers. Official spokesmen correctly pointed out that as long as blacks remained politically powerless, white businessmen would be able to manipulate them, to prevent the development of solidarity with white workers and to encourage the majority of the population to believe that black people were merely a useful economic resource. Yet because white philanthropy and black moderates remained aloof for the first year of the NAACP's existence, the press was unwilling to give it publicity, and because there was an informal understanding that the Association would not compete with the Urban League in the field of economic advance, no economic programme was evolved. This omission doubtless helped to restrain conflicting views among the membership about the merits of black integration or separation in the economic sphere, but it clearly limited prospects of achieving broad support in the cities, just as political radicalism was unlikely to appeal to the majority of Negroes in the South, where the NAACP was 'denounced violently'.[113]

Although it consolidated the efforts of earlier bodies, the Urban League made similarly slow progress before World War I. A typical 'federal' organization, centred in New York, it attracted 'socially prominent' reformers from both races and had no trouble in securing an encouraging press for its desire 'to promote, encourage, assist and engage in any and all kinds of work for improving the industrial, economic, social and spiritual conditions among Negroes'. Social workers were trained; scholarship aid was offered to potential leaders; advice, shelter and employment assistance was given to newcomers; and various social service projects were undertaken to help and counsel those already established in the cities concerning such matters as child welfare, housing and rents, health, dress and behaviour. Pressure was brought to bear by its representatives upon employers and urban authorities who discriminated against Negroes, but the League avoided political or legislative action, regarding this as the preserve of the NAACP, as well as out of a mistaken optimism over what could be achieved by personal persuasion and for financial reasons. Both societies had a great struggle just to establish and sustain branches; they were seeking to tackle racial discrimination and the problems of American cities at their worst point since the Civil War with annual budgets ranging from $15,000 to about $20,000, budgets which, in the case of the League, depended dangerously on the generosity of a few white philanthropists.[114]

Women lent their services to such activities—appropriately enough, considering their traditional interest in helping the young and the vulnerable. They made up about a quarter of the whites in the NAACP and the Urban League,[115] while black women were also involved in inter-racial work, though to a lesser extent, due to the persistence of those white prejudices which had kept the races apart in the women's club movement.[116] The female influence was not a radicalizing one, for the whites attracted to racial reform were college-educated and from good families, mainly seeking opportunities for employment and service, and black activists from comparable backgrounds could not afford to alienate the conservative men of their race, whose leaders seemed intent upon confining them to the role of noble preservers of home and virtue, a role which drove calculating nineteenth-century feminists to shape their strongly home-centred ideology.[117] Consequently, Negro women concerned to reject the twin burdens of racial and sexual prejudice achieved their greatest organizational successes through clubs, often affiliated to the non-sectarian and initially apolitical National Association of Colored Women (NACW), founded in 1896, and a variety of acceptable social-service and educational projects in their own localities. Nonetheless, experience in managing their own concerns outside the home produced greater militancy, and the NAACP, albeit with some misgivings, eventually called for women's suffrage, while the NACW spoke out against lynching, advocated boycotts as a means of combating discrimination and debated other national as well as international issues of the day.[118]

Success is difficult to measure, but by 1914, taking the most jaundiced view, it could be said that the NAACP had merely won a handful of discrimination cases; that the Urban League had helped a few blacks in a few cities, often in intangible ways; that neither could claim to be a national organization in any more than name; and that neither organization had been able either to resolve the ideological disputes within the black community or to convert the black majority to the merits of voluntary associations at a time when collective action to mitigate social evils was at last being accepted as efficient and legitimate.[119] Nevertheless, an educational campaign directed at black and white alike had commenced and would ultimately have its effect in more promising social circumstances. While demonstrating the inability of the Progressives to effect substantial changes in American life, each group also testified to the fact that urban liberals in the North continued to care about injustices that did not injure them personally, a fact which reflected the influences of religion, education and precedent.

In its work among city Negroes, as Nancy Weiss has pointed out, the Urban League was directly influenced by the operations of contemporary immigrant aid societies and settlement houses which offered shelter, employment bureaus, education, English lessons, recreational facilities and instruction in homemaking to immigrants, priding themselves on their up-to-date investigations and their understanding of urban problems and anxious to advance the acculturation of newcomers as well as their movement out of the slums. However, the general exclusion of blacks from such facilities (or their occasional admittance only on a segregated basis) made racial self-help of the kind fostered by the League a necessity.[120] It has already been suggested that acculturation was regarded as a one-way process; the host society set standards and the immigrants conformed to them.[121] Yet if they could not join forces with immigrant leaders, black activists showed a comparable desire to refashion the mass of their people to the extent that white prejudices would be soothed and then perhaps eroded. It is a sad fact that the enormity of the tasks facing all minorities in industrial America and the unpleasant tendency of whites to regard them 'in a common light' by the 1900s drove most minorities to exclusiveness. They often attempted to divert majority hostility from themselves towards other targets, as witness the abandonment by disillusioned feminists of the cosmopolitan views they had once held for a genteel brand of racialism. And unfortunately, white society sometimes encouraged these divisions, as when the anti-Catholic American Protective Association welcomed Negro support.[122] A common economic predicament still made the ethnic groups competitors and not comrades.

During the second half of the nineteenth century a host of organizations had sprung up dedicated to immigration restriction. They were somewhat similar to the racial societies in their attention to propaganda, lobbying, boycotts and fraternal activities, and their cautious approach to economic questions, despite their origins in economic adversity and change. Like the white reformers generally and the Progressives in particular, they set great store by political activity and legislative change, and at different times they operated throughout the country. In response, the immigrants combined their original village, regional, language and religious associations into national unions and turned these into vehicles of protest, getting up petitions, arranging meetings and lobbying Congressmen to resist immigration restriction and discriminatory treatment; they also had the inestimable advantages of the franchise and their own political representatives. But the immigrants shared some problems with the black population. For example they too produced 'marginal' leaders—men more anxious for acceptance in the larger society than loyal to the group. They, too, had difficulty in sustaining a national leadership, despite the initial strength of innumerable small community spokesmen; they, too, experienced conflicts 'between a leadership of accommodation and a leadership of protest' and between the poor and affluent; they, too, disputed the proper role of 'the homeland' in their affairs. Nor could adversity impose unity on immigrant communities, any more than on those of the blacks. Old immigrants would not join forces in the anti-nativist crusade with new arrivals from southern Europe, while in the pre-war years few outsiders acknowledged the sympathetic involvement with Negro reform efforts of Jewish groups or responded to the plea of Jewish intellectual Horace Kallen that ethnic diversity should be encouraged and America regarded as a 'democracy of nationalities, co-operating voluntarily and autonomously in the enterprise of self-realization'—the eventually influential doctrine of cultural pluralism.[123]

The Emergence of Western Protest Groups

In the West, where Mexican Americans had evolved numerous religious, mutual aid and even vigilante organizations, but where poverty, lack of education and parochialism militated against the development of what Hubert Blalock has termed 'pressure resources',[124] a sustained agitation from the 1850s onwards had forced Congress to enact legislation first excluding (1882) and then indefinitely suspending (1902) Chinese immigration. Foreign-born whites were among the most active nativists, seeking to protect their material interests and encouraged by labour organizations who at last found a unifying issue on which to campaign.[125] After their initial employment in the mining, lumber, railroad, construction and canning industries of the Pacific and Rocky Mountains West, the Chinese had been largely confined by native prejudice to domestic and personal service and agricultural pursuits, but they had nonetheless managed to develop their own small businesses at a rate far exceeding that prevailing in black communities. A similar economic cycle can be traced among the Japanese immigrants who were entering the United States at the rate of about 10,000 a year from 1900 and encountering the same white prejudices, now aggravated by fears of the growing power of Japan and the hardening of national racial antipathies. The Japanese exclusion leagues which sprouted in California were, however, supported by all elements of local society, and their pressures resulted not only in the curtailing of immigration (1907–8) but also in laws preventing the Japanese from acquiring land.[126]

Thus, like other American minorities, the Asiatic settlers

were faced with the alternatives of accepting restricted opportunities in the general labour market or developing their own economic sub-society, and that they were able to do with greater success than other non-whites, not because of their unique 'entrepreneurial individualism' but, as Ivan Light has argued, because of superior credit institutions, modelled on those existing in the home country and dependent on that mutual trust which is central to associations rooted in kinship and family ties. The social organizations of the Chinese and Japanese, the clans and Kenjinkai and their economic offshoots, also sought to control labour, to act as employment agencies, to intervene in labour disputes, to regulate wages and hours, terms of apprenticeship and prices, to provide welfare assistance, to give legal advice, to register and supervise the sale of businesses (among the Chinese) and to resolve commercial rivalries by appeals to duty, faith and honour. In these activities they were very effective, especially the Japanese associations, which did not have to contend with the tensions bred by congested living conditions and a severe imbalance between the sexes in their immigrant population. By contrast, black migrants to the North and those already established in the cities were not automatically drawn together by regional pride, by interest in Africa with the intention of returning there, or by the bonds of kinship and family, albeit these bonds were stronger than is often supposed. Moreover, as we have seen, the pioneer black pressure groups were small, elitist and sometimes involved with the white population, rather than invariably inclusive, popular, non-competitive and independent.[127]

Although voluntary associations had been an integral and accepted part of American life since the earliest days of the republic, ascriptive brotherhoods were generally regarded with considerable suspicion as encouraging divided loyalties. Those of the Asiatic immigrants were no exception. Contemporary observers referred critically to 'the channels of the quasi-Japanese government established in the towns and cities in California, and otherwise known as "The Japanese Association"'—a body established around 1900 and carrying out the same functions as the Chinese Six Companies, though operating through a network of societies quite independent of the

Kenjinkai, whereas the Companies directly represented the clans. The hierarchy, composed of consular office and central and local associations, supplemented by annual assemblies, was said to parallel California's political structure, and this, as well as Japanese propaganda, support for separate schools and apparent determination to introduce 'their peculiar civilisation' into the state rather than conform to local customs and standards of living, was strongly, if illogically, resented by the community, which discriminated against the newcomers. It was impossible to tolerate societies which aimed 'to defend, protect, and guard Japanese interests and privileges against the outside, and to maintain and establish unity and harmony in the inside, that they may enjoy full benefits'. All such bodies should be abolished and entire trust instead reposed 'in the American government and its educational system'.[128]

In fact, these fears were exaggerated, for though the Japanese government took an unprecedented interest in its American subjects, the Japanese Association was never directly connected with the home government; neither did it rule immigrant contacts with America or escape internal feuds and financial straits of the kind that afflicted voluntary associations. Its membership—which did not include all the Japanese on the West Coast—drew upon no tradition of protest, and if its publications did seek to put the Japanese case to the white population and defend the rights of Japanese immigrants, the Association also launched Americanization drives in the coast states, Nevada, Utah and Colorado, disciplined its supporters, made them aware of American laws, and successfully petitioned the Japanese government to amend its laws so as to allow the renunciation of dual nationality. During the first generation of settlement, however, when many immigrants returned to Japan, when nationalization was almost impossible and white animosity was intense, Japanese racial pride and personal deference dictated the establishment of inward-looking, generally apolitical sub-nations within the United States.[129]

Chinese Americans reacted in like fashion to comparable circumstances, accommodating themselves to those who resented equally signs of assertion and acquiescence, though adversity could not unite Japanese and Chinese or ally either with the growing black population,[130] and the Six Companies were rather more militant than the Japanese Association in opposing discriminatory legislation or treatment by the federal, state or local governments through protests and appeals. The organization also communicated to white society the desires and concerns, as well as the grievances, of the Chinese settlements. According to their historian, William Hoy, without having to rely on unpleasant coercive powers, an elaborate bureaucracy or an array of paid officials, the Companies, most active during the period up to 1910, represented 'self-government on a small scale and at its best' and were 'essentially democratic in form and function', a judgement which found some enlightened contemporary support. Unfortunately, there was a stronger native tendency to query the expenditure of Company fees, to allege involvement in illegal immigration and 'slave' labour, and to attribute its strength to 'the natural docility' of the Chinese and their veneration for men of power, which resulted in an organization so formidable that, according to one alarmist, 'the political influence of [the] . . . Chinese 130,000 . . . is more effective without the ballot than that of the entire Afro-American contingent, amounting in 1890 to nearly twelve per cent of the total population, or nearly 8,000,000 souls'. The Chinese 'machine' was credited by the same critic with fighting the passage and operation 'of restrictory legislation for over a decade', preventing 'unfavourable legislation for years' and taking its campaign to the courts with unparalleled astuteness and ruthlessness (although some whites felt the Chinese dangerously bypassed 'the American courts and tribunals'). Indeed, Chinatown supposedly was 'a factor in almost every election. Judges who have decided against them, Congressional aspirants who are anti-Chinese, and all candidates who have aroused their enmity, are liable to feel the effects of this influence always in the direction of corruption'.[131] Clearly, the 'unassimilable', however reprehensible in that condition, were expected to conform to type.

No doubt at the height of the Progressive crusade for clean government, any actually or potentially corrupt force in American politics was destined for criticism, but in this case ignorance and prejudice led to wild hyperbole about the efficiency and alien quality of Chinese associations. Cause crusades, particularly those of an abstract nature, were not popular among them either in China or in America, so that Chinese organizing abilities operated within narrow bounds, which may in turn have enhanced their effectiveness. Nonetheless, opposition to the exclusion law ceased once it was passed, contemporary assertions to the contrary notwithstanding. The Chinese Equal Rights League of America, for instance, founded in New York in 1891 and spreading to all larger cities, sought naturalization and full citizenship rights only for resident Americanized Chinese of 'education, property, energy, intelligence', promising to work for Americanization and appealing, like other racial reform groups, to justice and 'that idea of humanitarianism which has always characterized this Government'. Although the evidence is difficult to come by, there was even a degree of Chinese opposition to the Six Companies, which were regarded by some as expensive and possibly superfluous, and individuals who could find no appropriate clan formed another dissident element, occasionally taking to crime in the infamous *tongs*, though community and police opposition had broken the power of these by World War I.[132]

In the course of the nineteenth century voluntary associations developed among all American minorities and throughout American society, looking after the members' welfare and confirming their sense of separate identity. Although the black organizations did not generally feel the immigrant loyalty towards a distant country of origin before the Civil War, their conventions were beginning to entertain the prospect of emigration to Africa in the 1850s; later bodies, such as the International Migration Society, fostered this objective and indicated the growth of a strong nationalist tradition even in the black community, encouraged by a common history of oppression, segregation, and shared cultural characteristics.[133] However, the pressure groups that existed before 1914 (partly as a reflection of their middle-class leadership and white reformer influence) produced demands for American rights and committed their constituencies to Americanization. Ironically, it was white discrimination which not only triggered these demands but also ensured that the most they could achieve was a kind of unacknowledged cultural pluralism; this was what ethnic spokesmen generally settled for, uncomfortably seeking to reconcile two different worlds, though it is clear that blacks, Orientals, native and Mexican Americans alike were frequently convinced of the superiority of their own customs, the proof of which was their persistence.

With the passage of time the black and Indian aid associations evolved more elaborate bureaucracies and a national scope, but the former did not follow the normal tendency to become more moderate with experience. If urbanization facilitated the organization of ethnic groups, all except the Oriental alliances found it impossible to raise funds which matched their ambitions, and all suffered from leadership disputes, overlapping membership, a high failure rate, undue concentration in the North-East of the country, a vast gulf between activists and rank-and-file and an undue reliance upon what would follow from the dissemination of 'true' information about their situation. Economic competition and antipathies often learned from white men ruled out ethnic coalitions, and innate conservatism worked against an assertive role by black women in these societies, despite the steady growth of the feminist movement. Although collective action was greatly stimulated by the Industrial Revolution, the enormity of which was recognized, most Americans—race leaders not excepted—continued to believe that the lives of the majority could be fundamentally changed by orthodox political activity, legislation and individual exertion. Nevertheless, in a period when the Republican party had ceased to concern itself about racial justice and the Democrats remained indifferent (even if the two major parties competed for the immigrant vote), a political focus was both understandable and necessary to bring about wider access to the acknowledged institutions of power within the state. And while they frequently supported the conventional wisdom of their day, minority leaders at least established the possibility of organization, as well as the importance of resolving ideological disputes and challenging the popular prejudices which may be still more important than discriminatory laws in sustaining racism.

CHAPTER 4

Ethnic Pressure Groups in the Twentieth Century

The Impact of World War I

In a number of ways World War I transformed American society as pressure-group activity had never been able to do, creating new opportunities as well as problems for minority groups throughout the country. Various writers have pointed out that, since wars necessitate the participation of the underprivileged, the latter may hope in return for specific as well as incidental rewards; and, moreover, that such conflicts place great strains on existing institutions and attitudes, which may as a result be forcibly, if reluctantly, changed.[1] Thus in the nineteenth century, inability to fight for their country was made a reason for excluding women from the franchise, whereas black participation in the Civil War, although it was initially opposed, strengthened the case for extending civil rights to the freedmen and ensured their future service in the armed forces, albeit in segregated units.[2] When the United States entered World War I in 1917 Afro-Americans were divided about their proper course, but some 400,000 were eventually inducted into the army and the navy, with about half being sent overseas. Similarly, thousands of native Americans, though not liable to be drafted, volunteered and served during the war, following Civil War precedent and the later formation of all-Indian army units. The white ethnic role was, however, rather less promising from the point of view of improving relations between the minorities and the dominant society.

In May 1917 the Selective Service Act 'exempted enemy aliens and all other aliens who had not declared their intention to become citizens'; this exemption attracted more attention than the fact that 'quotas were appointed on the basis of total population' and that 'as the draft began to cut deeply into the country's manpower, it took a disproportionate number of citizens from communities with a large alien population'.[3] Resentment was soon expressed by the native-born, who feared that individuals whose loyalty to the country was suspect or barely established would enjoy the benefits of an expanding war economy, now deprived of the normal stream of immigrants. Discontent was also exaggerated by the movement northwards, between 1915 and 1918, of approximately 500,000 Southern blacks, lured by advertisements and labour recruiters promising jobs in the factories and war industries, better wages and freedom from discrimination. These migrants were generally young, predominantly male at first and unskilled or semi-skilled, and they settled in the already crowded and competitive cities. In time, skilled black workers, professionals and families all joined the exodus, which was encouraged by organizations like the Urban League.

Yet foreign-born and Negro Americans paid a high price for such employment advantages. Labour unions were still unwilling to recruit black members, whose use as strike breakers, often exaggerated, became a justification for established discriminatory practices. Living conditions for the newcomers were frequently appalling; they further strained the resources of the only partially reformed industrial cities, and their obvious poverty and different appearance and ways made them objects of suspicion, just as earlier European immigrants had been. The black ghettoes, which had rapidly developed in reaction to the institutionalized racialism and class tensions of the late nineteenth century,[4] were also enlarged and their problems proportionately increased, while closer Negro contacts with poor whites aggravated animosities which resulted in race riots throughout the North in 1917 and 1919. By the end of the war, alone among the non-white minorities, black Americans constituted a national rather than a regional 'problem' for whites, and their concentration into Northern settlements meant that in future they would find it as difficult there as in the South to win racial justice. And those who served their country found their rewards were segregation, unpleasant treatment by civilians at home and abroad and general confinement to the Services of Supply regiments.[5]

Although the number of aliens in key industrial posts was limited by 1918, native hostility towards foreigners—particularly those born inside the territories of the Central Powers—had been growing steadily since the outbreak of hostilities and was not easily appeased. Civil liberties were eroded by the zealous implementation of presidential powers or the Espionage and Sedition Acts, and by the state sedition and 'criminal syndicalism' laws; alien voting was restricted, the Press and films censored, and a host of societies exerted themselves, sometimes violently, against critics of the war, German Americans being the main objects of suspicion.[6]

If rising expectations among the unfortunate often generate militancy, their leaders may not automatically keep pace with this tendency, and at a time of national crisis it will in any event be checked by a desire to close ranks against external threats. Such a desire certainly manifested itself among the spokesmen for the nationality groups, and a similar caution is apparent in the black and Indian elites, necessarily concerned about the possible alienation of white friends and funds; by 1917 all ongoing reform movements were feeling the distracting demands made upon the American public by mobilization for war.

Black Groups in Wartime

The Urban League increased its affiliates by thirteen between 1916 and 1919, mainly in Northern cities; these branches had inter-racial executive boards and were staffed by paid professionals who dealt with the increased demands for social and employment services. It continued to emphasize the need for accommodation by black migrants to middle-class standards, while maintaining that adjustments would be easier for the Negro than for the immigrant, since 'he does not have to forget foreign customs and foreign loyalties for he is not a naturalized but a natural-born American citizen'.[7] During the same period the NAACP launched campaigns against lynching, the segregation of workers in the Civil Service, Jim Crow legislation in transportation, disfranchisement and residential segregation laws.

But although important victories were won by the Association's Legal Committee in 1915 and 1917 (the banning of grandfather clauses in state constitutions as a means of denying blacks the vote, for instance, and the invalidation of a Kentucky segregation ordinance), the Wilson Administration introduced segregation in federal government departments. Such action was taken despite the President's profession of sympathy with black aspirations before his election and his attempted recruitment of black voters from the Republican party, and despite protests from the NAACP and other black societies. These groups were unfortunately divided over both goals and tactics, besides being hampered by the still minimal 'educational level and political consciousness' of the black population as a whole and the particularly virulent contemporary racism which post-war tensions generated.[8] The transportation and lynching crusades both failed, not least because of inadequate legal resources in the case of the former, and undue reliance on publicity and denunciation in that of the latter. Ten years after its foundation the Association had more than 300 branches with over 88,000 members; following the death of Booker T. Washington in 1915 and the official reconciling of views among Negro leaders a year later, at the Amenia Conference in New York state, its position looked secure. The statistics were misleading. Many of the affiliates were inactive, like the rank-and-file membership in general, while early radicalism was muted by the attempts to develop an acceptable Southern strategy and resolve internal disputes (for example, about the wisdom of accepting a separate wartime training camp for black officers).

The NAACP journal, *The Crisis*, stressed that if blacks were to close ranks with other Americans to defeat the nation's enemies—a proposition endorsed by the rest of the black Press—certain concessions should be made by the federal government in return, to bring its domestic race policies into line with its lofty international objectives. There were no concessions, however, though Negroes during the war (notwithstanding considerable misgivings about the nature of the conflict) had again vindicated their claims to first-class citizenship. In 1919 the Pan-African Conference, which met in Paris to coincide with the peace discussions, was equally incapable of persuading the victors to accept a programme for the democratic treatment of coloured peoples in different parts of the world.[9] The disillusionment bred among black leaders by the betrayal of their wartime hopes would influence both their policies for the next two decades and their activities during World War II.

Indian Reform through the War Years

The white organizations working for the native Americans did not falter because of the European contest but, like all other pressure groups, they found it a disturbing influence. To the dismay of many supporters, in 1917 the annual Lake Mohonk Conference was postponed because of the outbreak of the war, and the war itself was made the occasion of scandalous neglect of the Indian Service by the government, with its employees leaving and crucial plant remaining unbuilt or unrepaired.[10] The IRA held a convention in 1918 with a view to preventing Indian affairs from being swamped by military issues, but clearly without success, and its hopes that the involvement of Indians in the world conflict would dramatically advertise their needs were destined for disappointment.[11] So, too, was this optimistic suggestion of the Massachusetts Indian Association: 'Surely in the world wide awakening to the rights of smaller nations Americans will no longer allow the Indian in his native land to be known as a wronged, helpless and oppressed people.'[12] Similarly embarrassed was the Society of American Indians (SAI), the first pan-Indian political protest association, which had been formed in 1911 and was active for some nine years.

Like most pressure groups of the Progressive era, the SAI was middle-class in composition, its members being drawn from medicine, law, the Church, education and government service, with whites admitted on an associate basis; the latter included individuals involved in Indian defence organizations, missionaries, clergymen, anthropologists and other academics, businessmen, Indian Bureau personnel and employees of Indian schools. There were no chiefs or tribal representatives among the activists, and the society was non-sectarian and non-partisan. By contemporary standards its delegates were well-educated, for many graduated from schools such as Carlisle, Hampton and Haskell, and they were individually successful, as well as anxious to conform to white ways regarding dress and social behaviour—something which was apparently thought worthy of remark, just as it had been at the early functions of black associations. As time passed the movement's assemblies went further westwards, though this shift did not stifle the complaints of critics that, meeting on university campuses and with a Washington office, it was not sufficiently in touch with reservation opinion, although there was something to be said for the suggestions that gatherings in cities ensured wide press coverage and white attention, while discouraging parochialism. Delegates to SAI conferences were not typical representatives of their various tribes, and their activities may be seen as marking a stage in the acculturation of the Indian elite.[13]

The Society sustained an annual conference, publicized its principles and goals, set up headquarters in the capital, produced a journal and lobbied or petitioned for changes in Indian legislation and administration in the manner of its day, but its members remained a collection of rather rootless individuals, anxious to change the Indian world substantially without forfeiting their acceptability to white society. Yet as Hazel Hertzberg points out, since the tribes had little basis for united action in language, customs or history, the formation of a federal, inter-tribal body was probably impossible, however strongly favoured by physician Charles Eastman and a few other prominent Indian spokesmen.[14] Society finances were always inadequate, reflecting the limited resources of the Indian elite, undoubted organizational deficiencies and the impact of the war. At the height of its strength, in the middle of 1913, the SAI could attract only a little over 200 active (that is, Indian) members and twenty-nine tribes to its yearly conference, primarily from Oklahoma, Montana, South Dakota, Nebraska and New York, although boasting at this time a white associate membership of about 400. By 1916 there were some twenty to thirty delegates in attendance at the conference, including associates; funds, which were chiefly derived from the $2 annual subscription, supplemented by occasional donations, were openly admitted to be short.[15] Associates were also playing a larger part in the Society's proceedings than had initially been visualized, but were not sufficiently representative of white opinion to compensate for the loss of its distinctly Indian quality.[16] As with the white pressure groups, most of the SAI's officers served without salary, but the full-time secretary-cum-treasurer eventually received a salary of $2000 plus expenses, which was a burden, and appeals for voluntary workers did not bring forth the desired response.[17]

These difficulties in turn meant that the Society was even more limited than its white counterparts in the number of individual short-term projects among the Indians that it could support, never managing to build up an effective legal aid department. The 69,000 pieces of printed matter the SAI proudly claimed to have circulated in 1916, though doubtless necessary to inform the public about long-term aims, to 'present in a just light a true history of the race, to preserve its records, and to emulate its distinguishing virtues', besides demonstrating the emergence of an acceptable leadership class among the native Americans, did not do anything for the sick or otherwise suffering reservation Indian.[18] All the Indian reform organizations, in both the nineteenth and the twentieth centuries, sustained some community centres, industries, missions, schools or training projects, but they could easily have spent their entire time and resources on meeting appeals for such help or on legal assistance of various kinds.[19] It is clear that most of the reformers' constituents preferred this sort of backing to any other and became disillusioned when they thought it had been promised but not given.

Regional or local ethnic associations have always been better able to keep in touch with the wishes of their supporters, despite having to compete with flourishing social clubs and fraternal societies. Thus the Alaska Native Brotherhood (ANB), established in 1912 by some Sitka (mostly Tlingit) Indians, though similar to the SAI in its emulation of contemporary white alliances, its reliance on a well-educated membership and its preference for Christian, pro-acculturation teaching, had several advantages over the national society. Having been able to establish itself as the bargaining agent with white industry and administrators in the territory, the ANB was able to persuade members of the local chapters, in the hope of gain, to pay its comparatively high dues ($12 annually, after a $10 initiation fee), and these chapters have retained membership loyalty by building up valued community centres. A few years after the Brotherhood, an Alaska Native Sisterhood was also founded, recruiting heavily from existing women's groups.[20]

The SAI, coming into existence after years of agitation by white reform associations, some of whose meetings its members had attended and whose efforts were frequently praised in the pages of its journal, evolved many comparable objectives and policy debates.[21] Much importance was attached by the SAI—and the Brotherhood—to the codification of Indian law and the recognition of Indian citizenship rights—for instance, by opening the US Court of Claims to the various tribes and bands instead of requiring special acts of Congress before grievances could be heard. It also wanted education designed to fit Indians for the white man's world, which specifically meant the extension of public-school instruction wherever possible, standard curricula and better provision for teacher training, together with higher education, for those who could benefit from it, in colleges and universities. Society literature urged the cultivation of such virtues as individual self-help, sobriety, hard work, race pride and faith in the future, to be facilitated through federal suppression of the liquor traffic, improvement of health facilities and the speedy allotment of Indian lands. Certain native customs and recent practices—for example, the use of peyote, alcoholism and participation in Wild West shows or exhibitions—were denounced with a puritanical zeal, and the influence was apparent of such white enemies of tribalism as Richard Pratt of Carlisle School, who described the establishment of the Society as 'the most momentous event in all Indian history'. Moreover, like the white 'friends of the Indian', SAI delegates disputed the value of the Indian Bureau, which continued to control native allotments and tribal funds. Some believed that it was no more necessary than an immigrant bureau would be and was wedded to advancing its own power, not Indian welfare; others were nervous at the prospect of its premature dissolution or advocated reform through increasing the number of native Americans employed by the agency.[22]

Considerable confusion prevailed about the appropriate means to achieve these ends. To encourage acculturation, the Brotherhood restricted membership to English-speaking Indians, notwithstanding protestations that a less exclusive organization might better advance the fortunes of the race; and with limited success in New York, Connecticut and Wisconsin, the Society pioneered the adoption by states of a national Indian day which, though designed to educate the public about the merits of Indians ancient and modern, was more backward-looking than anything else in operation.[23] While favouring the provision of educational facilities for every Indian child, the SAI was reluctant to tackle the controversy about the respective merits of day and boarding schools, from which many members had graduated, or to discuss the possibilities of joint educational programmes for blacks and Indians, as at Hampton.[24] Indeed, Indian and white associations alike were nervous about the subject of race relations. We have already seen that though many whites saw racial fusion as the solution to the Indian 'problem' and clearly admired Indians as a race more than Negroes, there was some reluctance openly to advocate intermarriage.[25] For their part the early native activists and their associates were unusual in thinking in terms of an Indian race at all, since tribal loyalties continued to prove so stubbornly resilient. They also acknowledged the cosmopolitan nature of American nationality and urged the logic of integrating Indians as well as blacks, suggesting impatiently that it might be as well to load 'all the Indians on board ships at San Francisco, send them around the "Horn" and bring them into harbor at Ellis Island as immigrants, in order that they might obtain their political rights'. But they attached particular importance to the Indian contribution, not least through extensive red–white intermarriage, and, like the women's movement of their day, they objected to being divested of all distinctive qualities and lumped together with other minorities, especially the blacks, whose difficulties were believed to be less complicated and oppressive in overall terms. More interest, during Society debates, was expressed in the fate of Indians in other parts of the world.[26]

The war gave Society leaders an opportunity to prove their claim to be good Americans by calling for Indian help in the war effort, by exhorting readers of the magazine to grow and produce for victory and by postponing the 1917 conference because of the involvement of many SAI officers in war work. The journal for that year looks appropriately thin. Nonetheless, if Indians were worthy soldiers, they deserved equal treatment by their government, and strong protests were made about the persistence of segregated military units.[27] Unfortunately, patriotism brought the Society no reprieve from its troubles, and it was moribund by 1920, though Indian military service contributed directly to the granting of citizenship to all in 1924, provided that the grant did not 'in any manner impair or otherwise affect the right of any Indian to tribal or other property'. Already advanced financial difficulties were aggravated by the conflict, despite brave claims at the 1918 convention that, even if the attendance was numerically small, it was strikingly representative and that new members had enrolled.[28] The leadership, like that of other protest groups, found the task of mediating between two worlds a daunting one, while slow progress encouraged ideological disputes and necessitated a dispiriting preoccupation with fund-raising and survival tactics. There were fewer common bonds in the Indian community than among members of any other ethnic minority, whatever concentration in Western settlements and instruction in English promised for the future, and the voting participation of Indians in federal elections, only just begun at the prompting of Woodrow Wilson's Secretary of the Interior, Franklin K. Lane, had quickly aroused local white opposition.[29] Poverty was a great impediment to voluntary work—individuals found it very difficult to travel to Society meetings, for example—and the cult of the individual was not easily grafted upon Indian cultures, although whites insisted on dealing with 'spokesmen' who were supposed to epitomize tribal opinion. After decades of reform agitation by bodies like Mohonk, and in spite of exaggerated claims about what they had accomplished, circumstances were not generally auspicious for the advent of a new association, even without the intervention of war, and disillusionment set in when Indian movements, especially those aiming at a national scope, emerged with a great flourish but promptly collapsed in a welter of personalities.[30]

The first issue of the SAI journal indicated the contrasting reactions the new venture had provoked:[31]

> Some fear we are trying to lead the Indian backward into the old condition, not realizing that such a fear is preposterous in its very concept. Some fear that the voice or act of one member is the voice of the Society. Some fear that we will become a church organization and the tool of a sect; some fear that we will not be a Christian organization. Some fear that we will become dominated by the government or the Indian bureau; some fear that we will become hostile to the government—some fear—but why proceed?

One of these fears eventually proved well-founded; the element critical of the Indian Bureau did come to the fore, but without appeasing those who wanted its prompt abolition or offering any alternative mediating institution for the duration of the reservations, an omission more understandable in the Society than among later Indian militants, who would also attack the Bureau.[32] Indeed, the Apache doctor and activist Carlos Montezuma was so dissatisfied about hesitation over this issue that in 1916 he launched his own magazine, *Wassaja*, with the sole purpose of rallying opposition to the Bureau as a barrier to native integration, tilting at the SAI, the IRA and Mohonk for their subservience to it, and accusing missionaries of supporting segregated schools and the Bureau because as long as the Indians remained 'wards' of the government, the philanthropist remained in business. In Montezuma's view, the Indian wanted 'freedom from the special government, under which we groan, over and above the ordinary government (to which we are also subject). We want freedom to develop normally. We want the CAUCASIAN'S CHANCE!' Reliant upon the relatively modest subscription of fifty cents a year, appearing at a bad time and preaching a message few reformers were then ready to hear, his journal had only a short life.[33]

Tributes were paid to the SAI by other 'friends of the Indian';

it seems to have enjoyed a favourable Press and contributed to a better reporting of Indian affairs, while its hard-pressed officers demolished the charge of their critics that native Americans were simply interested in having things done for them, in contrast, say, to the Oriental settlements, which looked after their own with very little call upon public resources.[34] Yet in trying to please as many interests as possible, they often gratified none. Moreover, it is difficult to give the Society specific credit for the eventual achievement of legislation favoured by most contemporary reformers, however valuable it was to whites to be able to cite educated Indian opinion. And ultimately, of course, the faith that all shared in the power of 'progressive' laws proved misguided: allotment failed because of Indian rejection as well as white rapacity, and the legislation passed by the states against the use of peyote (after unsuccessful attempts to secure federal action in 1916 and 1917) was ineffectual due to the medicinal, social and religious importance of the drug to the tribes.

Maturity in the Inter-War Years

Although the inter-war years posed great difficulties for all established pressure groups, because of the anachronistic reversion to *laissez-faire* politics during the 1920s and the customary drying up of funds available for voluntary work in the Depression that followed, such groups were also able to profit from earlier mistakes and concentrate on improving their organization after completing the initial, essential tasks of developing appropriate propaganda and establishing public credibility. Minorities once largely disfranchised by law or apathy—the Mexican Americans, the Indians, the Southern blacks and the Orientals—began to take an interest in politics. This involvement was encouraged by greater prosperity, occupational diversity and discontent with cautious first-generation leadership, as well as by the competition for new voters between the two major parties, especially in American cities. Such developments in turn produced a larger middle class among the ethnic and nationality groups, though if there were more individuals available with sufficient leisure for protest activities, they were still unable to attract mass followings. During the Depression the Democrats re-established majority-party status by putting together a coalition of the disadvantaged, but co-operation between its different elements continued to be slight, perhaps because it was at last clear that they were experiencing rather different rates of economic progress and degrees of acceptance by the larger society, and that this could not simply be explained in terms of when they had arrived in the United States or the colour of their skins.

Indian Organization

For the native Americans, however, these were politically difficult years, albeit marked by a heartening reversal of the long population decline, a religious renaissance and the passage of the most important Indian legislation since the Dawes Allotment Act. As a result of the Dawes legislation, Indian land holdings were severely reduced, but not all reservations had been destroyed (though some land within them had often been allotted). The severalty laws had proved difficult and disillusioning to implement, and the conditions of most Indians were sufficiently parlous, despite increased expenditure on education and health care, to make the case for looking again at established policies very strong. Accordingly, fresh campaigns were launched to arouse public interest and to pressure politicians and administrators into action, although it must be said at the outset that these were less important in producing a 'new deal' than the demonstrably enduring qualities of Indian cultures. Six years after the demise of the SAI, two of its former participants, Gertrude and R. T. Bonnin, both Sioux and she an artist and poet, he a member of the Indian Service, launched the National Council of American Indians which survived until the mid-1930s. Its title notwithstanding, the Council's following came mainly from South Dakota and Oklahoma, and its pioneering attempts to persuade the new citizens to vote did not continue after 1926. A newsletter was issued and, in marked contrast to the policy followed by the SAI, emphasis was placed upon representing tribal interests. But with even more slender resources than the Society had accumulated, the

Council was still less competent to help the Indians who came to Washington to 'secure . . . added recognition of their personal and property rights'.[35]

Fortunately, other associations appeared, operating primarily at the state or local level and in such numbers that their normally brief existence was dispiriting rather than disastrous. In New York a Society for the Propagation of Indian Welfare set out to improve red–white relations and obtain better law-enforcement, health and educational facilities on the state reservations.[36] When in 1921 New Mexican political interests pressed Congress for the transfer of large tracts of Pueblo lands to white intruders, there were protests from both whites and Indians; a Pueblo Lands Board was established to investigate territorial disputes, and an All-Pueblo Council formed to facilitate future political action. The crisis also produced a new white pressure group, John Collier's American Indian Defense Association. At meetings of the Society of Oklahoma Indians, resolutions were passed urging the state's delegation in Congress to prevail on the Secretary of the Interior to take action on their specific grievances and to expedite desired bills before the legislature, while the non-partisan Tushkahoma League, which brought together twenty-eight Oklahoma tribes, aimed at persuading Indians to vote and to elect men friendly to their special needs.[37]

In Chicago the Grand Council Fire of American Indians, which had functioned since 1923, drew up a long list of recommendations for the guidance of Hoover's Indian Commissioner, the Quaker philanthropist Charles J. Rhoads, who was urged to build more schools, to extend instruction at high-school level and to arrange for Indian attendance at public schools wherever possible, to increase the number of hospitals and the medical service, and to encourage and develop Indian libraries, employment bureaux, handicrafts and skills appropriate to native environments.[38] Indian women had long been the target for missionary and reformer propaganda, both as the moulders of the next generation and as having to make fewer adjustments to become 'Americanized' than their menfolk. By the inter-war years they too were organized in the National Society of Indian Women, which was modelled on white women's clubs, fostered self-improvement activities and welcomed white associates.[39] Meanwhile, established movements like the Alaska Brotherhood continued to work for assimilation of the native Americans, though they adapted their short-term objectives to changed times; the Brotherhood, by means of boycotts and court actions, was especially concerned to establish Indian voting rights, to secure the acceptance of native children in Territorial schools, to fight segregation and to encourage the formation of fishermen's unions.[40]

These endeavours undoubtedly contributed to a far-reaching investigation of Indian conditions authorized by the Secretary of the Interior, to the publication of the Meriam Report in 1928 and to a complete reorganization of Indian affairs in the 1934 Wheeler–Howard Act. There was by this time less unanimity among reformers than had prevailed during the nineteenth century, and a certain decline in white arrogance may be measured by the decision to apply the law only to those tribes where a majority voted in its favour. The new act at once acknowledged the failure of early policies to integrate and improve the fortunes of the Indian population and, without abandoning assimilation as the ultimate goal, allowed for slow progress towards this objective, constructing additional safeguards for native welfare in the process. In a sense, it marked a *rapprochement* between the conservatism which had lingered in the IRA, in journals like *The American Indian*, and in the House and Senate Indian committees on the one hand and, on the other, the flexible attitude to tribal practices epitomized by Collier and his supporters.[41] It was, furthermore, in tune with a growing public interest in Indian art and lore, which journalists were beginning to mine in a serious way.[42] The alienation of tribal land by allotment was now to cease; tribal corporations were to be formed for the acquisition and development of new lands which were to be exempt from taxes and placed under federal authority. In further recognition of the importance of the tribal units, they were permitted to contract for needed services and, subject to government direction, to establish their own form of government, to administer justice, to decide on tribal membership, and to levy taxes on Indians and those who did business on the reservations. This was no simple grant of the powers of self-determination, and once again the futility of general laws for diverse peoples was demonstrated. Nearly eighty tribes rejected the act, because many individuals who had prospered under the old policies resented as reactionary and personally damaging the return to communal activities, making their resentment felt through the 'progressive' factions which had once delighted the hearts of whites.[43] Others objected to the new leadership patterns which the act envisaged and the obstacles to the creation of tribal governments and party systems recognizable to the white world were initially underestimated. Although most of the Indian reform associations supported the 1934 legislation, taking pleasure in being consulted by those in power, the American Indian Federation of the 1930s gave organized expression to certain of these feelings of unease, while even generally approving bodies like the National Association on Indian Affairs (NAIA) felt the 'vital need for a powerful, well equipped national organization or union of organizations, capable of far-flung, constant field investigation as well as constructive field work', something which still does not exist and, due to inadequate funds, was not provided by the NAIA.[44]

Indian leaders recognized by the white world remained scarce between the wars, and it proved hard to galvanize Indian voters, only a tiny majority of whom had agitated for citizenship in the face of apathy, tribal opposition to the ending of their sovereign status and the unwillingness of some Western states to accept the 1924 act. There remained the old disparities between the tribes in terms of size and assets, the number of members living off the reservation, the extent of white influence and in modes of government; and such variety would have made common policies impossible for Indian spokesmen had they been seriously considered. Nonetheless, the articulation of tribal and pan-Indian interests had made considerable progress and it would never again be possible to pretend that the native Americans lacked political voices of their own, no matter how hard whites might try to ignore them.[45] There were similar signs of growing political consciousness among other disadvantaged elements in the West, again in response to social and economic change.

Pressures in the Mexican American Community

For the Mexican American communities progress was rendered more difficult by the constant increase in immigration from Mexico between 1900 and 1930, many of the new immigrants being illegal 'wetbacks', some of whom were brought in by American labour contractors. Reinforcing the existing heavy settlements in Texas, Arizona, California, New Mexico and Colorado, as well as moving in considerable numbers to Indiana, Illinois, Kansas and Michigan, their visibility was increased by their concentrated employment in the production or processing of cotton, vegetables, fruit and sugar-cane. The Mexicans came mainly into the race-conscious, economically slow-growing area (California excepted) of the South-West, a region badly hit by the Great Depression which bore down so heavily on agriculture in general and agricultural employees in particular, forcing many into unwelcoming urban environments. They consequently encountered discrimination from whites and provoked misgivings among indigenous Mexican Americans.[46] The romantic view of the region which was developing by the late nineteenth century in literary and conservationist circles had not displaced the stock image in the public mind of the Mexican as lazy, dirty, intemperate and violent.[47] An unfamiliar culture preserved by ethnic pride, inferior educational facilities and segregation, and epitomized by a foreign tongue, aggravated the economic fears of local poor whites and Negroes. Then dark skins, a high illiteracy level and an 'alien' faith—Catholicism, in a predominantly Protestant region—further stimulated Anglo prejudices and seem to have been more important than the numbers of Mexicans involved, some one and a half million by 1930, which made them the second largest minority in the United States. For their part the immigrants did not bring with them a tradition of political participation, and they arrived initially without their families; being both proud of their homeland and close to it, they frequently returned or hoped to do so. Their experiences in the United States scarcely encouraged a sense of belonging, and naturalization was a daunting process for those with little English or education.[48]

Yet there were many differences between the various areas

where Mexicans were established and within their own settlements, despite the factors making for cultural solidarity. Better economic prospects and a more open economic system prevailed in California than in the former slave state of Texas, which had once painfully secured its independence from Mexico.[49] Conversely, political participation was more widespread in Texas than California, perhaps because it seemed urgently necessary in that hostile land, and more general still in New Mexico, the only state with proportional representation and Mexican Congressmen from the 1930s.[50] Internal divisions, however, operated as the crucial brake upon pressure-group activity; the middle and upper classes experienced that tug of loyalties which affected their counterparts in other ethnic communities, deplored behaviour which lent credibility to Anglo myths and were tempted to distinguish between old and new settlers, between Hispanos, or Spanish colonials, and Mexicans. A familiar alternative means of escaping discrimination was full acceptance of white mores, although members of wealthy families might not even be conscious of its existence. In consequence, those most capable of providing leadership readily became estranged from the masses or lost interest in exercising power for fear of alienating white society, preferring to participate in Anglo voluntary associations.

Nonetheless, some middle-class activists did emerge from professional and business ranks, though their circumspection did not prevent the development of bossism in Mexican politics—for example, in Texas.[51] There illegal assistance was given in voting and in the purchase of poll taxes, and prosperous Latin Americans co-operated with whites to preserve the *status quo* in return for political offices in the counties where they were strong, the blame for such corruption falling not only upon the bosses but also upon their supposedly feudalistic followers.[52] Of course, complaints were made about the political manipulation of immigrants in the nineteenth century, but the big difference now was that, at a similar stage of acculturation, Mexican (and indeed black) voters were unable to extract much in return from their patrons because of historical racial prejudice, the relative decline of machine politics and the solidarity of their support—the Mexicans overwhelmingly gravitated to the Democrats, as the Negroes would do by the end of the inter-war period and as they once had backed the Republicans.[53]

Among the poorer elements of the Mexican population, immigrant or long-established, there was the usual preference for religious, mutual aid and economic organizations over any other, and while they evolved nothing comparable with the Six Companies, they did attach an importance shared by Oriental settlers to former community ties as well as kinship connections.[54] Challenging the patriarchal and political leaders for their allegiance was the *coyote* or *explotador*, who might have the advantage of the same class background and was reputed to help over jobs, housing and brushes with the law, but who also exploited his workers on payday.[55] The partial unionization of agricultural workers in California and elsewhere brought few tangible benefits in the face of much employer hostility, and loyal Mexican service during World War I could not even force their acceptance on equal terms in the veterans associations that were subsequently formed.[56] In these difficult circumstances the first major protest group to emerge, the League of United Latin American Citizens (LULAC), was sensibly cautious in its objectives.

Founded in Texas in 1929, out of a number of existing organizations, by 1934 the League could claim forty-three lodges, or councils. Building on the early efforts of the Catholic Church, and rather like the Japanese Association, LULAC hoped to promote Americanization and the exercise of citizenship rights; though non-partisan it was anxious to see Mexicans participate in 'all local, state and national political contests'. The organization welcomed politicians and office-holders as members if they were not seeking a platform for their political opinions, and particular store was set by jury service, non-segregated education, and the ending of 'every act of peonage and mistreatment as well as the employment of our minor children'. Attention was to be paid to the inculcation of race pride and the dissemination of propaganda through 'the press, lecturers and pamphlets', supplemented in due course by a monthly journal, but the League opposed 'any radical and violent demonstration which may tend to create conflicts and disturb the peace and tranquillity of our country'. In traditional American fashion, the LULAC council worked through various 'departments' concerned with matters like housing, legislation and education, while social and fund-raising activities enabled it to compete with less ambitious community clubs. During its first years of existence LULAC was influential primarily in Texas and was engaged in the difficult task of deciding on the best means to achieve its ends, tending towards negative protests against discrimination rather than the direct political and legal action it would later advocate. The League was certainly unable to transform Mexican attitudes, particularly towards compulsory school attendance, to disarm white critics, or to avoid the factional disputes which normally afflict such movements.[57]

Group Solidarity among the Chinese and the Japanese

Superior organizing skills and internal solidarity seem to account for the rather greater progress made by Oriental groups during the inter-war years, although distance from their homeland and the drying up of immigration gave them additional advantages, while success was enjoyed largely outside the political arena. At first, however, the prospects for progress could scarcely have seemed less encouraging, for native opposition had secured the termination of Oriental immigration in 1924 and had confirmed the exclusion of Oriental immigrants from naturalization, developments which had facilitated the spread of laws denying land-holding to Japanese Americans. These laws were both resented and flouted by their victims, thus intensifying existing white prejudices and dislike of the efficient Japanese farmers' organizations.[58] In time, persistent discrimination, as well as dissatisfaction with the cautious leadership of the Japanese Association among second generation Japanese (the *nisei*), prompted the formation of new movements designed to seek for their members full acceptance by American society. The American Loyalty League, founded in 1922 in San Francisco and soon spreading to other Western cities, survived for little more than five years, yet its demise stimulated the establishment of a similar but more successful voluntary association, which brought together surviving civic groups in a body known as the Japanese American Citizens' League (JACL).

By 1938 some thirty-five chapters were affiliated with the national League, which met biennially in conference, issued a journal in English only, became the recognized spokesman for the *nisei*, and made its major impact in the Western states, where it fought anti-Japanese legislation and discrimination in such matters as the provision of educational and recreational facilities. Like other ethnic pressure groups, the JACL was anxious to increase political awareness and, with this in mind, supported efforts to permit naturalization of Orientals who had served in the military forces of the United States and to amend the Cable Act of 1922. (The Act denied American citizenship to women who married aliens ineligible for citizenship.) These measures were secured in 1931 and 1935.[59]

Nonetheless, the League encountered familiar difficulties; despite its achievements in the fields of labour relations, community improvement and civil rights, only between a third and a half of the Japanese eligible to vote could be persuaded to register for that purpose during the 1930s and then they did not act as a block, even though interest was declining in the wealth of old associations—the prefectural, welfare, merchant, craft, artistic and patriotic societies—which had reaffirmed immigrant links with Japan. Normal generational differences were unusually marked in Japanese settlements, where a special terminology distinguished the first, second, third and fourth generations (*issei, nisei, sansei, yonsei*), so it was not to be expected that the JACL challenge to distant family or regional ties and the deference due to age and the ancient verities should develop unopposed. The willingness to accept non-Japanese members, the strength of the young, urban, Christian, comparatively 'high-status' element in League chapters, and their emphasis upon benefits (such as insurance) instead of mutual obligations were all controversial features of the *nisei* organization—though its inability to tap more than a fraction of its potential supporters or to convert more than a minority of its members to activists should have provided some reassurance that the early groups were unlikely to disappear.[60] Equally unacceptable to the older generation were the criticisms of Japan's activities in the international arena, the importance attached to 'socializing' activities away from the home environment, and the rejection of the advice of business spokesmen who saw no profit in minority protests, particularly during the adverse conditions of the Depression, and who by their control of employment opportunities were able to enforce this conservative philosophy.

However, it is possible to exaggerate the distinctions that were emerging between the first and second generations. Both expected and encountered hostility from the larger society, despite their declining family size and visibility as aliens. Both sought to achieve group solidarity through secular institutions, including the controversial Japanese-language schools which whites held to be 'proof of disloyalty to the United States', although, ironically, segregation in American public schools dramatically limited contact between the races and the prospect of Japanese assimilation through intermarriage. Both believed in their own superiority, as well as in the need to protect the 'Japanese image', and this conviction—more than family strength—sustained the exclusiveness of the *issei* and the integrationist efforts of the *nisei* alike, remaining unshaken by the bickerings of rival leaders and economic interests or the contrasting viewpoints of Christians and Buddhists.[61]

Between 1900 and 1930 the Chinese communities were shrinking rather than growing, like the Japanese settlements, and were less adversely affected by the alien land laws; but there were within them similar signs of discontent with established spokesmen and organizations, and a similar opposition to change was manifested by the Six Companies, or the Chinese Benevolent Associations, as they are now more commonly known. Indeed, in an attempt to remain all-inclusive in scope the Companies were obliged to embrace the entire range of Chinatown organizations: chambers of commerce, women's clubs, family and district alliances, *tongs* and even the Chinese schools and newspapers, all of whom paid dues to the Companies and were represented by their presidents at the federation's monthly meetings. Those not satisfied with first-generation leadership had already formed alternative societies by the beginning of the twentieth century, of which the most important has been the Chinese American Citizens' Alliance, incorporated in 1895. Like the JACL, the Alliance spread throughout the West, avoiding recruitment on clan lines and seeking to secure or defend the economic, educational and political rights of its members; it also built up a following among the educated, civically active and native-born and introduced popular insurance programmes. But it posed less of a threat to existing community institutions than its Japanese counterpart and, since membership was by invitation only and confined to Chinese, never attained the size of the League.[62]

With the greater prosperity and self-confidence of Chinese settlers during the inter-war years there was no resurgence of the violent manipulation by the *tongs* of prostitution and drug dealing, while social or professional organizations modelled on those of the white majority proliferated. Yet the overall prospects of the mass of Chinese Americans had not greatly improved by the time of the outbreak of World War II, any more than those of the Japanese. The society which had objected to Oriental migrants as clannish was not mollified by Americanization drives and proved unwilling to accept equality, resisting the admission of Asian children to white schools, retaining anti-miscegenation laws, and continuing to exclude Orientals from certain kinds of employment. After the Japanese attack on Pearl Harbor it proved to be an immense disadvantage to the Japanese in America that a whole range of farmer, labour and patriotic pressure groups still existed in the Western states which had campaigned—and were still willing to campaign—against allegedly unassimilable outsiders, some of them having renewed their anti-Orientalism between 1924 and 1934 in a successful crusade to halt Filipino immigration. Although this crusade depended on varied antipathies, it found much fuel in the competition for jobs between Filipinos and whites.[63] Similar economic tensions provide the key to an understanding of black protest activities between the wars.

Changes and Continuities in Black Protest

The increased prospects and expectations and the eventual disillusionment of American blacks as a result of World War I had a clear impact on the rhetoric of their established pressure groups, in addition to facilitating the rise of the Universal Negro Improvement Association (UNIA), the first national movement to capture the support of the black masses. A period of bitter reaction helped to trigger not only race riots but also the discussion by Negro leaders of the desirability of direct, possibly violent, protest against oppression, just as it had during the ante-bellum years of the nineteenth century and would again in the 1960s.[64]

Part of the greater militancy noticeable in the public pronouncements of the NAACP is, however, to be explained simply by the steady extension of black control over the organization—its field staff, secretariat and legal programme had all once been dominated by whites, notwithstanding a largely black membership from the outset. This erstwhile domination, initially necessitated by the dearth of black lawyers, their concentration in the North and public scepticism about their abilities, ceased because of both black resentment and a number of practical developments, including the emergence from Ivy League law schools of an elite of Negro lawyers, improvements in Howard University Law School, and the award of a $100,000 grant from the American Fund for Public Service to finance civil-rights litigation. In turn such developments were 'a function of the shifting social milieu in which the NAACP operated'—in other words: 'As the movement gained strength and achieved victories, and as the external society accorded greater legitimacy to the Negroes' demands, the usefulness of whites declined, and their role within the organization became constricted.'[65]

The actual machinery of the Association changed only slowly, nevertheless. Immense power was exercised by an educated, middle-class, New York element within the (still underpaid) national Board; rank-and-file members (still the main source of revenue) proved almost universally unwilling to attend the annual meetings in order to challenge Board policy or nominees for office; and the subordinate branches that were formed after the headquarters were established in New York often proved inactive or acquiescent.[66] Only from the 1930s, when the NAACP's lack of an independent economic programme seemed open to criticism and the existence of a reasonably sympathetic Administration in Washington encouraged black aspirations, was there progress towards making its annual convention the main policy-making agency.[67] Nor did the Association's aims change swiftly with changing circumstances, for it continued to give priority to protest, agitation, court action and lobbying for desired legislation in the field of civil rights, looking to the branches for funds, test cases from the lower courts and information, until pressure from within and outside the movement forced a major reappraisal of NAACP objectives after 1934.

Despite the attainment of a national reputation and bureaucracy, despite NAACP representation of the cause of American blacks at international conferences and the protesting of racial injustice in Panama and Haiti, despite its leadership of the domestic fight against lynching and barriers to equality, the Association, having failed to convert either of the major political parties to a civilized concern for the Negro, experienced serious doubts about its original integrationist goals and its early decision to leave economic policies to the Urban League.[68] Events made that decision unacceptable, for as the Depression deepened, unemployment among blacks reached a level twice as high as that among whites, and their wages were on average 30 per cent lower, while discrimination in relief payments was notorious.[69] All the efforts of the black middle class to create a viable black capitalism within the ghettoes had foundered on the rocks of white competition, the poverty and indifference of the Negro masses, and the limited scope and services offered by black businesses. Similarly, those who looked to politics as a way forward had found themselves obliged to repay patronage with loyalty to the party, regardless of racial considerations.[70]

No other Negro organization was so well placed to make an impact on race relations during the inter-war years. After the war the black-led Urban League did not even resort to threats of drastic action if its efforts should be rebuffed, but continued to collect information about black conditions, to intercede with employers, union leaders and public officials and to train social workers, making a limited number of job placements without being able to affect the basic patterns of Negro employment. Neither the NAACP nor the League was directly involved in mobilizing black labour, with the exception of the latter's seventy or so Workers' Councils in the mid-1930s, and the praise its activities won from 'both the white and black establishments', though to some extent deserved, gives a fair indication of the League's moderation.[71] Yet the experience of the UNIA, the most important radical black group of the 1920s, was not encouraging either and underlines the danger of supposing that there is a single strategy for securing racial advancement. Since his death the Jamaican founder of the Association, Marcus Mosiah Garvey, has become a hero for black nationalists in the United States and Africa alike, but he died in obscure exile from the country in which he had achieved his ephemeral successes, and during his lifetime Garvey was denounced not only by alarmed whites but also by the black elite in America and the West Indies.

After establishing an organization in Jamaica in 1914, Garvey transferred his main operation to the United States two years later; following an extensive tour and membership drive launched from New York, by 1920 he was claiming six million members in some 900 chapters throughout the cities of the nation, and indeed the world. Although these claims were clearly inflated, for the next five years Garvey enjoyed unprecedented influence in the black community, raising some $10 million from supporters. This success was not the result of exciting new methods, for the UNIA resembled other contemporary pressure groups in evolving an elaborate secretariat, in exacting dues revenue from its members, only part of which the local branches were allowed to keep, in offering unrealistic fraternal benefits, in publishing a periodical, in elaborating an ideology and in setting out a programme. Progress followed rather from the confidence of Garvey's message, his comprehensive exposition of black nationalism, and the immediate, tangible benefits which followers saw in the Association's network of black business enterprises. By no means the first black leader to try to resolve Negroes' emotional involvement both in their own culture and in that of the larger society, the Jamaican spoke in inspirational fashion to an aroused people of the need for racial pride, purity and solidarity to celebrate the African heritage, and to assert entitlement to a separate homeland in an Africa liberated from white colonial domination. If such a territory could not be acquired peacefully, then the need for military force should be accepted and applied by a whole range of Garvey units, among the African Legion, the Black Eagle Flying Corps and the Universal African Motor Corps.

The international aspect of Garveyism was vitally important to contemporaries and goes far towards accounting for its subsequent influence. Although it was not intended that all blacks should renounce their national allegiances or return to Africa, the organization of a steamship line to transport willing Negroes there and UNIA efforts to enlist support for the colonization project from the American and Liberian governments, as well as the League of Nations, aroused considerable alarm in Europe and Africa. The enterprise failed, like Garvey's other commercial ventures, because of lack of funds, expertise and precedent, and after his imprisonment in 1925 on a mail fraud charge of dubious validity, followed by deportation, the movement eventually split and went into decline. He made numerous mistakes, alienating black intellectuals, the black Press and many black ministers by his scathing criticisms of their moderation and his own tactics, not least his effective attempt to build a sect, the African Orthodox Church, at the expense of existing black congregations. The original demands for 'political justice and industrial rights' were dropped, and Garvey did not fully grasp the differences between the racial situation in Jamaica and America. While his rejection of inter-racial coalitions would be applauded by later black militants, along with his hopes of an alliance with Third World groups, opposition to integration brought him the unhelpful backing of white extremists, notably the Ku Klux Klan. Nonetheless, for the first time a national black organization had been forged which was able to recruit and rouse the interest of those unaffected or unimpressed by the ambitions and achievements of the small black middle class. Successfully bridging the gap between leaders and followers, between exhorting and achieving race pride, it stimulated the formation of a number of similar, if smaller, societies, and the intense white hostility Garvey excited confirmed the disturbing potential of mass demonstrations and marches in the race struggle, even when they were not effectively harnessed to a domestic political programme.[72]

The Depression Years which destroyed UNIA's financial base also dried up funds for philanthropic endeavour and discredited conventional liberal reform efforts. Yet for all the controversy aroused by the consequent extension of government power during the Roosevelt era, the blacks who had abandoned their traditional loyalty to the Republican party and had voted for Roosevelt so overwhelmingly generally failed to benefit from the social welfare programme and received only limited assistance from the other major legislation of the era. Under the circumstances, the Communist Party, which had committed itself to aiding the Negro struggle for equality in all its aspects and had adopted a Negro vice-presidential candidate, might have been expected to recruit the disenchanted black voters in large numbers. Such a switch did not take place, partly because of the normal reluctance of citizens to waste their support on minority contenders for political power. Many blacks, however, also felt as uncomfortable with the ideology of Communist Party leaders as they did with appeals for solidarity with traditionally hostile poor whites. Communists urged black advancement in associations where they were strong—the National Negro Congress, the American Negro Labor Congress and the Sharecroppers Union—and mounted some spectacular bi-racial hunger marches, strikes, and demonstrations, often against injustices meted out by the New Deal agencies. Nonetheless, their own internal disputes were hardly less damaging than those among the black leadership, while white opposition to the mobilization of the unorganized in agriculture and industry was bound to be intense at a time of economic adversity, even without the intrusion of the race question. The industrial unions formed during the 1930s admitted black members mainly because of their need to expand rather than in response to the Urban League or other pressure groups, readily confining them to poorly paid, unskilled work and denying them senior union posts.[73] Nor did the American Socialist movement, after a long period of indifference to minority-group problems, attract many Negroes, despite its belated efforts to enlarge its appeal.[74]

In desperation, new organizations were formed and fresh tactics tried. The Southern Conference for Human Welfare (1938) and the Southern Negro Youth Conference (1937) revitalized protest in a region whose political representatives in Congress constituted the chief barrier to civil rights legislation; and the National Negro Congress (1936) brought to the fight against segregation, lynching, the poll tax, inequitable relief payments, and union discrimination a number of associations representing different parties and classes. Building on precedents for non-violent, direct action dating back to before the Civil War, blacks also mounted 'Don't Buy Where You Can't Work' campaigns in certain cities between 1929 and 1941, campaigns which appealed especially to younger blacks and the entrepreneurial element, and may have received further encouragement from Communist ghetto workers, but which were certainly helped by the legalization of picketing in 1932 and 1938.[75] Designed to persuade firms heavily patronized by blacks to hire them too, the boycotts and mass demonstrations needed strong community backing to succeed; they frequently collapsed—despite some NAACP and more Urban League assistance—when supporters failed to agree, local courts proved hostile or the struggle became protracted.

The direct application of economic pressure outside the ghetto seemed a departure of uncertain value to the two major black movements, and until recently their judgement has proved correct. Successful boycotts opened up jobs in black areas but most achieved only modest results, and, taken together, these tactics could not reduce mass unemployment for blacks in the economy as a whole. Yet, there were other instances of direct action resorted to exclusively by blacks—protests against segregated public accommodations or schools, miscarriages of justice, the persistence of lynching—which, alongside the economic campaigns, were essential in preparing the public mind, black and white alike, for the greater militancy which developed during (and after) World War II. Meanwhile, the moderate approaches to the solution of their problems generally employed by ethnic organizations during the Depression were as much as the contemporary political climate would tolerate. And if hardship weakened them all, while government agencies or the new industrial unions undermined the influence of the old benevolent societies, the common interests of the poor, regardless of race or national origin, were at last persuasively demonstrated. In bringing this message home to moderate pressure groups, the Socialists and Communists did not win many direct converts, but they played an important part in widening the perspectives of such groups and in enhancing their ability to learn from others.

The Impact of World War II

Most of the American minority groups benefited economically and in other ways from the war, because of the needs of the defence industries and the armed services rather than through any deliberate concessions made by the federal government.[76] Women served as non-combatants in the forces, worked in jobs once reserved for men, and saw the inter-war prejudices against the employment of married women eroded; when the conflict ended the percentage of women in the labour force remained considerably higher than it had been in 1940. Many thousands of American Indians, Mexicans, and German and Italian Americans obtained jobs in strategic industries, and the black population made even greater gains when, after the failure of moderate protests against discrimination in employment by their prominent organizations, threats of a national protest march on Washington (orchestrated by journalist and unionist A. Philip Randolph) persuaded President Roosevelt to issue an executive order in June 1941 proclaiming Administration support for equal job opportunities, vocational training programmes, and anti-discrimination clauses in government contracts.[77] A Fair Employment Practices Committee was set up to investigate and remedy alleged violations of these provisions. Although the committee was small and short of funds and black personnel, and in spite of the fact that labour shortages were a more important source of economic gains, its very existence provided a long-needed and spectacular vindication of the efficacy of non-violent direct action, focusing attention as it did on black grievances and stimulating the passage of laws against discrimination in employment in certain states and cities.[78] Despite regional variations and continuing white prejudice, by 1945 there had been a marked increase in the number of black men and women in employment and of blacks in skilled jobs and government service. However it had been achieved, there would be no easy return to the conditions of the 1930s.

Nonetheless, progress was frustratingly slow. Wartime

migration by non-whites to the cities of the North and West aggravated housing problems and strained already run-down facilities, and those who joined the armed services faced segregation, discrimination and the risk of violent exchanges with white soldiers. Pressure on Roosevelt applied by spokesmen from the NAACP, Urban League and other organizations determined to amend military policy met with only a limited response, though the anger thereby aroused increased the financial contributions to the NAACP sent in by soldiers and civilians alike, its income rising from over $60,000 in 1940 to some $400,000 in 1945. The increase in membership was no less significant, for whereas in 1940 the Association claimed 355 branches with 50,566 members, five years later it could at last boast mass appeal, with just under 450,000 members in 1073 branches.[79] Neither the black leadership (including the now large and vigorous black Press) nor the black public was willing to give the war effort absolute priority as the President urged and as they had generally agreed to do during World War I, arguing instead that it was a patriotic duty to agitate against undemocratic treatment.[80] Thus while the March on Washington Movement achieved little after 1941 and had petered out by 1947, another wartime foundation, the interracial, largely college-based Congress of Racial Equality (CORE, 1942) was also able to build on Depression as well as Gandhian precedents for direct action, attacking segregation in public accommodations in Northern cities through pickets, boycotts and sit-ins.[81] Wide appreciation of such techniques would not come until much later (since they were difficult to popularize in wartime), but these were fruitful years, for acquaintance with new homes or new countries permanently stiffened the resolve of ethnic leaders and returning veterans, as did the continuation of economic prosperity after the war and the appalling treatment of the Japanese Americans throughout its course.

Although over 12,000 of them eventually saw military service, an exaggerated national response to the attack on Pearl Harbor combined with the entrenched hostility of many West Coast whites and the misguided patriotism of a few influential liberals to pressure the government into the mainly forcible evacuation of more than 110,000 people of Japanese ancestry (two-thirds of them American citizens) to guarded camps in Utah, Arizona, California, Idaho, Wyoming, Colorado and Arkansas. Twenty years after restrictions were lifted in 1945 the last compensation was paid for property lost during the evacuation; no restitution could be made for the miseries involved in a move that was entirely unnecessary on security grounds and an indefensible invasion of the civil rights of a peculiarly law-abiding and hard-working section of the population. German or Italian settlers in the United States were never subjected to such treatment during the war: it was clearly meted out for racial, not political, reasons; yet, ironically, the JACL successfully campaigned for the right of American citizens to serve in the army, besides organizing other expressions of loyalty. The League also petitioned Congress to finance compensation for evacuation losses, making up for its initial advice that removal should not be opposed.[82] Despite the criticisms which this counsel provoked, in the end the resourceful endurance of the interned Japanese seems to have done as much to break down white antipathies as the more militant activities of other oppressed elements in the population.

The organizational responses of these elements to the war were prompt but varied, reflecting their different attitudes to self-determination and participation in American politics. For many young and educated Mexicans military service brought an enforced realization that their future lay with the United States and that they would have to surmount both their own weaknesses and American injustice. Consequently, in Texas the non-partisan GI Forum was founded in 1948, soon spreading to other South-Western states; its objects were to fight discrimination against Mexican veterans of World War II and to 'develop leadership by creating interest in the Spanish-speaking population to participate intelligently and wholeheartedly in community, civic and political affairs'. Specifically, this has meant drives to get the electorate to the polls, the study of public issues and the devising of appropriate policies, the raising of money for scholarships and efforts directed at establishing fair-employment practices. Veterans and their wives have played an important part in other major Mexican associations. They were also instrumental in the formation of the National Congress of American Indians (NCAI) at Denver in 1944, and such militancy is particularly interesting in view of the allegedly invariable conservatism of veterans' groups as such.[83]

The first enduring political pan-Indian organization, the widely representative NCAI was open to tribes and groups as well as individuals, Indian and white, in a way that the Society of American Indians had aspired to be but could never manage. Nonetheless, the Congress resembled the SAI, in that it came to be seen by militants as acting primarily for prosperous and acculturated Indians and as being disproportionately influenced by the Bureau of Indian Affairs personnel within its ranks. In fact, low membership dues, intended to attract the largest possible membership, meant that the central office of both movements was short of both funds and staff. The main function of the NCAI was to lobby in Washington for desired legislation, to oppose measures against Indian interests, to scrutinize the activities of the Bureau and to develop legal assistance for the pursuit of necessary litigation; its focus on the national Congress reflected the importance of that body in shaping the fate of the reservation Indians and was crucial in view of the ominous wartime reduction in appropriations for the Indian Bureau.[84]

Through its newsletter and other publicity the new society hoped not only to reaffirm the importance of the tribal unit and the right to self-determination implicit in the Wheeler–Howard Act of 1934, but also to advance aims shared by earlier reform groups; it strove 'to enlighten the public toward a better understanding of the Indian race; to preserve Indian cultural values; to seek an equitable adjustment of tribal affairs; to secure and to preserve rights under Indian Treaties with the United States; and otherwise to promote the common welfare of the American Indians'.[85] A conference to plan for the post-war period held in April 1944 under the sponsorship of the American Civil Liberties Union, the Home Missions Council of North America, the American Association on Indian Affairs and the Indian Rights Association sounded a sympathetic note when its summarizing speaker suggested that to help establish a pluralistic democracy the native population needed to pass three milestones.

These were the achievement of economic status in the face of white exploitation, the acquisition of political experience despite the Indian scepticism of politics induced by such exploitation and the granting of complete cultural autonomy, which presented 'an especially searching challenge to Indian missionaries and to the generally accepted Western Christian axioms of American culture'.[86] Progress towards the first milestone was dramatically assisted by the establishment in 1946 of the Indian Claims Commission, a body for which the NCAI had quickly agitated and which was empowered to judge suits from identifiable Indian groups for adequate compensation for earlier land cessions.

Post-War Trends

Black Pressures Set the Pace

So much attention has been accorded by scholars to black protest movements since the war that the briefest account of these will be offered in order to chart the main changes in Negro pressure-politics as a whole, and in the durable national societies in particular, as well as their influence on other minority crusades.[87]

Enough has been written about the complexity of early black thought, tactics and organization to suggest that we cannot simply interpret these years in terms of a progression from integrationist to separatist thought, from moderate effort for rights to radical demands for power, accompanied by a proliferation of radical, exclusively black groups. Whites have always preferred to deal with a select few, supposedly representative and preferably moderate ethnic leaders; yet to suggest that the influence of Douglass or Garvey, Washington or DuBois, King or Malcolm X has been exaggerated is not to diminish their stature or that of their supporters but to place in proper perspective the activities of innumerable community alliances encouraged by the American setting and by subsequent urbanization. The comparative multiplicity of associations committed to race betterment in recent years has marked an important shift in priorities, and a confirmation that black interests are different in different parts of the country, rather than any dramatic conversion to the merits of voluntary concerns, which have always been numerous in twentieth-century black communities (in 1937, 'when Chicago had only 275,000 Negroes, an actual count revealed more than 4000 formal associations among them').[88] Whites who have noted startling shifts in post-war black ideology have frequently failed to realize the deep historical roots of nationalist thought, and there has been a similar tendency to see the tactics of the 1960s as unprecedented, when in fact there has been a long tradition of direct action, both violent and non-violent, the latter sometimes supported even by so-called moderate or legalistic organizations.

What has clearly taken place since the war, however, is an upsurge of Negro activism comparable with that of antebellum and Reconstruction years, the period after World War I and the 1940s, when changing white attitudes to race, an expanding economy and rising black expectations also generated impatience with the customary pace and vehicles of reform. As on these former occasions, although the value of racial integration has been questioned as never before and confrontations have overshadowed other forms of direct action for the first time, realism has remained the hallmark of most protesters, no matter how intense their disillusionment with inter-racial co-operation or piecemeal progress. In other words, there has been, as always, only limited support for an all-out campaign of violence to overthrow the power of the white majority; even in the race riots of the sixties, the primary target was often white property, not white people.[89] Moreover, the suggestion that the 'failure' of the civil rights movement has necessitated subsequent bids for black power is based on an unduly high expectation of what could be achieved by that movement, engendered partly by the idealism of the civil rights workers and partly by the way in which politicians have conceded their demands—that is, slowly and cautiously, as if yielding immense benefits. As Martin Luther King put it in 1957:[90]

> Give us the ballot and we will no longer have to worry the Federal government about our basic rights.

> Give us the ballot and we will fill our legislative halls with men of good will.
>
> Give us the ballot and we will place judges on the benches of the South who will do justly and have mercy.

The crusade for civil rights specifically aimed at the relatively limited (and ultimately practical) goal of abolishing legal segregation; it was widely (and wrongly) believed that other barriers to equality would speedily fall. That they have failed to do so should not be made a reason for condemning the crusade.

In many ways the recent phase of the black struggle has resembled the last stage of the women's suffrage campaign, when frustration with years of moderation produced challenges to the prevailing feminist ideology of the Progressive era, the diversification of tactics, and new factions justifying competition with established associations on the grounds of the impotence of the old guard, although in fact both were essential to victory and taken together they made up a social movement of potentially profound impact. Among the black and women's groups alike, the elaborate structures of their major national organizations have made them only slowly responsive to changes in American society, just as their knowledge of how past victories have been achieved and of how white politicians expect them to behave has become a restraint as well as an inspiration.[91] Hence, as Rudwick and Meier have shown, the centralized and bureaucratic NAACP, with its dominating national office, special departments and subordinate branches, its stable leadership of middle-class, college-educated blacks and its appeal to a wide cross-section of black opinion, has found radical departures from precedent difficult, despite pressures within its ranks during the 1960s from a youthful element advocating greater reliance on direct action. Such pressures were successfully restrained by procedural means, although since 1965 the Association has paid added attention to economic programmes, encouraging branches to initiate ghetto projects which might receive outside funds and helping black businessmen to compete for federal contracts.[92] The Southern Christian Leadership Conference (SCLC), founded by Martin Luther King in 1956 to agitate against segregation in all its forms, has remained similarly wedded to traditional techniques of overcoming discrimination, to co-operation between the races and to non-violence, as befits a coalition led by Church ministers.

Conversely, a body like CORE, with a small, fluid and youthfully intense membership—some 5000 to the NAACP's 500,000 by the 1960s—has been unembarrassed by a conservative Southern wing or a cautious, highly professional staff. And with great power residing in the democratically run local affiliates, in addition to the self-financed national office, the Congress has found it much easier to respond to public apathy (as during the late fifties) or frustration among race leaders by making constitutional changes, by abandoning its initial pacifism and inter-racial composition, or by advocating black community control and black capitalism rather than integrationist goals. Similar alterations in outlook have affected the Student Non-violent Co-ordinating Committee (SNCC) (1960) and the Black Panther Party (1966), though major changes in personnel have taken place within the latter organization, notwithstanding its centralized structure and overtly strict rules for members, as a result of enforcement difficulties and official harassment. Both groups are anti-capitalist, the Panthers from the outset but becoming less aggressively so by the 1970s, when priority has been given in California and by the local chapters to black community work. The SNCC, like CORE, was first reanimated and has since been disillusioned by civil rights operations in the South, turning in the process from a middle-class student alliance to a federation of full-time field secretaries, hostile to the white volunteers they attracted in the beginning, aware of the international scope of the race struggle, and in search of emancipation from both white racism and class exploitation.[93]

The division between separatist and integrationist race associations has been accompanied by divisions within the two major camps over the best means to achieve their ends and the question of which elements should take control. Such advocates of a Socialist solution as the Panthers and the SNCC, despite their telling indictment of many features of American society, have signally failed to show how poor whites and blacks are to be persuaded to form an alliance, political or otherwise, to demonstrate what the interests of the white business community are in maintaining the permanent under-consumption of black workers, or to indicate how 'the system' is to be overthrown by concentrating on self-determination inside the black ghetto, a tactic which achieved very little during the inter-war years. Exponents of black power have never been clear whether separation from white society is to be permanent or a temporary phase before activists return to pluralistic politics from a position of strength. The distinction between black power and black nationalism has also been blurred, not least over the question of territoriality, though it seems fair to suggest that black power has meant the strengthening of existing black enclaves in the larger society, whereas nationalists hope for the destruction of those exploited black 'colonies' through revolution or the establishment of a separate state outside or within America. This last objective is cherished by the Republic of New Africa (1968) and, like the proposals for compensation for black deprivation during and since slavery, or United Nations sponsorship of referendums to establish black preferences regarding their future status, it is an unrealistic demand in the present political climate, albeit designed principally to rally black support and not to convert white politicians. It has also drawn from and stimulated similar claims by Indian tribes which, because of the Indians' original occupancy of the continent and their distinctive relationship with the federal government, have already resulted in some major land settlements.[94]

Moderate organizations such as the SCLC have likewise experienced schisms as new leaders and contentious issues have emerged; but it would be a mistake to regard these too gloomily, because the last few years have seen an unprecedented willingness among black leaders to praise each other's endeavours, despite the endemic ideological feuding between revolutionary nationalists and cultural nationalists opposed to playing down the importance of race in the search for class allies and solutions.[95] All can see the necessity for economic programmes not simply dependent upon inevitably limited periods of liberal reform and economic prosperity. Poor housing, unsuitable and sub-standard education, high unemployment, inadequate medical care, police brutality and brutalizing prisons were all problems which the civil rights revolution could not cure and which were at their worst in the cities where more than half the population lived by the 1960s, necessitating sustained community campaigns. These represent more than a retreat from the extreme aims of black nationalism, and in cities like Chicago and Newark they have been devised with varying degrees of success by men as politically far removed as the Rev. Jesse Jackson and Imamu Amiri Baraka.

Breaking with SCLC's Operation Breadbasket, Jackson, an active preacher and former associate of Martin Luther King, built up a strong following on Chicago's South Side in the 1970s, seeking to use his young operation, People United to Save Humanity (PUSH) to pressure local white businessmen into hiring and dealing with blacks and to influence the policies regarding minorities adopted by the city machine. From its foundation in 1971, the organization emphasized the black 'need for economic power', stemming from 'a strong economic base within the Black community, not least as a means of disturbing political apathy among Negroes, and helping to support better schools and housing, especially in the cities'. At a 1975 PUSH fund-raising exposition, whose 500 or so exhibits included fourteen by major white manufacturers, plans were announced to mobilize black consumer support 'behind the products of companies who are helping blacks', using the 'power of the positive dollar' to supplement that of the negative boycott. Three years later some thirty chapters had been established nationwide, claiming 65,000 members 'from all walks of life'. By this time, in addition to its services for Chicago blacks, PUSH had assisted poor home-owners to file for federal grants and had persuaded the department of Housing and Urban Development to 'declare a moratorium on the foreclosure of multi-family dwellings'. It had also participated in numerous political education and voter-registration drives, had helped in the election campaigns of many black officials, and had set up a Washington bureau to raise minority issues 'before Congress, the Executive and the Regulatory agencies'.[96] In New Jersey Baraka's Committee for a Unified Newark brought together a number of city associations in civic activity, to obtain state support for a new corporation involved in low-cost housing projects, to control the city anti-poverty fund, to put blacks and Puerto Ricans on the school board, and generally to influence the council in their favour.[97]

While the post-war and existing black associations have, since the 1960s, made a clear impact on the political programmes of the major parties and have created a degree of racial unity and support for nationalism in the black community that once seemed impossible, many familiar obstacles still remain. Whites who could accept black enfranchisement as harmless or in accordance with American democracy, or who have been shocked by media exposure of bigotry in their midst, have drawn the line at integration and a collective redistribution of social advantages.[98] This was only to be expected, since escalating demands for change backed up by violence invariably encourage a hostile public reaction, especially if they generate similar demands from other disadvantaged groups, as was the case by the 1970s.[99] Militant protest leaders have not yet been able to build large and enduring operations among the 'street blacks' comparable in effectiveness with the Urban League and the NAACP, the latter, with its strong Church and fraternity support, being the largest and wealthiest as well as the oldest of the black organizations. They have been quite successful enough to generate unrealistic black expectations and white hostility, as witness the reactions to the Congress of African Peoples (1970) and the Black Political Convention (1972), which sought to establish a Negro political assembly and party respectively.[100]

The proliferation of black migrants in closely contested political districts throughout the Northern states between 1940 and 1970 enhanced the ability of black voters to influence the political parties on their own behalf and that of the disfranchised Southern Negroes. Yet though this influence eventually helped to procure civil rights legislation, better laws and services in black communities and a marked growth in the number of black office-holders, North and South, increases in black voter turnouts tended to be offset by a parallel extension in white voting and to have little impact on any forms of discrimination in the private sector or, lately, upon the securing of new laws, as opposed to the just administration of those already in existence. Moreover, since the 1960s many policy initiatives have come from the professional welfare advisers in government and the universities rather than from the dispossessed groups themselves, whose spokesmen may consequently feel as much the pawns of sympathetic 'experts' as of their political enemies. And the now permanent importance of federal government intervention in the economy demonstrates the continuing necessity for blacks to enlist white allies, not only at the local level but in Congress too, and such allies will probably remain liberal elements, often on the fringes of power. They will be no more able than the Black Political Caucus (1970) or other black politicians to devote themselves exclusively to race issues, and a great deal less willing. The overwhelming loyalty Negroes still show to one party, the Democrats, further reduces their political leverage in many areas.[101] The very improvements in status that blacks have achieved in terms of politics, education and the emergence of a large middle class have strengthened white faith in established political institutions and ideologies.[102] But if a recoil from the prospect of 'reverse discrimination' in favour of blacks is natural, in view both of its novelty and of its expense, its necessity has not been disproved, since blacks are seeking redress for historic injuries quite unlike those endured by white immigrants at a time when the political machines and unskilled job opportunities which benefited more fortunate minorities have largely disappeared.[103]

Indian Pressure Groups since World War II

Indian leaders in the post-war period, like most other ethnic spokesmen, have been embarrassed by the rapid expansion of the urban population and all the attendant problems of ghetto living. There has been a need to break down understandable cynicism about the value of political involvement and to resolve the mounting disputes between young and old, rural and city dwellers, over the nature of progress, its desirability and the means by which it may be achieved. During this period the NCAI has come fairly rapidly to occupy a position similar to that of the NAACP, the Chinese Benevolent Associations and the JACL, one which no association has yet achieved in Mexican American communities. And if there is nothing quite like the black arguments about separation or integration in Indian protest ideology, for even reservation progressives and urban leaders emphasize their distinctive 'Indian-ness', there has emerged a familiar impatience with long-accepted negotiating procedures, the federal bureaucracy and political compromise (although, ironically, the most spectacular recent victories have been achieved through just those court cases of which many minorities were tiring).

Two policies in particular were challenging the ingenuity of the NCAI by the 1950s, one being the relocation by the government of reservation Indians in certain cities, where they received an initial subsidy and welfare assistance before adjusting and finding jobs. The movement was designed to relieve unemployment among the tribes and to reduce future responsibilities for the native population, but many of those who had been uprooted had neither the skills nor the taste for city life. They quickly sank into poverty and disorientation or were driven to return home, while those who stayed might find themselves involved in wretched conflicts over a share of distant tribal assets.[104] Even more resented was the attempt by Congress, begun in 1953, to terminate the special legal and social status of the reservations and their governments and to allow some states to assert jurisdiction over them, ignoring their previous poor record in Indian affairs, past treaty commitments and Indian opinion.[105] These measures marked the beginning of a new campaign by the American government to assimilate the tribes, preferably with—but if necessary without—their approval, in line with Republican distaste for large federal budgets and paternalism of the kind epitomized by the Bureau of Indian Affairs (BIA). Although ostensibly encouraging the extension of ordinary citizenship rights to the Indians, something which the NCAI did not oppose, such legislation actually encouraged the squandering of tribal resources (divided on an individual basis in a manner unpleasantly reminiscent of the Dawes Act of 1887) and repudiated the Indian entitlement to self-determination which the association was pledged to defend.

The response of the NCAI, with backing from concerned white associations, was to extend its fieldwork by establishing a trust fund and by mounting community organization 'workshops' designed to encourage native leadership and research into a variety of Indian problems. It tried to press on Congress and the public a 'Point Four Program for American Indians', along the lines of 'the technical assistance and Point Four programs which this nation has found to be good business in underdeveloped countries abroad'; to provide advice on how to establish Indian centres; and to oppose termination vigorously at its conventions and in its literature, offering to help tribes threatened by the policy. Much time was also taken up by those procedural matters which can determine pressure-group success or failure. The work priorities and structure of the NCAI were adjusted as it grew, and there were disputes over whether it should help non-member tribes, in order to advertise the work of the Congress, and over the related question of finance. By the late 1950s upwards of $30,000 was being disbursed, but in 1958, when a deficit occurred, contributions and dues amounted to only $16,372.57 (including $1479.66 from non-Indian members). Since the society was pledged to work within the political and legal system to influence the nation's law-makers, to encourage the generosity of other reformers and to rally white opinion, it is perhaps not surprising to find that it was prepared to co-operate with the anthropologists and ethnologists who had been regarded with so much suspicion by the SAI and would be resented for rather different reasons by later Indian militants.[106] It was likewise ready to condemn confrontation tactics, such as the picketing of the White House in 1959 by an 'unrepresentative' deputation of New York Iroquois, as 'irresponsible and disgraceful' and 'out of Indian character'.

As a result of these careful strategies the NCAI clearly came to be 'recognized by the committees of Congress as the responsible Indian voice on matters affecting their welfare', developing a greater seriousness in planning and discussions, so one of its leaders, D'Arcy McNickle, suggested. In after-hours activities members turned increasingly to 'Indian forms of socializing'—drumming and singing, recording the sessions and circulating them informally to other Indian gatherings—and starting 'to discover that they were all Indians together'. At the beginning of the 1960s, McNickle felt, pan-Indianism was a force to be reckoned with; and at least among the membership of the Congress (which attracted women as well as men), the 'passion for separatism' was 'yielding to a growing interest in discovering and exploring areas of shared problems and mutual action'.

By 1960, both presidential candidates had been willing to condemn the forcible termination of federal Indian responsibilities, something for which the NCAI could claim considerable credit, although organized Indian opposition at the local level and the sufferings of some of the sixty-one terminated tribes also helped to produce an official reaction. In 1963 Attorney General Robert F. Kennedy, in an address before the NCAI, reaffirmed his brother's campaign pledges to the Indian peoples, promising much that the Congress had been asking for: a substantial area-redevelopment measure; increased credit assistance, not least to help Indians retain their land, which was seen as of paramount importance; a vocational training programme; increased expenditure on Indian education; community development schemes worked out in consultation with those to be affected; and a new emphasis upon 'genuinely co-operative relations between federal officials and Indians'.[107]

Despite these signs of significant change, however, the more militant elements of the Indian population—younger people and those whose acquaintance with city life had enlarged their understanding of white society—were becoming discontented with both the methods of composition of the Congress and the enormity of the challenges which it still faced. Among the groups that have arisen out of this discontent are the National Indian Youth Council (NYIC), founded in 1961, and the American Indian Movement (AIM). Originating in 1968 in Minneapolis, spreading its influence to various government task forces and eventually establishing a number of autonomous chapters in the Mid-West, the Movement attracted a young, urban-reared and tribally mixed membership, a number of whose spokesmen are suspect in the eyes of older leaders because of their unconventional, even criminal, backgrounds. In return, AIM spokesmen have been bitterly critical of existing tribal leadership and government—for instance, during the investigations into the affairs of the Richard Wilson regime at the Oglala Sioux Pine Ridge reservation in South

Dakota.[108] By contrast, the NIYC, based in New Mexico rather than Washington, which remains the centre for national protest associations, claims that it believes in tribalism and is simply attempting to take the 'functions of decision-making away from the expert administrators and put it in the local communities where it belongs'. Like those of the AIM, Council members are frequently young, urban, and (intermittently) at odds with the NCAI. Ironically both young and old, 'traditionalists' and 'militants' are concerned about the efficacy of tribal governments which some regard as creatures of the BIA, some see as destroying ancient forms of authority and speaking largely for 'progressive' elements, and which some feel represent only reservation opinion.[109]

In general it has proved easier to tap the pool of Indians dissatisfied with the *status quo* than to devise new national societies. The AIM has demonstrated great skill in devising a series of spectacular protest demonstrations—the occupation of Alcatraz in 1969, the 'trail of Broken Treaties' march on Washington in 1972, the occupation of the village of Wounded Knee, South Dakota, in 1973—but inevitably it has suffered from its brushes with the law. The NIYC has done better in some ways, because it has been rather less alarming, growing rapidly from a staff of three to one of over twenty by August 1975. It has concentrated on research into key issues, on developing a litigation programme, supporting a manpower scheme designed to raise the level of Indian employment in New Mexico, assisting two community schools (in Albuquerque, New Mexico, and Hammon, Oklahoma) and providing services to help ex-offenders. Like all such associations, the Council has been obliged to respond to changing constituency pressures and national crises, so that at the time of writing, for example, educational and civil rights activities have been somewhat subordinated to the fight—conducted especially through the courts—against white exploitation of Indian economic resources and for the maintenance of the hated but essential 'special relationship' with the federal government. Funding sources for the NIYC include a variety of white foundations, Indian associations, appeals through the mail, Church bodies and the federal government, and it has clearly benefited from the increased responsiveness to Indian pressures which had become marked, in monetary terms at least, by the mid-1960s. Even so, there has been neither money nor time to accept individual cases for litigation, while much of the Council's strength has come from its state base, despite the support given to many out-of-state protest campaigns.[110]

However, the need for unity, notwithstanding these new approaches to Indian problems, was stressed in the literature of the older organizations. When calling for an Indian 'summit conference' during 1966, the NCAI was once more suspicious —like its young rivals—of a federal government anxious to shed its responsibilities. Accordingly, the Congress continued to agitate for voting and social security rights for Indians, better health care, professional and vocational training, the development of employment opportunities within Indian communities, and the adjudication of land or resource disputes in the interests of the tribes, as well as to conduct a more positive campaign to convince the public of the Indian right to self-determination, in part by re-educating people through media campaigns about native American history and culture.[111]

Although an ambitious attempt to form a national alliance of existing Indian city community centres came to nothing in the late 1960s, due to the lack of 'a central ideological foundation and a sense of common purpose', various local urban movements have enjoyed considerable success, notably Oklahomans for Indian Opportunity and the United Indians of All Tribes in Seattle, which has employed direct action to obtain land for community projects. By 1971 the influence of non-reservation Indians had so far affected the NCAI as to precipitate the establishment of a more conservative National Tribal Chairmen's Association (NTCA), soon representing leaders of some two hundred authorized tribal governments. Moreover, growing acceptance of the need for organization among Indians resulted in a good response to NCAI efforts to reconstruct legally recognized tribes and units in the East and in the cities, that would have access to funds unavailable to private individuals. Similar objectives were embraced by the Coalition of Eastern Native Americans, while the specialized National Indian Education Association sprang up to act as a clearing-house for information about federal legislation, educational opportunities, programmes and organizations, working 'through technical assistance, communication and oversight' and relying on a Board of Directors elected by mail vote, executive officers and committees, annual conventions and a newsletter.[112]

All these groups were faced with the difficult fact that, if the continuing domination of Indian affairs by the BIA and the federal government required them to look to Washington for legislative change or finance, their local workers and constituents were increasingly demanding programmes in which they could take a personal interest or from which they could personally benefit—hence, in part, the greater immediate appeal, in cities such as Los Angeles and Chicago, of urban centres and Indian projects than of national associations and, indeed, the attraction of fraternal pan-Indian bodies, meeting for religious or social reasons at pow-wows or fairs and providing not only obvious enjoyment and the opportunity to meet Indians from many different areas but also a stimulus to a number of neglected tribal practices.[113] By the mid-1970s Chicago's Native American Committee, with financial aid from the Office of Native American Programs, was publicizing the activities of a variety of local Indian agencies in the fields of employment, education, counselling, health and social services, hoping itself to develop in these areas a 'professional-credentialed leadership from within the community who is accountable to the community' and to 'create and develop a workable network of stable institutions and agencies in the Native American Community in order to make self-determination and local control a day-to-day reality'.[114] But although the objectives of the local and regional movements may sound more modest and practical than those of the national concerns, they are no more able than similar alliances in, say, the black community to demonstrate that self sufficiency does not depend to a dispiriting degree on money rather than ethnic unity, pride or numbers.

The urbanization of a large part of the Indian population has helped to draw its members into a closer involvement with the political process; especially women, who often exerted considerable influence in traditional Indian societies and have recently begun to reassert themselves, despite some masculine hostility. If in the process uncomfortable divisions have emerged between urban and reservation Indians, they still share a desire to retain their distinctive identity, while their leaders frequently advance the same material objectives.[115] Both also return repeatedly to the necessity for clarifying Indian status and the need to change the structure and scope of the BIA. For the past few years some hopes have been expressed of finding a hemispherical solution to American Indian difficulties, and no doubt in this widening of horizons we can see the influence of other militant ethnic groups who appeal for external support. The NCAI and the National Indian Brotherhood of Canada continue to adhere to the traditional recognition of a dependent economic Indian position, but they give new emphasis to 'a yet legally undefined and refined separate social, cultural, religious and self-governing "national" autonomy for each tribal culture', grounded in its land base and, it is hoped, to be recognized by the United Nations. Among more radical groups, the AIM in particular goes further, maintaining that 'contemporary Indian reservations are "island nation societies" under international law, and that each separate Indian tribe or nation by right is entitled to a full-member seat in the United Nations'.[116]

In seeking such objectives—though well aware of the barriers to hemispheric co-operation among Indians—the AIM, the NCAI and others may be seen as genuine social movements, and they can take encouragement from the recent success of a number of important resource and land cases in the courts which confirm the special status of Indian peoples within the United States, originally defined in treaties which fortunately survive to the present.[117] Nonetheless, the need to devise solutions for immediate domestic requirements remains overwhelming, and it is tempting to see these as being best achieved through litigation accompanied only by the reform of existing institutions.

As long as the BIA dominates tribal affairs, the Indians are likely to be accorded low priority from other federal agencies which help minorities—for example, the Small Business Administration and the Office of Minority Business Enterprise. Nor do special investigations of their problems offer the tribes much hope of swift practical assistance. The eleven task forces of the American Indian Policy Review Commission, established in the summer of 1975 to investigate a wide range of urgent questions, began its work with charges that, though mainly Indian in composition, it was 'apparently designed to avoid a confrontation with the pressing issues of the day' and was not sufficiently representative of radical and traditionalist opinion, a familiar complaint against the BIA, despite the increasing numbers of native Americans on its payroll. Although it seems essential to reform the Bureau's elaborate bureaucracy, which impedes action, and to end its dependence on the conservative or indifferent committees of the Indian section of the Bureau of the Budget and the Department of the Interior, which often face a conflict of interest between their Indian and other responsibilities, there is no agreement about whether the BIA should simply become a service agency or should be abolished outright. Some Indians—including members of the NCAI, the NIYC and the NTCA—feel that abolition would not speed progress towards genuine self-sufficiency but would constitute a step back down the road to termination. Some also fear that the occupations and demonstrations organized by militants since the late sixties against the Bureau and other targets will alienate white Americans, undermine the authority of bodies operating 'through peaceful and traditional channels' or cause Indians to be seen as merely imitating the tactics of other impatient ethnic leaders, when in fact their grievances are quite distinctive. Clearly, the vast media coverage which these activities secure is not equivalent to support (nor sometimes even sympathy), and if violent actions contributed to the setting up of the Review Commission, its recommendations, presented to Congress in 1977 and eventually regarded by many whites as too sympathetic to the Indian side of the questions investigated, have yet to be implemented. The suggestions that an independent BIA should be instituted, and that the tribes should be given full jurisdiction over taxation, the trial of offenders and natural resources in Indian territory, have proved particularly controversial.[118]

There are, then, no easy ways forward in Indian pressure-politics, and the best hope at the moment is perhaps that a combination of issue-orientated groups which may enjoy only a short life, radical shock troops like the AIM spokesmen and a few more conservative national organizations may finally bring home to white legislators the need for varied approaches to Indian needs and may demonstrate, as the success of current educational programmes should already have done, the practical possibility as well as the value of Indian control of their own affairs. A level of political involvement has now been reached in Indian communities (thanks in part to the national civil rights legislation and the passage of the Indian Bill of Rights in 1968, extending to the reservations the rights guaranteed in the first ten Amendments to the Constitution) such that the vulnerability of particular protest groups or the unreal expectations with which Indian leaders have had to contend are no longer a primary cause of the slow progress of reform.[119]

Although dependent to some extent on the generosity of white foundations as well as on the skills of white lawyers, the Indian reformers have also outgrown their initial dependence on white allies in the field, and militants have even added anthropologists to the list of suspect, self-styled 'Indian experts'. As obnoxious as are all summer visitors to quiet places, the anthropologist is further regarded with caution on the reservations because he makes a living out of his Indian 'observations', allegedly regarding people like chessmen available for experimentation and manipulation, focusing on the past and failing to use his knowledge to influence beneficial changes in government policy.[120]

Western Post-War Developments

In spite of the entrenched hostility displayed towards them by the white population and the traumatic Japanese experience of internment, the post-war progress of Oriental Americans has been enormous. Indeed, even during the war—in 1943—the repeal of the Chinese exclusion acts had been achieved. This achievement followed partly from changing American attitudes to China, a variety of strategic considerations and a nation-wide tour by Mme Chiang Kai-shek. But the activities of a Citizens' Committee formed to secure repeal were, as Fred Riggs has shown, similarly important in 'counteracting the opposition of traditional exclusionists' and in establishing 'liaison with certain Congressmen who helped to mobilize support in the legislature itself.' Among the commercial, religious and idealistic groups supporting the campaign was the Chinese Benevolent Society of New York, and since the war such societies have remained supreme in Chinese communities. However, the number of competing voluntary associations has continued to increase, actively involving women for the first time and concentrating on family affairs, sport, educational and community-improvement projects. If numerous Chinese still congregate in the great Chinatowns of San Francisco, New York and Los Angeles, in a form of voluntary segregation which facilitates group solidarity, eases the language problems of newcomers and affords them non-competitive economic opportunities, their dispersion has nonetheless proceeded rapidly. It has done so without destroying among the younger generations the cohesion provided by a distinctive culture, a strong family tradition and a commitment to achievement and acceptance in America outside the political sphere.[121] The repudiation of the laws against intermarriage between whites and Chinese after 1945, like the erosion of the Chinese 'ghettoes' has been both a cause and an effect of improved ethnic relations, as has the low incidence of crime in the settlements of Chinese and Japanese alike, regardless of their frequent location in high-crime areas.

The restrictions imposed by living in segregated districts were ended for many Japanese with evacuation; since a return to the old occupations and ways often proved impossible, more determined efforts had to be made to break down the prejudice of white employers, and these were gradually successful. Moreover, educational opportunities (including veterans' benefits) were so avidly exploited that since 1940 the Japanese 'have had more schooling than any other race in the American population, including whites', and women are gaining on a par with men (instead of more quickly than men, which is usual among racial minorities). And while the power of the Japanese Associations has declined as the Japanese population has moved about or changed, strong community organizations, including the JACL, have not ceased to provide a remarkable degree of discipline and support for their members, with a view to protecting the group 'image' and securing its civil rights. Most notable, since the war, have been the JACL's effective efforts to obtain 'naturalization of *Issei* and other Asians as well as a quota for Japan . . . [in] the Immigration and Nationality Act of 1952.' Yet as the need for such efforts has diminished and the influence of the third and fourth generations has grown, the League's dominance may be coming to an end without any comparable form of community leadership emerging in its place.[122]

Among Mexican Americans the years after 1945 witnessed a considerable multiplication and diversification of voluntary associations, initially encouraged by dissatisfied returning veterans. Even so, differences between the major areas of settlement have persisted, along with the old barriers to complete acculturation: prejudice, rooted in a conflict of cultures, large-scale Mexican immigration and poverty, inadequate education and segregation. Although large numbers of workers had returned to Mexico during the Depression, World War II saw the launching of the *bracero* programme, an agreement in force until 1964 between the American and Mexican governments which allowed Mexican agricultural labourers to work in the United States for specified periods in return for guarantees over fair wages and living conditions. Many permanent settlers also came, often to cities within and outside the South West, but this scheme, together with the continued influx of 'wetbacks' (despite official attempts to end the traffic from 1953), confirmed the erroneous public impression of the average Mexican as an impoverished migratory worker. The shifting composition of the Mexican American population, however, its rapid post-war expansion and the fact that most of those living in Texas and California crossed over into the United States after 1900 or are descended from people who did have made Mexican group progress, in American terms, a comparatively recent phenomenon.[123]

Commentators have noted especially the damaging economic effects of poor educational attainments as well as discrimination, and the adverse political consequences of a low naturalization rate.[124] We have already seen that reformers from the nineteenth century onwards saw the school as an important agent of assimilation for immigrants; but when ethnic characteristics survived despite the efforts of teachers and civic leaders, and despite the challenge in the work place of alternative ways or values, the doctrine of cultural pluralism began, in the 1930s, to pass from the realm of theory to that of practical politics. Unfortunately, as the case of the native Americans makes plain, it proved very difficult to devise the necessary measures for ensuring the cultural independence which had been so long denied. In particular, Jennifer Hurstfield reminds us, there was a failure

> to examine whether the schools would have to be changed to realise the goal of cultural pluralism. This is an important issue since traditionally the schools have propagated the dominant economic, political *and* cultural values of the wider society. Therefore unless the schools were to make conscious efforts to inculcate equal respect for different cultures, then cultural pluralism would mean in practice that, within the schools, ethnic cultures would still be perceived as inferior to the culture of the dominant White majority.[125]

The domination of local school boards by Anglos, the small number of Mexican American teachers, deliberate and *de facto* segregation, and the reluctance to see Spanish used in the classroom even though it is the first language of the majority of Hispanos—all these factors have predictably resulted in educational programmes geared to the needs and preferences of white Americans. Since 1945 major efforts have been made by the Mexican Americans themselves to change this unpleasant state of affairs, though with limited success to date. A number of state and federal court cases challenging segregation have been brought in Texas, California and elsewhere, while a range of pressure groups have given priority to educational improvement, including the development of Parent Teacher Associations and the election of school board officials. Among the activists we may count LULAC, the Community Service Organization (CSO), founded in California in 1947, the Council of Mexican American Affairs (CMAA) formed in 1953, the California Mexican-American Movement, the GI Forum, which originated in Texas in 1948, and the Arizona Coordinating Council of Political Education. There are, in addition, a number of more ephemeral societies primarily concerned with raising funds for scholarships, and specialist bodies such as the Latin American Education Foundation and the Association of Mexican-American Educators. Despite their efforts, the habit of categorizing Hispanos as 'white' allowed whites to claim compliance with desegregation orders when black and Mexican American schools had been consolidated but their own institutions remained unchanged, while the female domination of school teaching was just one more feature of American society which threatened traditional patterns of authority in Hispano communities.[126]

If low expectations have to some extent produced low performance in the area of education until quite recently, there is a similar cycle of frustration in politics. This is because a restricted level of naturalization—and consequently of voter registration—results from white hostility, a continuing attachment of many settlers to Mexico and the difficult procedures involved, from the point of view of the poorly educated, in qualifying for citizenship. A feeling that little will result from going to the polls is also important, and is partly the consequence of the Mexican Americans' giving such solid support to the Democrats (notwithstanding the successes of the independent La Raza Unida Party in Texas), that there is little contest for the Hispano vote. Though common among the isolated poor or oppressed of all races, such feelings may strengthen Anglo prejudices against Mexican Americans as a people resistant to assimilation. This cynicism in turn increases the difficulties of potential leaders, and as late as the 1960s their scarcity was deplored in the scholarly literature. It is clear that, up to the present decade, no single group has been able to speak for the Hispano population in a particular locality, although it has been suggested earlier that the search for definitive ethnic spokesmen is often undertaken primarily for the convenience of the dominant society. Moreover, as the Mexican settlers have spread out across the country, organizational difficulties have increased, while class and factional divisions within Mexican American constituencies have prevented them from giving unanimous support to Hispano candidates where their united votes would have been sufficiently numerous to ensure success.

In addition to LULAC, various societies have attempted to educate Mexican American citizens in their political 'rights and duties', persuading them to register, pay their poll taxes and vote, to agitate for admission to jury service and political office at every level, if necessary by demonstrations in or against places and agents of discrimination, and to seek more equitable employment and social security provisions. They include the CSO, the CMAA and the GI Forum, as well as the Pan-American Progressive Association (1947), the California Mexican American Political Association (1958) and the Texas Political Association of Spanish-Speaking Organizations (PASSO) (1960). Many of these bodies are regional in scope and claim some contact with the Hispano masses, but they have been largely unable to attract outside aid (because of their lack of co-ordination) or to manage on what they can raise from their members, not least because the small-business and professional class remains nervous of protest activities which might jeopardize its limited status or resources, and disappointing results may impede the collection of membership dues after the first year of operations. Lack of funds means that a proper office cannot always be maintained and publicity suffers; there is no national or regional medium of communication to make good the loss, and thus the work of Mexican American pressure groups is frequently little known among those they are designed to serve. In such circumstances any rash project may be fatal to the organization, while the frustration of large designs, impatience with the traditional deference due to age, and the example of the black power movement has led discontented Hispano youths to join 'Brown Beret' clubs, which have used direct action to force change, especially in school programmes.

The most radical and distinctive of all the recent Mexican American movements, however, has been the Alianza Federal de Mercedes of New Mexico (or Federal Alliance of Land Grants), established in 1963. Aiming to improve the economic position of lower-class Hispanos, the Alianza was also unusual for its extreme demands, millenial message, and dynamic leader, Reies López Tijerina. In pursuit of their main aim—the recovery of some 4,000,000 acres of land grants taken from the original Mexican owners after 1848, in defiance of rights guaranteed by the Treaty of Guadalupe Hidalgo and the allegedly unabrogated 'Laws of the Indies', by which the Spanish Crown had ruled its American possessions between 1598 and 1821—the dues-paying members of the Alianza (perhaps 10,000 by 1967) financed a propaganda campaign, petitioned the Governor of New Mexico and the President of the United States, and attempted to initiate judicial investigation of their demands. These efforts having failed, the Alianza increasingly resorted to violent demonstrations, in the process alienating both whites (who thought the cause had attracted many supporters with no land entitlement at all) and more affluent Mexican Americans (who felt embarrassed by its style). Although the peculiar circumstances of New Mexico, particularly its high proportion of Hispanos and the widespread unemployment among them, explain much of Alianza's urgency, the emphasis upon a messianic deliverance from persecution, together with the focus on land ownership and the need to expel those who intrude upon that land, were reminiscent of pan-Indianism. But the legal basis for the Alianza campaign was more vulnerable, so that its only tangible achievements were to mobilize and gain publicity for a section of the Hispano poor and to precipitate some of the young into reform activities—no mean feat, albeit far short of its original objectives.[127]

So far the impact on American politics of these various associations is uncertain. They have probably played a part in procuring the extension of the 1965 Voting Rights Act to Mexican Americans in 1975, yet coverage was simultaneously given to Alaskan natives, American Indians and people of Asian ancestry, and the work of *their* leaders, as well as the impact on legislators of a more sympathetic media attitude, cannot be discounted. Despite the use of new techniques and the appeals to a wider constituency, there has been some reluctance to abandon the moderate, non-partisan approach of such early organizations as LULAC or to welcome the full participation of women in political affairs, although this is happening, notwithstanding opposition. Since conservatism springs from an entrenched desire not to sacrifice Mexican American values in the fight for full acceptance in the Anglo world, it is a formidable obstacle to reformers.[128] Nevertheless, the success of union organizers since the ending of the *bracero* programme has been encouraging, and there are signs of a greater willingness among political leaders to seek influence within the two major parties and at least to contemplate coalitions with other sympathetic interests, namely, white liberals, labour and ethnic minorities.

Black leaders have also considered such coalitions, of course, the Black Panthers especially having inspired and kept in touch with similar groups in the Hispano, Chinese and Puerto Rican communities, enjoying their chief success in co-operative work with Puerto Ricans on community projects in New York and Newark.[129] But solidarity is not easily created between black Americans and those who have seen a comparatively light skin as a means of escaping the worst white prejudice and of protecting their own social position, or when many ethnic spokesmen resent what they regard as a disproportionate amount of public money being made available for Negro projects, at their expense and to the detriment of those thus discouraged from self-help. As the *Latin Times* put it in 1966, 'whatever is done to assist the under-privileged Negroes will inevitably be done at the expense of equally under-privileged Mexican-Americans'. If the PASSO has been willing to admit Puerto Rican and Cuban members, while the NIYC has made use of tactics favoured by other minorities (and its first leader, Clyde Warrior, compared the Indian experience with that of Negroes, Mexican Americans and Puerto Ricans), some activists have opposed collaboration, in part as a distraction from their own distinctive priorities. Competition for jobs places an additional strain on relations between the minorities, despite certain evidence of class sympathy across race lines, and none relishes playing down those appeals to racial pride upon which their organizations have been built.[130] For the moment, however desirable liberal–ethnic coalitions may be, it is difficult to see them emerging in areas where any minority has strength in numbers, and their value to whites has yet to be proved; so they remain, along with many more radical pressure-group aspirations, mainly a matter of rhetoric and threat rather than fact.

During the early twentieth century the voluntary associations already established in the Negro and Oriental communities grew and multiplied, gaining something of that reputation as useful sources of specialist information and potential 'negotiators' which makes government today seek out the advice of interest groups instead of merely responding to their lobbying activities. Yet in the process they developed bureaucracies that were slow to respond to demands from their constituents for change, as well as reputations they were reluctant to hazard (although there is no automatic correlation between bureaucratization and increased conservatism).[131] Consequently, the proliferation of ethnic protest groups continued, further encouraged by the fact that leadership of such groups was one of the few executive roles within the grasp of most of the members as long as discrimination and segregation persisted. Organizations designed to engage in pressure-politics were also established among the native and Mexican Americans, and while at first they followed other early ethnic associations in urging accommodation to white society, from the inter-war years onwards there was a growing emphasis upon the right to self-determination. Such an emphasis aggravated existing generational differences, especially among the Oriental and Chicano minorities, with the latter facing the additional problem of a constant enlargement of their numbers by immigration. However, this heightened race pride and group-consciousness fostered both concerted opposition to discrimination and fears among ethnic spokesmen that wholehearted participation in American politics, when negotiating terms were still laid down by dominant whites, might erode their own cherished cultural values.

Pressure-group operations, in the present century as they were in the nineteenth, have been directly shaped by political and economic changes or crises. In particular, two world wars enlarged expectations among returning veterans and migrants who had moved in search of lucrative war work, both of which groups had hoped to benefit from expanded opportunities and national gratitude, and therefore proved intolerant of attempts to reimpose second-class citizenship. The Depression similarly transformed expectations among white as well as non-white minorities, notably those concerning what might flow from political action and union membership.[132] Unfortunately, since the thirties the increasingly solid support shown for the Democratic party by one minority after another ultimately reduced their political leverage, and the return of the

Republicans to power in 1953 brought a lean time for all of them, just as the decline of the old party machines reduced the immediate benefits available to individual members of any group in return for political support. Moreover, a frequently hostile white reaction to ethnic politics sometimes led either to a recurrence of apathy or a greater willingness to advocate militant tactics which, though by no means new, were still not acceptable to the larger society.

By the 1960s a fairly extensive mobilization of the once unorganized, combined with a widespread resort to confrontations and even violence, had contributed to the passage of a plethora of civil rights and anti-poverty legislation. But these achievements brought the real danger of a white reaction based on the argument that the courts and government had been moving too fast in pursuit of a redefined ideal of equality, although in fact statistics about income distribution alone indicated how wide the gap remained between white and non-white, despite minority pressures.[133] Nor have activists yet managed to come together in many practical projects, notwithstanding vocal expressions of mutual sympathy, such as those one also now finds among once opposed women's organizations, or to build mass followings in support of the new protest tactics. For it has, except in a few cases, proved difficult to demonstrate that lower-class elements really can participate in decision-making, however much economic change may have revealed the common interests of the poor.

CHAPTER 5

The Less Privileged Half: Women's Suffrage, Temperance and the Women's Movement—and the Case of California

Environment and Opposition

The women's movement, aiming at the overall enlargement of the opportunities and activities of women and encompassing a variety of pressure groups designed to achieve such specific objectives as the suffrage, operated against an even greater array of institutional and environmental obstacles than those which faced the ethnic minorities in the United States. Paradoxically, it could also appeal to a number of factors and traditions which appeared positively to encourage the aspirations of its members.

During colonial times and outside the ranks of the prosperous landed and mercantile families, married women took care of their households as well as providing a whole range of goods in daily use which would otherwise have been unobtainable, such as clothes, shoes, soap and candles. In a new country most of the additional opportunities for women lay, in fact, in the field of employment as, in addition to their own duties, they helped their husbands and carried on the family farm or business in the event of early widowhood. However, although most of those concerned have left no record of their feelings and we must acknowledge the depressing consequences of a rigid sexual division of labour at a later date, we should not value too highly the right of frontier women to work themselves into premature old age while bringing up large families, any more than we would extol the equal exploitation of the sexes under slavery or the indentured labour system. Material conditions were undoubtedly better than those prevailing in Europe, but expectations were much higher in the New World, and the economic versatility of women does not seem to have led men to reassess other aspects of feminine worth. Thus when white and Indian women compared notes about their circumstances in the early years of the Massachusetts Bay settlement, the male conclusion seems to have been that white women could simply count themselves as fortunate 'as . . . in old *England*.'[1]

Attitudes to marriage, for example, survived the Atlantic crossing relatively intact. Under the Common Law doctrines imported from England, married women were denied an independent legal existence: they had no title to property, their own earnings or children upon legal separation, nor could they sign contracts. Divorce, almost impossible to obtain in England and in most of the colonies, was granted in New England, though sparingly, and a distinct sympathy was manifested towards male petitioners. If eventually the hearing of matrimonial cases in equity courts brought greater liberality to the Common Law, comparatively few women could afford the time and expense they involved.

At a time when interests rather than individuals were still represented in government and the arguments about the need for an educated citizenship in a democracy were yet to be developed, it would be unreasonable to expect strong pressure from women for either the vote or better educational facilities, however unsatisfactory their position was in relation to that of men or from the point of view of a few enlightened individuals. Women, who in New Jersey and Virginia had enjoyed the suffrage until the Revolution, were not protected in their rights when the new state constitutions were drawn up, despite the contribution they made as agitators and suppliers of the army during the struggle for independence. In New England, their exclusion from political rights was explicitly justified in the Essex Result of 1778, a statement produced by conservatives during the debate on the Massachusetts constitution and in which a striking comparison was made between women and slaves.[2]

Although primary schools admitted female pupils from the first, less importance was attached to the instruction of women, some 40 per cent of whom remained illiterate even in colonial New England. Those who benefited from any kind of secondary education were the well-to-do, and the syllabus provided for them was designed to foster gentility rather than intelligence. The Churches provided no relief for the discontented since, apart from the early Baptists and Quakers, they excluded women from active participation in religious meetings and from ordination as ministers, emphasizing the special duties and virtues expected of the most faithful part of their congregations—virtues which, if practised, would ensure their permanent subordination in society.

There were obvious advantages to be won from acquiescence by the resentful in this state of affairs, though we have no means of knowing how many women submitted gladly. Much has been written about conscious or unrecognized role-playing by black slaves as a means of securing both white approval and personal survival. The same process was no doubt at work when women agreed to cultivate the art of domesticity in deference to the strength of their oppressors but also, equally clearly, in return for male good will, courtesy and protection. Yet in handing over to the most ignorant and conventional members of the community the preservation of personal purity and family stability, organized religion and the refinement of civilization, men both ensured the elevation in these matters of conformist mediocrity and laid the foundation of their personal discomfort, not least in matters of sex and etiquette. This unsatisfactory bargain has proved to be at once the most enduring single obstacle to the development of a radical feminist ideology which would minimize the consequences of biology, and the greatest possible encouragement to female self-sacrifice and service, from which the vulnerable and unfortunate have so long gained assistance. Thus, if the leading agitators for the suffrage during the nineteenth century demanded it as a right, the diplomats within their movement requested it so that women might be better able to protect their children.

Once enough women enjoyed enough leisure to consider and protest their position, however, they could find various causes for optimism. As the United States approached political democracy in the 1830s, and the major parties committed themselves to the enlargement of economic opportunity, though by different means, the gulf between the principles of the Revolution and the practice of the republic towards women seemed deplorable to thoughtful members of both sexes, especially those in the anti-slavery movement, who were already preoccupied with minority rights. The movement was never concerned with the specific objectives of feminism, nor did it produce the first women's organizations, for these already existed to foster the literary interests of members and to raise money for religious or charitable purposes. Rather, it precipitated far-reaching debates about the validity of segregating and ranking workers according to sex in a common cause, while drawing attention to the similarity of the arguments used to justify Negro slavery and the subordination of women.

In defending their rights to speak against slavery in public, before mixed audiences, female abolitionists such as Angelina Grimké stressed that there were no sexual or racial rights but only God-given human rights, grounded in the common nature of all human beings.[3] By so doing they evolved what was to be the most powerful argument of later feminists, encouraged a far wider discussion of women's role in society than had previously occurred, enlisted crucial male allies to their cause and strengthened their own self-confidence. Even where women continued to work through separate societies, they risked mob violence, like other early abolitionists, yet did not disband; they helped with slave escapes, circulated petitions, wrote for and to journals, went out alone—and survived. Ultimately it was the exclusion of women from participation in the 1840 World's Anti-Slavery Convention held in London, involvement which would scarcely have been attempted without such prior activities, that provoked Lucretia Mott and Elizabeth Cady Stanton into calling the first women's rights assembly.[4] Feminine resolution was also stiffened by experiences in other reform movements, notably temperance, where women were expected to remain aloof from meetings and policy-making, though they were valued as members, propagandists and fund-raisers.[5]

During an era of growing equality, when religious teaching as well as political doctrine emphasized individual worth, these slights gave unusual offence. So, too, did the obstacles still placed in the way of individual pioneers who sought access to the professions and the frequent ridicule of women writers who might be deficient as novelists or poets but whose productions for religious, children's and reform publications, besides general magazines and newspapers, were scarcely more sentimental and ornate than those produced by their male counterparts.[6] A further stimulus to group awareness was given by the expanding opportunities for women to work outside the home (although these opportunities were partly counterbalanced by the increase of immigration and the decline in the number of tasks now performed at home). But while wages were welcome, the new industrial order imposed strain upon the family and increased the exploitation of women, who were not paid as much as men for the same work, were frequently regarded with suspicion by male employers and were more easily intimidated as a result of their greater ignorance and their conditioning in the ways of servility. Attempts at organization, even in the once inviting New England textile mill towns, were doomed to failure not only because of the inexperience, inadequate funds and limited leisure of the women involved, but also as a result of the public disapproval, hostile courts, indifferent governments and fluid economic situation which impeded the progress of other early labour organizations.

Of all the factors making for the formal organization of women in their own cause during the summer of 1848, however, the most important was the contemplation, as the New York feminist Elizabeth Cady Stanton put it, of constraints imposed by their 'position as wife, mother, housekeeper, physician, and spiritual guide'. Certainly the movement before the Civil War, reflecting its overwhelming middle-class composition, did not offer a serious critique of those aspects of the changing economy (notably the creation of a gulf between 'the world' and 'the home', where women continued to work according to the patterns of a pre-industrial era) which were fostering a restricting 'cult of domesticity'. Instead, feminists strove to re-shape this cult by frankly debating such questions as the proper condition of married women and the grounds for divorce, the need for education and the place of women in the professions, the Churches and society at large. And from the outset they disagreed about when they might properly press for the suffrage. Their protest activities, not inappropriately, were similar to those of free blacks at this time, namely, a series of conventions, both national (from 1850) and local in scope, which provided opportunities for the clarification of ideas, the development of leadership and contacts between women in different parts of the North and the assessment of public response to their objectives. Almost every demand made by the early feminists was, like those of the abolitionists, rejected by their critics on the grounds that these demands were opposed to Scripture, nature or the existing order of society. Despite that sympathy from their husbands and liberal male reformers without which the conventions would have been almost impossible, their organizers were hampered by lack of funds, the timidity of the mass of women and the prejudices of the majority of men. Scarcity of money is always a problem for reform movements, but the dependent status of women (and in the case of the blacks, their poverty) made publicity, travel and administration peculiarly difficult to finance.[7]

Interested women in the South had to contend with the reasonable belief that feminism was yet another example of the modernizing Northern spirit which endangered the patriarchal society of their own region, and they had to combat a particularly stifling view of the role of privileged women, which was unusually effectively enforced. The idealized Southern lady could indeed scarcely be improved from a masculine perspective: beautiful yet modest, amiable and submissive, devoted to God, husband, children, servants and suffering humanity, 'pious but not austere; cheerful but not light; generous but not prodigal; economical, but not close; hospitable but not extravagant . . . Everything under her care went on with perfect system'.[8] The struggles to live up to such foolish expectations and to reject the species of slavery they entailed, despite constant indoctrination at home, in the Press and from the pulpit, have been graphically detailed by Anne Firor Scott, who also demonstrates that in reality most married Southern women led much less pleasant and sheltered lives than their menfolk suggested, not least because of their frequent responsibility for slaves. Moreover, the parallel between the lot of slaves and women was not lost upon them, although, of course, some slaveholders' wives shared in the maltreatment of the enslaved, while the sexual abuse of female slaves was resented as an injury to the women of both races. Even when men acknowledged the need for improved educational facilities—and a number of new academies for women were founded between 1830 and 1860—they remained generally opposed to the enlargement of the woman's sphere.[9] In this unpromising environment, where economic opportunities and outlets for those of reforming bent were equally limited, determined suffragists did not emerge, though women lent their support to moral, humanitarian and civic improvement movements which did not endanger the South's distinctive social order.

By the Civil War the women's rights movement sustained no national organization beyond a central committee comprising respresentatives from states where there was activity. Nonetheless, by means of lectures, petitions, conventions and newspapers, as well as the aid of sympathetic men, it had been possible to make some progress in opening the professions and colleges to women, to persuade certain state legislatures to grant married women control of their wages, incomes and property and to enlarge the grounds for divorce.[10] The events of the Civil War and the Reconstruction years combined to galvanize feminists to fresh efforts to help themselves and others, while disappointment with the results brought new organization and a greater acceptance of its utility, though still no unity. Women in each section predictably supported the war efforts of their governments through nursing, forming hospital or soldiers' aid societies, helping families whose breadwinners were away fighting, taking on jobs normally filled by men and learning in a thousand ways to manage without male counsel. In the North, however, between 1863 and 1864, the Women's Loyal League had circulated a petition urging Congress to approve the Thirteenth Amendment which eventually secured nearly 400,000 signatures from men and women, an indication not only that normal pressure-group activity did not have to be suspended in wartime but also that support for the Republican adminstration was not unconditional. When in 1865 the Amendment was adopted and the slaves emancipated, and when, in the ensuing years, an appropriate national definition of citizenship rights was sought, women's leaders—supported by a number of liberal men—naturally expected that their work during the war and on behalf of abolition would find recognition in the extension to them of such rights. These expectations, if natural, were naive.

While the early reformist Republican party contained many opponents of slavery (though comparatively few converts to the radical Garrisonian belief in racial equality), there were far fewer advocates of women's suffrage. The case for the black vote was difficult enough to make in the 1860s, with the Democrats hoping to use the issue as a means of discrediting the victors, the Republicans still not assured of a national political base and various states in their heartland voting against Negro suffrage in referenda between 1865 and 1868. Whether the Republicans eventually opted for the Fifteenth Amendment to increase voter support both in the South and in such marginal Northern states as Connecticut, Indiana and Pennsylvania or out of a genuine idealism—and historians are divided on this point—political risks were clearly involved, and the resulting nervousness was reflected in the tentative wording of the Amendment.[11]

It was understandable that the party should be wary of tackling more contentious reform and that male reformers would sooner secure one desired goal than sacrifice both to principle, especially in view of the limited interest taken in women's rights even in the anti-slavery movement. Only a minority among blacks and women alike were actively campaigning for the vote, and in the women's case this was a decisive factor. White politicians opposed to extending the suffrage presented it as something to be worked towards, a prize rather than a right, for which neither group was yet prepared.[12] If the newly enfranchised might be expected to vote for the party which conferred that right, women did not offer a voting bloc in the same way as the freedmen, being less ignorant, geographically more scattered and not bound together by class or common memories of servitude.

Moreover, the majority had husbands who could represent their interests and save them from distracting or degrading political involvements, an argument which sounded less hollow during the Gilded Age than at most other times. The black women who had worked for abolition were as powerless as white campaigners to challenge male conservatism.[13]

Undoubtedly, some of the staunch, well-educated and middle-class advocates of votes for women shared contemporary racial antipathies towards the blacks, the Chinese, ignorant foreigners and other social 'misfits' excluded from politics at the end of the Civil War, and they resented being classified with them in any respect: a similar charge of prejudice was, of course, levied against Republicans by Southerners far more effectively opposed to the proposition of human equality. But a greater part of their bitterness sprang from the sense of an opportunity missed and the realization that the political obstacles in the way of female suffrage were huge, now that the word 'male' had appeared in the Constitution as a prerequisite for citizenship. Although Wyoming territory granted women the vote in 1869 and Utah in 1870, these victories can be explained in terms of purely local efforts to attract settlers and recruit conservative votes in the face of serious threats to the *status quo*.[14] More indicative of the swift retreat from Republican radicalism was the hostile response to women's efforts, during the 1872 presidential election, to register and vote as 'persons' under the Fourteenth Amendment, the first clause of which extended citizenship to 'persons' without the addition of the word 'male', as in the second section: the Supreme Court speedily endorsed the judgement of the registrars who refused to admit their claims.

In 1866 the women's rights movement had generously broadened its objectives with the formation of the Equal Rights Association; by 1869 it had split apart over the race issue but also over tactics. The New York-based National Woman Suffrage Association (NWSA), directed by Elizabeth Stanton and Susan Anthony, favoured the adoption of a constitutional amendment to enfranchise women, whereas the Boston-centred American Woman Suffrage Association urged state action. While both organizations had their male supporters, the more radical National Association did not recruit them as officers. This division of forces, aggravated by disputes over 'associated' issues such as temperance, continued until 1890, when a merger produced the National American Woman Suffrage Association (NAWSA); but before the vote was achieved through the Nineteenth Amendment in 1920, yet another schism occurred in the movement, when in 1913 a breakaway group formed the Congressional Union for Woman Suffrage, aiming at bringing more militant pressures to bear to achieve the passage of the proposed Amendment.

The persistence of women in seeking the vote, despite innumerable setbacks, is not at all mysterious. In a country pledged to defend individual rights and where steady progress towards a democratic suffrage had been made since the eighteenth century, the exclusion of women seemed more unreasonable than anywhere else in the world. As black clamour for enfranchisement after the war had shown, the vote was a well-understood symbol of emancipation (albeit its benefits are as invariably exaggerated by those who do not possess it as they are undervalued by those who do). If women had their own special civic concerns and disabilities, it was reasonable to suppose that desired social legislation and reform would follow most readily from their direct involvement in politics. It is also generally agreed that of all feminist objectives, the suffrage was the one upon which more women could agree than any other. Yet during the years between 1869 and 1920 the ideology and composition of the suffrage campaign, let alone the wider women's movement, changed enormously, and some of these complexities may fruitfully be explored by looking first at the experiences of one state, California—at its relations with the national organizations, and the reasons its workers offered for their initial failures and ultimate success. In this way we may come to a closer understanding of the length of time required before the national victory could be achieved.

The California Campaign: First Phase

There were forty-one state amendment campaigns after 1869, with thirty-two defeats and nine triumphs before 1916, while for fifty years, from 1867, there were fifty-six referenda on female suffrage.[15] In California, a spirited campaign during 1896 ended in disappointment for the suffragists. It was not until 1911 that their determination was rewarded, by which time representatives from the national societies had visited the state; an elaborate range of state and local societies had been developed; support from the political parties, other reformers, the Press and influential men had been strenuously canvassed; and a number of vivid leaders had emerged who deserve more attention than they have hitherto attracted.

Activity in the state was under way by the early 1870s, when Susan B. Anthony first visited the Pacific Coast, enjoying a mixed reception there and a limited response in California; by the following decade a state suffrage league was in being and an effort had been made to extend women's rights in the Constitutional Convention of 1878–9, though without much success.[16] In 1894 the Republicans had adopted a strong plank in favour of female suffrage, while the next year a number of prominent suffragists attempted to secure from the Republican legislature a bill enfranchising women. Although their efforts were unsuccessful, that body did submit a constitutional amendment to the voters, to be acted on in 1896. Miss Anthony visited California again for a few weeks during the preceding year, together with Dr Anna Shaw, returning in 1896, and other outside workers came to help with the preparations for the testing vote. But most of the efforts in the eight-month campaign were made by local women, channelled through a joint committee and state central committee, formed out of officers from the state suffrage and amendment associations and in touch with societies in each county. Meetings were held in all towns with two hundred inhabitants, on a precinct basis, as well as in every county in the state; special attention was given to the county seats, and a highlight of the campaign, in May 1896, was a Women's Congress on the theme of women in government, described by one observer as a suffrage convention in disguise.[17] Visits were made to newspaper editors, for the importance of a wide Press coverage was fully recognized, and delegates attended the conventions of the various political parties.[18]

Feminists often argued that the West was in general less reactionary than the East, and such claims amounted to more than the natural desire of developing pressure groups to encourage their members and to challenge a distant, old-established leadership.[19] In political terms, their validity is at first sight borne out by the success of suffrage referenda in Colorado (1893) and Idaho (1896), as well as by the retention of women's suffrage by Wyoming (1890) and Utah (1896) when they attained statehood. Yet recent scholarship suggests that these gains owe less to the efforts of the women themselves or Western egalitarianism than to a conviction that female voters could be relied upon to reinforce elitist opposition to the ascendancy of immigrants and urban values. They were also influenced by the vagaries of party conflicts in Congress and the needs of local political parties. In particular, the emergence in Colorado and Idaho of the Populists, with their sympathetic attitude towards the women's cause and their divisive impact on the two major parties, was crucial to the victories of the 1890s. Political issues were equally important in California but ultimately proved too complex to offset the effects of a hastily organized campaign and united opposition from the liquor interests.[20]

Minority-party support was forthcoming, for such groups were eager for any votes, even if the women were careful to make no promises in return for endorsement of their cause; but more important than sympathy from the Populists, the Socialist Labor Party, the Single Taxers and the Prohibitionists were the attitudes of the Democrats and Republicans. A declaration in favour of women's suffrage, though predictable after the action of the legislature, was greeted with elation as 'the first time that the Republican party of any State, in advance of the election, has endorsed a pending Constitutional Amendment enfranchising women . . . It is the first public recognition of the fact that a majority of the Republican voters of the North and West are in favor of woman suffrage'.[21] The Democrats, always more conservative on feminist matters (especially in Congress, where Southerners feared the women's vote would reopen the question of black enfranchisement), voted by three-quarters to a quarter against the amendment at their convention, despite the presentation of a petition in its favour signed by 40,000 Californian men and women. A victory here would have been extraordinary, since this was the first occasion on which a Democratic gathering had entertained such a resolution, and hostile forces among the delegates had been well organized.[22] Moreover, the politics of the 1896 campaign were complicated as well as assisted by its coinciding with a presidential election. Anxious to improve their prospects and finances, Populists fused with the Democrats and subsequently toned down their support for the women, while the Republicans, in their bid to retain power, did not want to give undue publicity to a constitutional amendment which was being vehemently denounced by the well-organized alcohol concerns of the state. As a result, they were reluctant to have women speak at their campaign meetings; the suffragists were in fact obliged to beg time to be heard at political gatherings of any complexion.[23]

It is worth considering in more detail the reasons why the pressure for woman's suffrage made such rapid ground in California, only to be defeated in November 1896 by 26,734 votes out of a total of 247,454. Independently of the women's rights movement, though from about the same time, temperance forces were beginning to gather momentum, seeking support from feminists by advocating votes for women which might in due course be turned against the liquor interests. The first northern California branch of the Woman's Christian Temperance Union (WCTU) was formed in 1874, with a state union following in 1879; the southern part of the state was organized in 1883 and functioned separately from 1884, the need for two societies being dictated by the size of California. At the 1883 annual convention, after some hesitation—for the cause was not yet popular—a commitment was made to women's suffrage, and in 1886 it became one of the organizational departments of the northern body. In the south the cause was endorsed a year later. By 1889 temperance workers were lobbying for municipal suffrage and women's school suffrage, for the full vote in 1891 and for school suffrage again in 1893; indeed, from 1889 the WCTU asked for some sort of suffrage from the legislature every year.[24] Despite repeated failures, the guarded sympathy of the state Senate had been demonstrated by 1895, and the women of the Union pledged themselves to work for the amendment campaign. But the alliance brought difficulties for both sides.

In each movement there were those who favoured single-issue campaigns so as not to dissipate their strength or alienate elements opposed to the secondary goals.[25] As far as giving offence was concerned, the suffragists had most at risk. Saloons were particularly popular in comparatively recently settled regions where recreational alternatives were few, and by the end of the century, with the exception of Arizona and Nevada, California had more saloons in proportion to its population than any other area in the United States, and San Francisco boasted more saloons in proportion to population than any other city. During the 1870s, when the women's temperance drive for local option laws got under way, the liquor dealers were not similarly aroused, but by 1896 the alcohol wholesalers and retailers were united in the California State Protective Association, dedicated to pressurizing their outlets in the hotel, saloon, grocery and drug businesses and to tackling their adversaries in the courts and at the polls, whether these were suffragists or prohibitionists.[26] The liquor interest inevitably looked askance at votes for women when WCTU literature maintained that the result would be temperance legislation.[27] Feminists like Susan Anthony, long sceptical about the reliability of temperance support,[28] therefore asked the organizers of the WCTU convention planned for California in 1896 to hold their meeting elsewhere and urged women to seek the franchise not as a measure 'for temperance, social purity, or any other reform' but because of 'the right of every individual to have his or her opinion counted at the ballot-box, whether it is in accordance with ours or not'.[29]

In this instance Miss Anthony's scepticism seems out of place; the WCTU assembly meant for San Francisco was held in St Louis, and though the two questions were deliberately not confused, Sarah M. Severance, suffrage superintendent for the Union, noted after the election was over that the counties carried for the amendment were those 'in which temperance and Christian sentiment are strongest'.[30] Nonetheless, the women placed much of the blame for their defeat on the liquor lobby, and it may well be that the crucial hostile vote of San Francisco and Alameda counties can be explained by the association of the two women's campaigns in the minds of voters. Yet suffragists needed all the help they could get; while workers at the time might take pride in the activities of 1896,[31] the historians of the movement later complained of 'insufficient organization, too small a number of workers, lack of necessary funds, [and] the immense amount of territory to be covered'.[32] Susan Anthony attached particular significance to the failure to carry out 'house-to-house educational work throughout every voting precinct', not only to counteract the committees of the 'liquor man' in 'every saloon, "dive" and gambling house' but also to persuade party conventions, state legislatures and Congress that woman's enfranchisement was a matter which interested rank-and-file voters.[33] Without twenty years of temperance agitation by California women, it is doubtful whether there would have been enough workers to undertake even the inadequate canvassing of 1896.

The other allies of the women's cause, by their own reckoning, were the 'colleges, the churches, the teachers' conventions, the philanthropic societies, the women's clubs, the educated and respectable people generally'.[34] The Press approaches paid off in an unprecedented amount of free publicity. Some 250 papers declared editorially for the amendment before the campaign ended; only two journals were markedly hostile; and those of the Spanish, French and Italian groups, labour, the Socialists, temperance, and the anti-Catholic American Protective Association were allegedly staunch in their support. The backing of the latter association apparently waned, however, for reasons that remain obscure.[35]

The attitudes of the 'foreign' elements, especially in the cities, are likewise in doubt. Women experienced in Chinese mission work were delegated to canvass the Chinese voters, but though the women had allied with them during the Kearney riots, the largely male Chinese settlement was hardly famous for its progressive views about the position of women.[36] The very much smaller Negro community was not neglected; a black woman lecturer worked hard among her people, and the Afro-American League, reportedly in favour of the suffrage, permitted a debate on the subject at its Los Angeles convention.[37] Even so, the conservative scepticism of that gathering was noted, and when defeat finally became apparent it is not surprising if some conventional antipathies surfaced among the disappointed feminists. According to one San Francisco Press woman present at the count:

> Some Negroes who came in and stood behind my chair were delighted that the vote was going against us, and they laughed and made remarks about women's not knowing enough, etc. That from men whose fathers and grandfathers were slaves, and who were freed by the pen of a woman! One native-born Chinaman said, 'Oh, woman no vote, she no lead (read) enough!' There is a sweet pill for you to swallow! Oh, why won't people see that women are degraded by their position?[38]

Considering the leadership of the suffrage movement, in which journalists, social reformers, teachers and club-women predominated, such feelings are to be expected, while the group which had worked for the slaves and freedmen and which sympathized with the Chinese cannot be blamed for hoping for a *quid pro quo*.[39] When none was forthcoming, the fact that Chinese labour posed a far greater threat to the employment prospects of white women than they did to those of white men may have given an added dimension to their resentment, for women were now organized in the sewing, shoe and printing trades, and there was sympathy among the middle-class suffragists for the eight-hour day and the minimum wage.[40]

Many women eventually developed a concern about the economic exploitation of their sex and of children, as well as a host of civic questions, through the club movement. A General Federation of Women's Clubs was founded in 1890, and by 1900 its convention brought together perhaps 150,000 women. One of the best-known organizers in California, Caroline M. Severance, who had begun her activities in this field in 1868 while living in New England, was instrumental in the formation of the first Los Angeles women's club in 1878, and by 1891 was presiding over the Friday Morning Club of that city, which was among the earliest members of the General Federation. The initial aim was simply to bring women into closer contact and sympathy with each other, breaking down prejudice and ignorance, the great obstacles to progress; no one interest or topic was to be made paramount at club gatherings, a rule designed to promote the recruitment of the widest possible membership. Yet horizons broadened only slowly.[41]

Elizabeth B. Harbert, who, like Mrs Severance, had moved to California after a career of public service elsewhere, noted the 'timidity and conservatism' of the early women's movement, and suggested that since 'it was essential to the growth of . . . pioneer clubs that they . . . avoided the rock and whirlpool', 'the consideration of politics and religion were excluded'.[42] The essential benefit of the woman's club, as Charlotte Perkins Stetson averred, was that it trained women 'in the great human force of organization', gradually teaching those 'whose range of life was wholly personal . . . to care for the general good, and to work for it';[43] in this sense clubs certainly exerted a radicalizing influence. But their initial proponents equally resented the efforts by the advocates of consumer protection, peace, temperance, suffrage and other reforms to make use of the fledgling clubs, believing that 'the great mass of women' could not 'be plunged into what must be a propaganda'.[44] Certainly, the Federation did not advocate female suffrage until 1914, after much pressure both from outside and within its own ranks, though caution here arose partly from a desire to encourage the growth of clubs in the South, which in turn produced a timid attitude to race questions. Except in Massachusetts and a few other Northern states, black women were not received into the clubs of white women and fears were entertained that mixing in clubs would lead to fraternizing in private houses, even though organizers might discount them as groundless. Separate associations provided the way out of this dilemma, and the Federation retained the right of deciding whether or not to admit black groups to the larger membership.[45]

It was during the first two decades of the twentieth century that the club movement really became concerned that women should 'advance and progress in every line of thought and action', working to create, in addition to a taste for better literature, art and music, 'the improvement of conditions affecting the home, the perfect development of the child, and the citizen'. Their efforts, however, were still presented as conservative, 'more remedial than original'[46]—hence their sucess in the Progressive era; they would only serve to fit women 'to be mothers of heroes and noble men'. The results of this continuing emphasis on conciliation were epitomized in a plaintive request for a suffrage speaker from a Pasadena club woman in 1909, on the grounds that 'our women have to be educated up to much that is already accepted elsewhere'.[47]

In the end the favourite verdict on the defeat of 1896 was that it was engineered by the twin forces of ignorance and vice, united in the city slums of San Francisco, Oakland and Alameda;[48] moreover, the masculine support vital to success was so far little in evidence, either in the form of separate organizations or as financial contributions.[49] Yet in San Francisco and Oakland, according to some sources, the richest and poorest wards were equally opposed to the suffrage amendment, suggesting that if active feminists were ever to carry the day, they would have to convert men of the middle and 'respectable' working class.[50]

The California Campaign: The Successful Phase

The years between 1896 and 1910 were extraordinarily bleak ones for suffragists; not one state enfranchised its women during that period.[51] Although the two national associations had come together, many tactical and ideological conflicts remained to be settled, while the national political environment was less promising, with the decline of Populism and the disfranchisement and segregation of the Southern Negro. Nonetheless, the California women were not entirely dispirited after their narrow defeat in 1896, accepting the necessity for long preparation before any suffrage success[52] and at once devising a new plan of work envisaging the organization of every county and precinct to correspond with, and make the maximum impact upon, existing political districts. These units would, it was hoped, facilitate home calls, the distribution of literature and the recruitment of audiences for meetings; systematic Press work would be assisted, as would the presentation of the suffrage case at public functions and before other organized bodies (including women's clubs), the conversion of young people through a variety of entertainments, and the establishment of district institutes to be conducted by qualified instructors.[53] There were, however, many roads towards the ultimate goal, including club membership and civic activities, in addition to service with the California Equal Suffrage

Association, the College Women's Equal Suffrage League, or local suffrage groups. Apart from broad educational efforts, the women again directed their energies to lobbying activities in Sacramento; they remained true to the classic pressure-group profession of bipartisanship, and both parties flirted with the petitioners, though neither was in full support until the upsurge of Progressive reform sentiment in the state threw its policies into the kind of flexible condition last witnessed during the 1890s.[54] And if Progressives were at first cautious in their approach to those pressing for a new women's suffrage amendment, their belief in direct democracy could eventually only help the fight for extension of the franchise.[55]

Operations in California, duly encouraged by the political situation, expanded considerably from 1910, even before the passage of the suffrage amendment by the legislature in 1911 necessitated another drive throughout the state. Old organizations revived and new ones were founded; notable among them were the Votes for Women Club, formed to agitate among self-supporting women, a Wage Earners' League, the Club-Women's Franchise League, and the Political Equality League of California (PEL), established by a wealthy Los Angeles banker, John Hyde Braly.[56] The determination of this Republican millionaire played a large part in reanimating the state movement during 1910, when he decided after attending a dispiriting suffrage meeting, that he must arouse 'the attention of strong men whose opinions would attract and influence women of intellect!'[57]

In April a banquet in Los Angeles for about fifty such individuals led to the formation of the PEL, later supplemented by a separate Men's Equal Suffrage Campaign League, involving some of the most prominent men in the city. There followed an information-gathering visit to the national suffrage convention at Washington, DC; then the opinions on women's suffrage of legislative candidates all over the southern counties of the state were established, which encouraged the undertaking of similar inquiries in the north, all with a view to guiding the votes of those sympathetic towards the women. Delegates to the 1910 Republican Convention managed to get a suffrage plank written into the platform—though that party's awareness of Progressive strength no doubt influenced the decision—and Braly subsequently funded another well-publicized dinner, this time for the newly elected legislators and state officers of the South. He afterwards joined representatives from the women's groups in canvassing legislators at Sacramento during the vital votes on the amendment. Close attention was paid by the men's League to precinct work; appeals were sent out to the clergy to preach and campaign for the franchise; an automobile tour took some of the drudgery out of operations in a large state; and Mr Braly paid all his own expenses.[58]

In the banker's opinion, California men were instrumental in forcing the 1911 suffrage battle, while female efforts secured the victory, a judgement endorsed by women co-workers, who welcomed his wealth, political acumen and ability to muster support from influential citizens, even if they did not always appreciate his independence.[59] Mrs Braly was said to be 'equally ready to work and sacrifice for the cause', but most often it was the sympathy of husbands that was essential to both the harmony of suffragists' households and the success of their activities.[60] Conscious that women busy outside the home were ever suspected of neglecting their families, the national spokesmen for the movement were at pains to point out the exemplary home life of leaders like Mrs Stanton, although concern for masculine goodwill did not break down NWSA's reluctance to admit men to official positions in the Association, on the grounds that they '*cannot make women's* disfranchisement hurt them—*as it hurts us*—hence cannot be our guides & ultimate appeals—as to principles and policies of action'.[61] California feminists similarly paid tribute to the 'time and means and service' given to the crusade by their own menfolk, although there was some impatience with male supporters who only spoke out in the safety of suffrage meetings.[62] Nonetheless, tensions inevitably arose within marriages; thus the correspondence of Mrs Severance, despite assertions that her husband 'was in sympathy with her in all her efforts' and that theirs had been a 'very bright and happy' home, contains some poignant letters suggesting that Theodoric was accustomed but still not resigned to her frequent absences from Los Angeles, just as she was irritated by his reproaches.[63] Furthermore, even when widowhood released women from domestic disapproval and opposition, the need to make a living could detract from full-time suffrage work, as in the case of the outspoken and vigorous Clara Shortridge Foltz, whose five children, aged mother and law and business interests kept her, so she modestly believed, from winning the vote in California single-handed.[64]

During 1911, as in 1896, the sustained wooing of local newspaper editors resulted in a large Press coverage of suffragist endeavours; individual voters were canvassed and circularized with thousands of leaflets; temporary offices were taken in prominent locations to attract the passer-by, despite the heavy expense incurred; and, in the view of one worker, '*meetings, meetings, meetings* were what finally won us the victory', whether in parlours, halls or the streets. An elaborate system of departments was developed by the major suffrage groups, of the kind favoured by other women's movements of the day, and a co-operative council established comprising representatives from sympathetic clubs and bodies not affiliated with the state association. The national organization sent literature and funds, and money was also gathered from prominent California women, as well as at the clubs and mass meetings.[65] As usual, the role of the outsider in state suffrage campaigns was controversial, but though the representatives of the national association might traditionally be resented as self-serving 'professionals' who alienated the local workers, they were at least prepared to take on unpopular touring duties.[66]

In the course of all this activity some familiar enemies and objections were identified; feminist arguments were slanted accordingly. The extremes of wealth and poverty were once more ranged against the women. It proved difficult to arrange suffrage meetings with commercial leaders, and men of wealth were offended by the movement 'because their own womenkind are economically dependent and in their judgement do not need "rights" for self-protection. Moreover people of this class have a stricter code of social behavior and measure women, especially, by it'.[67] Although some rich men like Mr Braly, and women like Mrs Sargent, Mrs Sperry and Mrs Goodrich, were generous contributors to the cause, as they had been in 1896, this was not the normal practice of the affluent, and Clara Foltz was particularly scathing in her comments on the ineffectual support given by the 'passee relics of distinguished and defunct spouses', unable any more 'to appear in decolleté gowns' but dissatisfied simply with basking in the glory of 'their illustrious male ancestors'. However much the California women may have contrasted their techniques with those of Eastern, let alone English, suffragists, Brian Harrison's recent work on the opposition to women's suffrage in Britain notes a similar antipathy towards the cause among the fashionable classes there (and likewise among many suspicious brewers and working men).[68]

Equally suspicious of feminism were the foreign-born, 'who still retain the foreign ideas of the necessary subordination of women. To this . . . class suffrage is not only offensive but preposterous.'[69] Special leaflets in foreign languages were distributed among the ethnic groups, though women continued to resent 'the bitter irony of the appeal to the ignorant immigrant to permit us a voice in the land of our forefathers';[70] not surprisingly, this appeal was pressed with difficulty among the Chinese, and the French, German and Italian newspapers often proved hostile or at best ambivalent.[71]

Nor had the 'liquor interest' been routed since 1896, any more than the debates over the wisdom of a link between suffragism and temperance agitation had been settled. In 1911 the WCTU endorsed the fight for the franchise alongside the Federation of Parent-Teacher Associations, the California Federation of Women's Clubs, Jewish organizations, college clubs, the State Nurses' Association, women's organized labour and leaders in the arts, science and philanthropy.[72] The Union was given the task of enlisting for the campaign the backing of the Churches and religious and philanthropic bodies; it duly involved itself in house-to-house visiting, co-operating with the many other women's groups in the field and keeping WCTU interests in the background.[73] Although temperance advocates might proudly suggest that to the Union 'more than any other organization belongs the glory of our . . . [1911] victory. It educated and organized women',[74] the liquor lobby could only be alarmed by the support of the normally single-minded Anti-Saloon League at its 1911 convention (given in the belief that the female vote would be dry) and by the continued claims of prohibitionist newspapers like the *California Voice* that 'we could, at once, abolish the rum traffic and the rum devil and the rum hell on earth, if women were allowed to vote'.[75] The suffrage-temperance alliance was also likely now, as at any other period, to repel the foreign element in the state, regarded by both movements with mixed feelings. The WCTU had departments devoted to missionary activities among immigrants and Negroes, but progress was particularly difficult in cities such as San Francisco where, in 1910, 68 per cent of the population were foreign-born or the children of the foreign-born, and foreign influences were closely associated with the saloon.[76] This association prompted the *California Voice* to indulge in unashamedly nativist outbursts to the effect that 'every sot who beats his wife, every ignorant beer-swilling Mexican, Italian, Polack and other savage, and every illiterate Negro, believes solemnly that women will never know enough to be fit to vote'.[77]

If, then, suffragists persisted in trying to discredit their opponents as the worst sections of society—'the ignorant, the depraved, the tyrannical, the bum and the thug, and the saloon element'[78]—and club-women might not fully appreciate the viewpoint of working-class men, no matter how strong the theoretical commitment to socialism of some among them and the fears of contemporaries that 'the cause of socialism [would] . . . be advanced by the vote extension to both sexes', they believed they had won masculine sympathy 'in the comfortable, hard-working American middle class and in the upper organised labouring group'.[79] These elements were used to making women partners in their concerns and to seeing them struggle for the family welfare or share their own exertions for better wages, hours and conditions. In Los Angeles, the 'striking shopmen of the Southern Pacific put in their best efforts for suffrage', working 'shoulder to shoulder with the women' at the polls.[80] Just as club activities had ceased to be a conservative alternative to suffrage endeavours by 1911, so these endeavours now involved, and were directed towards, the working-class constituency neglected during the nineteenth century.[81] And while the leaders of the suffrage movement remained middle class, their open-air meetings, state tours and precinct work reveal a new energy and political awareness. However, this greater dynamism did not destroy their essential caution; the California feminists continued to congratulate themselves on having avoided recourse to unseemly British militancy of the kind that was beginning to affect the national leadership.[82]

Although it may be true that women's suffrage was carried in the West partly because the political opposition was less united than in the East and because there were fewer diverse cities to win over,[83] the very fact that experience was producing better, more confident organization intensified the efforts of the California opposition forces.[84] In 1911 the pro-suffrage lobby at Sacramento was for the first time joined by a hostile delegation, and some journalists suggested that the 'good looks, handsome gowns and "feminine tactics" of these ladies' were 'in marked contrast with the "old-time shriekers for the ballot"!'.[85] Denunciations of the female vote were still published, despite the general sympathy of the California Press, particularly after 1905. Indeed, as in Britain, organized opposition to women's demands grew as general hostility to them declined and their chances of success correspondingly increased.[86] Objections related to the likely effect of enfranchisement both on politics and on women themselves, or focused upon the weaknesses in the feminist ideology. And by now women and their male allies were shaping their debate not simply according to the early natural rights argument, but with reference to a whole range of practicalities.

The franchise, critics maintained, far from being a right was a privilege and a burden, one to which women were not entitled, since their frailty prevented them from bearing arms to defend their country and since they could not even wield the police power that was needed in the last resort to uphold unpopular laws. Too much was claimed for the vote and the average voter: middle-class suffragists might be high-minded reformers but the mass of their sex was as ignorant as the mass of men, and would in any event assert no beneficial influence by going to the polls because the 'influence of the voter on the law-maker [was] infinitesimal'. Moreover, although politics was 'a matter of business, not of morals', economic progress was alleged to depend on 'the education and enlightenment of public sentiment' and the organization of labour rather than on the passage of new laws. In states where female suffrage had been enacted social abuse had not been curbed, nor had the standard of office-holders risen. It was suggested that the majority of women did not seek the ballot, aware that they already enjoyed favourable treatment under California laws, and were always accorded superior status by chivalrous men. Feminists, by contrast, were hostile to men, it was claimed, neglectful of their domestic duties and bent on procuring partial laws which would raise taxes, close legitimate businesses, and scare away settlers. Whether or not they recognized it, the charge ran, suffragists were supported by all the political opportunists in the state, and their cause might lead them into militancy and political radicalism. It was up to men who opposed that cause to protect women 'from a threatened invasion of the priceless heritage of rights now theirs'.[87]

The debate about the effect of female voting was particularly important since, like the spokesmen for all other pressure groups engaged in a long struggle against daunting odds, feminist leaders had often exaggerated their case. Fortunately, if the best that had been hoped for had not come about, then neither had the worst, and male sympathizers were produced who would say so, though public debates with the 'antis' were avoided, as it was considered that they gave undesirable publicity to the forces of reaction. While the political world remained imperfect, the feminist reply went, women voters had supported good laws, and refrained from infringing masculine rights and had neither neglected their homes and families nor 'become frenzied for office': indeed, the debate about protecting womanliness and the home had acquired a rather quaint ring by 1911 and was attracting fewer contestants than formerly. Reforms were usually initiated by small minorities, and 'wicked' women would certainly not be interested in the franchise, as was sometimes supposed; but innumerable petitions to Washington and the clamour of thousands of women's groups throughout the country —groups which had already demonstrated their sense of civic responsibility and efficiency in public service—indicated a widespread desire for the suffrage. The privileges enjoyed by dependent groups were not only demeaning but also far outweighed by the benefits enjoyed in freedom; furthermore, since men and women had different interests and aims, the former could not adequately represent the latter. Where there were laws favourable to women, they had usually been hard-earned, and the involvement of women in politics was essential as city life produced new problems and at a time when the state intervened in a host of matters once exclusively the concern of individual households. Military duty and voting were not co-extensive, as the 'antis' alleged, only about a third of voters being subject to that duty, and though the law might ultimately have to be upheld by force, this crucial coercion was not exerted by the law-makers themselves and by only a fraction of the voters. Finally, of course, there were the classic arguments: those required to obey the laws should have a say in their making; those who paid taxes to support the government should be represented in that government; unfair legislation still remained on the statute books; those who had charge of homes and children should be equipped in every way to safeguard their interests; and working women needed the vote for their protection.[88]

In the end, it seems, the woman suffrage referendum was carried—though by the frighteningly small margin of 3587 votes—because of the favourable political situation, Western precedents, the feminists' long-established and increasingly efficient organization, the favourable impression created by their activities in other fields, and the development of a set of arguments which appealed to many different groups among the electorate. No miracles were achieved, however; the urban vote remained hostile, while in some counties attempts were made by unfriendly political and economic interests to tamper with the returns, and despite the enlargement of their support during the few years before victory, many of the activists in 1911 were veterans. In the verdict of Selina Solomons, ex-president of the San Francisco Votes for Women Club, it was 'inevitable that in the main . . . [reform] work has to be finished by these same hands, hearts and brains that have directed it from the first'.[89] This fact, together with the moderate nature of the campaign, does much to explain the limited consequences of the franchise.

Aftermath of Victory: California and the Wider World

Early in 1912 the California suffrage association decided to continue operations for another two years to help other states mounting campaigns, and political clubs as well as non-partisan women's leagues were formed to mobilize the new voters.[90] The leaders of the movement involved themselves in the professions, in club work, journalism and civic affairs (the *Woman Citizen*, edited by Mrs Arthur Cornwall, once president of the Woman's Franchise League, was specifically designed to educate the women's vote). California women were said to register and to go to the polls in about the same proportion to their numbers as men, dividing their patronage between all the parties, but they did not produce many office-seekers.[91] In 1920 the pioneering California Civic League merged with the national League of Women Voters, which succeeded NAWSA on the adoption of the Nineteenth (suffrage) Amendment to the United States Constitution, and the more militant, nationally orientated National Woman's Party (NWP), stemming from a group which in 1913 had broken away from NAWSA, was also represented in the state.[92]

The divisions which had plagued the feminist movement in the second half of the nineteenth century erupted again just when women in nine states and a territory enjoyed the vote and were in a position, in a politically strategic region of the country, to make a direct impact on national elections. The disagreement was essentially between the advocates of an all-out drive to secure a federal suffrage amendment and the stalwarts of the national association who continued to value campaigns to secure amendments to state constitutions while abandoning their policy of 'almost exclusive concentration on the states'. But it was also a contest between old and new styles of leadership: between the advocates of 'militant' tactics and those who abhorred them, between those who urged a continuing aloofness from party politics and those in favour of threatening the party in power, the Democrats, with the claim that women's votes in the West would be used to topple them from office unless the national amendment was given official support.[93]

There was, furthermore, a bitter debate among feminists over the proper attitude to adopt towards World War I. That conflict diverted funds, workers and interest away from the women's movement and, as Alice Park maintained, robbed women of actual or potential husbands while enriching profiteers and discrediting 'cooling-off' periods and international arbitration.[94] Nevertheless, it is apparent that, apart from the new political tactics they adopted, women at this time advanced their cause most dramatically by their contribution to the war effort.[95] Those suffragists (mainly in the NWP) who joined the Socialists, Industrial Workers of the World and conscientious objectors in maintaining that democracy should begin at home soon found their civil liberties and motives under attack.

Although both NAWSA and the NWP played a crucial part in securing the Nineteenth Amendment, the divergent views they represented were not reconciled, and after 1920 women continued to debate the purpose and results of the vote and the best ways of organizing themselves in a still male-dominated world. We have already seen that, to broaden the base of their support, many feminists had played down their threat to existing marital and family arrangements, evolving instead an ideology based on womanly self-sacrifice which, in its political ramifications, emphasized their unique interest in social reforms of various kinds. Nationally women had already been involved in the successful Progressive effort to establish a federal Children's Bureau, which did sterling work in persuading states to outlaw child labour, and had supported Office of Education efforts to encourage compulsory school attendance. They had contributed to the crusades against liquor and prostitution and to those pledged to initiate sex education in schools, to establish kindergartens and nursery schools and to secure the protection of working women; many had found social work a rewarding career, and the increasingly outward-looking club movement went from strength to strength, 1919 witnessing the formation of the National Federation of Business and Professional Women's Clubs. Having thus proved their 'fitness' for the vote they once claimed as of right, feminists predictably continued to concern themselves with such matters. In California Mrs Park maintained that five years after their enfranchisement, and without neglecting their home responsibilities, women had been able to gain membership of school boards and other similar bodies, in addition to influencing the passage of laws giving parents equal guardianship rights, outlawing houses of prostitution, providing pensions for teachers and needy mothers, raising the age of consent and punishing offences against young girls. It was also more than coincidental that a long-needed state industrial school for girls was being built and a minimum wage commission had been appointed.[96] Were not women thus acting as they had claimed they would do—with moderation, humanity and concern for their special sphere? What need of anything beyond this 'social feminism' and hopes that in time direct involvement in politics would increase? As Clara Foltz confided to Mrs Park in 1923, personal efforts at improvement rather than further legislation would ensure respect for women's work and advice: 'We have a whole lot more rights than we can exercise—the same can be said of men, for that matter; for on the whole, they are as inefficient and unqualified for any civic duties as are women.' And encouragingly, the participation of American women in voluntary associations was to prove greater than in many other parts of the world.[97]

Throughout the country similarly decorous and specialist reform activities were undertaken by social feminists; moderate as they were, they frequently aroused opposition, and their achievements should not be underestimated. Support for home economics teaching was justifiable as part of a general effort to improve vocational training for the masses during this period, though it prompted the writing of much pretentious nonsense about the household arts as higher arts. If there was still nostalgia in the South for the gracious lady of tradition (and it was necessary for feminists there more than anywhere to conform to 'genteel' patterns of behaviour), women's groups in the region campaigned for state and municipal reform, children and women's legislation and even inter-racial co-operation.[98] Elsewhere traditional pressure groups such as the League of Women Voters, the American Association of University Women, the National Consumers' League and the General Federation of Women's Clubs, worked successfully for the passage of new marriage and divorce laws, state welfare codes, and maternity and infancy protection legislation.[99]

Interest in the temperance question likewise persisted. The prohibition amendment had been enacted in 1919–20 in somewhat similar circumstances to those surrounding women's suffrage, though through a different combination of forces and in order to restrict rather than to extend personal freedom, despite the mutual support of feminists and temperance advocates and their comparable expression of middle-class aspirations. Thereafter prohibitionists were embarrassed by enforcement problems, scandals which discredited the Anti-Saloon League, and the inevitable falling away of support which affects any cause that has achieved its primary goal.[100] Nonetheless, the WCTU survived both these developments and the changing attitudes to moderate drinking which would soon undermine its greatest achievement. It did so by aiming at a lower middle-class and working-class constituency, focusing its attacks on middle-class alcohol consumption, and contributing eventually to 'arousing public sentiment upon moral and social issues, such as gambling, venereal disease, the narcotic evil, and . . . securing legislation restricting such anti-social activities'.[101] In addition, and apart from the education work slanted towards youth which had assumed an ever larger part of its operations, the Union was seeking, by the 1960s and 1970s, the better enforcement of laws against drinking and against the advertisement of liquor and its effects. It was also helping the foreign-born to become 'Americanized' citizens, subsidizing relief programmes at home and abroad, supporting child-welfare work, helping the blind, endorsing pacifism and its implications, and agitating for uniform marriage and divorce laws, the suppression of obscene literature and measures to contain juvenile delinquency. Its official publication was now appropriately subtitled 'A Journal of Social Welfare'.[102]

Such an enlargement of its original scope did not seem outlandish in the Union, which had always entertained large ambitions and co-operated with friendly interests.[103] Before the revocation of the Eighteenth Amendment in 1933, achieved partly with the assistance of middle-class groups like the Woman's Organization for the Repeal of National

Prohibition, the WCTU found employment for social feminists in a variety of good works, as well as labouring for the better enforcement of prohibition, pressing the local unions for funds to this end and launching a new membership drive.[104]

In Washington, however, the NWP remained dissatisfied. It had taken forty-two years to obtain the woman suffrage amendment, first introduced into Congress in 1878. Victory had been achieved, as in California, through a combination of persistence, improved organization and fortunate political circumstances, despite the opposition of Southern racists, commercial and liquor interests, defenders of states rights and other diehards. Yet, even after 1920, women remained outside the benefits of the Fourteenth Amendment, which secured for male 'persons' the 'due process of law' and 'equal protection of the laws'. Years of concentration on the suffrage had been at the expense of all other women's rights, urged radicals, and without these even the moderate goals professed by many suffragists would be unobtainable. In the view of a contributor to *Equal Rights* (the NWP journal) in 1923, the 'maternal instinct of the world' was being wasted:

> the augmented interest in the special concerns of women [that is, education and social and moral work] reflects itself faintly in American life. This is because as our Declaration of Principles says: 'Women today, although enfranchised, are still in every way subordinate to men before the law, in government, in educational opportunities, in the professions, in the church, in industry and in the home'.[105]

Moreover, expression was also given to more alarming sentiments, of a kind that had been muted in the later stages of the suffrage movement when radicalism had become a matter more of tactics than of ideology. The NWP was, in a sense, conventional in its methods, pressing for an Equal Rights Amendment to the Constitution from 1923 (an almost identically worded amendment eventually went to the states in 1972) and favouring traditional pressure-group tactics—for example, state campaigns to achieve a variety of legal changes and the formation of permanent councils for each profession to investigate discrimination and agitate for its removal.[106] But in the context of the political reaction which set in at every level of government during the 1920s, equal rights seemed revolutionary, suffrage a conservative concession to keep the peace with a traditionally conservative group in society. If women were going to complain of being too 'cumbered with much serving', if they were going to demand 'power, not protection' and to regard not superior home-making and social reform but 'the status of women' as 'the paramount issue until that status has been raised to one of absolute equality', then traditional family relations and masculine comfort would be threatened as they never could be by occasional trips to the polling booth.[107] The chief argument used against NWP—namely, that the Equal Rights Amendment would deprive working (especially married) women of a mass of protective legislation secured with difficulty during the Progressive era—fails to do justice to its radicalism. For the party wished to improve benefits for all rather than simply exclude one category of women from employment under certain conditions; it was not 'opposed to industrial legislation', merely advocating 'the removal of sex in protective laws'.[108]

Understandably, the controversy aroused by the new amendment drive, so soon after the 1920 success, caused the supporters of more conservative bodies such as the League of Women Voters to protest in bitter terms. As NAWSA leader Mrs Catt complained to a correspondent in 1925:

> The National Woman's Party is by no means the successor of the ideas of Miss Anthony, although they have tried to claim that this is true. While they have been trying to get an equal rights amendment introduced into Congress the League of Women Voters has secured the passage of more than four hundred bills in the various legislatures, and little by little the old discriminations which made the civil status of women so unjust are being removed. No other organisation agrees with the National Woman's Party amendment because it includes so many things that are not a part of the woman movement that we believe it means endless litigation. We all believe in equal rights, but we think we are getting it by a much faster process.[109]

Nonetheless, while this disagreement was very harmful to the activities of moderates and radicals alike, by the end of the decade a *rapprochement* was under way between the NWP and other business and professional women who had become increasingly uneasy about the effects of protective legislation.[110]

Contemporaries focused further attention on female radicalism after the war by making much of the so-called revolution in morals and fashions, and historians have subsequently concerned themselves about its extent and duration, generally coming to the comfortable conclusion that, having had her fling, the flapper gave way to woman as consumer and professional housewife whom, on shopping-basket issues, the politician or manufacturer ignored at his peril. Yet at the time the 'New Woman' tag became a trap and a distraction, along with the notion of a 'New Negro'. For just as the position of both groups was similar in terms of discrimination and separate socialization, so their members were equally incapable of embarking on a path of new freedom after 1920—though many women, unlike most blacks, obviously did not reject their circumscribed role in society—unhampered by male or white disapproval, economic or legal barriers, educational or media conditioning, and ancient stereotypes of appropriate female or Negro behaviour. Women also had to carry the burden of entrenched attitudes towards their biological role, which remained unchallenged (even by many feminists) at a time when nineteenth-century racism appeared to be under attack from the teachings of contemporary science. The pattern of race relations was not affected by Garveyism or the Harlem Renaissance, and the basic pattern of sexual relations was not altered by changes in fashion and etiquette or even by the self-help activity undertaken by women in all aspects of public life.

Moreover, the most significant changes in the Victorian moral code had been accomplished by the Progressive era, as is illustrated, for example, by recent work on the purity movement which culminated during those years.[111] Labour-saving devices, smaller families, the relaxation of the divorce laws, less constricting clothes and less ignorance about sex had emancipated some middle- and upper-class women before World War I, giving rise to what Walter Lippmann called the 'amateur male' long before the advent of the flapper. Yet the strong-minded heroines of Realist fiction, who rebelled against Victorian morals, do not illuminate the general condition of women at the end of the nineteenth century, any more than the plays or novels of the 1920s, which depict women in masculine roles—the aggressor in sex, the breaker of marriage ties—prove that moral changes which gained publicity then were actually significant outside a small urban elite. There is certainly little about the emancipated women of post-war fiction to rejoice the hearts of feminists, and those who abandoned public duty for private satisfaction were largely presented as enjoying sexual liberation within the confines of domesticity, variously assisted by leisure, cosmetics, short skirts, drink and the motor car. We shall never be able accurately to assess the importance of liberated individuals in the Progressive era or the twenties, but the imitation of the dominant section of society—namely, white men—which has been a feature of most emerging sub-groups was probably no more characteristic of either period than the use of time-honoured protest tactics: involvement in distracting civil activities, the vocal or unstated assertion of moral superiority and the withdrawal of sexual 'favours'.

Wider opportunities for working outside the home had also presented themselves from the late nineteenth century onwards, with the development of the typewriter, the telephone exchange and the business office, and during World War I attitudes to the propriety of such work and to women's abilities seemed to undergo a change. But the growth in the female labour force was a temporary phenomenon, while old attitudes returned with 'normalcy': women discovered what it was to be a pool of cheap labour for times of economic emergency, something American blacks had always known. The author, editor and sociologist Charlotte Perkins Gilman, in her striking 1903 analysis of the iniquities of the average home and the waste entailed of nearly half the world's labour, had not foreseen the failure of an economy dominated by mass-production industries to provide opportunities for women more attractive than those offered by the poor, antiquated domestic industries she so despised.[112] The new openings for women from the war years onwards seldom required more than manual skills and were poorly paid; women were discriminated against in appointments and promotions, and where they worked alongside men they failed to obtain equal pay. The twenties witnessed an increase in unemployment which was both structural and regional, matched by a resurgence of court and employer hostility towards union claims. In this inhospitable climate the Women's Trade Union

League, which from 1903 had attempted to organize separate unions or to force entry into existing ones, was attacked by right-wingers and other struggling labour organizations. For although most surveys carried out in the twentieth century suggest that those women who work do so, like men, primarily for money and company rather than for luxury or 'fulfilment', society continued to expect women to retire from work at marriage and exploited, to their disadvantage, the 'lump of labour' fallacy from which immigrants had once suffered; that is to say, it was assumed that each new woman added to the work force took a job from a man—this despite their concentration in industries where few men were employed and which were notorious for a high labour turnover. The coming of the Depression intensified prejudice against working (particularly married) women and resulted in dismissals from the civil service and schools, while many kept their jobs only by accepting lower minimum wages. In a nice revenge upon women who had once argued that their voting would reform the world, men threatened with unprecedented unemployment blamed working women for everything from declining national morals to male indentity crises.

It would not have been easy for women to make an impact on national politics even without the inevitable onset of disillusionment and boredom with the issue among both sexes after 1920. Women did not make startling gains in the exercise of political office or voter turnouts—indeed, no newly enfranchised element in American history has done so. Women in politics certainly failed to check the post-war forces of political reaction, and some of their organizations, notably the Daughters of the American Revolution, set a record for extreme militarism, nationalism, isolationism, anti-radicalism and expulsion of internal dissidents. If sympathy for women's suffrage had been loosely associated with the Republicans,[113] though achieved nationally when the Democrats were in power, neither party had seen any overriding case for enfranchising so large and heterogeneous a group, whose loyalties would be accordingly difficult to calculate and secure. Consequently, neither became the woman's party after 1920, and women for once demonstrated the truth of the customary pressure-group disavowal of partisanship.[114] Nevertheless, female enfranchisement was a further step in that progress towards democracy which had been under way since the eighteenth century, though the process was still incomplete; it marked another crucial step in the modernization of American political institutions, as well as contributing to the continuing agitation for the humanizing of industrial society through the intervention of the state.

As a result of decades of tedious and tiring work in the face of fluctuating apathy and opposition, American feminists had by the 1920s achieved one spectacular political victory and many minor gains. But they remained to some extent enthralled by the tactics and ideas which had brought them success. Having—like all effective pressure groups—framed their arguments with close reference to those of their critics, it was difficult for women's organizations quickly to overcome what had eventually become their own preferences for moderate responses to discrimination, which emphasized rather than overcame biological factors. The relationship between wife and husband in the home might be akin to that between proletariat and bourgeoisie, and the dependent wife might only spend the family wealth, not control it; however, there was little incentive to make feminists urge long-term alternatives to 'conventional' marriage, such as communal living and collective child-rearing, alternatives that would have horrified most of their contemporaries, when so much still remained to be done before women could enjoy life to the full in the wider world.

The women's movement had proved itself able to foster group-consciousness for limited ends among a group which, unlike the ethnic minorities, lacked cohesion although it was similarly constrained by ascribed characteristics. After the disappointments of the inter-war years feminists were increasingly concerned to persuade other women of the need to join them, for apathy was encouraged by the fact that their treatment in society was benign by comparison with that of other disadvantaged elements. There was also a need to frame an ideology which came to terms with the fact that equality was not an unchanging ideal based on rights defined in the eighteenth century, but one clearly shaped by a changing environment; to recognize, therefore, that in removing some of the old barriers to individual advancement women had not fundamentally weakened the collective restraints imposed upon them by education and the media, as well as by the economy. And it has become the task of the present generation of women, operating in a more promising social climate, to persuade men at last to welcome their companionship and competition outside the home.

CHAPTER 6

The Less Privileged Half: The League of Women Voters and Other Twentieth-Century Groups

It would seem to be a truism that, in virtually all the Western countries where the struggle for the vote took place in the first part of the twentieth century, the attainment of that privilege was an end unto itself and provided little of a political follow-up, apart from the emergence of a token number of women activists in this field. Even today, over half a century after the establishment of the vote for women in Britain and the United States, an event like the elevation of a woman to the leadership of a major political party is still looked upon as remarkable. In the United States, women state governors such as Mrs Grasso of Connecticut and Dixie Lee Ray of Washington are still rarities; for some time there were no women in the Senate (between Margaret Chase Smith's defeat in 1972 and the election of Nancy Landon Kassebaum in 1978), and it would require a major shift of attitude to persuade one of the two major American political parties to nominate a woman for the vice-presidency, let alone the presidency. Yet the United States has witnessed the development of women's pressure groups to an extent unknown in other Western countries. One of them has a continuous history of well over fifty years, and it has now been joined by a number of newer groups which encompass a wider range of political belief; the common denominator is the belief that women remain, to some degree, second-class citizens in the republic. Possibly, the peak of pressure applied by women's organizations is past for the moment; the relative diminution of their influence on the main political parties could be judged, for example, by the small impact made by women's groups who tried to alter the rules at the 1976 Democratic Convention to allow for women to be more fairly represented at the quadrennial gatherings of the party. On the other hand, at this same Convention one of the largest ovations was given to keynote speaker Barbara Jordan from Texas, one of the small group of black women in the House of Representatives who are bringing new stature to their race and their sex. Women's organizations, then, have more than 'come to stay' as far as political pressure is concerned; they have been around for some time and have proliferated in number while increasing their range of activities over the last ten years.

With the attainment of the right to vote, it might be felt that it was inevitable that the suffrage movement would disintegrate, much as it did in Britain. It is, however, an interesting point of comparison to note that, unlike the other major Anglo-Saxon country, there was an attempt in the United States to keep alive the spirit of the suffrage movement by creating a women's organization that would encourage its members to make full use of the new power which they had obtained. Certainly, as we have noted earlier, the women's movements in the twenties and thirties made few real strides towards the sort of equality that their younger sisters have recently been demanding.[1] The National Woman's Party, set up before the vote was secured, remained a small, though highly articulate, group, notable mainly for its advocacy of an Equal Rights Amendment.

It may be that American women in the early decades of this century were too busy adjusting to a new and freer set of conventions to be as preoccupied with their political status as their descendants were to be more than a generation later. The newspapers and journals of the day made much of the propensity of the flapper and her successors to swig bootleg gin, smoke in public and indulge in courtship practices formerly avoided by respectable girls and the Press consequently virtually ignored the very occasional incursion of women into active political roles.[2] As in most historical periods, the stereotypes scarcely reflect the attitudes of all of the age groups described therein, and a strain of definite activism persisted through the twenties—and the thirties—among American women of all ages. Yet it made little impression at the time, as the comments of one distinguished newspaper reporter, writing as the thirties began, suggest:

> The American woman . . . won the suffrage in 1920. She seemed, it is true, to be very little interested in it once she had it; she voted, but mostly as the unregenerate men about her did, despite the efforts of women's clubs and the League of Women Voters to awaken her to womanhood's civic opportunity; feminine candidates for office were few, and some of them—such as Governor Ma Ferguson of Texas—scarcely seemed to represent the starry-eyed spiritual influence which, it had been promised, would presently ennoble public life.[3]

Another reason for the limited impression made by women on the politics of the period—one which invariably affects the ascent of underprivileged groups—is that legislation is inadequate by itself to alter public attitudes all at once. In fact, it has taken decades for these attitudes to change, despite the high proportion of women among the American population. The low self-regard of women as far as public life is concerned has also been one of the great hindrances to female advancement in politics and business in the United States, as in most countries.

However, when all of the above has been admitted, one can still identify groups of women between the two world wars who tried to persuade their sex that a concern with public life would neither soil their hands nor label them as over-earnest and somehow 'non-feminine'. Most of these groups tended to coalesce around the League of Women Voters (LWV), which dominated the field, as far as public-spirited women's groups were concerned, for over forty years. It grew directly out of the suffrage movement, the last convention of NAWSA in February 1920 also acting as the first convention of the League. Its most prominent spokesman was Carrie Chapman Catt, former president of NAWSA, whose early pronouncements tended to set the tone of the League for some years. In particular, she played down the purely feminist orientation that had permeated many of the pre-war suffrage groups and balanced the need for advancing the status of women with the intent that the newly enfranchised sex should act as citizens in the fullest sense. In a statement made in 1919, she declared: 'We propose to get into the great parties and to work from the inside. We do not fear issues, and we do not fear the future. We'll not vote as women, but as American citizens, and we are unafraid.'[4]

One of the problems of the early League, though, was to establish how women were to vote and generally to operate in the political field 'as citizens', and to decide how the League could help them here in a way in which other groups, including political parties, could not do. In other words, the League in its formative years (and, indeed, until after World War II) found it difficult to define its role and, in retrospect, it concentrated too much on areas where its presence was least effective. Initially, its three purposes were 'to foster education in citizenship, to promote forums and public discussions of civic reforms, and to support needed legislation'.[5] In 1920 Mrs Catt put a slightly different gloss on the League's aims, which she outlined as follows:

> (1) To use its utmost influence to secure the final enfranchisement of the women of every state in our own republic and to reach out across the seas in aid of the woman's struggle for her own in every land; (2) to remove the remaining legal discriminations against women in the codes and constitutions of the several states in order that the feet of coming women may find these stumbling blocks removed; (3) to make our democracy so safe for the nation and so safe for the world that every citizen may feel secure and great men will acknowledge the worthiness of the American republic to lead.[6]

Much of the effort of the League in the inter-war years went into what would then have been termed 'the cause of peace', with more support being given to the League of Nations than was usual among other groups in the United States at the time; the LWV backed wholeheartedly American membership of the League of Nations in 1932, and went on to endorse a foreign policy which inclined more to the interventionalist cause in the late thirties than was current even in the official utterances of the Roosevelt Administration. Although history has tended to justify the wisdom of the LWV's support for a foreign policy which strengthened the forces trying to check German and Italian aggression, there is little evidence that the League had much influence on the framing of national policy in the area of foreign affairs; it could have better utilized its efforts in pushing for the many domestic reforms that were contained in the programme passed by successive conventions. Interest in international relations has continued in the post-war period, although on the whole it does not loom as large as in the 1930s—perhaps for other obvious reasons, but particularly because there is a feeling that awareness of the dangers of international strife was then low in the United States, whereas it is more than evident today.

Much of the activity of the League during the first two decades of its existence was devoted to social issues, including the support of programmes such as that resulting in the Social Security Act of 1935; it also developed an interest in governmental reform which has remained with it ever since. The League's official history notes that:

> The League was the only citizen group acting consistently for the merit system in those years. Contests for slogans brought catchy phrases which are still in use, among them 'Good Government is Good Politics' and 'Find the Man for the Job, not the Job for the Man'.[7]

Historians have generally praised the organization for its reformist attitudes at a time—in the 1920s especially—when American social and political attitudes were essentially conservative.[8] However, it could be argued that these attitudes were rather superficial and that the organization generally reflected contemporary conservatism. The League had already begun to elaborate its policy of selecting issues that seemed to concern its members, making a detailed study of all the implications and then taking a stand based on a degree of rational judgement. Many critics of the League, as we will see later, have condemned this approach as slow and not necessarily rational, and this seems to be the view of contemporary scholars who believe that commitment is a vital part of the investigation of an issue. One historian argues: 'the problem was that lengthy inquiry delayed taking a firm stand on any issue. It also re-enforced the belief that women were insecure in the political world and ignorant about politics.'[9] Nonetheless, the surprising fact is that the League survived the inter-war years as a viable organization and did achieve certain successes, although it must be admitted that in the 1930s, for example, it was the rest of American society, due to the circumstances of the Depression, that caught up with the League in supporting the economic and social welfare legislation of the New Deal. As far as the critique of League procedure is concerned, it is difficult to see what alternative technique for defining policy would have worked, at least in the period under review. The admittedly middle-class ladies who formed the backbone of the League until comparatively recently were neither sympathetic to ideological stance nor prone to swift emotional responses. However, they could be persuaded that the systematic study of an issue was intellectually defensible as the basis of a call for action.

Even World War II did not fundamentally change the nature of the League. It did reorganize itself in 1944 and 1946, dropping the word 'National' from its title so that the National League of Women Voters became the League of Women Voters of the United States. There was a limited amount of centralization, in that the national League became the body that individuals joined first and foremost (though the main thrust of the individual member's activity was still directed towards local and state Leagues), but its technique of study for action remained virtually intact. Perhaps one of the strengths of the League as an organization today is that it mirrors the federal system so effectively and, as with the federal system, new courses of action that initially have little success at one level often succeed at another level. But it is the consensus that has so often come in for ridicule as a significant part of the decision-making process of the League. It does not rely on majority voting as such but on sounding the 'grass roots' until a wide measure of agreement is ascertained. It depends especially on a variety of different types of local Leagues reaching their own separate accords, so that the final decision is made by a cross-section of the membership. Obviously, the League does not wait for unanimity on an issue about which it takes a stand but, equally, it is doubtful whether an issue for which there was only paper-thin majority support among League members would be included in the League programme.

An example of this procedure in action can be seen in the League's reaction to the Bricker Amendment of the early 1950s, a proposed constitutional amendment that would have restricted the power of the president to enter into treaties and agreements (and of the Senate to uphold the treaties), ostensibly to ensure that the federal government kept to the Constitution but in reality to try to limit the internationalist tendencies of post-1945 foreign policy.[10] In 1952–3, shortly after the second attempt of Senator Bricker to carry his amendment through the Congress, the League held a series of meetings at the various levels of its government—Convention, Council, National Board—which discussed the amendment and publicized both sides of the case extensively in its publication *The National Voter*. It was January 1954 when the National Board announced that the consensus of the League was that the Bricker amendment should be opposed (in fact, neither it nor its variant, the George Amendment, was ever carried).[11] Because of this somewhat laboured process, the League is not a body that can be made to operate quickly.

It is the disadvantage of a group so patterned on the federal system that it is slowed down by the need to consult at every level, though it must be admitted that its integration with the federal system gives the League definite advantages over those pressure groups which centre all their activities on Washington. Many issues ricochet between state and federal level, with regulation being mooted at both, and it can be of inestimable value to a pressure group to be able to exercise persuasion at each level—and occasionally locally as well. The 'federal' nature of the League does tend to make up for its obvious shortcomings as an operator on the national scene. Pressures in Washington cost money, if only expenses incurred in the maintenance of an office, staff and actual lobbyists on the Hill and elsewhere. Fund-raising is essentially a local task and is something of a strain on the local Leagues which contribute to the national office. There is an obvious tendency for the large economic pressure groups, with financial resources of a reasonable size, to be more effective in Washington, other things being equal, than groups of more modest means. In fact, this point was made by a one-time executive director of the League in a 1972 interview made just before she left office:

'Washington is a very big pond and the League has only limited resources.'[12]

At state and local level particularly, the League can call on the services of dedicated and intelligent members who operate the administration and maintain much of the contact with those who make the decisions at governmental level; mostly, these women are volunteers and they provide a rare reservoir of talent missing from many pressure groups staffed by professionals alone. What the national office can do admirably, even with its modest funding, is to act as a clearing-house for the state and local Leagues, circulating information about local successes and difficulties when dealing with particular issues; this is in addition to its liaison with Congress and other national bodies. This combination of voluntary worker and professional, of local, state and national initiative, makes the League quite an effective organization, despite the difficulties that its relatively slow processes may produce. Many women's organizations of a newer stripe have questioned its commitment to the women's cause as they see it—that is to say, in their eyes it has seemed to proceed not only too slowly but also without the degree of radicalism that some of the newer groups have shown. In fact, this criticism has been less evident of recent years than it was at the beginning of the 1970s and, as we shall see, there now seems to be some consensus among most of the women's groups active in the field of political pressure.

During the post-war period much of the League's efforts in the several states has been directed to the reform of state government, and the state Leagues have become expert in monitoring the performance of the various branches of government at state level. In many cases, state Leagues were in the vanguard of schemes to alter the constitutional structure of state government in order to make that government more responsive to the public will and to eradicate waste, misgovernment and corruption. State government in the United States has tended to be more susceptible to these faults than the federal government in Washington, although inevitably scandals in the federal government make the headlines more readily. A good example of this involvement may be seen in the Massachusetts League, which carried through a number of schemes associated with constitutional reform, especially in the 1960s. At the beginning of the decade the state was regarded as peculiarly susceptible to corruption and a whole spate of scandals were uncovered during that early part of the decade, giving rise to magazine reports suggesting that it was a 'state on trial'.[13] Over several years the state League participated in campaigns to break the power of the archaic Governor's Council, to establish four-year terms for constitutional officers and to provide for the election of the governor and lieutenant-governor as a team instead of separately. The culmination of this streamlining process was to be the reduction in size of the state House of Representatives from 240 to 160.

The Massachusetts campaign illustrates the way in which the League at state level enters a contest to accomplish a reform. The case for a reduction in numbers in the House was not clear-cut, for it depended on the ratio of voters to state legislators in the state House of Representatives. League propaganda in the 1960s made much of the fact that the House was the second largest in the Union (only New Hampshire's was larger at that time) and also that its ratio of one state representative to 22,240 constituents contrasted with those of many other states where the ratio was much higher. California had one representative to 225,050; New York, one to 119,000; Texas, one to 69,300. Of course, these are the large states of the Union and, as the staff of the then Speaker of the House pointed out, their elimination for comparative purposes brought Massachusetts much closer to the norm.[14] However, the state League had prepared a clearly argued case which, when presented to the legislature and the voters, listed certain obvious advantages that would follow from the reduced membership of the House:

> A cut in the size of the House would increase its responsiveness, effectiveness, and efficiency. Proceedings and debate are shorter and sharper in a small body. Reponsibility of individual members is more clearly focused and the power and prestige of each member is enhanced.[15]

The brief pointed out that dispensing with a third of the House members would save money which could be used to increase the provision of supporting staff for the representatives.

Since the proposed bill involved the presentation of an

initiative petition to the voter, the process by which it could become law was a lengthy one. To appear on the ballot, the petition had to pass the test of raising a 25 per cent vote at two joint sessions of the Senate and the House in the legislature. In February 1970, at the second of these votes, a degree of what appeared to be unethical coercion by the House leadership left the petition one vote short of the seventy it needed; but perseverance paid off in the long run, for the referendum was eventually on the ballot paper for the election of 1974. On this occasion two-thirds of those voting were for a reduction of members in the House, effective from 1978, and this level of voting justified the pressures brought by the League and other interested organizations.[16]

Another state where constitutional reform was a major preoccupation of the 1960s was Illinois, though here the effort centred not on piecemeal reform but on the need for a constitution convention that would revise the whole Constitution. This state was a more difficult proposition for the League than Massachusetts because of the relative remoteness of the state capital (Springfield) from the main centre of population (Cook County), which contained about 40 per cent of the 22,000 members of the state League at that time. Piecemeal reform had been tried in the 1950s, when there seemed little chance of a constitutional convention being called; but the fact that the Constitution had been written in 1870 and, though occasionally amended, had never been thoroughly revised (attempts to do this in the 1920s were defeated by the electorate) kept the hope alive in some quarters that a convention would eventually take on the important task. The League kept up pressure as far as it could with well-argued literature and lobbying; a leaflet of this period listed the following defects of the 1870 Constitution:

(a) 'Hampering details' such as a limitation on the State debt.
(b) Inflexibility, such as the construction that powers could only be used where expressively granted.
(c) Lack of clear administrative and legislative responsibility.
(d) Limitation on taxing power which made financing of new programmes difficult.[17]

Eventually the General Assembly of the state was persuaded by the League (and other civic organizations) to set up a

Constitutional Study Commission (in 1965) which included as one of its more active members an ex-president of the state League, who had become a member of the state Assembly. The electorate ratified an Assembly recommendation that the Convention be called, and a new constitution was ready to go before the electorate at the end of 1970. It was in the form of a central 'package', which included the now familiar device of strengthening the executive branch by establishing four-year terms and a joint election for the governor and lieutenant-governor, greater prospects for 'home rule' for municipalities, provision for more flexible taxation systems and even the basis for support of a 'healthful environment' as part of public policy.[18] Where the Convention had been unable to agree on an issue the electorate was allowed to vote separately, as over the removal of the death penalty or the electoral device of 'plumping' whereby, in multi-member districts, the voter could give all his votes to one candidate.

The League pushed for the adoption of the new Constitution by advocating the creation of 'community committees' drawn from local organizations with a civic purpose; as well as League members, the committees were composed of representatives of groups such as the Parent Teachers Associations, the Lions, veterans' associations, Chambers of Commerce and the Churches.[19] The unanimity of central package support on the part of the Convention seems to have swayed the voters who upheld it at the polls, but the four separated items (lower voting age, single-member districts, nomination of judges, abolition of the death penalty) all failed, despite League support for all but the last one, on which it took no stand.

The League was only one organization out of many active in the ratification process and it is not easy to evaluate its leverage. Nevertheless, there is little doubt that its published literature on the issues involved was read by opinion leaders in the state and was regarded as informed and fair. The League is still especially important on the information side of pressure-group activity, even if its actual influence is often less marked than that of better-funded and larger groups. Curiously, however, recent developments in Illinois illustrate the possibility that, in this respect, the League may be less effective in the future than it has been in the past. Both the executive and the legislative branches in the state are employing more staff, and they are developing expertise in areas where the League has been especially prominent in research in recent years; it could be that the Illinois League saw its finest hour in the campaign for a new state constitution.

Although constitutional reform has been a major plank in the programme of most state Leagues in the late fifties and the sixties, it has certainly not been the only one. The Florida League, for example, succeeded in its campaign for a revised constitution, which was adopted in 1968, but it has also been active in many other areas. A critical question was that of the judicial reform of dated practices and some contribution was made to modernization. This involved change in the system of electing justices to inferior courts and the simplification of the practice of 'fragmental jurisdiction', by which a suit may have to be pursued in different courts at the same time, via the amendment of Article V of the old Constitution, which was left intact in 1968 but revised in response to a referendum in 1972. Because of its complexity (the League needing to consult expert opinion), tax structure may seem to be an unlikely field for the League to take up, but the early seventies found the League pressing for a corporate profits tax on the basis that it would increase prices only marginally, while the alternative—a sales tax—would put them up by considerably more.[20] The state League provided a mass of informative literature, pointing out the contrast between these taxes and their effect on prices—the corporate tax would be partially absorbed by federal tax exemption, for instance—and it was felt by many of those who worked in the State House at this period that League propaganda had played some part in the victory of the constitutional amendment which led to the adoption of the tax.[21]

On other issues of the time the Florida League was less successful; for example, it supported 'busing', but this device was rejected by the voters in an anti-'busing' decision of March 1972, when it was on a presidential primary ballot; the American public tends to oppose 'busing' when given the chance, despite its support by liberal groups and some civic organizations. With another topical issue, that of the preservation of an amenable environment, the League did give general support to a conservation programme, but it was rather eclipsed by the emergence of a more specialized pressure group in 1969 called 'Conservation 70s Inc.', which was not a direct-membership group like the League and which had its policy determined largely by a Board of Trustees with thirty-one members. As one newspaper put it in the summer of 1970, referring to the general issue of conservation: 'It shows that conservation as an issue has been accorded a niche alongside motherhood and the flag in the eyes of Florida's senators and representatives.'[22] In its first year, Conservation 70s managed to put a package of bills through the state legislature which were designed to protect various aspects of the state's wildlife, beaches, water and air. The Florida League certainly supported this type of legislation but it did not research or publicize these bills as thoroughly as other issues which it wanted to see defined in law.

It may be that specialized groups like Conservation 70s will be in the forefront in pressing certain types of citizenship issues in the future, rather than general-purpose associations such as the League. This is already happening to some extent in Washington as well as in the states and may lead to some modification of League attitudes, as well as to a reduction in its role. Another factor that restricts state League programmes is the general political climate prevailing in the state at any one time, and its worth noting that in Florida 'reform' forces were running quite strongly by the end of the sixties and during the early seventies. Reuben Askew, the governor elected in 1970, had been voted in on a reform platform, while at the same time a similar tide flowed in the legislature, especially under Speaker Dick Pettigrew (1970–2). When there is an 'open door' of this nature, it is obvious that League programmes are going to be much more successful than if public and governmental attitudes are resistant to change.

A look at another state League, that of California, a year or two on shows further how the balance in programmes had begun to alter. Although the state programme contained items on revision of the state Constitution and reform of the tax system, it also included a major plank about environmental quality, which was adapted from the national League's programme and was summarized as:

> Action to achieve a physical environment beneficial to life, including improvement of water and air quality, promotion of wise use of water resources, progress in recycling and reduction in generation of solid wastes.[23]

In the same period (*circa* 1974) the California League produced an action kit that set out positions and possible lines of action on air quality and transportation problems, which are inevitably linked through heavy dependence on the automobile; the United States is the automobile society at its most highly developed, and, as the kit pointed out, 'in automobile consumption, California is the largest marketplace in the US'.[24] As one might have expected, the state League's position was that on the one hand it aimed to emphasize the need for strict control of pollution, and on the other it sought to encourage the development of an integrated transportation system, using trains, buses, moving sidewalks, street cars and bicycles to cut down the dependence on the automobile. Rather more than its Florida counterpart, however, the California League appears to have taken the initiative in the fight for a more satisfactory environment—and this despite the fact that there are many other active groups in the state (such as the Sierra Club), which are primarily concerned to bring pressure over environmental issues to bear on government.

If state Leagues provide much of the 'meat' of the LWV structure, one must not forget that there is still a third tier to be considered, that of the local Leagues. On the whole, and despite their large number, these are less prominent than the structures on either of the other two levels because of their small size. There are some exceptions to this rule, for local Leagues that are established in major cities are organizations of some membership and power as compared with those in rural areas or smaller towns. In California again, both Los Angeles and San Francisco have local Leagues, as do many smaller communities such as Palo Alto or Napa, to take two that are not far from the city on the Bay. Yet both large and small local Leagues in California, the biggest state of the Union, tackle a wide range of questions—education, governmental structure, land use, parks, planning, sewerage, youth problems, to name just a few. All over the United States local

Leagues decide what programme items they should study, some suggested by the state or national office, some developed locally; there is always a considerable overlap, however, dozens of local Leagues in one state and hundreds over the whole of the country tending to tackle similar problems at any one time.

Although the League is very much a 'grass-roots' organization, the national office has a range of essential functions; one of the most important is that of co-ordinating activity over the country, disseminating information about the work of individual Leagues at state and local level in order that a degree of cross-fertilization can take place. Nationally produced literature is obviously of enormous value to local and state Leagues with less well-organized research units than the national League. The national office has, as one of its sub-units, an Education Fund which is technically separated from the lobbying activities of the League. The fund is a research organization and thus tax-exempt, unlike lobbying organizations. Its research findings are published in pamphlets and leaflets, which allows the League at its various federal levels to find a position on specific issues. Once the position has been reached by debate and, preferably, consensus—since the League does not care for positions to be determined by narrow voting decisions—a specific issue will pass to the lobbying stage, known in the national office as Legislative Action, although the process might also involve the Litigation Department, since the League is finding that the courts can also be used as what one of the senior League officers in Washington has termed 'an agent of change'.[25] Some of the titles of the Education Fund literature in the 1973–5 period give an idea of the range of its research—'Open Communities; Metropolitan Housing Exchange', 'Congress; A Time of Renewal', 'Elections '74–'76; Turning People On'.

It will be noted that, like many of the Washington-based public-interest groups, the League has become increasingly interested in the workings of Congress and, more recently, in the operation of the executive branch of government, possibly under the influence of the Watergate disclosures. Another fairly new development has been the active entry of the League into the Clearing-House of Women's Organizations, which includes a number of the other women's associations to which we must shortly turn. The Clearing-House tries to pool information and plans for action held by each group in order to improve their overall efficiency. It has been particularly concerned in recent years with consumer issues and the Equal Rights Amendment, two areas in which all the women's organizations share a strong interest. Although it is not an executive organization as such, it does help in co-ordinating what has become a multifarious set of groups whose only common purpose is to promote the interests, or supposed interests, of women.

As one of the longest-lived of the women's movements in the United States, the League retains pride of place amongst pressure groups functioning in that overlap between women's associations and what can still be termed loosely 'good-government organizations'. It still dislikes to be thought of as being solely interested in women's affairs, and in fact some local Leagues now accept men as members with the agreement of the national office. It could therefore be regarded as a hybrid body—not that this fact detracts in any way from its effectiveness. It seems evident that in a pressure group world which boasts far more organizations than a few years ago, the League must stress one of its twin aspects rather than the other and to some extent the feminist side of its character has been emphasized of late, perhaps because of the competition from the newer women's 'movements' such as the National Organization for Women and the National Women's Political Caucus. Yet the admission of a few 'token' men and the balancing of, say, interest in the Equal Rights Amendment campaign with the maintenance of the LWV's preoccupation with standards of governmental practice and behaviour suggests that there is unlikely to be a complete commitment to one side of the fence or the other; 'straddling' may be undignified for the ladies, but it is still desired by the majority of the membership.

It is not only from the newer women's organizations that the League may face competition. As we have already seen, the other strain among its main interests is being catered for by consumer groups like Common Cause and the Ralph Nader Organization. There is also the fear that members may 'drop out' because of general disillusionment with the progress of the League programme. The League's own self-study of 1974 summarized this concern:

> All voluntary organizations tend to be anxious that there may be an overall decline in membership—particularly these days as two factors may siphon off members. First, there is the growing number of organizations and citizen interest groups; second, there is the growing sense of disillusionment with politics and politically relevant participation.[26]

In fact, the League increased its membership in the early 1970s, and the main reason for defection, where it occurred, appeared to be growing job or family commitments, not transference of allegiance to other organizations.[27] However, the self-study report did recognize that some of the newer public-interest groups have the advantage of being 'top down' organizations, which can move faster than the League over specific issues. It was suggested that the membership of the League should be 'given a greater sense of belonging to a national organization'.[28] If this could be done without destroying some of the practical aspects of the 'grass-roots' structure of the League, it might indeed make this unique federation even more effective than it is now. No one seemed surprised that it was the League that sponsored the Carter–Ford debates at the time of the 1976 presidential elections, and this is some indication of the respect in which the League is held in public circles in the United States.

Even at the time when the League seemed almost unchallenged as an active pressure group involving women, it was not the only group of its kind. However, its political activities were always much more prominent than those of the others, which included the Business and Professional Women's Clubs and the American Association of University Women. In the mid-1960s this pattern changed, and a number of new women's groups emerged to take their place among those exerting pressure on American government. Although the 1964 Civil Rights Act contained a ban on discrimination by sex, the well-known 'Title VII', many activist women felt that little was being done in the year or two following the bill's passage to implement its intent. In 1966 the Third National Conference of the State Commissions on Women met in Washington, voiced this discontent and decided that something should be done about it:

> The consensus was that there was need for an organization to pressure the government on behalf of women in the same way that the civil rights organizations functioned for blacks. These forces came to a head in [Betty] Friedan's hotel room, where plans were formulated for the National Organization for Women.[29]

Founded in 1966, the National Organization for Women (NOW) claims to be the largest women's movement in the world (it argues that the LWV is not a 'movement'); it had about 70,000 members in 1975 (it was about half the size of the LWV), organized in 700 chapters.[30] Betty Friedan was its first president and its early headquarters were split between New York, Chicago and Washington, the latter gaining in importance since it was designed to monitor federal legislation and to see that the organization gained suitable publicity in the nation's capital. It has used volunteers as legislative co-ordinators in Washington to follow the progress of any legislation in which NOW has an interest.

The main areas of interest have, perhaps, been predictable. Task forces on health and education have been active, and another has even challenged the Federal Communications Commission over the restricted status given to women on TV commercials. The passage of the Equal Rights Amendment through Congress in 1972 gave the organization a fillip, bringing new members and a cause with which vast numbers of American women could identify. One of the Amendment's aims, according to a NOW spokesman, was to 'raise the consciousness' of women to the constraints under which they existed as compared with the relative freedom of the male sex. NOW operates in much the same way as other similar organizations—that is, it has regular national convention meetings with major direction between the conventions being in the hands of a board which meets on average once every two months. It considers itself very much a 'grass-roots' movement, with its local chapters and its state organizations that supplement the local ones. The organization's thesis is essentially the one summarized by one of its later presidents, Karen DeCrow: 'Gender should not be a very important aspect of how one functions in society today.'[31] In little more than ten years NOW has certainly tried hard to reduce the gap in opportunity and status that exists between women and men in American society.

It tends to be a feature of organizations which try to change the *status quo* in some way that many of those who join them are soon dissatisfied with the pace at which change is taking place and wish to set up splinter groups to hasten or moderate the process. Alternately, an issue arises over which one group of members takes a line so different from that of the main body that friction grows and the group secedes in order to retain its 'purity' on the particular issue. In 1968 such an issue arose within NOW: the issue was abortion and 'a woman's right to choose'. Some members of NOW who felt that the organization should not put too much emphasis on the abortion issue set up a new group of their own, which came to be called the Women's Equity Action League (WEAL). It sprang initially from a group of Ohio academics and lawyers led by Elizabeth Boyer. It did not 'go national' until 1970, when it made its mark with a campaign directed at the academic community from which many of its members came. On 31 January 1970 WEAL filed a charge in the courts claiming that an Executive Order outlawed sex discrimination on American college campuses, despite the fact that it had originally been issued primarily to protect certain categories of blue-collar workers. None of the other legislation available at that time covered this type of discrimination but a series of enactments in 1972 extended considerable protection to women in this field.[32]

WEAL concentrated initially on economic issues and although a comparatively small organization (considerably smaller than NOW, for example, though its actual membership is not published), it has become very much a civil rights group functioning in the interests of women. It operates in what seems to be an almost standard way, with national president, national board, state and local chapters; policy options are first drafted by the board, then discussed and finally decided upon by the convention. Perhaps because of the way in which it was set up, with a number of lawyers in its first wave of membership, it frequently works through the courts, filing suits based on state and federal legislation which purports to outlaw sex discrimination. A case in point is the 1975 action based on Title VII and VIII of the Public Health Services Act, when WEAL, in association with NOW and other organizations, accused the Department of Health Education and Welfare of illegally giving funds to schools which practised sex discrimination in their hiring practices or which discriminated between boys and girls in the context of educational opportunity (Title IX of the 1972 Education Amendment Act was also used). Sex discrimination at all levels of American society is very much the central inspiration of WEAL's activities and the enemy at which its efforts are aimed. It is obviously a less radical organization than, say, NOW, even if the difference may seem minimal to an outside observer.

The third organization which must be mentioned, although it differs more from NOW and WEAL than they do from each other, is the National Women's Political Caucus (NWPC). The Caucus is not primarily a civil rights group but is dedicated instead to placing more women in positions of political power by helping them to become elected to public office. It was formed in July, 1971 and seemed the pinnacle of the drive for women's rights at that time, for NWPC was the final outcome of that phase of disenchantment with the cautious approach of older organizations catering to women which took place in the 1960s and which had led to the setting up of NOW and WEAL. There is little doubt that the Caucus was regarded both by its founders and by most observers as a relatively radical organization when it was formed, though by about 1975 it had moved over towards the middle ground of politics. It found that it was necessary to operate through the political parties if it wanted action; otherwise it would be no more than an irritant, a useful function perhaps but not fully satisfying to NWPC members. It would also be fair comment to suggest that an organization like the League had become more consciously 'feminist' by the mid-1970s, and the various women's pressure groups were therefore less divided ideologically than they had been when the decade started. The Caucus, as we have noted, started with what was virtually a single aim—to see that more women were elected to office at local, state and federal level in the United States. However, when the proposed Twenty-Seventh Amendment to the Constitution—the so-called Equal Rights Amendment, which stated that 'equality of rights under the law shall not be denied or abridged by the United States or any state on account of sex'—passed through the Congress in 1972, it became a second major plank in the programme of the Caucus, and the group worked in conjunction with about thirty other organizations to try to see that thirty-eight states ratified the amendment before March 1979, the legal limit for ratification (since extended until 1982).

The Caucus, like NOW, started life more as a 'movement' than as an organization, though by the mid-1970's it was beginning to adopt the same type of structure as those of the other groups described above—president (Frances Farenthold at that time), national board, convention, local and state chapters; the danger of bureaucratization was felt to be outweighed by the need for greater continuity and effectiveness in the organization. About 80 per cent of the 30,000-strong membership was either Democratic or independent in affiliation, which reflected to some degree the radical residue in the 'movement'. (There is a distinct impression that the Democrats are more responsive to the Caucus then the Republican Party; on the other hand, as Ms Farenthold pointed out in 1974, Mary Louise Smith had become chairperson of the Republican Party without experiencing the hostility that Jean Westwood had faced when she took over the chair in the Democratic Party.)[33] In 1974 the election of Ella Grasso as governor of Connecticut—the first woman governor elected in her own right, and not, for example, following on from her husband—plus other victories at federal and state level, led the Caucus to feel that some headway was being made. There were still, however, only 610 women out of about 7500 in state legislatures all over the country which meant that there was a long way to go. The view of the Caucus staff was that women face two major problems in becoming effective candidates for office—credibility and fund-raising—but that publicity, some of it organized from Washington, could increase the credibility of women candidates. A fund-raising drive in 1974, with money coming in from a few 'big givers' and groups such as environmental organizations, did help marginally to alleviate the shortage of money that women candidates continually face when running for office. It is still a major problem for the Caucus, for it believes that it cannot hope to attract funds commensurate with those available to most men candidates. However, this is likely to be less true as more and more women run for elective office and 'givers' become more attuned to this development.[34]

The Caucus does do a limited amount of lobbying through its 'legislative component' but only on specially selected issues, such as the establishment of day-care centres or the vocational training programme which was being discussed by Congress in 1975. At that time one of the main Caucus aims was the setting up of a consultancy service for women candidates, staffed by women who would offer help on advertising, registration and the other problems that candidates encounter on a short-term basis, in order that they could assist a considerable number of candidates during the election period. With only a few full-time staff (three or four in 1975), the Caucus is probably wise to keep a relatively narrow frame of reference, though a statement of the chairwoman at that time indicated Caucus interest in issues ranging from abortion to campaign financing.[35]

By the later 1970s all the major women's organizations had settled into the familiar pattern for pressure groups that try to further limited and non-economic 'courses'. Many of their interests overlapped with those of 'public-interest' groups described in the next chapter but, strictly speaking, their main aims were closely linked with the common denominator of their membership, the fact that, with few exceptions, all are women, and this can still be regarded as a 'special interest'. However, unlike most 'special interests', women's concerns can be said to involve a majority rather than a minority of the American population, since women account for about 51.3 per cent of all Americans, even though there are many of them who deplore the activist stance of the women's groups and even some who oppose the ratification of the Equal Rights Amendment. Women may be a majority in the population, but it is difficult to ignore the discrimination that they have suffered in the past, which has not been dissimilar to that meted out to real minorities such as the blacks, the Mexican Americans, the Orientals or the native Americans.

The LWV provided the main outlet for activist women for many years. It has now been joined by three newer groups working in the political arena, while a host of other women's groups operate sporadically on governmental organizations. As we have noted, the organizations reviewed in this chapter appear to have settled any differences that arose between them initially and there has been a real *rapprochement*, resulting in co-operation over the Equal Rights Amendment and the major issues concerning women. This was due partially to the general decline of radicalism in the seventies and the realization that traditional pressure-group tactics were usually more effective than confrontation.

The potential for the exercise of power by women in the United States should be considerable when one considers how well-organized they have become compared with their opposite numbers in other Western nations or, on the face of it, anywhere in the world. It is true that the sheer size of the female population makes it almost inoperable as a pressure group—Mancur Olson has commented on the problems of pressure groups that begin to approach the general population in size.[36] In practice, large numbers of American women prefer to remain unidentified with any of the pressure groups which emphasize the feminist dimension of their claims, although, of course many pressure groups concerned with other issues rely largely on the female half of the population to support them. Consequently, probably no more than 250,000 American women belong to the politically oriented groups that we have described, though many more belong to less overtly political women's groups, such as those which supported the passage of the Equal Rights Amendment after its passage through Congress and while it was being considered by the states.[37] However, the groups discussed in this chapter form the spearhead of activity for those women who feel that considerable discrimination against their sex still exists within the United States and that organized groups are the only way in which it can be combated. It is possible, but unlikely, that there will be some merging of the groups discussed; unlikely, because their aims are far from identical and, as one official has pointed out, Americans like to have a choice of groups to join even if there is considerable overlap between them. If the League has a long and honourable history of pressure in connection with worthy causes, the several women's associations now operating almost exclusively in the political field are certain to be able to exercise even more powerful pressure in the future; and women in the United States, even if still under-represented in Congress and elsewhere, will remain at the very least a force in the political system.

CHAPTER 7

Reform and the 'Public Interest': The Quest for Good Government and Consumer Protection

It is often suggested that corruption in American public life is as old as the republic itself, the only likely modification being the counter-suggestion that it goes back beyond the American Revolution to the very early days of the first British colonies in the New World. Did it, as has been suggested, enter the North American continent with the first regular officers appointed by the British Crown to administer the Colony of Virginia?

> The principle of personal gain in public office, which was in his day as firmly fixed an element of British government as the English tradition of liberty . . . bloomed luxuriantly in the fertile soil of the New World.[1]

Certainly, the history of British government down to the mid-nineteenth century, and occasionally thereafter, contains many examples of the use of public office for private profit but, as it tapered off in Britain with the advent of Victorian concepts of public morality, it appeared to be on the increase in America. The British civil service developed a reputation for probity, one that it carried into the colonization of the Second British Empire, while Parliament reformed itself and eliminated most of the corrupt practice which had marked the eighteenth and early nineteenth century. In contrast, or perhaps because it was a 'younger' country, major American political corruption reached a height first in the Grant administration following the Civil War and then at intervals thereafter, especially perhaps at the time of Warren Harding's Administration and its subsequent Teapot Dome Scandal, involving the sale of governmental oil reserves. Britain could contribute an occasional scandal like the Marconi affair, but the older Anglo-Saxon nation was closer to a model of honest national government than was the government in Washington. Although there has been a gradual improvement in standards at the national level in the United States during the twentieth century, the most blatant patterns of corruption were to be found at state and (especially) city level and these have been slower to respond to pressures for improvement. It was, after all, in the lower tiers of American federal government that the distinction between 'honest' and 'dishonest' groups was often made:

> The neat distinction between honest and dishonest graft was drawn a great deal in the 'eighties and 'nineties. Blackmail, protection money from prostitutes, thieves, gamblers and saloon keepers, outright pay for a vote—these were dishonest . . . Honest graft was where the big money lay . . . Contracts for government work, wise use of advance information on legislation and, above all, co-operation with industrial and financial magnates—these were the paths to wealth.[2]

Corruption at national level, whether it be the individual lapse of a Sherman Adams or the more pervasive departure from accepted standards of morality that Watergate represented, is usually remedied by public disclosure, either by the Press or by other means. When this happens, resignations follow and, for a time at least, government reforms itself and Washington seethes a little less with rumour. At local level it has always been difficult to 'root out the rascals' and provide any programme of sustained reform in civic life. This difficulty is in part accounted for by the very nature of American cities in the later nineteenth century and much of the twentieth. Outdated models of government, a general lack of understanding among the business community of the problems of urban management, indifference toward the plight of the newer immigrants who were often discriminated against because of their accents, religion or unfamiliarity with American life: all of these factors encouraged a state of affairs in which only blatant wrongdoing on the part of those responsible for municipal government could rouse public anger and then usually for a limited time only.

The classic period for civic corruption in the United States was the thirty or so years after the Civil War:

> The era, 1865 to 1895, was one of tremendous physical growth of cities and expansion of municipal activities. From the standpoint of administration, it was a period of disintegration, waste and inefficiency. Political machines and bosses plundered many communities . . . The period has been justly described as the 'Dark Ages' of American municipal history.[3]

Such is the most common view of the period, though it should be noted that this viewpoint is being revised somewhat by those who feel that the price extracted by the city bosses and machines of the period was moderate when compared with the economic and physical development of the cities which the 'corrupt' politicians pushed through.[4] However, much as one now wishes to put municipal corruption in a more balanced perspective, it is difficult to be completely tolerant of the excesses of those years. Nor had the phenomenon ceased by the 1890s—indeed, one of the most effective exposés of city corruption, dating from the early 1900s, is still read for its pungent assessments of American cities:

> All our municipal governments are more or less bad, and all our people are optimists. Philadelphia is simply the most corrupt and the most contented. Minneapolis has cleaned up, Pittsburgh has tried to, New York fights every other election. Chicago fights all the time . . . Philadelphia is proud; good people defend corruption and boast of their machine.[5]

What did happen by the early 1900s, though, was that corruption was less accepted as an inevitable concomitant of city life. Reform groups sprang up as early as the 1870s, but it was not until the end of the century that they became prevalent. Municipal Leagues, good-government associations and other similarly titled organizations had by then become part of municipal life, most of them dedicated to the improvement of city government by constitutional change, by raising the standards of administrative officers, by making the machinery of government more responsive to pressure from the voters and, of course, by attempts to remove the worst of the machine politicians and replace them with more scrupulous civic leaders. Many of these efforts were concerted by the National Municipal League, which grew out of the First National Conference for Good City Government held in 1894. Its broad objective was the improvement of municipal government, and it pursued this by holding periodic conferences and by the publication of literature on municipal reform—in fact by generally acting as a co-ordinator for the municipal reform movement. The League was in the vanguard of the move towards strong mayor systems and the various experiments in city manager and commission forms of civic government: 'As a leader in municipal reform, the League had a prominent part in most of these developments.'[6]

Individual reformers, especially when they reached office as mayors of important cities, were also vital in the civic reform movement, since they could put into operation what the groups could only advocate. Some reform organizations counselled changes in the structure of city government, while many of the turn-of-the-century mayors realized that this would have to be accompanied by social reform which would improve the condition of the poorer inhabitants of the city:

> The programme of the social reform mayors aimed at lower gas, light, telephone and street railway rates for the community and higher taxes for railroad and business corporations. . . .
>
> The whole tone of the social reform movement was humanistic and empirical. It did not attempt to prescribe standards of personal morality nor did it attempt to draft social blueprints or city charters which had as their goals the imposition of middle-class morality and patrician values upon the masses.[7]

Of course, both streams of reform were of use in improving the standards of civic government, but the value of the social-reform approach lay in the realization that, for all its faults, the 'machine' form of government did provide some basic service for the immigrant community, a service that would have to be assumed by an arm of government if machine politics were to be successfully suppressed. It has taken generations, in fact, to phase out the machine approach to urban politics, and it is often suggested that it needed developments like the 1935 Social Security Act and welfare legislation passed since 1945 finally to demolish this style of political response (if, in fact, it has completely disappeared). Robert Merton's classic analysis of the difference between 'latent' and 'manifest' functions is perhaps the best explanation of the persistence of the urban machine into the post-1945 era. He has argued that since the machine satisfied 'basic latent functions' not satisfied by other 'patterns and structures' in the political system (such as the acculturation of immigrants), then it was not reasonable to expect it to disappear until something new was forthcoming to carry out these functions.[8]

What was especially important in this urban reform movement from our point of view was the creation of the reform groups themselves, inadequate as they often were as vehicles for lasting reform. They tended to establish public expectation that, if conditions in government deteriorated sufficiently, or an evident abuse arose which might be eradicated by popular pressure, then it was a matter of time before these instruments would appear and that, at least, there would be certain forces to balance and combat the worst excesses of governmental abuse. As we have noted, reform at the national level—as, say, in the Progressive Era—very often came about as the result of Press campaigns and general public revulsion over some gross injustice in the political system, with leading politicians of the day (President Theodore Roosevelt in the Progressive period, for example) tending to give a lead in the hope that this would advance their reputations as representatives of the people who were responsive to public demands. Though some of the reform mayors may have come into this category, civic change was often difficult without consistent support from groups in the local political system; in many cases, politicians and reform groups could not make progress without one another.

Much of the stream of effort that went into civic reform at the turn of the century (there were over seventy citizens' associations working for the improvement of conditions in the cities by 1895) flowed into the larger river of the national Progressive Movement in the first fifteen years of the twentieth century. Its development is summarized by one of its best-known chroniclers, Richard Hofstadter: 'If one examines the historical course of Progressive politics, one finds that the Progressive movement began in the cities, spread rapidly to the states, and reached the federal level most effectively in its later phases.'[9] Hofstadter has also noted the point that was made earlier about the change in the nature of reform when it moved from the civic via the state to the national sphere, a transition resulting in the increased importance of the Press:

> The fundamental critical achievement of American Progressivism was the business of exposure, and journalism was the chief occupational source of its creative writers. It is hardly an exaggeration to say that the Progressive mind was characteristically a journalistic mind, and that its characteristic contribution was that of the socially responsible reporter–reformer. The muckraker was a central figure. Before there could be action, there must be information and exhortation. Grievances had to be given specific objects, and these the muckraker supplied. It was muckraking that brought the diffuse malaise of the public into focus.[10]

The Press still remains a vital channel of information, ensuring that the public is aware of corruption, wrongdoing or incompetence in government (*pace* Watergate), and it is used extensively by contemporary pressure groups to convey their knowledge and information to the public to persuade it, via the pressure that can be put on to legislators and administrators, that specific actions are needed.

America's entry into World War I undermined the reform wing of the Progressive movement, even though some interest in reform lingered on into the twenties to link up with the New Deal of the thirties. As one writer remarks: 'It seems clear that the war marked an abrupt decline in the liberal as distinct from the nationalistic side of Progressivism.'[11] Whatever activities persisted after the war were certainly less evident than in the Progressive years, and when reform was in the air again in the 1930s, it had changed its style and, to some extent, its shape. Much of it was directed from 'the top' and was aimed at restoring and refining the economic system, so that on the one hand private enterprise would be preserved but, on the other, some of its excesses would be curtailed and both sides, labour as well as capital, would be given a fair chance to develop their interests. For perhaps the first time in American history, the trade unions came to be recognized as a crucial part of the economy and, gradually, there developed what it was fashionable at a later date to term 'countervailing power', that balance between capital and labour which prevents either wielding unique power to the detriment of the other. Although many Americans could be seen to adopt the roles represented by one or the other for much of the time, and even the farming interests were more and more to be seen in terms of the two sides of industry, many people adopted neither and others embraced them only intermittently.

One role which began to form the centre of concern (because of its lack of representation) was that of the consumer. As late as 1945 Stuart Chase could still state: 'There are no lobbies representing the whole consumer interest . . . Special groups of consumers have lobbies in Washington, some weak, some strong; but no pressure group so far as I know is looking out for all of us.'[12] Chase had been one of the advocates of organizing for the wider interests of the public, though he acknowledged that the large pressure groups of that time, whether they were the 'Big Three' (business, labour and farm) organizations or more specialized groups like professional men (or even reform organizations), already argued that they operated in the 'public interest', even if they represented select and specialist groups of people:

> All pressure groups protest that they are concerned with the 'public interest'. This comes as naturally to them as for a person to declare himself against sin. They let it be known that they are making this splendid fight for the common good at great personal sacrifice to themselves. This makes it hard for the rest of us to discuss the public interest without acute nausea.[13]

In fact, the tendency in Roosevelt's Washington seems to have been for a wider range of pressure groups than hitherto to appear and to vie with each other for a share of the New Deal cake. If one could organize, finance an operation and present a case, it appears that there was a good chance that one could gain at least some of what one wanted from the proliferating governmental agencies. A historian dealing with this period has summarized the situation aptly:

> Roosevelt's predilection for balanced government often meant that the privilege granted by the New Deal was in precise proportion to the strength of the pressure groups which demanded them . . . Those [causes] which relied on a mythical 'consumer interest' fared poorly, as the history of the NRA Consumers' Advisory Board and the sad saga of Tugwell's futile attempt to get an effective pure food and drugs bill amply demonstrated.[14]

Despite this trend, however, it is noticeable that the thirties did see the emergence of organizations which had some concept of the 'public interest' in mind. There had been a 'People's Lobby' in Washington since 1928, though its nature was more akin to a radical political movement than a pressure group operating in the public interest. It lingered on into the 1940s, when, presumably, it died under the weight of suspicion attached to all radical movements as the country lurched towards the McCarthy years. The Lobby's executive secretary, Benjamin C. Marsh, made its platform clear in a letter to the *New York Times* in 1946: 'We are working for public ownership and democratic controls of natural resources, natural monopolies and basic industries, and taxation of ability to pay, and benefits received from Government, as we believe in an economy of abundance.'[15]

Much closer to the mainstream of American reform interests was the Consumers' Union, formed in 1936. It was not the first organization to test products for their value, safety and efficiency, but it became the most effective and has lasted until the present day. The Union has been described as 'perhaps the only new reform movement of the thirties to survive the Great Depression'[16] and was once branded as subversive, but it is now regarded as reliable and respectable, with a circulation of somewhere between one and two million for its main publication, *Consumer Reports*. It is true that for most of its existence Consumers' Union has hardly been a pressure group in the strict sense of the term. Though a widely based membership group, its main task has been to supply information on industrial products such as automobiles or home equipment (cookers, washing machines and similar items) to its members and to let them assess the desirability of these products in terms of value for money. Nevertheless, its results have sometimes been used by other associations which, unlike the Consumers' Union, have used direct lobbying techniques. By the 1960s the Consumers' Union was beginning to play a more active role in 'consumerism', as the summary phrase is now, partially prompted by the increased interest activated by Ralph Nader, who secured a seat on the Consumers' Union board.[17] Therefore, a movement concerned with industrial standards which can be said to reach back in American history at least to the time of the muckrakers and Upton Sinclair's *The*

Jungle, to have been fuelled by the 1927 book *Your Money's Worth* (writted by Stuart Chase and F. G. Schlink), seems to have fused with other related movements in the sixties or seventies to reach a sort of maturity.

One could make the generalization that much of the 'public-interest' pressure of recent years has grown out of the two earlier lines of reform that we have touched upon: first, governmental reform as such and, second, reforms that would give Americans as consumers in the market place a fairer deal than hitherto. Therefore, there is some degree of dichotomy which is not always fully appreciated by the main participants in the field, and it is one which has had some curious results, including the incapacity of some groups to transfer their abilities and expertise from the political to the economic arena or vice versa. The amount of overlap between political and economic activity in American life has made the duality of reform an inevitability, though one stream often reacts on the other.

After World War II there was no great interest in the United States in thoroughgoing reform of the political or the economic system, despite the paying of occasional lip-service to both, such as the 1952 Republican allegations of Democratic corruption, implied in their election slogan 'Corruption, Communism, Korea'. The latter two of these three 'planks' were perhaps more potent as war cries than the first, and Communism as a domestic and an international threat certainly muted, and often defeated, attempts to create a public more aware of governmental malpractice, outright corruption and economic sharp practice. It is true that there were many exposés of corruption during these years and, especially at state level, many administrations within the United States became bywords for corrupt practice. Most of these 'scandals' were contained at the local or state level, though often enough general interest was aroused for this or that state to become notorious.[18] Individual states contained local organizations that tried to combat the conditions which encouraged misgovernment and corruption—taxpayers' federations, state and local Leagues of Women Voters and the like—but there was little concentrated effort on a national scale to tackle basic inequities in the political system as seen through the eyes of an individual voter. The Eisenhower years were ones of domestic complacency; the fear of nuclear warfare and 'international Communism' acted as brakes not only on political reform but also on any type of reform movement which could even remotely be thought of as radical or 'subversive'. It has been said that the post-war period 'was one of general quiescence for consumer protection (as well as many other reform issues) until the early 1960s'.[19]

Why did reform issues, especially those connected with consumer needs and questions of good government become salient in the 1960s? The author of the above quotation, Mark Nagel, suggests that, as far as the promotion of consumer issues was concerned, the sixties witnessed a useful combination of factors, including the complexity of many consumer durables (like colour TV), the brief re-emergence of an 'active' presidency, growing public consensus on the need for consumer protection, resulting in pressure on politicians to achieve legislative action to this end, and the emergence of a few crusading individuals like Ralph Nader to spearhead the new wave of reforming zeal.[20] Certainly, all of these points have a certain validity, but it may be that they are symptoms rather than causes of a larger phenomenon, namely, a gradual reassessment of priorities in American life which started some time in the early or mid-1960s and is still taking shape. To a certain extent, the Cuban Missile Crisis may have been the turning-point, for before it a continuous atmosphere of 'cold war' had stretched back to the 1940s, with the effects that we have noted already. Since 1962, in contrast, overt tensions of this kind have lessened (though they have not disappeared), and public attention has gradually turned inwards to the domestic problems of the United States—which is why the Vietnam intervention eventually came to appear such an anomoly. With United States public opinion becoming increasingly averse to physical intervention overseas in recent years (providing critical areas such as Western Europe and South America are not threatened), energy has been released for the devising of internal rearrangements to protect the interests of 'the public' in a range of economic and political matters. Other changes in the public attitudes of the sixties and seventies were also obvious contributors to this move, especially the so-called

'Youth Revolution', for when this had cooled down after its more violent phase, it left a number of young or youngish people ready to commit themselves to long-term causes such as the pursuit of the 'public interest'.

We have suggested that reform, as a precursor of the appeal to the public interest, has had both an economic and a political aspect. This duality has been reflected in the organizations that have emerged in recent years to defend the public at large against the encroachment of the 'special interests'. The two points of emphasis are best represented, on the economic side, by Ralph Nader and the network of organizations which he has sponsored and, on the political side, by Common Cause, the brainchild of John Gardner. Neither of these groups is exclusive in its field of operations—Nader, especially, has been almost as involved in the political as in the economic field because of his desire to see industry and commerce more strictly regulated by government; similarly, Common Cause has become embroiled in issues such as the environment that have an economic dimension. It is exceedingly difficult to divide economics and politics into discrete compartments in contemporary American life; one does it heuristically, but in practice the two overlap considerably. This is especially true when one considers that in this chapter we have used the term 'economic' as one of convenience and not in any way that it has generally been employed in the discussion of pressure groups. Reform movements in the economic field have been essentially consumer-oriented, whereas it is usual to describe economic interest as stemming from one's mode of employment or sustenance, whether as an operative or as a dispenser of capital. It is this fact which (as we saw in Chapter 1) was the main motivating force behind group interests until recent times, and the whole crux of our argument is that the range of pressure-group activity is dominated less by the capital–labour axis than was the case a generation or two generations ago.

We have noted before that 'consumerism' was a reform area which thrived for perhaps the first time in the New Deal period. This pattern of reform was opened up considerably in the 1960s, most dramatically by the emergence of automobile safety as the kind of public issue that it had not been in previous times. The *cause célèbre* which catapulted the issue into the public eye, transforming the automobile from a status symbol to an unpredictable weapon of deadly dimensions, was, of course, Ralph Nader's book *Unsafe at Any Speed*, published first in 1965. At the time Nader, a young lawyer of Lebanese descent born in Connecticut, was a recent graduate of Princeton and Harvard Law School. He had become interested in what he termed 'public-interest law' as a reaction to the tendency for most lawyers at an elite school such as Harvard to be trained to work for the great private corporations. In particular, and perhaps as the result of witnessing one or two highly unpleasant accidents which seemed to be due to design faults rather than driver error, he became concerned with highway safety and slowly amassed as much expertise in this area as a non-technical layman could.[21] The 1965 book, although it criticized the whole system by which automobile safety was accorded low priority by the giants of the automobile industry, was especially notable for its exposé of the Corvair, General Motors' 'sporty' rear-engined car introduced in 1959. This was a vehicle which, by 1964 or so, had developed an underground reputation for its lethal tendencies, including a propensity to roll over because of the design of the rear axle. Pointing out that car accidents caused a third of the injuries necessitating hospital treatment in the country, Nader pleaded for government to lead the fight for safer automobiles:

> Only the federal government can undertake the critical task of stimulating and guiding public and private initiatives for safety. A democratic government is far better equipped to resolve competing interests and determine whatever is required from the vast spectrum of available science and technology to achieve a safer highway transport environment than are firms whose all-absorbing aim is higher and higher profits. The public which bears the impact of the auto industry's safety policy must have a direct role in deciding that policy.[22]

Nader's position as an advocate of the interests of the public versus the automobile manufacturers was boosted, paradoxically, by the industry itself. Because of his book and his subsequent appearances before Senator Abraham Ribicoff's Sub-Committee on Executive Reorganization, at least one of the major automobile companies mounted a secret investigation into Nader, his background and private life in such a way as to suggest that they were looking for some way to 'smear' him. The subsequent apology by the president of General Motors, James M. Roche, and Nader's suit against General Motors (which won him a settlement of $425,000, largely used to finance further inquiry into automobile safety and other public interest projects), made Nader into a figure who enjoyed considerable public respect.[23]

Since the initial public tangle with General Motors, Ralph Nader has become one of the most visible public figures in the United States. While part of that tradition which reaches back through the consumer movement to the early-twentieth-century 'muckrakers', he is nonetheless very much a contemporary person, using the communications network of late-twentieth-century America as a vehicle for his beliefs. As one journalist admitted:

> Nader pursues his objectives on many levels and through many stages of action, including hard pressure for remedial legislation. Nader is not only a researcher and a journalist but also an innovative lawyer; beyond this, he is a highly skilled publicist who knows how to make the most effective use of the electronic and print media on behalf of his cause. Finally, he is a deft behind-the-scenes negotiator and skilful congressional lobbyist.[24]

To understand the influence that Nader has exercised over the development of the concept of 'public-interest politics' in the later sixties and the seventies, it is important not only to appreciate his many capabilities described in the above quotation but also to be aware of the philosophy which has driven his endeavours and of the machinery which has now become known as the 'Nader Network'.

Nader is no overgrown campus radical—in fact (since he was born in 1934) he graduated before waves of student activism arose in the sixties and early seventies, though his ideas have canalized many of the more lasting efforts on college campuses directed at furthering the public good. Similarly, he is not a left-wing critic of the free enterprise system as such. He sees his attempts at protecting the consumer as a way of making the private sector of the American economy guarantee those good things that rhetoric once claimed it could—service, quality, low prices, safety—and if governmental control and regulation is the only way in which the private sector can be cajoled into operating in this manner, then so be it! He stated in 1968, referring to his 'consumer crusade':

> It's a disservice to view this as a threat to the private-enterprise economy or to big business. It's just the opposite. It is an attempt to preserve the free-enterprise economy by making the market work better; an attempt to preserve the democratic control of technology by giving the government a role in the decision-making process as to how much or how little 'safety' products must contain.[25]

Nader appears to feel that as technology has become more complex, and marketing techniques more subtle and more dominant in the industries that they are supposed to serve, the older constraints of the market place no longer operate; *caveat emptor* should not apply where the buyer cannot compare accurately or assess competently—through no fault of his own. In his view, the 'corporate economy' has depressed the standard of life; much of what the consumer spends is so much wasted money, for he receives far less for his outlay than he should. Many factors have contributed to this state of affairs—products that are sold under false pretences, short weight, badly designed or defective items, arbitrary price increases, tax dodges by the consumer industry, discrimination in favour of rich customers and against poor ones. In a 1971 article Nader quoted Senator Philip Hart, who estimated that 'of the $780 billion spent by consumers in 1969, about $200 billion purchased nothing of value', and he advocated regulation of the American economy to balance the power of the great corporations and to reduce their exploitation of the consumer:

> The lesson of this story is that we can no longer depend, as classical market theory held, on consumer response alone to encourage efficiency and competition that will result in higher quality. In a complex multi-layered economy it is necessary that countervailing economic power be brought to bear at each level of the buying and selling process, however remote from the consumer. This is the only way to prevent excessive transfers of costs and to encourage efficiency and innovation.[26]

In the past the term 'countervailing power' has been used to describe the balance between capital and labour as exercised by the owners and management of business and industry on the one hand, and by the labour unions on the other. It is often argued that both labour and capital have a common interest today in maintaining relatively high price levels and in giving the consumer the minimum for his outlay, both sides of industry then dividing up the spoils. The myth of free competition and corporate responsibility as bulwarks of protection for the consumer has been described by Nader as 'The Great American Gyp', and he has claimed that, as an issue, consumer protection is more important than 'crime in the streets' in American life: 'What the consumer movement is beginning to say—and must say much more strongly if it is to grow—is that business crime and corporate intransigence are the really urgent menace to law and order in America.[27]

The empirical pattern of Nader's work permits one to point to a number of specific governmental actions where his ideas have had some effect. Automobile safety is an obvious example, stemming from Nader's original appearance before Senator Ribicoff's Sub-Committee on Executive Reorganization and the confrontation with General Motors outlined above. The 1966 National Traffic and Motor Vehicle Safety Act resulted from these events, and it is suggested that a number of other Acts that passed through Congress over the next few years were influenced by the evidence and the advocacy of Nader and his assistants, among them the Natural Gas Pipe Line Safety Act, the Radiation Control for Health and Safety Act, the Wholesome Meat Act, the Federal Coal Mine Health and Safety Act and the Consumer Product Safety Act.[28]

Of course, as we have suggested earlier, the late sixties and early seventies were more auspicious than the two post-war decades for legislation of this nature (and despite the relative coolness of the Nixon Administration). As well as Ribicoff, a number of Senators and Congressmen have been active in the consumer field—Senator Warren Magnuson of Washington state, chairman of the Senate Commerce Committee, for example, is someone with considerable experience in this area; as one reference book puts it: 'Long before Ralph Nader was heard of, Magnuson was fighting for proconsumer legislation, and he continues to do so with great effectiveness.'[29] Other activists include Republicans Javits and Percy in the Senate and Congressmen such as Benjamin Rosenthal, and all of these legislators saw the culmination of their efforts to protect the consumer take shape in the Consumer Protection Bill of the late 70s, which would have become law in the 94th Congress but for the opposition of President Ford. This bill came to receive the support of President Carter and would have created an agency for consumer advocacy that would:

> . . . represent consumer interest by participating in Federal agency proceedings and activities and in resulting judicial review.
> . . . obtain and disseminate information important to consumers.
> . . . serve as a clearing-house for consumer complaints by receiving, reviewing and transmitting complaints from the public.
> . . . conduct studies and surveys to assure that it understands consumer preferences.[30]

Together with the appointment of Esther Peterson as the President's consumer adviser, the climate for consumer legislation at the beginning of the Carter Administration seemed set fair. The combination of a sympathetic Administration and a Congress which had already expressed some willingness to set up a consumer agency promised much, and all the elected politicians involved would have agreed that Ralph Nader had been at least a reinforcing agent in this whole process. When he became the Democratic nominee, Jimmy Carter appeared (in August 1976) at the Public Citizen Forum to advocate the setting up of the agency and undertook to 'consult Ralph Nader while making appointments to government positions in the consumer field'.[31] In the later stages of the 95th Congress, however, the legislation was killed by pressure from special-interest groups, although it is unlikely that the last has been heard of it. This was a considerable blow to consumer advocates in Congress and indicates that resistance to extended consumer protection is still active.

Today much of Nader's influence is exercised through the 'Network', a range of public-interest groups inspired by Nader but now often quasi-independent, though staffed by like-minded persons:

> Scattered throughout the nation—in basement suites, rundown storefronts, dilapidated row houses, and low-rent office buildings—are the various subsidiaries, divisions and affiliates of Ralph Nader Enterprises. What began in the sixties as a one-man crusade has grown in the seventies into the country's leading public interest conglomerate.[32]

The beginning of the Nader 'Network' lay with the group of law students that he collected together in 1968 to make a study of the Federal Trade Commission; their report gave fresh publicity to Ralph Nader's goal of enhanced consumer protection (ironically one of the writers of the final report was Edward Cox, who was to become Richard Nixon's son-in-law).[33] By the summer of 1969 the student group had grown to over a hundred and had become known as 'Nader's Raiders'. Charisma was eventually routinized and institutionalized in that year by the creation of the Center for the Study of Responsive Law, a tax-exempt (and therefore not a lobbying) organization. The Center was used as a research organization and produced a whole range of reports on the Food and Drug Administration, Anti-Trust Enforcement, the Interstate Commerce Commission, Air Pollution and Water Pollution.[34] It tended to decline in relative importance during the early 1970s as other sub-groups proliferated. One can now only understand the ramifications of the Nader 'Network' by means of a sketch or flowchart such as the one provided by Susan Gross in her 1975 article and reproduced here (see figure).

The different functions of the Nader organization are now becoming specialized and to an extent enmeshed in bureaucracy, rather in the way that contemporary administrative theory suggests is inevitable in modern large-scale organizations, especially those with quasi-governmental connections—and the Nader efforts are directed mainly at governmental activity (Fred Riggs' prismatic analogies would suggest that the various groups under the Nader umbrella have now become relatively 'refracted' in their degree of specialization).[35] Public Citizen is the chief fund-raising arm of the organization, while the main lobbying office is Congress Watch which, as its name implies, pressures Congress, with the aid of impressive factual data, by reminding those on the Hill of the citizen interest in a range of legislation, and also encourages the citizenry themselves to support 'good' legislation broadly in the consumer field by writing to their Congressmen. Other Nader groups handle litigation and specialized issue areas like health, tax reform and pollution. The Center for Auto Safety is still active, as one would expect, since this was the area which first brought Ralph Nader into the public eye. New organizations tend to emerge from time to

THE NADER NETWORK

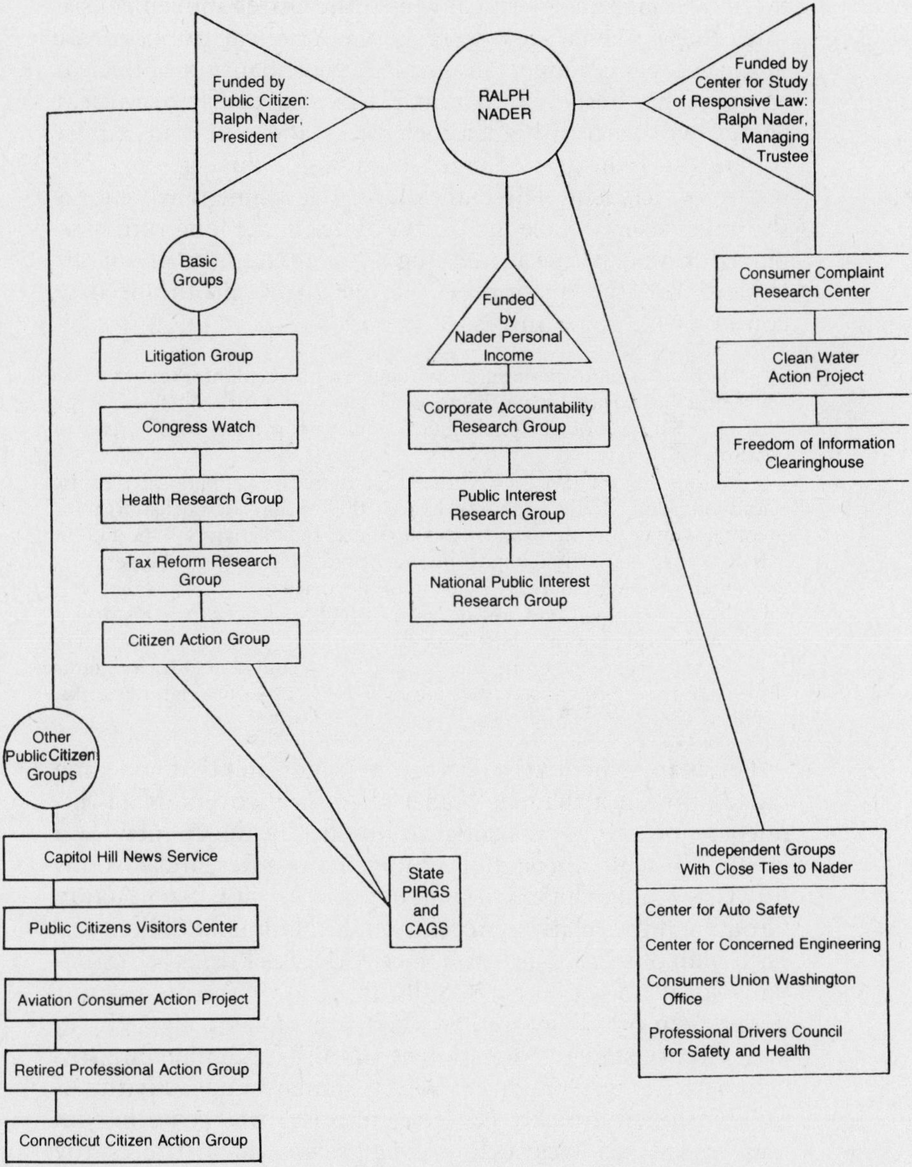

From Susan Gross, The Nader network. *Business and Society Review*, Spring, 1975.

time and take their place in the 'Network'; one which is not in the 1975 diagram is Critical Mass, 'the citizen movement for safe energy', which seeks to make the American public aware of the costs and dangers involved in the expansion of nuclear energy. The thesis here is that the expanded use of nuclear energy will lead to higher fuel prices and will also expose Americans to the grave dangers of radiation through contamination or accident. These allegations, at a time when energy shortages seem to face the United States in the long run, have played a crucial role in the ongoing debate there about the expansion of production on the one hand and the need to conserve energy resources on the other:

> The building and operating costs of nuclear power plants are skyrocketing, and the consumer pays the price in higher utility bills. Nuclear energy is now also bad for our pocketbooks, quite apart from serious risks to health and safety.
>
> Many scientists have long warned that atomic power plants are unsafe and environmentally unsound. Every 1000–megawatt nuclear reactor contains over one thousand times as much radioactivity as the fallout from Hiroshima. These huge amounts of radioactivity must be perfectly contained forever. A major accident, initiated accidently or by saboteurs, could cause human and soil devastation unparalleled in the history of civilian disasters in the United States.
>
> Yet the utilities and the nuclear industry claim that nuclear plants produce energy so cheaply that lower electric costs outweigh any risks. This is simply not true.[36]

This involvement in the energy issue indicates that widening range of interest that the Nader 'Network' covers. It has influence not only in Washington but also in the country as a whole, especially through the Public Interest Research Groups (PIRGs). Though linked to some extent with the Citizen Action Group and the relatively recent (1974) National Public Interest Group of the Washington 'Network', the PIRGs are essentially local and resulted initially from a 1970 campus tour undertaken by Nader and two of his associates. By 1975 at least twenty states had a student-run PIRG, channelling student activism into practical projects similar to the activities of the Washington-based Nader enterprises but centering on local and state issues such as drug pricing, interest rates, toy safety, nuclear waste disposal and the setting of interest rates. Research, publication and lobbying are the three main steps in the process and many PIRGs have seen real achievements in such areas as holding down telephone rate increases, preventing the destruction of historic sites, and exposing sex discrimination in the consideration of job applications and credit availability.[37] Since the PIRGs are student-financed in the main, they are in a state of perpetual financial crisis; nevertheless, they appear to be surviving the inevitable dangers of relying on short-lived student generations to supply cash and manpower for the running of a public-interest group (perhaps because a few professionals are hired for rock-bottom salaries). By 1977 there were over thirty PIRG's active in the United States and Canada. Nader and the individual PIRGs insist on their independence from him and this they technically enjoy, but the initial inspiration was, and the continuing ethos is, directly related to the doctrine of political accountability that Ralph Nader has fashioned into an effective political weapon. This is a real 'countervailing force' in the American political system, although it would be unwise to overrate it, as the following comment by an Indiana University economics professor tends to do:'The greatest new influence upon higher education today is Naderism. The greatest new influence upon the socio-economic system for the remainder of the twentieth century may well be Naderism.'[38]

It would, in fact, be very easy to overestimate the effect that the Nader movement has had on the body politic. Nader is highly visible and has gathered around himself a group of dedicated and effective young people who have experienced some genuine success in altering political outcomes, but not everything that the Nader 'Network' attempts is carried out efficiently. The study of Congress which produced a series of profiles covering the majority of the members of both Houses and a book which received indifferent reviews was regarded in Washington as a patchy affair; some summaries of individual legislators were telling, but some were slipshod in execution, and it is noticeable that the exercise has not been updated (nor does there seem to be any intention of doing this).[39] The range of issues in which the Nader 'Network' is now involved is extensive and tends to overlap with a number of pressure-group concerns, from the environmental lobby via the other consumer-oriented groups to the 'good government' area. The

'Network' has appeared to be at its most effective and persuasive in the consumer field from where its initial impetus sprang and—if we can regard it any longer as an entity—the organization seems less sure of itself when involved with the machinery of government as such or even with the environmental area (it is likely to lose some allies in its efforts to outlaw nuclear power). However, Nader obviously feels that technology has become too large, too impersonal and, because of these factors, too dangerous to the welfare of the individual not to be checked. One remedy is a pattern of decentralization and a return to smaller units; in a 1975 interview he commented:

> I think in the next decade we're going to rediscover smallness. We're going to rediscover it in technology—already there are movements around the world calling for an appropriate smaller-scale technology which is more responsible to self-control and local control.[40]

That this is still in the forefront of the projected programme of the Nader 'Network' is indicated by the response of one of the senior aides to a query about the future priorities of Public Citizen:

> Probably the greatest effort will be in the field of energy: pushing for conservation; fighting oil and gas deregulation; pointing out the hazards and economic impracticality of nuclear energy; and urging solar energy use. Solar in its different forms fits into the 'small is beautiful' concept with which we are in agreement.[41]

Although there are now many independent organizations active in the consumer field, among them the Consumers' Federation of America, Consumers' Union, Consumer Action Now, the Nader groups, perhaps partially due to the evident charisma and public following of Ralph Nader, have tended to be in the vanguard of the consumer movement. There is not likely to be any shortage of issues in this area because of the increasing complexity of what one might term consumer technology and, whatever its difficulties in other fields, the Nader organization is still achieving much in consumer affairs. Obviously, major industries and government departments which have come under attack cannot be expected to share the views of liberal legislators who usually welcome Nader-style help and expertise, but even those who have been criticized for their performance should appreciate that Nader is not a critic of the system as such, only of its inconsistencies and shortcomings; as long ago as 1967 he stated:

> the upshot of consumer protection, when it succeeds, is simply to hold industry to higher standards of excellence, and I can't see why they should object to that kind of incentive. And hopefully, as it gains momentum, the consumer movement will begin to narrow the gap between the performance of American industry and commerce and its bright promise.[42]

Perhaps both consumers and producers could agree with this point of view!

As suggested above, the Nader efforts have become diverted to some extent into purely 'political' paths in recent years, but this is an area where they tend to be overshadowed by the other major newcomer on the public-interest scene, Common Cause. Like the Nader organization, Common Cause stems from the impetus of one man in particular, an older one, a very different character in many ways from Nader, though similar in possessing that reforming spirit which believes that society can be changed for the better by concerted moves on the part of the community.

John Gardner, the founder and first chairman of the Common Cause organization, had a long career as a bureaucrat and university teacher even before he entered Lyndon Johnson's Administration as Secretary of Health, Education and Welfare. Subsequently, he was chairman of the Urban Coalition from 1968 to 1970, an organization with an educative function connected with the problems of cities which had an offshoot, an action council, which was a 'lobby' in terms of the Internal Revenue Service regulations. (Many public-interest groups organize in this way because contributions to an educational organization such as the main Urban Coalition are tax-deductible, while contributions to lobbying organizations are not.) Gardner was a prolific writer at this time and produced several books with catchy titles—*Self-Renewal, Excellence, The Recovery of Confidence, No Easy Victories*—which sound almost like Moral Re-Armament tracts but which on examination turn out to be critiques of late twentieth-century America, calling for a range of specific reforms together with a revival of that sense of community and participation in the affairs of the nation which seemed to have become a waning force in American life. It was particularly this lack of a sense of community and mutual assistance that seemed to trouble him most:

> Everything about modern life seems to conspire against a sense of community, and as a result we have lost something that most of us need very much.[43]

> A man feels constrained by the conformity required in a highly organized society, but he also feels lost and without moorings. And both feelings may be traced to the same cause: the disappearance of the natural human community and its replacement by formula controls that irk, yet give no sense of security.[44]

Like many other thoughtful Americans in the late 1960s, John Gardner recognized the shortcomings of American life, the apparent failure of political action to remedy them, understanding, without condoning, the frustration which often led to violence. He felt that it should be possible to canalize the zeal and effort applied—and sometimes misapplied—by the protest movements into a quieter but perhaps more effective movement for political change, which in turn might shift the balance in public life away from the dominance of a few political elites and more towards the interests of the general public, an aim often voiced by reformers but difficult to realize in practice. He has placed Common Cause within the context of this upsurge of protest, though not as an integral part of it:

> in the 1960s a feeling for citizen action reappeared with extraordinary vigor. It was foreshadowed in the 1950s in the civil rights movement. In the 1960s the students raised the cry of 'participatory democracy'. Among the poor the phrase was 'community action'. The peace movement, the conservation movement, the family planning movement emerged as potent elements in our national life.[45]

John Gardner was one who believed that the means for translating public discontent into effective action was at hand. By adapting the concept of Urban Coalition's Action Council to a new organization, which he left the Coalition to lead, he felt that the old concept of lobbying for improvement in governmental standards and practices could be wedded to new techniques, and that the result would work—his was to be an 'independent citizen's lobbying organization supported by membership dues', new not so much in concept as in the more efficient vehicle it offered to the concerned citizen:

> Common Cause is pursuing an old American tradition; hard-hitting pressure on politicians to bring about results desired by citizens. It is better organized than most citizen's groups have been; and it is using techniques of professional organizing and lobbying that the citizen has rarely used in the past.[46]

Because the fee set for individuals wishing to join the new organization—$15 per year—was not especially high, there were to be few problems over finance in the initial stages when the organization was being launched, and its dues-paying membership allowed Common Cause to lobby without contravening tax regulations.[47] In fact, dues came in so quickly that a campaign to raise $500,000 in gifts for 'seed money' was soon abandoned as unnecessary.[48] 100,000 members were recruited in the first twenty-three weeks of operation, indicating that there *was* something of a demand for the organization whose official date of birth is given by Gardner as 18 August 1970.

With the creation of Common Cause, its aims needed to be clarified. In particular, it was to put pressure on government to improve the machinery of administration so as to make it work for the citizen. Gardner isolated four components of self-government which were essential attributes, in his view, but were not being maximized—effectiveness, access, responsiveness, accountability.[49] Specific campaigns undertaken by Common Cause could be seen to come under one or more of these headings. Thus the early fight to reform the seniority system in Congress was mainly a question of accountability and effectiveness, while access was especially represented by the long-running battle on campaign spending. In Gardner's terms, this method was known as 'focused action'—taking a general principle and translating it into a specific goal which can only be realized by vehement lobbying techniques and by mobilizing public pressure on the governmental machine.

The effectiveness of Common Cause was clearly shown in its first few years of operation, during which it recruited over 300,000 members (it dropped back a little after the Watergate crisis was over, but seems stabilized at about 250,000, despite a certain turnover of membership). For example, in January 1973 a major blow to the seniority system in Congress was effected with the House vote to choose committee chairmen by secret ballot of the Democratic caucus, and in March the secrecy procedures were heavily dented by the House's adoption of a rule which required all committee meetings to be held in public unless a majority of the committees decided, in open, recorded vote, to 'close' them.[50] These were issues over which Common Cause had lobbied extensively, and when in 1975 three chairmen were removed from their positions in committees or sub-committees, one of them specifically blamed Common Cause for his removal.

Some of the Common Cause battles have been won and are part of history. The efforts to bring the United States out of the Vietnam War—perhaps a case of 'pushing at an open door' by the 1970s, when Common Cause came into existence—the 18-year-old vote, feuds with such individuals as Wayne Hays and Robert Sikes, whose dubious ethical practices became public (Common Cause filed complaints against Sikes with the House Ethics Committee over conflict of interest), and the cessation of work on the supersonic transport aircraft (SST) are perhaps the major victories, although there were also occasions when Common Cause did not get what it wanted. The lawsuit against the Committee to Re-elect the President (CREEP) played an important part in uncovering the secret financial gifts which partially financed the illegal acts eventually coded under the general heading of the Watergate break-in. As part of the reaction to the latter affair, amendments were passed to the 1971 Federal Election Campaign Act, amendments which allowed public funding of presidential primary and general elections, a procedure which is likely to be extended to congressional elections in the future.[51]

Other issues are being resolved, chiefly through what Common Cause calls the OUTS programme (Open Up The System). Seniority reform now appears to have been secured in the senate where, in February 1977—and for the first time in history—committee chairmen were elected by the Democratic Conference instead of by the old escalator system within the committees themselves. The 1977 'pay hike' for Congress was tied to a new ethics code, a measure which Common Cause had long advocated (the most controversial item being the restriction of outside earned income for legislators in the Federal capital to 15 per cent of salary). The pressures for fiscal reform in the post-Watergate era has been a great boon to the campaigns fought by Common Cause. On the ethics code, one newspaper phrased it thus:

> It has, in the eyes of some members of Congress, elevated Common Cause from the status of outside adversary to sudden political parity in its field—ethics—with special interests as the oil and maritime lobbies in their legislative terrains.[52]

Certain campaigns have benefited from catchy titles. 'Sunshine' was the name given a few years ago to the efforts to open up committee and agency meetings both at national and at state governmental levels. 'Sunset' is the name given to the pressures on government to evaluate programmes and agencies periodically to ensure that they continue to perform a useful function and, if any can be proved to have outlived their day, to terminate them. Although this drive to bring 'Sunset' legislation on to the books gives, in one sense, a new guise to Common Cause, as an enemy of waste and the unnecessary expenditure of public money, it could lose the organization allies within the governmental structure, especially where members of Common Cause work in government and might conceivably find themselves eased out of a job by the very organization that their contributions support.[53] Common Cause has claimed that it has 'no permanent allies, no permanent adversaries',[54] a fact which is sometimes a strength but also a potential weakness, since it can only operate on its own when there is a strong wave of public feeling upon which it can capitalize. The organization has, for instance, worked closely with the labour movement, but it has clashed with it at times, notably over the Bolling Committee recommendations for congressional reorganization, and, to some degree, on energy policy, where this overlaps with environmental issues. Another aspect of the difficulty of preserving a consensus on issues has been raised in a case study on Common Cause which points to its high annual turnover of membership (supposedly 40–50 per cent) and its shifting priorities (though this weakness is often due to its very successes):

> there is the valid question of how long any populist activity can be sustained when the issues to which it attaches itself keep changing . . . Turning this many-faceted speculation another way, if a business proprietor joined Common Cause in 1973 out of disgust at the Watergate revelations, what would his loyalty be towards Common Cause if and when its focus turned to the reform of tax inequities, which called for assessing more of the burden to business firms?[55]

Those problems lie in the future—perhaps even the distant future—rather than in the present, when Common Cause still seems to be able to win important battles and to preserve a substantial following. It has a long list of current and 'developing' policies, that is, ones that are still being studied, the latter including electoral college reform (which is now likely to be a current issue), civil service reform and private sector accountability which will probably focus on corporate disclosure in particular.

The resignation of John Gardner as the first chairman early in 1977 and his replacement by Nan Waterman of Iowa prompted speculation about the nature of the organization, the 'elitist people's lobby', as David Broder termed it (in Washington it is often sneered at as the 'Commie Cause' or the 'Common Curse').[56] It is true that although it regularly polls its members on the issues that concern them, Common Cause tends to be a 'top down' organization because, as Broder points out, perhaps as few as 10 per cent of its members do more than pay their dues (he quotes from David Cohen, the group's president), and the lobbying in Washington is mainly carried on by professionals these days, with volunteers filling in on the more menial roles.[57] There is a sixty-strong board of directors, voted in by the membership (plus a few co-opted members); the list of board members reads like a sampling of representatives from other public-interest organizations, labour, management and education, together with prominent 'concerned' citizenry, and it is useful for setting long-term priorities, though little more. There was a regional organization for two years (1972–4), but it was phased out because of its relative ineffectiveness. The Washington-based organization is basically a highly specialized one dedicated to the achievement of Common Cause's goals in that city in particular—it includes sub-divisions directed at field organization, legislative oversight, litigation and issue development. However, perhaps the most interesting developments among Common Cause activities over the last few years have been at the state level, where quasi-independent Common Cause organizations have been set up.

The state-level Common Cause units began to emerge fairly early in the history of the movement. By 1974, it was noted that:

> In the last year or so [i.e. 1973–4], Common Cause state units claim credit for helping pass laws in 25 states that curb legislative secrecy or reform campaign financing. A few state units have grown into substantial operations. In California, for example, the Common Cause unit operates with $125,000 budget and is pushing a 'clean elections' referendum in the November ballot that, among other things, would bar campaign contributions by lobbyists, limit overall campaign spending and require public officials to disclose their personal finances.[58]

Common Cause's own figure for the number of states in which it was involved in the mid-seventies was twenty-eight if rated by active pressure in the state legislature. Among this number were Colorado (particularly effective under lawyer Craig Barnes), Ohio, New Jersey, New York, Massachusetts and Florida; Common Cause also monitored spending and contributions in three major mayoralty elections, in Detroit, Houston and New York City.[59] Since Common Cause remains active (to a greater or lesser degree), in the great majority of the American states, in the state's own political processes, it is impossible to do more than take a fleeting glance at these endeavours. Generally, the state operation is financed by contributions separate from the main organizational dues, in the form of an annual payment or monthly pledge from Common Cause supporters in the state, and the organization is therefore usually rudimentary compared with the Washington operation and more heavily dependent on voluntary and part-time assistance.

Few state reforms in recent years have been more far-reaching than the Political Reform Act in California, secured by a 69–31 per cent ballot victory on Proposition 9 at the General Election of 1974. Its many ramifications included full public disclosure of lobbyists' spending, full disclosure of financial holdings by public officials, full reporting of contributions and spending by candidates for office and the establishment of a Fair Political Practices Commission to ensure compliance with the new law; Common Cause in California headed the drive for this law. Colorado Common Cause drafted the bill which acted as the main piece of 'Sunshine' legislation requiring open meetings, financial disclosure by elected officials and regulation of lobbyists, and it also lobbied successfully for the state's Campaign Reform Act of 1974. Between 1973 and 1976 Common Cause Massachusetts lobbied effectively for campaign-financing statutes, a freedom of information Act, open meeting rules and an open-budget law which would provide for public hearings at both the agency and the legislative levels and the full disclosure of all budget details. In 1977 Common Cause New York persuaded two assembleymen to introduce a bill (S412A–S518A) 'that would terminate thirteen agencies over the next three years', an example of 'Sunset' legislation.[60] These achievements could be reproduced in the great majority of states and indicate the very real progress made by Common Cause units at this level, progress which, in some cases, has been greater than that achieved on the same issue in Washington.

It might be argued that Common Cause is similar to the Nader 'Network', in that its aim is to tinker with the system rather than to reform it radically or to replace it with something different. Yet few Americans, even today, would wish to see anything approaching a social or political revolution and would agree with Gardner that the United States would be a finer place if it only lived up to its professed ideals:

> First make the system work. Make it so that an individual can hold his government accountable, so that it's responsive, so that he can have access to it . . . When citizens begin to feel that they can have an impact on politics and government, they're going to send better people into politics and government. . . . Then we'll get some traction. We'll get our feet dug in and we can begin to tackle the problems. That's where you start.[61]

Gardner believes that there are substantive problems to be tackled—arms control, racial justice, tax reform, law-and-liberty and equal opportunity are all high on his agenda—and Common Cause, in which he will still hold a highly important emeritus position, is beginning to move into certain of these areas as the more procedural or systematic issues reach some resolution. The problem, as we suggested above, is whether the consensus inside Common Cause, as represented by the retention of a substantive membership, will hold or fragment:

> 'If the group moves towards involvement with "single issue" fights,' one knowledgeable observer predicted, 'it's size and scope are going to shrink'.
> 'You've got to have a vast pool of national feeling on which to draw for successful major changes,' he said, 'and that is difficult on specific issues.'[62]

After only eight or nine years Common Cause has become far more than a lusty infant—it is a force to be reckoned with in Washington and in some state capitals, and legislators usually prefer to have it on their side rather than against them. We have exposed a possible problem area for the future, but it could be that Common Cause will surmount this and will preserve its consensus; if this is so, it is likely to be an ingredient in the American political process for a long time to come.

Although the two organizations to which we have devoted most space in this chapter are the two most highly respected and influential in the pursuit of the 'public interest', they are not the only ones. In the consumer field, for example, the Consumers' Federation of America is now almost as highly regarded as the Nader 'Network'. It claims to link 200 consumer organizations and to be the largest consumer association lobbying Congress. Unlike most 'public-interest' groups, the Consumers' Federation of America has begun to endorse or oppose Congressional candidates (via its 1976 Political Action Fund) according to whether or not they support consumer interests, though it is debatable whether this has had much political effect.[63] Like some of the other 'public-interest' groups, the Federation is beginning to feed its own executives directly into the governmental machinery; the Federation's executive director, Carol Tucker Foreman, left it to enter the Department of Agriculture as Assistant Secretary for Food and Consumer Services early in 1977 (at roughly the same time as Joan Claybrook of Congress Watch also entered the Carter Administration). It also goes without saying that, as well as a range of other lobbying activities, the Federation was in the forefront of the fight for the creation of a consumer protection agency which seemed likely to be won in the course of 1977, but which, as we have seen, was lost in 1978.

New groups appear all the time claiming to be in defence of the 'public interest'. At the beginning of 1977 an association called New Directions was launched that was quite different from the other groups that we have described in that it emphasizes global solutions to international problems, but not entirely new, in that other groups, the United Nations Association for one, have long emphasized the interdependence of people and problems all over the world. A safe energy future, United States assistance for programmes designed to foster self-reliance and the reduction of overseas arms sales were the three primary objectives chosen at its first governing board meeting held in December 1976.[64] The organization will complement the work of the domestically inclined 'public-interest' pressure groups and seems, in part at least, to have 'spun off' them. It has, for example, attracted some personnel from these groups, the governing board chairperson being Jack Conway, first president of Common Cause and a former labour leader. New Directions' full-time president is Russell Peterson, formerly governor of Delaware (1969–73) and chairman of the President's Council on Environmental Quality, while its council was initially chaired by none other than that best-known of contemporary anthropologists, the recently deceased Margaret Mead.

Public interest groups now tend to cover a variety of fields. A national directory, prefaced by the Committee for the Advancement of Public Interest Organizations and some 999 pages in length, lists the plethora of minor organizations that exist, ranging from those that advance the expected liberal causes, including the issues pressed by Common Cause and the Nader 'Network', to far less liberal ones, such as those that pressure for more military spending or for an end to compulsory busing designed to reduce racial segregation in schools. The vast majority of the organizations are either politically insignificant or highly localized, or both. A study by J. M. Berry suggests that there were only about a hundred effective 'public-interest' organizations operating in the Washington area in the early 1970s (he looked at eighty-three which, in his view, accounted for 80 per cent of the serious activity).[65] Successful 'public-interest' groups need to combine the command of a moderate amount of resources (active helpers and money) with a programme that will receive support from a local or national public, since otherwise there will be little reaction from law-makers who respond to the concern of their constituents.

On a national scale, Common Cause and the Nader 'Network' have so far dominated because of their prominence in the public eye, their archetypal position (to which other groups may aspire) and the role that both organizations have played in dramatizing specific issues in the recent past. Apart from Washington, the hubs of 'public-interest' pressure-group activity tend to be either the state capitals, to which we have already referred in commenting in particular on the state-based arms of Common Cause, or those of the larger cities which have a tradition of civic intervention by concerned citizens, as noted earlier in this chapter. In New York City, for instance, a number of civic reform groups have a long and honourable history. The City Club of New York, founded in 1892, still presses for the general improvement of the standards and services associated with municipal government (recent reforms have included one concerning the public hospital system and another concerning municipal labour policy). As long ago as 1879 an offshoot grew in the form of the Citizen's Union, which differs from the City Club and similar associations in its endorsement of candidates for local office, supporting those who (it feels) will deal honestly and efficiently with the many problems that face modern city government. Many other large cities have comparable organizations, and although one cannot claim that their influence, even in proportion, rivals that of the better-known national organizations, they do form a channel of information independent of the politicians and their party apparati for voters who are trying to make an informed choice at election time or who wish to check politicians' performance between elections.

Much of American public life is now touched by the concept of the 'public interest', and although there is a continuing dispute about its exact meaning, some consensus has been reached which allows at least a restricted definition for the term in the context of 'good government' and consumer affairs. Whether the consensus can hold for much longer is conjectural, and there is evidence that it is already cracking under the combined weight of its own contradictions and renewed pressure from the special interests. Even if there is a decline in the relative power of the 'public-interest' lobby in the near future, what is certain is that two major organizations described in this chapter have had a lasting effect on American politics and that the cause of good government and the cause of consumer protection have both benefited considerably from the intervention of the major 'public-interest' groups during this period of intense activity.

CHAPTER 8

Radicalism as Dissent: Ideology in Recent American Politics

Migration from Europe, that great reservoir of those who wished to start a new life where opportunity was greater than in the homeland, was always an ambivalent process. Since the slowing down of migration by the Quota Acts, Americans have rediscovered their ethnic origins, but in the nineteenth and early twentieth centuries, while not abandoning language and customs entirely, non-English speaking immigrants in the United States tended to try to slough off certain aspects of their European origins. In particular, they were pleased to leave behind the rigid class hierarchies of Europe, an aspect of life which, for those who stayed behind, helped to fuel that growth of socialist and radical thought which has been a feature of life since the industrialization process took place. The immigrant from southern and eastern Europe, who dominated the latter-day pattern of mass migration into the United States, was unlikely to reflect the radicalism occasionally found in earlier, mainly northern European migrants:

> In the case of the Italians and other central Europeans, the revolutions of the mid-nineteenth century had added fear of the pillaging reds to the traditional suspicion of revolutionaries. All the old misgivings crossed the ocean to the New World. Conservative enough at home, the peasants had become more conservative still in the course of migration. They dreaded political change because that might loosen the whole social order, disrupt the family, pull God from His throne; the radicals themselves talked that way and confirmed the worst such suspicions.[1]

Cases like the Brockton, Massachusetts, robbery of a

paymaster, which resulted in what many think of as the 'judicial murder' of Nicola Sacco and Bartolomeo Vanzetti (because they were professed anarchists), indicate the fear that could be aroused over radical thought in the 1920s, and even the Depression did not bring a party like the Communist Party more than a small core membership (30,000 in 1935). Though many flirted with communism during the New Deal period, few stayed with it long. Neither communism as a creed nor anarcho-syndicalism (despite the prominence given to the Industrial Workers of the World in some history books) more than scratched the surface of twentieth-century America in the four decades prior to Pearl Harbor. Even during the Cold War, the publicity given to the case of Alger Hiss and a few others who had been tempted to ascribe the domestic and social problems of the 1930s to the ills of the capitalist system was more an incident in postwar history than anything of greater import.

Once the tension over relations with the Soviet Union grew into the enveloping near-conflict of the Cold War, however, radical or left-wing sympathies became more suspect than ever in the United States. Communist Party candidates largely disappeared from the ballot paper in those American states where they had contested for office in the late thirties and early forties, while the Communist Party itself came under legal anathema, from which it was only saved by a belated decision of the Supreme Court.[2] Until the early 1960s the general assumption inside the United States (and elsewhere in the world) was that there was a high degree of consensus in the country over the unacceptability of left-wing thought and that it barely impinged on American intellectual life; patterns of immigration and a reaction against 'European' ideologies saw to this.

The socialist tradition in the United States has always been weak and to some extent overshadowed by Populism which flourished from the 1890s to the early 1920s. Like socialism, Populism believed in a conflict of interest between the class represented by the 'people' and that represented by those who possessed the means of capital investment by which labour is turned into wealth. Historians such as Christopher Lasch have distinguished between the two traditions by stressing the limited ideological content of the Populist thought:

> What distinguished populism from socialism was not that the former was reactionary or that the populists were incurable individualists who did not see the need for counter-organization against the power of organized wealth. . . . The difference lay rather in their confidence that these changes would be brought about without a fundamental re-structuring of American society or a long period of tutelage during which the victims of capitalism would have to be gradually made aware of their victimization not by unscrupulous 'interests' but by capitalism itself. The populist lacked the socialist conception of ideology.[3]

It can be argued, therefore, that Populism itself upheld the consensus epitomized by the liberal centre of American beliefs about the nature of the political system. By the 'objective' standards of Marxism, there may have been a sense of self-deception, a 'false consensus' here, but the belief in the near perfectibility of the American system, both political and economic, was certainly sincerely held by the mass of the population.

'Consensus', in fact, came to be an accepted code word in American political thought, one which stressed a general belief in a 'liberal' idea of American democracy, but it was a term which the 'New Left' of the 1960s, for example, came to think of as highly conservative. It reflected an attitude that was empirical and pragmatic, essentially Anglo-Saxon in its roots and opposed to the European romantic traditions upon which the young radicals of the sixties seemed to draw.[4] Slow change and gradual reform of the political and economic systems were acceptable, but the country had been through its revolutionary period in the 1770s and 1780s and a further revolutionary upheaval was allegedly unthinkable. Even more than the Anglo-Saxon strain in its homeland, the mode eschewed formal ideology for the reasons suggested above. It is ironic, therefore, that many years after mass immigration into the United States had ceased, the European (Beitzinger suggests essentially German) 'mode of thought' should have entered the American intellectual consciousness to disrupt the aforesaid consensus.[5] Yet it is not easy to put one's finger on the exact causes of the revival of interest in radical solutions to political problems that swept through the American campuses in the 1960s, a wave which seems to have abated in the 1970s but which could return.

A few generalizations are almost universally accepted. The

year of the Port Huron Statement by the Students for a Democratic Society, 1962, was also, coincidentally, the year of the Cuban Missile Crisis although the Statement preceded the Crisis by four months. Although the Cold War lingered on for years after 1962, overshadowed and translated into an Asian context by the Vietnam build-up, it never produced a direct confrontation on the scale of that experienced in the spine-chilling week in October 1962 when global nuclear war seemed imminent. By the end of the Kennedy Administration, and still more as the Johnson Administration waned amongst the ruins of LBJ's Vietnam policy, the Cold War seemed dated and *démodé* to many younger intellectuals, particularly as a *raison d'être* for preserving a strong strain of consensus in political thought. The work of an admittedly elderly writer such as Herbert Marcuse, who stressed feelings, emotion, love and instinct rather than reason and self-restraint, gave some intellectual validity to the move, if any was needed. But to some extent there was a predictable reaction to the perhaps over-complacent acceptance of the 1950s as marking the 'end of ideology' in the Western world. This phrase had been popularized by Daniel Bell and Seymour Martin Lipset in particular, though it formed the basis of a debate which went on well into the sixties. Bell put it tersely: 'one simple fact emerges: for the radical intelligentsia, the old ideologies have lost their "truth" and their power to persuade.' Bell's argument was that disillusion with communism, the 'God that Failed', to use Koestler's term, was evident in the rejection of the doctrines and practice of the 'Old Left', particularly as exemplified in the Soviet Union; this process started with the show trials of the thirties and ended with the Hungarian Revolution of 1956. The newer states of Asia and Africa might still look to Russian and Chinese experience in their quest for modernization and rapid industrialization, but the intellectuals of the Western world apparently no longer see anything much worth emulating in the established communist states. What is occasionally missed in critiques of Bell is that he did envisage the rise of a 'New Left' to fill this void, even in the United States: 'In the U.S. too there is a restless search for a new intellectual radicalism.'[7]

Although Bell successfully forecast the emergence of a new

radical force in American politics, he could not have envisaged, when he wrote *The End of Ideology* in 1960, how far this movement would travel in the ensuing decade or how far his own predictions would be stood upon their head, providing a rallying cry for the new dissenters who wished to bury the title of his book as just an empty slogan of the fifties, whether or not they had read it. Few decades have rubbed up against each other in such an antipathetic way as did the American fifties and sixties, even though the latter seems to have been compressed into its its middle years, while the former seems to have persisted at least until the occasion of John Kennedy's assassination in Dallas late in 1963. As the 1960s lurched towards their last few years, marked by incidents such as the Chicago police–student confrontations at the time of the 1968 Democratic Convention, or the final blood-letting between students and National Guardsmen at Kent State University in 1970, a new interpretation of the Bell–Lipset viewpoint arose: they had put forward a tacit ideology in their defence of American pragmatism. In the view of many mid-sixties radicals, a clear set of values was present in the attitudes of those who had defended American stances in world politics between 1945 and, say, 1962—values which approximated to a conservative ideology:

> But now young people have discovered that pragmatism too, has the characteristics and effects of an ideology. They have observed, in particular, its low resistance to a new, toughened strain of tyranny.[8]

That 'tyranny' was, in particular, embodied in the demands of a technological society which imposed rigidity of thought in the name of stability and controlled economic growth, for technological progress needs this stability if long-term plans are to be realized. Much of the life-style that came to be regarded as typical of American youth in the mid- and late-sixties seemed to be a reaction to the demands of a society in a 'post-technological' phase of growth. The emphasis placed by at least a section of the young on 'alternative life-styles'—eschewing a wide range of material possessions, emphasizing the ultra-casual in dress, 'deviating' into patterns of behaviour which were designed to shock their elders, though this occurs to some degree in most generations—was to an extent a hostile response to the placid non-ideological domestic conformity of the preceding generation. When this rejection happened it came as a surprise. Clark Kerr, later to be a noted protagonist in the California student troubles of the 1960s, had commented complacently at the end of the previous decade: 'The employers will love this generation, they are not going to press many grievances. . . . They are going to be easy to handle. There aren't going to be any riots.'[9] Yet within a few years student dissent in the United States was more strident than at any previous time in the history of American higher education. Why was this, and why was there so little warning of the unrest to come, as the fifties slid into the sixties?

We have already pointed out that the Eisenhower years constituted a highly conformist period. In the first half of that eight-year cycle the country was still intensely disturbed by the anti-communist hysteria provoked by the unexpected turn in post-war international politics, which appeared to have given the advantage to the USSR and the new communist state set up in China. Joseph McCarthy gave his name to that period, although he was not the only person to trade on American fears of a third world war precipitated by communist forces overseas and supposed communist subversion inside the continental United States. McCarthy was no ideologue himself, and it is probable that he merely stumbled on an emerging fear of communism as a barely understood 'threat' to the United States. There may even have been strands of decayed Populism in the loose coalition of right-wing and other groups which came together under the tattered banner of McCarthyism, for the Populists had been highly suspicious of that Eastern Establishment who were now supposed to have 'sold out' American security to the major communist powers, the USSR and China. However, during these few years in the early and middle 1950s left-wing ideology in the United States was at a very low ebb because the label 'subversive' was feared, and a number of years elapsed before it was possible to encourage the discussion of these ideas in an atmosphere free from antagonism and hysteria.

After 1954 McCarthy's power was broken and McCarthyism was on the wane, though it did not mark the end of right-wing radicalism in the United States. Generational change in the United States takes place more quickly than the actual turnover of generations would suggest, however short a 'generation' may be nowadays. By 1960 or thereabouts the fear of communism had diminished somewhat, though trouble in Berlin and the Caribbean continued to stimulate it for a few more years; certainly the threat of 'internal' communist subversion seemed less real than it had in McCarthy's heyday, even to that mass of people who still felt the menace of communism in Europe, Asia or the American hemisphere outside the United States. Perhaps the very straightjacket of political belief over those fifteen post-war years made the eventual breakout appear more dramatic than it was in actuality.

For the student generation the trappings of post-war American political thought were less constricting than for their elders, who had more of a past to constrain their viewpoints. For students coming of age in the early 1960s, the anti-communist hysteria mentioned above was a vague childhood memory which had probably passed them by unless some member of their immediate family had been affected by it. During the Eisenhower era the mass of American students and young people generally had followed the conformist line, full of the belief that American values had to be preserved from communism, anti-Christ and anti-civilization as Americans knew it. The new generation of students quickly abandoned these consistent attitudes, and many rejected them outright. Some of the reasons for this have been mentioned, ones which affected most Americans to some degree, but others were perhaps peculiar to the campuses.

Undoubtedly, one factor which rocked American intellectual and campus life in the late fifties was the realization that the technological know-how, which itself seemed to underline the moral superiority of American civilization, had been overtaken by the Russians, at least in the attempt to conquer space. 1957 was the year in which the Russians launched their first orbiting satellite, Sputnik I, and the effect of this was to create in the United States a certain disillusionment with its educational standards, especially in the technological field. It was remarked that the 'American Century' which many thought had been born in 1945 had lasted for only twelve years (exactly as long as Hitler's 'Thousand-year Reich', as some cynics pointed out), and a degree of self-criticism resulted, particularly on college campuses. Alexander Werth, attached to Ohio State University as a visiting professor at that time, commented on the students he met there:

> Previous inquiries have called this generation 'silent' and 'unthinking' and even 'scared'. I found that they were none of these things. On the contrary they were not silent (far from it), still less were they unthinking. . . . The first sputnik, which the Russians launched only a few days after I arrived in Columbus, made these young people think furiously about the future of the world, about the future of America.[10]

Over the next few years the mood represented above intensified; criticism became more vocal and more specific. One of the catalysts of this transitional period in the American college community appears to have been student intervention in the civil rights movement. The modern civil rights movement, despite a long history of protest by organizations like the NAACP, can be said to have emanated principally from the effects of the Supreme Court decision in Brown *v.* Board of Education in 1954. In the wake of this historic decision it was evident that the South would not give in gracefully to the desegregation that it implied, not only in educational facilities (the specific subject of the Court's judgement) but in the whole public arena. The Montgomery bus boycott of 1955 and the Greensboro lunch-counter sit-ins were comparatively quiet affairs, and only the integration of Little Rock's Central High School in 1957 brought the risk of violent conflict in the decade preceding the turbulent 1960s. By the early sixties, however, it was not unusual for Northern students with a social conscience, inspired by the attempts of blacks to end segregation to go down to the South in the summer vacation to help in the struggle, and before long the non-violent ethos of Martin Luther King and other black leaders was being severely strained by the violence perpetrated against them by such men as Sheriff Jim Clark and Police Chief Bull Connor or the assassins of Chaney, Goodman and Schwerner in Mississippi in August 1964.

By this time a sizeable black student population could be found in the Northern universities, and the civil rights movement led to the creation of new student organizations drawing most of their support from this group. Perhaps the best-known of these in the early sixties was the Student Non-Violent Coordinating Committee (SNCC), an organization which has been described as having passed through three phases, integrationist, community-organizing and black power.[11] White students as well as black participated in the first two of these phases but were excluded, or excluded themselves, from the third phase, which predominated by the end of the decade. Much of the later radical passion must have stemmed from the frustrations engendered by the failure of the earlier, less extreme phases to achieve the goals which the SNCC had set the movement. Even though 1964 and 1965 saw the enactment of the two major pieces of civil rights legislation of modern times, SNCC leaders felt that progress on the ground was too slow and that a new countervailing force to white power was needed. This was articulated especially by SNCC activist Stokely Carmichael, who gave this force the inevitable title Black Power. Many Americans were alarmed at this concept which seemed to spell extreme militancy, not least because of the rhetoric and style of the young black spokesman, though it is worth noting that it was espoused in the original book of that name (co-authored by Carmichael and Roosevelt Univeristy political science professor, Charles V. Hamilton) with reference to the writings on pressure-group activity and political modernization by such mainstream academics as the late V. O. Key, Jr, and David Apter. Carmichael and Hamilton denied that Black Power was 'racism in reverse', or that it would of necessity be violent, although they made it plain that they advocated self-defence if necessary. In some ways their work embodied an old-fashioned concept of the group basis of much political activity in American society:

> Black Power recognizes—it must recognize—the ethnic basis of American politics as well as the power-oriented nature of American politics. Black Power therefore calls for black people to consolidate behind their own, so they can bargain from a position of strength.[12]

Despite the qualifications of Carmichael and Hamilton, Black Power came to be regarded as placing the SNCC and other advocates of this approach in the radical vanguard of student politics and post-civil rights activism. By the end of the decade the organization seems to have dwindled to a relatively small hard core, with far less of a generalized influence on student radicalism than had been the case in the mid-sixties. By 1969 the 'Non-violent' portion of the SNCC title had been changed to 'National' (thus leaving its familiar set of initials intact), and SNCC became a marginal movement; unlike the abolitionist movement of the mid-nineteenth century, the 'new abolitionists', as Howard Zinn termed them, had lost much of their constituency without gaining their ends (their practical and ideological problems have been discussed elsewhere).[13] The drift to the far left, and the transformation of large-scale, would-be 'mass' movements into radical spearhead groups had been notable features of the student protest movements and of those civil rights movements that overlapped with them.

The other major catalyst of student activism in the 1960s was, of course, Vietnam. Of little or no concern to student leaders at the beginning of the decade because of its low public salience at that time, within a few years it became the all-consuming interest of activists amongst radical groups in general, surpassing even the race issue as militant blacks slowly squeezed whites out of many race organizations. By 1967, when the 'Americanization' of the war in South-East Asia was at its height, the names of 100,000 Americans had appeared in the casualty lists, and what became known as the anti-war movement was emerging in the mainland United States. The effects of the war on ideological thinking in the country was considerable: 'Non-political people were being radicalized by the war and ex-radicals repoliticized.'[14]

The escalation of the war ordered by President Johnson during the first few months of his second term on the advice of those, military and lay, who felt that it was the only way to end it, seemed to demonstrate only the apparent invincibility of the Viet Cong to the highly technological American war machine, a fact grimly confirmed by the flow of GI coffins back to the United States, to end up in cities and small towns all over the country. As a result, radical opposition to the war grew in 1967 and 1968. It led to Johnson's withdrawal from the 1968 election and the defeat of his supposed surrogate, Hubert Humphrey. The anti-war movement recruited a wide range of ages and interests, but much of the energy came from the student activists who now dominated life on many college campuses. As we shall see, the opposition to the Vietnam War and the American military machine became the main focus for student (and adult) radicalism over the late 1960s, stretching into the first Nixon Administration and culminating, at one point, in the Kent State College massacre of 1970. Only when American forces started pulling out of South-East Asia in the 1970s did the anti-war movement dwindle away.

As well as the race and anti-war issues, the two important stimulants of student radicalism in the 1960s, a whole host of minor issues augmented youthful disaffection with the American establishment. Notable among these was the frustration with the 'mass universities' that had grown up in post-war America, run, in the view of many students, by faceless bureaucracies and by academics who largely left undergraduate students to their own devices, prepared to surrender the teaching experience to graduate assistants and to the mass lecture, while they themselves chased research grants, governmental contracts and other aids to advancement and promotion. Where California led, the rest of the United States followed; for a number of years, from the Free Speech Movement of 1964 to the People's Park demonstrations of 1969, Berkeley in particular was the focus and symbol of student unrest.[15] Students extrapolated from the university as a bureacracy or degree mill to American society in general. Eventually, some concessions were offered by university teachers and administrators to contain student pressures—they absorbed student representatives in decision-making bodies, they permitted some form of rating of professors' teaching prowess, and they inaugurated schemes of study relating to the problems of minority or disadvantaged groups (black studies, women's studies and so on). It is evident that the causes of student radicalism in the sixties were as many as its overall life was relatively short. George Kennan tried to list them:

> The ubiquity of conscience; the unwillingness to recognize any clear delinations of function and responsibility in public life; the strong feelings about the negro problem and Vietnam; the extremely disturbing effect of the draft; the sensitivity of what is felt as sinister interference of the government with life on the campus; and the demands for greater personal license and administrative authority on campus.[16]

As would befit such a disparate movement, the sources of its ideology were also many and various. There were Populist strains native to the United States, in this case tending to be left-wing radical rather than deriving from the 'decayed Populism' mentioned already in the comment on Joseph McCarthy. There were a number of variants on Marxism, often loosely applied and diffused through the writing of men like C. Wright Mills. There was, overlaid on this mishmash of social and political theory, a distinct 'life-style' which proved to be more longlived than the general theoretical construct. This was the whole 'counter-culture' drive prevalent among the young of the sixties, taking some of its inspiration from the 'hipster' approach, first adopted by postwar blacks (especially musicians), later taken over and changed to some degree by middle-class white youth who associated it with soft drugs, beat music and a general suspicion of American materialist culture. As a general ideological framework, many Europeans would find the ethos too eclectic and to be somewhat lacking in intellectual rigour when it began to sweep into their universities in the later sixties, but in the USA it sufficed for a time to give some sort of credence to the movement's attack on the structure of American society. Although still of considerable academic interest, it is doubtful whether this framework of ideology was ever powerful enough to fuel the movement without the causes listed above and it is not our aim to analyse the ideology itself in further depth.

The archetypal radical student organization of the 1960s was undoubtedly Students for a Democratic Society (SDS). It had a long, if somewhat tenuous, provenance, supposedly stretching back to Upton Sinclair's Intercollegiate Socialist Society in the early 1900s, but it was more firmly an outcrop of the student wing of the League for Industrial Democracy (SLID).[17] SDS proper was born out of SLID in 1959 but only came fully into prominence from 1962, with its convention at Port Huron, Michigan, when Tom Hayden, soon to be one of the best-known of the white student radicals, presented an outline policy which came to be known as the Port Huron Statement (later to be regarded as a significant manifesto of early sixties ideals before the drift towards more violent expressions of feelings took place). Violence and communism were eschewed in the Port Huron Statement, which looked instead to the older roots of American radicalism such as the Populist tradition, with its campaign for a reinvigorated democracy. Participation in decision-making was to be a goal of the 150 SDS members who supported Hayden's document at the Port Huron convention; depersonalization, privilege and the existing power structure were to be opposed. Much of the inspiration of the early leaders came from their admiration of SNCC, but they felt that the new organization needed a wider frame of reference than the civil rights movement which was one of the principal motivating forces of its sister organization.

Like the SNCC, SDS moved across the spectrum from non-violence to violence as the 1960s wore on, or as its main chronicler has summarized it: 'The three R's for SDS began with reform, led to resistance, and have unofficially ended at revolution.'[18] The 'reform' phase did not last more than three years after Port Huron because by 1965 SDS was heavily involved in the anti-war movement as a result of the escalation that had taken place in American intervention in Vietnam. During these three years SDS became increasingly active in community action programmes, especially through its creation of groups financed by a United Auto Workers Union grant (something the Union seems to have later regretted): the general programme was named the Economic Research and Action Programme (ERAP). By 1966, when SDS is reputed to have been supported by 20,000 dues-paying members, it had 300 full-time field workers in a number of major cities under ERAP.[19] However, it was as one of the main props of the anti-war movement that SDS sprang into national and international prominence, with its support for the 1965 March on Washington, among other 'peace' groups, the teach-ins, free universities and eventual draft-card burnings as milestones along the way. The fact that students formerly able to avoid the draft became eligible for it gave wider support to the anti-war movement than would otherwise have been the case.

As the general air of dissent over the Vietnam War deepened into near-crisis in the country overall, so the progress made by SDS across the reform–revolution spectrum quickened. The anti-war movement came to present many faces and to include diverse groups, including academics, some ex-servicemen, giants of the literary and aesthetic establishment such as Robert Lowell and Arthur Miller, Church dignitaries and many ordinary people. Of course, they were countered by equally sizeable blocs—not only Republicans and 'hardhats', either—who were in general support of more hawkish views, even to the extent of advocating 'bombing the Viet Cong to the conference table'. Among the anti-war groups, students and blacks appeared in quite disproportionate members, even if the activist students were always a minority among the student body as a whole. However, it should be remembered that this was a more massive number in the later sixties than ever before. Pressures of the type that we are describing are inevitably initiated by minorities, however much these activists—as in this case—aspire to mass following.

Nineteen sixty-eight proved to be a highly significant year for student radicalism in general and for SDS in particular. The California troubles which had once led the field now gave way to outbursts in many Eastern schools, especially the notorious series of confrontations at Columbia University in New York City in the spring of that year. Here SDS was heavily involved in a campaign which only partially reflected the group's preoccupation with Vietnam. The university's proposal to build a gymnasium on land which was being used for a park in Harlem (Columbia lies just south of the great Negro ghetto) was contentious, although SDS leader Mark Rudd admitted that it was only peripheral: 'The gym issue was nothing. We manufactured it. I'd never even seen the gym site before we marched there.'[20] A number of other issues, such as recruitment on the campus by Dow Chemicals (manufacturers of napalm) and the university's connection with the Institute for Defence Analysis, an organization with some Pentagon links, were also brought into the argument, which developed into a general confrontation with the university as a bureaucracy, a growing feature of student demonstrations in the late sixties and since. Whereas governmental organizations were usually well guarded and difficult to influence, the university was near at hand; it represented (via its academic and administrative staff, and even though many academics had opposed the extension of the Vietnam War) the older generation which made the decisions disliked by student activists; and it sometimes had government (and particularly defence) links, which could also be exploited as a grievance. At Columbia, in late April 1968, the SDS-led demonstration eventually occupied the president's suite of offices and other faculty rooms; a police charge exacerbated the situation, and the direct confrontation dragged on for several weeks. It became a symbol for the New Left—as suggested, for example, in Tom Hayden's article 'Two, Three, Many Columbias'—and the argument seemed to be that if the SDS and its allies could not bring down society, they could at least bring down the university world, which was seen as its surrogate. The validity of such an argument, of course, depends on the accuracy of the diagnosis; perhaps a more rational view is enshrined in Daniel Bell's comment based on the incidents at Columbia:

> But the university is not the microcosm of the society; it is an academic community, with a historic exemption from full integration into the society, and having an autonomous position in order to be able to fulfill its own responsibility, which is to conduct untrammeled inquiry into all questions.[21]

But the Columbia crisis, despite the enormous publicity it enjoyed from the media, was relatively small-scale compared to the disturbances at the Democratic Convention in Chicago in the summer of 1968. Like the black wing of the civil rights movement, student activism was showing signs of strain by 1968, splitting into wings with differing attitudes towards the need to alter society. But this factionalism was still muted at the time of the Convention, as one of the more literate observers of the 'Siege of Chicago' noted, while detecting the conflicting pressures that were to drive wedges into the movement:

> By mid-summer, the wings of the MOB (National Mobilization to End the War in Vietnam) and Yippie army were more or less ready. On one flank was the New Left, still generically socialist, believing in a politics of confrontation, intelligent programmatic warriors, Positivists in philosophy, educational in method, ideological in their focus . . . on the other flank, Yippies, devoted to a politics of ecstacy, programmatic about drug-taking, Dionysiacs, propagandist by example, mystical in focus.[22]

Yippies gained their name from the title of their party—the Youth International Party—and were regarded as the political expression of the hippie movement, composed of those neo-bohemian young (and a few not-so-young) who repudiated the values of mid-twentieth century America, money, possessions, success—and, so their critics felt, even cleanliness! Their gentle nihilism broke out on occasion into facetiousness: at the time of the Chicago Convention they produced a live pig as the presidential candidate in the place of Hubert Humphrey. The 'realism' of the New Left and the hashish-induced euphoria of the Yippies were both smashed during the Convention by the anonymous police of Mayor Daley's Chicago. Daley seemed determined to drive them out of Lincoln Park and the city, despite the worldwide notoriety the action conferred on him (paradoxically, Daley had been a Robert Kennedy supporter and disillusionment over the latter's death, after which he moved into the Humphrey camp, may have contributed to the savagery that he condoned). The Chicago days, as well as aiding Richard Nixon's bid for the White House, destroyed any optimism that student activists may have possessed that they would change the direction of American affairs by love and persuasion. In their turn, the Chicago authorities had shown a rare capacity for overkill; the student demonstrators were a nuisance even to the McCarthy wing of the Democrats but never a real threat to the city:

> The demonstrators were middle-class and idealistic. Whatever their intentions they were not capable of putting Chicago to the torch or numerous enough to disrupt the city significantly. Treated with good humour and tolerance their protest could have become a demonstration of American political maturity and democratic ideals. But the Chicago authorities did not have the wit to see this possibility, nor had the police the discipline to achieve it even had they been instructed to do so.[23]

Although it was far from evident at the time, the influence of SDS was at its height in 1968, certainly in its effect on national events; a peacable Chicago convention might well have allowed the Democrats to retain the White House.

SDS was back in Chicago in October 1969, encouraging 'days of rage' to keep up a concerted opposition to the Vietnam War, but only a fraction of those expected to participate actually turned up for this particular wave of confrontation with the city police and administration. Much had happened in the year or more since the Convention. At that time the dominant faction inside SDS was Progressive Labour (PL):

> PL was a disciplined organization with a specific ideology which advocated revolution through the agency of the American working class. PL came to dominate SDS and its criticisms of the Black Panther party and the governments of Cuba and North Vietnam caused embarrassment to SDS leaders. The Revolutionary Youth Movement (RYM) faction which opposed PL saw SDS as being capable of becoming a mass revolutionary organization of white students and workers, which could promote not a national but an international revolution.[24]

This summary condenses several years of in-fighting between the factions inside SDS. The activists within the organization had moved across the reform—revolution spectrum so rapidly that many became disoriented, sometimes dropping out when the degree of violence advocated by the leadership became unacceptable. With no real revolutionary tradition in American student circles, the activists were constantly borrowing from abroad, sometimes hoping for a more effective version of the short-lived student-worker coalition that existed in France in April 1968, sometimes reaching for a dream world which would materialize once violence had brought down the existing social order—a dream world based on peace, love and grass. SDS tried to contain as wide a range of ideology as almost any left-wing movement could encompass, from anarchism to the mildest type of socialism, and eventually one organization could not straddle the whole range without collapsing.

At a June 1969 meeting of SDS, also held in Chicago, PL lost control of SDS to the RYM faction. This latter group was also in the process of dividing into two sections, which meant that SDS was losing what limited cohesion it had possessed in 1967–8. It was RYM which evolved quickly into the Weathermen for whom violence was the main immediate aim, preparatory to, and designed to hasten, the world revolution that would destroy imperialism in the United States and elsewhere.[25] After a final public conference in December 1969, in Flint, Michigan, the Weathermen went underground and commenced the series of bombings which made them the 1970 equivalent of the thirties 'public enemy' category, though this time the *raison d'être* was politics and not crime.

Although May 1970 saw the shootings at Kent State University—the most visible example of the massive student protest against the Cambodian bombing ordered by Richard Nixon—it proved to be something of a watershed. The mass of student opinion appeared to be moving away from the extreme solution advocated by the Weathermen who, as in the Greenwich Village explosion of March 1970, often succeeded in blowing themselves up instead of the symbols of the imperialist oppressor—or even killing innocent fellow students, as happened in an incident in Madison, Wisconsin. When the bombing campaign proved to achieve nothing except the alienation of the Weathermen's peers, it simply petered out in 1971.

With the end of the Vietnam War student activities seemed to die down as well. A tighter job market in the 1970s obviously contributed to the situation, with fewer students enjoying the luxury of enough spare time to involve themselves in political activity. This is not to say that American student communities are ever likely to relapse into the political apathy of the 'pantie-raid' times of the post-war years but, temporarily at least, active radical politics have slipped into the background of student consciousness. The more moderate of the student activists had certainly left a mark on the politics of the sixties. SDS and its allies, prior to their disintegration as effective apparati, had canalized much of the opposition to the war in Vietnam, at least among the young, and had helped (however indirectly, and in the face of the reluctance of the political and military elite) to create a situation in which peace was an attractive alternative to a hypothetical military victory. However, the inexperience of the student activists in handling ideology or the rhetoric of revolution encouraged the slide into excess and cut off groups like the Weathermen from any type of mass base. In fact, the question hanging over American left-wing radicalism is whether it has any chance, at any foreseeable time, of creating enough of a following to dent the American political system in any durable fashion.

Many commentators have noted the struggles that every left-wing radical movement has faced in the course of American history. While recognizing the similar 'political technology' exercised by extremist left- and right-wing movements in

American history, Lipset and Raab have noted that 'extreme *rightist* movements have been more indigenous to America and have left more of a mark on its history'.[26] With the consensus that exists about the difficulties that the far-left wing faces in the American context, it is hardly surprising that the radical movement did not succeed in its objectives; it *is* surprising that it made as much impact as it did in the 1960s. Lipset and Raab also comment that 'extremist politics is the politics of despair',[27] but this was only true of the later stages of student dissent, especially the phase which led to the emergence of the Weathermen. It was by this stage that what has been termed 'punitive moralism' had pushed out any remnants of compassionate feeling that the radicals had retained for their fellow men.[28] When this seemed a dead end there appeared to be a retrenchment and a general disillusion with anarchist techniques generally, especially as overall support for student radicalism was on the wane. Yet something remained. Most chronicles of left-wing extremism in the United States suggest that it is basically alien to American practice. This seemed to be true, for example, of the history of the Communist Party, which virtually died before the New Left was born. A historian of the Party has argued that the New Left was different, that it has left a deeper impression on American society than its predecessor movements. He writes:

> The new left has made radical ideas legitimate in the land, something which older radicals never quite succeeded in doing and because the democratic roots and processes are alive and operative, this legitimized radicalism has already diffused itself throughout the society and transformed the way of life of millions of Americans.[29]

There are some elements of exaggeration here, but as a basis of comparison it is relevant and close to the truth. Left-wing radical thought is no longer bizarre or quite as repulsive to the American ethos as it was a generation ago. After crises such as the Vietnam War and Watergate, Americans are less confident in the previous liberal consensus and more willing to accept that criticism, even from the Left, may have some validity.

National consciousness of the left-wing point of view is some compensation for the radicals' years of struggle, though it must be scant recompense for those who hoped to change society during those few, heady years in the late sixties. The brief history of the New Left and student radicalism of this period illustrates by example some of the generalizations one is inevitably led towards when considering protest movements in the United States. Those that are prepared to move relatively slowly, to use persuasion rather than coercion, to mobilize large numbers, or those in elite positions, or both, are more likely to achieve results than those who drive full tilt at the mechanics of the system, hoping to demolish it and erect some braver, newer world in its place. The concept of consensus, so unfashionable in the later 1960s, may need to be resurrected to explain why a movement like the radical students could achieve a few limited aims but eventually came to grief when they overreached themselves with more grandiose visions of a future suffused with some nobility but also with some misconceptions and a clouded viewpoint. Consensus was the favourite apologia of that earlier period to which we have referred. It was purveyed by those academic writers who dominated political science and contemporary history and also by their brethren who contributed to the media at that time. It was a comfortable belief, buttressed by the 'end of ideology' theory referred to above, and suggested that Americans broadly believed in the *status quo* and in a limited amount of incremental change; the implication was that domestic politics in the United States would continue much as it had in the first half of the twentieth century. Perhaps some of the consensus theorists forgot the stories of the Depression and the New Deal period, although many of them would have argued that the strength of the American system was in its ability to survive such strains without radical alteration.

As we have seen, the sixties' radical movement, largely fuelled by the young, did not accept the validity of consensus politics and tried, without success, to inspire a desire for fundamental change in the American political and social system. That it failed to do so indicates that the concept that fuelled the movement, although not entirely incorrect, was inflated. On the one hand if America could weather the 1930s, when at least some of the classic requirements for a revolutionary situation were present—for example, a domestic decline in the living standards of many people after the relative prosperity of the 1920s—how much less likely was the intrusion of a real revolutionary situation into the politics of the 1960s! On the other hand, revolution did seem possible in the black ghettoes, where despair was prevalent—but even here the minority nature of the protest was evident. Certainly, a student-led revolution was far less likely in the United States than in many less developed countries. Once the Vietnam crisis declined in importance, students became integrated into the general political culture once more—and this is less than revolutionary, as we have suggested.

One must return to the generalization, complacent as it may seem, that radical movements of the left are not typical of protest and pressure groups in the United States. Of the groups reviewed earlier in this book, it *is* the moderate ones that have increased and which have had the most considerable long-term effect (although many movements produced fruitful contests between their moderate and radical elements, while many groups considered moderate by modern commentators appeared radical in their own day.) This is even true for ethnic pressure groups, among which frustrations can easily boil over into demands for radical solutions. For the women's movements it is especially true, for few of their activists appear to relish an out-and-out sex war which most women, as well as men, would abhor. The reactions against the ratification of the Equal Rights Amendment in the later seventies, such as the attack led by Phyllis Schafly, would tend to support this. For governmental reform groups incrementalism is the name of the game; their very ethos is one of gradual reform and therefore in many ways they are supportive of the system and anathema to radicals in the same way that Social Democrats are anathema to the revolutionary Marxists of Europe.

This is not to say that consensus politics has returned completely to the United States and that the radicalism of the sixties can be forgotten. We commented above that it has left its mark, if only in the wider range of ideas in circulation and in that distrust which Americans now seem to have for leadership and for extensive political action in general. It may be that a crisis that one cannot foresee (just as writers in the fifties could not envisage the circumstances of later years) will reactivate radicalism, unlikely as it may seem at the present time. Yet the consensus that does exist in American political life, limited and uneasy as it is, does explain the relative success of many of the organizations described earlier. They laboured as hard as the radical groups, but over a longer period and more systematically. They have settled for less, but their achievements survive in the shape of a moderate amount of real and durable reform of the American political system.

CHAPTER 9

The Power of the Group: Has it been Overrated?

Any study which purports to see alterations in the shape of the American political system must leave itself open to the accusations of special pleading. Minor trends come and go, but there does appear to be a case for our contention that certain social and political trends have intensified over the years and now present us with an altered picture of the way in which power is exercised in the United States. The constitutional system alters only slowly, but the way in which pressures are brought to bear on that system can differ considerably from generation to generation.

Even inside this time-scale, however, it generally takes a few years to detect the relative efficacy of new patterns of pressure. For example, it may have seemed in the 1960s that the 'young', as represented by the student radical groups of that period, would have a lasting effect on the direction of American politics. It is true that their efforts may have hastened the end of the Vietnam War and may possibly have contributed to the decision of an American president not to seek re-election (although Lyndon Johnson would have denied this). It is also true that they effectively articulated and diffused many contemporary criticisms of American culture, thereby giving encouragement to other radical organizations while stimulating the discontent of a 'wider public', and that various student leaders of the 1960s have gone on to fashion public careers for themselves in the 1970s. Yet the student movement failed to find the means for linking its sometimes successful demands for cultural change to a programme for political or economic change and has left no substantial organizational legacy to the present decade.[1] And it is doubly ironic that one of the best-known student names in 1977–8 should be that of Allan Bakke, whose case before the Supreme Court rested on the illegality of reverse discrimination, stemming from the attempts of American colleges to admit blacks and other 'disadvantaged' youths with lower scores than those normally required from white entrants.

Other ironies abound in the world of pressure-politics. If the activities of youth-orientated organizations have diminished, at least for the time being, the tactical lesson that they—and other minorities, such as the blacks—have taught the rest of society seem to have been well-learned. Who would have imagined, a generation ago, that the elderly would try to become a mobilized force in the United States political system? Some were involved, of course, in the various protest movements of the 1930s and, often via trade-union financed groups, in the fight for socialized medicine thirty years later; but it was not until 1973 that an organization pressing for new benefits for old people appeared—the Grey Panthers. As the 1970s waned, it seemed to be about to take its place among the other 'new' pressure groups, by which time there were an additional fourteen associations acting in the interests of the elderly in Washington. As one of the (young) Grey Panther leaders explains:

> We Panthers are the big new movement. After black rights, after women's rights—then comes the claim of the old. We've had enough of 'help the elderly' schemes. The Panthers aren't in the begging game. We're about ageing—you, me, everyone, all the time—and getting society to build housing, health, pensions, education and politics right around that basic process.[2]

The Grey Panthers are much more likely to exercise sustained power than were, say, the ill-fated Black Panthers of the 1960s, and the reason for this is obvious. The black group appeared to represent a relatively small percentage of Afro-Americans, the bulk of whom would not have supported the extreme tactics advocated by the Panthers, though they may have agreed with many of their objectives. On the other hand, a group voicing the disquiet of senior citizens that they were not being fairly treated by the social and political system has inevitably gained widespread support from the elderly and from many younger people, if only on the grounds that 'we will all grow old if we live long enough', and reflecting the expanding number of old people in the population as the capacity of medical science to prolong life has steadily improved. (Similarly, during the 1960s, when the youth group was larger than usual, its organized endeavours were more than usually marked.) In other words, group pressures will succeed more easily when they accord with the prevailing cultural winds rather than when they go against them. But it should be made clear here that success depends only in part upon the size of the pressure group. As Brian Barry, commenting on Mancur Olson's work, has phrased it, there is 'a fallacious assumption that any significant shared interest is likely to give rise to a pressure group whose strength will in some sense be proportional to the aggregate strength of the interests affected'.[3] In reality, small pressure groups can be very effective if they reflect some strand of contemporary thinking. Although this fact should be self-evident, many newer pressure groups prefer to ignore it or hope that the wind will change and that their efforts will help it to do so.

Among the pressure groups reviewed in these pages are a number that seem destined to retain their power to influence decision-making for some time to come and, in most cases, these are groups that strike deep into the American unconscious, perhaps animating regrets about the neglect of the past or fears for the future (for instance, black organizations on the one hand and Nader-type public-interest associations on the other). However, it sometimes appears that certain group styles are not making as much impact as one would have expected a few years ago. By the late 1960s it looked as though the environmental groups were poised for a great breakthrough. The old-established Sierra Club, as well as new organizations like Friends of the Earth, alerted Americans to the despoilment of what was left of the wilderness and the possible deterioration of all the amenities of a natural life—pure air, water and food. Unfortunately, other counterpressures appeared, such as the shortage of energy, which made the 1970s less immediately responsive to measures designed to retain the natural heritage but at the expense of dearer fuel, higher taxes or some similar outlay, none of which could be described as being in the public interest. Such conflicts understandably intensified the arguments about whether there was a public interest at all. The barriers encountered by certain of the environmental crusades also illuminate the relationship between what has inelegantly been called 'non-decision-making' and the exercise of power in American society. For, as Matthew Crenson has argued in his study of organized attempts to reduce air pollution, the large corporation (specifically US Steel, in the author's case study of Gary, Indiana) is able to affect policy-making on a question crucial to its interests without direct intervention in the political arena. It may do so by relying on its importance to the local economy and by reacting to proposals for controls first with delaying evasion and then with disapproval. In addition, Crenson's work raises valid doubts about 'the pluralist view that different political issues tend to rise and subside independently', since pressures for economic development and environmental control are plainly both related and at odds.[4]

The whole question of the impact and significance of the public-interest groups is a difficult one. As Jeffrey M. Berry pointed out in his investigation of these concerns, many of them are very conscious of the magnitude of the tasks they face, even in the 1970s, and have yet to perfect their organizations, relying at the outset on young or inexperienced staff who may not—in view of the poor pay they receive—be committed to working for the association as a permanent career.[5] More than most pressure groups, they have depended upon a sympathetic climate of opinion and a conviction among leaders and rank-and-file members alike of the importance of their activities. The satisfaction to be derived from participation in such campaigns for the public interest may ironically have been reduced, as the passage of time has brought to the successful alliances a greater degree of bureaucracy and a diminished sense of pioneering, while success has led to the proliferation of competing groups in the field. For several of the smaller operations it is a struggle simply to keep going. The lofty moral tone adopted by some of the best-known public-interest lobbyists has inevitably lost its appeal with familiarity and the advent of a more conservative Congress than those of the 1960s, just as direct mail appeals bring in less funds and fewer members than they once did, not least because they have been tried by so many pressure groups in the last decade that recipients have become unresponsive and because they are now much more expensive to mount. Moreover, the cynical can make much of the fact that a number of the employees in the offices dedicated to working for a better world have recently been agitating for improved conditions of employment, while some (perhaps as many as half) of the new councils and centres have no membership at all or are middle-class enclaves dependent upon small oligarchies for the choice of issues and tactics. This lack of members in turn causes money-raising difficulties, which may only be solved by an undue reliance upon foundation assistance, inevitably conferred with conditions and restricted by the increased demands on such bodies as well as by an unpromising economic climate.[6]

However, if the first period of growth is clearly over for the public-interest groups, they have just as clearly filled a vacuum and are likely to take new forms in the years to come, though they will encounter greater practical difficulties of the kind already described. Thus while problems of population growth, for example, may have ceased to attract the interest they once did, concern over the danger of nuclear power is still growing and 'liberal' reform efforts may give place to more conservative endeavours such as the successful Proposition 13, reducing the ability of the state of California to assess property taxes. These endeavours will probably be more manifest at the local, city and state level than in Washington, but they have already received 'institutionalized' status in the capital, in the sense that some thirty-five federal agencies responsible for consumer matters and specialist bodies providing legal and public assistance to the public-interest lobbyists have been established there, among them Public Interest Public Relations and the Center for Management Services. Universities have even begun to offer special graduate degrees for those intending to work in this area. Many large corporations have now set up consumer complaints departments in recognition of the strength of the movement, and consumer cases, together with suits brought by the public-interest organizations, have been effectively prosecuted during the last few years, although the latter have experienced some difficulty in first establishing their standing to sue.[7]

It is evident that whatever adjustments may be in store, the pressure group universe will not revert to the apparent predominance of 'economic' group exertions that existed prior to World War II. If the size and the financial muscle exercised by the large economic-orientated associations will inevitably give them a commanding position in decision-making in the United States, their influence is now consistently being challenged by the newer pattern of group activity which we have described. Such activity is doubly necessary as a countervailing force at a time when economic pressure groups are becoming more complex and more powerful organizations, often international rather than national in scope. According to one of the best of the Washington research agencies:

> A complicating factor in the 1970s was the upsurge of multinational corporations, companies whose interests extended far beyond national borders. Including in their ranks some leading United States corporations, these concerns exerted important influences on American trade and other policies.[8]

The 'international' dimension of pressure-group politics is seldom revealed in detail, though some disclosures have been made in one or two cases during the mid-1970s. These have concerned not only multi-national corporations but also American firms trading abroad (as witness the Lockheed scandal), foreign commercial activity aimed at the United States and even governmental lobbying by countries with a special interest in Washington decision-making, notably such 'client states' as Taiwan, South Korea and Israel. After the publicity afforded the Tongsun Park affair, the *Congressional Quarterly* commented:

> The South Korean lobby itself is a good example of that commercial bent [evident even among official foreign delegations]. Leaving aside the allegations of bribery and favor—currying of members of Congress by Tongsun Park and others, the South Koreans have put in place an extensive network of trade promotion offices. Nine such offices are now in operation from Seattle and San Francisco to Atlanta and Miami. Three different Washington law firms represent specific Korean commercial groups such

as the Korean Stainless Steel Flatware Manufacturers Association and the Korea National Housing Corporation. In all, 23 agents represent disparate, presumably legitimate South Korean clients.[9]

Moreover, not only are virtually all major corporations now retaining lobbyists in Washington, but the largest of them employ teams of experts to look after their interests on Capitol Hill, investments which they were reluctant to make a decade or so ago, with the United States Chamber of Commerce (in the key position once occupied by the National Association of Manufacturers) effectively acting for and against relevant legislation on behalf of thousands of corporations, professional and trade associations, as well as its own affiliates, local and regional. In addition to the AFL–CIO spokesmen, some fifty trade unions are independently represented in Washington, though lacking the degree of influence enjoyed by the conservative groups, with their vast resources and newly cultivated links with like-minded Congressmen.[10]

In the light of the expanding activity among economic lobbies of all kinds, it is not surprising that pressures from the rest of the community continue to grow and to become better organized. A literate and increasingly highly educated public, the absence of that deference to authority still found elsewhere and the tradition of group effort described in our first two chapters all combine to make the work of organized groups operating on political decision-making seem highly natural. Other and newer factors have lately encouraged the growth of lobbyists and their employers. We have already suggested that the failure of the two main parties in the later twentieth century to provide the urban poor with immediate, tangible benefits has contributed to both cynicism about political involvement and the adoption of more militant tactics to exert some influence over the political system. This disillusionment with the effectiveness of the parties has taken a different form among less alienated citizens, for Congress has become more open to their pressures because of the reform of the committee and seniority system, and the greater role of legislators in policy and budget-making since the recoil from the 'imperial presidency' of Richard M. Nixon. Furthermore, the impact of federal spending and regulations on all aspects of American life make the lobbyist as valuable to many groups in the post-industrial society as the 'expert' was to the harassed administrator of the Progressive era struggling with the complexities of the industrializing world.[11]

The members of the groups that we roughly classify as 'non-economic' and that are engaged in this complicated and progressively more competitive area of political pressure may be spurred on by their knowledge that the economic lobbies spend huge sums of money, much of which is not filed publicly as required by the 1946 Federal Regulation of Lobbying Act and which they must somehow try and match. As the *Congressional Quarterly* manual on lobbies states, 'Loopholes in the federal law allow many organizations engaged in major lobbying efforts to avoid filing spending reports altogether. Other interests report only a portion of their lobbying expenses.'[12] The reason for this lies in a 1954 Supreme Court interpretation (United States versus Harris) of the 1946 law which allowed, for example, the continued concealment of the financial details of what is known as 'grass-roots' lobbying by organizations among their own members, who then try to pressurize legislators. The 1973 figures of the twenty-five top spenders on lobbying produced a list which placed Common Cause first; but closely followed by a number of trade unions and union federations, such as the AFL–CIO and the American Postal Workers Union.[13] An organization like the National Association of Manufacturers argues that it is not covered by the law, since its main purpose is not the influencing of Congress to pass favourable legislation. At the time of writing it is clear that lobbying reform, after a defeat in 1976, has again failed to pass the Congress. The aborted measure, which would, among other things, have required organizations to report expenditure on 'grass-roots' lobbying, was successful in the House but became bogged down in committee as a result of the objections brought to bear against it by a coalition of lobbyists.[14] Yet sooner or later it seems that we will know how much money is spent by all the major associations that involve themselves in exercising pressure on Washington legislators. If anything, this is likely to increase the incentive for groups professing to operate in the public interest to attempt to offset the power of the major economic groups, though, ironically, Ralph Nader was among the activists opposed to the move requiring lobbyists to account publicly for their funds. His stance is an indication of the importance of financial resources to all kinds of modern pressure organizations—more than was the case in the nineteenth century—but it is a stance which has nevertheless done nothing to improve the reputation of that advocate of open government.

In the opening chapter we attempted a rough working definition of the circumstances which allow some pressure groups to profess that they operate in the public interest. It is not our intention to attempt a closer definition of the hallmark of many of the newer groups operating in the current climate of opinion, a climate which still seems to favour organizations which collate strong public feelings on a variety of issues, if not quite as powerfully as a few years back. Yet it must be recognized that the debate will continue until there is some consensus on what the public interest signifies, how it can be described or even defined. Against a style of analysis of the political system which was, especially in the heyday of group theory, essentially behavioural, it is now sometimes suggested that public interest politics involve a quasi-normative choice made in the name of the political system as a whole. Virginia Held has claimed: 'The polity may be understood as a system which validates public interest claims.'[15] However, like so many other writers in this field, Professor Held is reluctant to equate the public interest with the majority will, pure and simple. Thus there is a danger of tautology in stating that the public interest is decided upon by the polity but that it is the polity that determines the public interest by its very nature. It would seem to be self-evident that there are political systems in many parts of the world which do not operate in the public interest and that it is only in a political system where there is relatively free access to decision-makers for a multiplicity of groups that such a concept can have much applicability.

Within this model it is more difficult than some writers on the subject realize to produce a public interest theory in which the sum is greater than the parts. Bargaining, which appears to have become something of a dirty word in the ears of certain normative theorists, still seems to be used in the attempt to delineate what is, or is not, in the public interest. James Q. Wilson has commented 'There is not and there cannot be any wholly satisfactory solution to the problem of how best to aggregate political preference.'[16] Wilson goes on to point out that the American political system favours the group that is well organized, that 'broader harder-to-organize constituencies' may be left out of the reckoning and that demagoguery among associations in the latter category is certainly a possibility. But even he concludes: 'The policies of mass mobilization of media appeals and social movements, and of ideologies and personal followings, will often produce a wider public-interest debate, place new issues on the public agenda and call into question accepted but perhaps morbid institutional arrangements.'[17]

This is the sort of dilemma that Robert Dahl highlighted in the 1950s, since which time twenty years of discussion have done little to dispel the problem, except that—and it is an important exception—observers acknowledge that the 'constituencies' have become considerably extended in the interim.[18] We are approaching the position where very few Americans will not potentially have access, via an organized group, to the decision-making of the political system. In fact, it can be argued that pluralistic theory has received a new lease of life just because of the proliferation of new groups during recent decades, and although some individuals still find it difficult or even repellent to identify themselves with a group formed to bring pressure, in general the pressure group appears to be an ascendant vehicle for political power in the United States. Many have associated its growing importance with the relative decline of the political party as a political force, which decline stems from a number of causes, including the increase in the number of presidential primary elections and, consequently, the more important role of the individual voter. This trend is in strong contrast to the situation in Britain where, as Graham Wootton remarks, the political parties have become steadily more programmatic from the second half of the nineteenth century, assuming 'much of the load previously carried by the great campaign groups', albeit leaving some social reform issues to be pursued by the latter, particularly those regarding the liberalization of the sexual code.[19] If there is an argument for the rise of the concept of public interest in American pressure-group politics, it lies surely in the growing range of groups now active, a range which perhaps at last provides a real form of countervailing power—a forum, indeed, in which public issues are debated among groups and individual actors in the political process, leading to some consensus which does have a high degree of community feeling. Yet as we shall now suggest, and as Todd Gitlin reminds us, 'different groups contending for supremacy does not mean that their respective powers cancel out', and as far as the poor and non-white are concerned, pluralism provides far too optimistic a view of their situation and potential.[20]

It may be pointed out that many of the groups mentioned in these pages are as highly 'special' in their interests as any economically orientated pressure group of the past; hence black and Indian spokesmen tend to be active in remedying past wrongs committed against their respective racial minorities, just as women's organizations have concerned themselves with the affairs of their own sex. Certainly, this categorization is adopted by the Carter Administration, and the members of ethnic groups particularly do tend to belong more exclusively to their own associations than is usual among other American citizens, though they may belong to more than one racial alliance. Moreover, the tendency to treat all petitioners as essentially the same, or equally selfish, can only be encouraged by the growth of pressure groups. However difficult to resist, this tendency must be protested; for minorities and women alike, as they have long complained, have unfairly been obliged to make a special case for rights supposedly guaranteed to all Americans—in other words, for equality. Thus the black Representative of South Carolina, R. H. Cain, declared in a speech to Congress in 1875:

> Let the laws of the country be just; let the laws of the country be equitable; that is all we ask, and we will take our chances under the laws in this land. We do not want the laws of this country to make discriminations between us. Place all citizens upon one broad platform; and if the negro is not qualified to hoe his row in this context of life, then let him go down.[21]

Consequently the protest and other organizations of such 'excluded' groups may be seen as having an integrative function, and even their more threatening campaigns may be regarded as justified in terms of the American political tradition, however unwillingly this may be acknowledged by those in power.

Commentators have suggested that black successes during the 1960s not only provoked resentment among less 'visible' ethnic groups, white and non-white, but also stiffened political resistance to further expenditure on their behalf. Similarly, though the forces in favour of 'women's liberation' may still receive favourable media coverage, the organized opposition to the Equal Rights Amendment continues to block its adoption, while the publicity given to recent native American militancy and litigation to recover lost resources has produced a dangerous reaction in Congress. (It is worth noting that, according to recent findings, this more sympathetic media response to minority affairs has had little impact on the operation of the media themselves. Thus in 1977, whether because of the scarcity of suitable recruits, financial stringency or the decline of militant pressures for change, 'Less than one per cent of the newspaper and three per cent of the broadcast media staffs are minorities.' And like other elements in society, the media have tended to support only moderate protest activities, despite giving publicity to violent demonstrations, presumably on the classic principle that there is no news like bad news.)[22] In specific terms, the anti-Indian backlash has taken the form of bills introduced in Congress to remove or buy out Indian hunting and fishing rights guaranteed by treaty and ultimately to abolish all treaties between the United States and Indian tribes, as well as to extend the control of federal courts over crimes committed by Indians and to subject Indian tribal governments and peoples to feared state laws and courts, in violation of their right to self-government. Unease about the effect of pending tribal claims on white property values and titles, ancient white prejudices, and the desire of white entrepreneurs to begin or to continue to exploit those native American land, water and mineral deposits which are their greatest potential source of power, have unpleasantly combined to produce a campaign which some believe is financed by the 'multi-national energy corporations'.[23]

At first sight this phenomenon seems exactly equivalent to the drive to define 'affirmative action' for blacks as 'reverse discrimination', a denial of equal opportunity, according to the brief in the Bakke case, which cannot be justified even as compensation for generations of gross discrimination against those whom affirmative action programmes would assist.[24] But the anti-Indian sentiment is more dangerous in the short term, because of the comparative recent political mobilization of the native population and its lack of unity and friendly representatives in Congress. There are only sixteen women and sixteen blacks in that body at present, although members of both groups have slowly been admitted to top federal jobs since the New Deal, and from the late 1950s have held a growing number of key political offices at the state and city level. Given a total congressional membership of 535, these numbers are not impressive, yet they are sufficient to allow each group to act as a caucus on issues that concern it, albeit many minority politicians must also consider the wishes of non-minority constituents. The Indians, however, have no representatives of their own, and in this respect they are worse off than they were in the early part of the century. Furthermore, it is difficult to find white Congressmen sympathetic to native American pressures now that Representative Lloyd Meeds and other once friendly politicians from states affected by 'reparations' suits have joined the backlash forces, followed by the retirement, so far without the emergence of similarly committed replacements, of chairman of the House Indian Affairs Subcommittee, Teno Roncalio, and chairman of the Senate Select Committee on Indian Affairs, James Abourezk, although the latter was able to secure an extension of the life of his committee.

Their lack of friends in Congress might not be such a serious liability were the Indian protest organizations able to speak with a single voice, in the manner beloved of busy legislators, but they are less able to do this than any of the other interest groups reviewed here. In the case of the native Americans conflicting objectives are inevitable, because of both urban–rural rivalries and tribal divisions which mean that even now the National Congress of American Indians, their only registered lobby, represents a mere 154 of the nation's 483 tribes. While the 1970s have witnessed some reduction of Indian hostility to coalitions with similarly 'disadvantaged' sectors of the population, and the same group of liberal Congressmen is associated with all of them, the special legal status of many Indians sets them apart from the rest. Unlike the homogeneous, predominantly middle-class public interest concerns, among whom coalitions flourish, the most the members of different ethnic groups have in common is a sense of outrage at how easily their courted voting support is discounted in times of economic adversity. In the words of Congressman Parren Mitchell, chairman of the Black Caucus, 'No one cares if the black unemployment rate is twice as great as the white unemployment rate. We are to be the sacrificial lambs on the altar of American economics, to keep inflation down. "High unemployment" is "justified" by economic theory which holds the system superior to the man. And we pay the price. We pay the price.'[25] In November 1978 this sense of outrage led to the formation in Washington, by the national leaders of black and Spanish American groups, of a Working Committee on Concerns of Hispanics and Blacks, its task forces designed to identify and promote 'mutual national policy objectives', to strengthen the participation of both minorities in policies 'at all levels of government, beginning with voter registration drives', and to 'seek to ensure that our constituencies do not bear the brunt of a restrictive economic, social and political climate'. While the coalition may achieve little, its formation is an important event and may help to reduce the difficulties such co-operation has so far encountered at the local level. Although there seems generally to be less friction between non-whites and other ethnic groups than there once was, and all face the problems posed by increasingly bureaucratic organizations and the consequent 'fading of a visible national leadership', co-operation among them has not yet reached the stage where it has produced major payoffs.[26]

There are a number of traditional tests of power in society. They include effective participation in decision-making conflicts and a role in determining the 'predominant values, beliefs, rituals and institutional procedures' of that society. Those playing such a role may in turn hope both to confine the scope of decision-making to safe issues and, in a host of ways, to keep 'potential issues' out of politics.[27] On application of any of these tests, the Indian organizations—whether active behind the scenes or involved in such demonstrations as the July 1978 'Longest Walk' on Washington—have only just started to acquire some share of power at the national level, a process which began at the tribal level in the 1930s and which essentially means more autonomy for the reservation Indians and more assistance for those in the cities. Yet without denigrating self-help efforts, this breakthrough is partly due to the existence of old but valid treaties with the Indians, which petitioners can argue have been flouted, and partly to the fact that some of the landless Eastern Indians have discovered overlooked transgressions against the Indian Non-Intercourse Act of 1790, which required that Congress approve all land deals between whites and Indians. Nonetheless, the continuing supervisory role played by the Interior Department's Bureau of Indian Affairs and the March 1978 ruling of the Supreme Court that Indian courts have no jurisdiction over non-Indians indicate that a great gulf separates the Indians from their political objectives of self-determination. Meanwhile many activists take comfort in their ability to wait out anything the impatient white civilization can offer or in the conviction that an apparent detachment from politics may actually be a positive vote for an alternative society to which such organized civic activity is alien.[28]

The national black associations, which have moved, over a longer period and to better effect, from appeals for justice to direct action designed to achieve power, have also been assisted by a more enlightened white population and international concern. Unfortunately, because of their frequent geographical separation from other citizens, the tribes have gained less from this liberalization of racial attitudes, and although the hardships of the American Indian population were cited by foreign critics to try to discredit United States interventionist foreign policies after World War II, and Indian leaders drew inspiration from their counterparts in other countries, such external interest has not been sustained. One reason for this may be that the Third World countries in the United Nations which might be expected to support American Indian claims to autonomy have their own embarrassing difficulties with oppressed indigenous populations.[29]

For most urban Indians and the other ethnic community organizations, the local political response to their demands still appears to be the 'symbolic reassurance' which in the twentieth-century democracies has become the most common means of social control employed by those in power, though state force, by the nature of things, will always be employed in overwhelming fashion against truly dangerous social protest. (The argument that all 'legitimate' channels must be exhausted before others are tried, and the encouragement of the belief that failure is inevitable are both additional and very useful forms of state 'coercion', to be seen operating particularly effectively at the local level of politics.) Reassurance has involved the concession of such small practical—and individual—favours as remain within the urban politician's grasp combined with a refusal to concede anything which would stimulate further substantial claims or alienate the party leaders and powerful city interests. Official appointments for a few prominent agitators, the setting up of time-consuming investigations of well-known problems, and the enlargement of palliative relief appropriations have been among the more successful ways of resisting serious change. Strikes and other forms of non-violent direct action by non-whites in the inner cities, though now regarded as 'permissible' forms of dissent due to earlier community efforts, nonetheless continue to produce much the same reaction as they have always done from municipal landlords, public officials, courts, police and political machines, and no new means exist of changing the rules of political exchange except a more systematic application of violent demonstrations than was feasible in the past or is desired by many of the powerless. The poor and non-white may indeed by excused for believing that, contrary to pluralistic theory, the inequalities of potential resources for political influence are cumulative and concentrated rather than widely dispersed.

In other words, the outcome of pressures mounted by such groups does not basically depend upon the efficiency of their organizations, though these are, of course, most unlikely to be either stable or effective in the face of frequent defeats by the attitudes and forces described above, with only the better-off ghetto dwellers resisting doubts about the efficacy of voting.

The latter, however, are reluctant to get behind third-party bids for office, lest by doing so they should bring the Republicans to power (notwithstanding growing minority disillusionment with the Democrats). The device of dividing their vote between the major parties in order to increase their political leverage has only slowly been gaining respectability. Consequently, local community groups among minorities will probably be as 'unrepresentative' as many of their larger organizations, although consideration of how democratic they are seems somewhat irrelevant, since for material reasons larger numbers cannot usually be mobilized, while the largest turnout would not in the end change the position of the poor as a minority at odds with the majority in American society. For all these reasons, the active life of an ethnic community leader is liable to be exhaustingly short, or at least interrupted by time out: witness Imamu Baraka's frustrated move from Newark politics to college teaching and the Revolutionary Communist League, or the retirement of Dennis Banks from the directorship of the American Indian Movement to teaching at the D-Q Indian and Chicano University in California.[30]

Opting out of political competition may be deplored by middle-class commentators seeking and overestimating their own values in lower-class constituencies, but it seems to remain a fact—though it might be noted in passing that since 1960 the number of non-voters to be found among the comparatively affluent, educated suburbanites has grown steadily, and it has long been suggested that most citizens vote as a result of habit rather than rational reflection, being thus as 'apathetic' as the poor non-voters.[31] Nevertheless, we have already shown that organization as such has not been lacking among ethnic and inner-city groups, however alien its forms and purposes to majority opinion; and, as Michael Parenti reminds us, apathy over politics should not be confused with lack of awareness of political problems or of the system of government which compounds them, certainly among the black population.[32] Although the preceding chapters on dissent among American minorities have not tested systematically the theory of 'non-decisionmaking', the statements of protest leaders constantly reveal a belief that the weight of unresponsive institutions and inactivity on the part of people in power serve quietly to limit their political access. Indeed, it is difficult for more fortunate individuals to resist forming the opinion that many urban governments would be unable to solve the difficulties they face if they were genuinely responsive to them; even Edward Banfield concludes that most of his solutions to the ills of 'the unheavenly city' are politically impracticable.[33]

The comparative success of PUSH in Chicago, noted in Chapter 4, appears to depend not only upon the charismatic leadership of Jesse Jackson and the tradition of black organization in Chicago, but also very much upon the tempering of anger with moderation. Thus its literature condemns 'cultural decadence and dependency', emphasizing the importance of self-help generally, but especially the need to 'instill within each student a will to ascertain self-discipline, self-confidence, and self-motivation in the pursuit of educational excellence'—all of which is in the mainstream of black and white reform endeavour and difficult for anyone to criticize.[34] In contrast are the experiences of the American Indian Movement, like PUSH an essentially urban association, though with aspirations to national influence. Working out of the 'red ghetto' of Minneapolis, the Movement has also been concerned with the same problems—unemployment and poverty, alcoholism, sickness and crime. But AIM is more stridently committed than the Chicago group to offering its people alternative services to those provided by the government (and the BIA), including local schools, alienating the white citizenry by its tone and tactics. In its hopes for a radically different society, AIM might in fact be better seen as a social movement than a pressure group, if its local programme did not qualify it for that title.[35] Neither organization can yet be said to have fundamentally altered the conditions of daily life for the majority of their constituents, and wherever one stands on the debate between pluralist and stratification theories, it is clear that none of the community associations exercises real power as it is generally defined. Nor until very recent times—and unlike the other pressure groups we have considered—have they made a major contribution to the modernization of government by enlarging its role because, excluding the case of the native Americans, governments have not specifically assumed responsibility for such services as these alliances offer and demand, except insofar as the services are provided for the population as a whole. Indeed, they have often been denied, or been extended to them at an inferior level of benefit. Thus in the expanding spectrum of American pressure groups, it is primarily the ethnic organizations which continue to sustain that 'push towards equality' once associated with these groups in general on both sides of the Atlantic, hoping that limited concessions will lead to broader ones, as they have so often done in the history of reform, including their own experience. They have also sought, more than any other organizations with the exception of the trade unions, to transfer egalitarianism from the political and legal to the social and economic realms, and, like the women's alliances, have a record of solid achievement in obtaining incremental benefits and increasing group solidarity among those elements of American society which are most notoriously difficult to organize.

In some other respects, British and American pressure groups have problems and tendencies in common, and the work by Graham Wootton and Patricia Hollis on the development of those associations in Britain will be used here as a basis for comparison.[36] As we have previously indicated, there was in the nineteenth century, and it has been sustained in the twentieth, a close connection between political radicals and religious dissenters in the two countries, and a common vocabulary of reform, as agitators pitched their appeals at a lofty level, urging the primacy of moral over political considerations and claiming to be operating in the general good against the entrenched forces of monopoly and corruption. If the ethnic organizations have generally fared badly at the hands of politicians, both they and the women's movement agitated successfully for the vote, that vital though disputed stake in government, while good-government and women's groups have, like British pressure groups, contributed in time to the creation and extension of a modern civil service and more complex, departmentalized governments, in the process themselves evolving elaborate bureaucracies. The desirability of the latter development, we have suggested, has been the subject of debate, with pluralists maintaining that some democratic activity persists within the competing interests, despite their elite leadership, and some of the newer (ethnic and women's) associations rejecting elaborate organization altogether because of the twin dangers of ossification and oligarchy. But they, in their turn, must face the question of whether they represent consenting or merely 'claimed' supporters and the ironic fact that the better their organization has become, the more they have encouraged fresh organizational activities and voter turnouts on the part of their opposition. However, the very complexity of modern governments, to which the pressure groups have added, appears to necessitate their continued existence in the United States, with its weak parties and federal system, not least to provide legislators with much of the practical information they need to draw up workable laws and to stay in touch with the innumerable 'public opinions' existing in a complex society.[37] And even if the British political parties have usurped many of the functions formerly exercised by interests outside Parliament, they remain strong enough to arouse, as in the United States, fears about the nature of their relationship with government, in the way that they have always done.

On both sides of the Atlantic the growth of pressure-politics has also served to increase the power of the central government and the necessity for lobbying in the capital; but the federal structure and size of America will long necessitate vigorous 'provincial' activity in a way that modern British politics does not. Despite the relative failure of community efforts by non-whites, the consumer and women's organizations can still operate effectively at the state and local levels—in fact, often more effectively than on the national scene. If the South remains something of an exception to this generalization, with the breakdown of the one-party system, greater prosperity and urbanization, the situation there is already changing.

The role of religious influences and pressure groups in the American reform tradition has only been considered in Chapter 2 of this work, but J. R. Pole has recently demonstrated the importance of their pressures in sustaining both religious freedom and sectarian claims to protection under the law.[38] Nonetheless, the involvement of such groups in bringing about the secularization of politics has evidently not been as protracted in the United States as in Britain, since the commitment to equality of conscience secured by neutral governments had been won in the New World by the end of the eighteenth century, and the major nineteenth-century reform campaigns were avowedly non-sectarian as well as non-partisan. Professor Pole's work has also highlighted a distinctive feature of the American search for equality, namely, the propensity to turn to the courts for redress, a propensity which raises problems because the Constitution is bound to protect the individual and class legislation has therefore been abjured, whereas pressure groups of all kinds, impatient with gains made available only to the individual, have advocated legislation in the name of equality between the different classes in society. Similarly, in the United States, because of the early separation of Church and state and the rapid emergence of government based on the active consent of the governed, there was not the British tripartite association of parliamentary reform, free trade and dissent, although in both countries there was a comparable overlapping membership in voluntary associations and interchange of ideas among their leaders.

In conclusion, something must be said about why the pressure-group developments we have studied took place and about their general political inventiveness. Economic and social disturbances contributed, as we have seen, to the emergence of the non-economic pressure groups in the United States, and these groups (for example, the abolitionists, temperance advocates and feminists) frequently hoped to secure material benefits from their agitation. But they have primarily offered either ideological satisfaction, a gratifying association with individuals of the same persuasion and a sense of personal fulfilment to their active members, or they have been engaged in crusades so vast that they have transcended fluctuations in the economy.[39] This is not at all to deny the importance of fund-raising difficulties associated with depressions, or the fact that it has been thought desirable in difficult times, by spokesmen for the ruling classes, that efforts which might otherwise have been directed towards changing prevailing economic institutions and theory should be deflected into less dangerous channels. Even so, the moral reform groups drew upon their own logic, finding inspiration in the contradiction between professed American egalitarianism and the increasingly democratic institutions of the country on the one hand, and the reality of American prejudice on the other. At first neglectful of the importance of political decision-making, they were at the same time (and accurately) aware that power in society was also manipulated by alternative means, though able to agitate as they did in part because of the early establishment of a democratic suffrage and political system. In various ways, techniques of persuasion have not greatly changed since the mid-nineteenth century, with the initial work of arousing public sympathy—education via the pamphlet and platform—followed in due course by the establishment of a network of local branches, albeit some organizations were national in name only, their branches being merely dead wood. Once political activity was seen as legitimate, attempts to send in the lobbyist and get out the vote were accordingly made, and have been ever since, along with drives to recruit the widest possible spread of members.

More important as a new departure than the recent partial rejection by ethnic groups of these classic forms of organization and pressure would seem to be, at the tactical level, the greater 'legitimacy' and use of violence (or threats of violence), curiously balanced by a renewed interest in reform through the courts since World War II. Perhaps the most interesting post-war developments, however, have been the rapid changing of issues, ideological fluctuations and the inclination to radicalism among many pressure groups, formerly so securely pledged to middle-class values and liberal reform, to reaffirming with subtle amendments rather than challenging the prevailing ideologies of their day. It is difficult to judge whether these are more than temporary phenomena, which will ultimately be confined mainly to the frustrated ethnic organizations, themselves once roughly to be classified as separatist or integrationist, depending on the economic situation and the intensity of white prejudices. Yet this 'instability' at present affects the women's movement too, while the recent student movement was chiefly concerned to evolve a radical new ideology that would facilitate cultural change rather than political concessions in the face of intractable social problems and individual alienation. Though doubtless necessary because of unprecedented impatience among their constituents, such deviations by pressure groups from conventional protest strategies are not normally a recipe for American political success. They may also be, together with the decay of the parties, the isolation of city dwellers and blue-collar workers and the disillusionment with the benefits of 'universal' education, economic growth and expensive defence policies, just another factor making for conflict in the politics of post-industrial society.[40]

Throughout this book we have attempted to chart the changing shape and significance of pressure group protest in the United States, concentrating on the underestimated non-economic groups. Our title may suggest to some, however, that the focus should have been more directly on the general distribution of power, following the example of a succession of writers in the last generation or so. In particular, a dialogue or contest has been built up between scholars who feel that American society is basically 'elitist', stratified into those who have power and those who have little or none, with only a slow replenishment of the top level and then by the same type of people; and other theorists who follow the 'pluralist' line. Group theory is frequently regarded as an apologia for the pluralist thesis but it is also an effort to fit the growing power of the group into an analysis of the American polity; we have tried to use it in this context, rather than to enter into the larger contest, which might have distorted our examination of the workings of individual pressure groups. The latter are obviously only one ingredient in the overall distribution of power in the United States, although an increasingly important one. Indeed, many of the American radical commentators who were prone to criticize the social structure of their country as elitist, now seem to find dangers in the expansion of the power of groups that cannot be seen in a strictly elitist setting:

> Interest group identities—alliances of class, women, youth, or what have you—may turn out to be a crucial aspect that could make any real future identification with the American polity as a whole extremely difficult. There are many ways societies fall apart even as they satisfy great numbers of wants and needs.[41]

This pattern of participation is, therefore, one that can be seen as giving rise to new problems (some legislators complain, for instance, about the growth of 'single-issue politics') but it is still too early to say, with the above observer, that there is any real possibility of the American polity 'falling apart' due to the efforts of interest groups; despite their growing postwar radicalism, such a consequence seems intrinsically unlikely.

Notes and References

Chapter 1

1. Clayton Jones, Citizen activist groups forced to cut crusades. *Christian Science Monitor*, 20 June 1975.
2. Alexander Hamilton, James Madison, and John Jay, *The Federalist Papers*, (New York: Mentor, 1961), p. 78.
3. *Ibid*., p. 79.
4. Alexis de Tocqueville, *Democracy in America* (London: Fontana, 1968), Vol. 2, p. 662.
5. James Bryce, *The American Commonwealth*, 3rd edn (London: Macmillan, 1909), Vol. 2, p. 278.
6. Arthur F. Bentley, in Peter Odegard, ed., *The Process of Government* (Cambridge, Mass.: 1967, orig. publ. 1908), pp. 208–9.
7. Robert A. Dahl, *A Preface to Democratic Theory* (Chicago: University of Chicago Press, 1956), p. 132.
8. Peter Odegard, *Pressure Politics: The Story of the Anti-Saloon League*. (New York: Octagon Books, 1966, orig. publ. 1928); E. Pendleton Herring, *Group Representation Before Congress*. Baltimore, Md.: Johns Hopkins University Press, 1929.
9. David Truman, *The Governmental Process*, 2nd edn (New York: Alfred A. Knopf, 1971), p. xx.
10. See Gabriel A. Almond, A functional approach to comparative politics. In G. A. Almond and J. S. Coleman, *The Politics of the Developing Areas* (Princeton, N.J.: Princeton University Press, 1960), pp. 33–8.
11. Truman, *op. cit*., p. 502.
12. Earl Latham, The group basis of politics: notes for a theory. *American Political Science Review*, Vol. 46, June 1952; reprinted in H. R. Mahood, ed., *Pressure Groups in American Politics* (New York: Scribner, 1967), p. 28.
13. Harmon Zeigler, *Interest Groups in American Society* (New York: Prentice-Hall, 1964), p. iv.
14. *Ibid*., p. 25.
15. W. J. M. Mackenzie, *Power, Violence, Decision* (London: Penguin, 1975), p. 79.

16. David Easton, *The Political System*, 2nd edn (New York: Alfred A. Knopf, 1971); David Easton, *A Systems Analysis of Political Life* (New York: Wiley, 1965); Karl Deutsch, *The Nerves of Government* (New York: The Free Press, 1963); Gabriel A. Almond and G. Bingham Powell, *Comparative Politics* (Boston: Little Brown, 1966).
17. Gabriel A. Almond, Scott C. Flanagan, and Robert J. Mundt, *Crisis, Choice and Change: Studies in Political Development* (Boston: Little, Brown, 1963), esp. Chap. 1 by Almond—Approaches to developmental causation.
18. Maurice Duverger, *Party Politics and Pressure Groups* (London: Nelson, 1972, transl. from *Sociologie Politique* 1972), p. 101.
19. V. O. Key, Jr., *Politics, Parties and Pressure Groups*, 5th edn (New York: Crowell, 1964), p. 17.
20. *Ibid.*, p. 18.
21. Samuel Eldersveld, Interest group theory. In Henry J. Ehrmann, ed., *Interest Groups on Four Continents* (Pittsburgh, Pa.: University of Pittsburgh Press, 1958). Reprinted in B. E. Brown and J. C. Wahlke, eds, *The American Political System* (Homewood, Ill.: Dorsey Press, 1971), p. 113.
22. Theodore Lowi, Groups and the problems of governing. *Midway*, Vol. 9, No. 3, winter 1969. Reprinted in R. E. Morgan and J. C. Connor, eds, *The American Political System* (New York: Harcourt Brace Jovanovich, 1971), p. 144.
23. Truman, *op. cit.*, Introduction. Truman draws here upon Mancur Olson, *The Logic of Collective Action: Public Goods and the Theory of Groups* (Cambridge, Mass.: Harvard University Press, 1965); Anthony Downs, *An Economic Theory of Democracy* (New York: Harper and Row, 1957), p. 254.
24. Lester Milbrath, *The Washington Lobbyists* (Chicago: Rand McNally, 1963), p. 276.
25. *Ibid.*
26. Alec Barbrook, *God Save the Commonwealth: An Electoral History of Massachusetts* (Amherst, Mass.: University of Massachusetts Press, 1973), pp. 68–70.
27. Harmon Zeigler and Michael Baer, *Lobbying: Interaction and Influence in American State Legislatures* (Belmont, Calif.: Wadsworth, 1969), p. 190.
28. See James C. Scott, *Comparative Political Corruption* (New York: Prentice-Hall, 1972), esp. the diagram on p. 32.
29. For a listing of these terms, see Krishan Kumar, The industrializing and the 'post-industrial' worlds: on development and futurology. In E. De Kadt and G. Williams, eds, *Sociology and Development* (London: Tavistock, 1974), p. 329.
30. Daniel Bell, *The Coming of Post-Industrial Society* (London: Heinemann, 1974), p. 14.
31. Kumar, *op. cit.*, p. 341. Also see Alain Touraine, *The Post-Industrial Society* (English transl.) (London: Wildwood House, 1974).
32. Bell, *op. cit.*, p. 481.

33. Touraine, *op. cit.*, p. 163.
34. Edward C. Banfield, *Political Influence* (New York: The Free Press, 1961), p. 315.
35. James Q. Wilson and Edward C. Banfield, Public-regardingness as a value premise in voting behavior. *American Political Science Review*, Vol. 58, December 1964, pp. 876–87.
36. Robert C. Wood, *Suburbia: Its People and Their Politics* (Boston: Houghton Mifflin, 1958), p. 189.
37. Joseph Zikmund, II and Robert Smith, Political participation in a middle-class suburb. *Urban Affairs Quarterly*, Vol. 4, June 1969, p. 456.
38. Dahl, *op. cit.*, p. 138.
39. See, for example, the introduction to Nathan Glazer and Daniel P. Moynihan, *Beyond the Melting Pot*, 2nd edn (Cambridge, Massachusetts: MIT Press, 1970).
40. Glendon Schubert, *The Public Interest* (New York: Free Press, 1960), p. 227.
41. Daniel Bell and Irving Kristol, What is the Public Interest?', editorial, *The Public Interest*, 1, 1965, p. 5.
42. Walter Lippmann, *The Public Philosophy* (London: Hamish Hamilton, 1955), p. 42.
43. See Brian Barry, *Political Argument* (London: Routledge and Kegan Paul, 1965), ch. 11; also J. W. Roxbee Cox, The Appeal to the Public Interest, in *British Journal of Political Science*, 3, pt 2, April 1973, pp. 229–41.
44. Roxbee Cox, *op cit.*, p. 234.

Abbreviations Used in Chapters 2, 3, 4, 5, 9

A.P.S.R.	American Political Science Review
C.Q.	Congressional Quarterly
I.R.A.	Annual Reports of the Executive Committee of the Indian Rights Association
J.A.S.	Journal of American Studies
J.N.H.	Journal of Negro History
J.S.H.	Journal of Southern History
L.M.C.	Proceedings of the Annual Conferences of the Lake Mohonk Conference of the Friends of the Indian
M.V.H.R.	Mississippi Valley Historical Review
W.M.Q.	William and Mary Quarterly
W.N.I.A.	Annual Reports of the Women's National Indian Association

Chapter 2

1. Quotation from H. R. Mahood, ed., *Pressure Groups in American Politics* (New York: Scribner, 1967), p. 77; and for definitions directly influencing these paragraphs, see P. Hollis, ed., *Pressure from Without in Early Victorian England* (London: Edward Arnold, 1974), editor's introduction; G. Wootton, *Pressure Groups in Britain, 1720–1970: An Essay in Interpretation with Original Documents* (London: Allen Lane, 1975), General Introduction, esp. p. 7.
2. See Rudolf Heberle, *Social Movements: An Introduction to Political Sociology* (New York: Appleton Century Crofts, 1951), p.9; a useful introduction to this subject is provided by J. R. Gusfield, *Protest, Reform and Revolt: A Reader in Social Movements* (New York: Wiley, 1970). Organization of a conventional sort is not always involved in a social movement, although shared beliefs and action are: see R. Ash, *Social Movements in America* (Chicago: Markham, 1972), p. 1.
3. See pp. 285–6, 296–303, 306 below and *passim*.
4. Michael Guillaume Jean de Crèvecoeur, *Letters from an American Farmer, etc.* (London: Lockyer Davis, 1782), pp. 49, 52.
5. For the standard economic interpretation, see V. O. Key, *Politics, Parties and Pressure Groups* (New York: Crowell, 1964), pp. 17–18 and *passim*.
6. Quoted in C. P. Nettels, *The Roots of American Civilisation: A History of American Colonial Life*, 2nd edn (London: George Allen & Unwin, 1963), p. 349; see also Wootton, *op. cit.*, p. 3.
7. T. Archdeacon, *New York City, 1664–1710: Conquest and Change* (Ithaca, London: Cornell University Press, 1976), pp. 26, 29–30, 108–9, 113–15, 133, 147–9, 152–7. I am indebted to Dr P. Haffenden for drawing my attention to Archdeacon's work.
8. See P. Maier, *From Resistance to Revolution: Colonial Radicals and the Development of American Opposition to Britain, 1765–6* (New York, London: Routledge and Kegan Paul, 1973), pp. 196–7.
9. Maier, *op. cit.*, Pt 1 and *passim*.
10. A. G. Olson, *Anglo-American Politics, 1660–1775: The Relationship between Parties in England and Colonial America* (Oxford: Clarendon Press, 1973), pp. 162–72.
11. Freedom now: the intellectual origins of American radicalism. In A. F. Young, ed., *Dissent: Explorations in the History of American Radicalism* (Dekalb, Ill.: Northern Illinois University Press, 1968).
12. Quoted in B. Bailyn, *The Ideological Origins of the American Revolution* (Cambridge, Mass.: Harvard University Press, 1967), p. 20.
13. See R. P. McCormick, *The First American Party System* (New York: W. W. Norton, 1973) and W. N. Chambers, *Parties in a New Nation: The American Experience, 1776–1809* (New York: Oxford University Press, 1963), pp. 24–5.
14. See E. Foner, *Tom Paine and Revolutionary America* (New York: Oxford University Press, 1976); J. Lemisch, Jack Tar in the streets:

merchant seamen in the politics of revolutionary America. *William and Mary Quarterly*, Vol. 25(3), July 1968, pp. 371–407; The American Revolution seen from the bottom up. In B. Bernstein, ed., *Towards a New Past: Dissenting Essays in American History* (New York: Vintage Books, 1968), pp. 3–45; B. Bailyn, ed., *Pamphlets of the American Revolution 1750—1776*, Vol. 1 (Cambridge, Mass.: Harvard University Press, 1965), pp. 581–3; R. B. Morris, We the people of the United States: The bicentennial of a people's revolution. *American Historical Review*, Vol. 82(1), February 1977, pp. 1–19.

15. See below, pp. 236–61, for an account of some recent public interest groups.
16. For a survey of some 'extremist' groups, see below, Chapter 8. See also S. M. Lipset and E. Raab, *The Politics of Unreason: Right-Wing Extremism in America, 1790–1970* (London: Heinemann, 1971), pp. 6ff.
17. Hezekiah Niles in *Niles' Weekly Register*, December 1815, quoted in G. R. Taylor, *The Transportation Revolution, 1815–1860* (New York: Harper Torchbooks, 1968), p. 4.
18. For a summary of some of the findings on this point, see Robert Lively, The American system: a review article. *Business History Review*, Vol. 29, March 1955, pp. 81–96.
19. See F. G. Castles, *Pressure Groups and Political Culture* (London: Routledge and Kegan Paul, 1967), pp. 74–6.
20. See N. J. Ware, *The Industrial Worker, 1840–1860* (New York: Quadrangle, 1964).
21. See Walter Hugins, *Jacksonian Democracy and the Working Class: A Study of the New York Workingmen's Movement* (Stanford: Stanford University Press, 1960); Edward Pessen, *Most Uncommon Jacksonians: The Radical Leaders of the Early Labour Movement* (Albany: State University of New York Press, 1967).
22. See articles by Richard P. McCormick and Lynn L. Marshall in E. Pessen, ed., *New Perspectives on Jacksonian Parties and Politics* (Boston: Allyn and Bacon, 1970), pp. 11–20, 38–65; and see Wootton, *op. cit.*, pp. 3–5, and below, Chapter 3, p. 85 for explicit fears about employing lobbyists as late as the 1880s.
23. See Perry Miller, *The Life of the Mind in America: From the Revolution to the Civil War*, Bk 2 (London: Gollancz, 1966).
24. *Brooklyn Daily Eagle*, 28 July 1846; quoted in C. Rodgers, ed., *The Gathering of the Forces: Editorials, Essays, Literary and Dramatic Reviews and Other Material Written by Walt Whitman as Editor of the Brooklyn Daily Eagle in 1846 and 1847*, 2 Vols. (New York and London: Putnam's and John Black, 1920), Vol. 1, p. 11; Miller, *op. cit.*, Bk 1, Chap. 11.
25. See H. R. Niebuhr, *The Social Sources of Denominationalism* (New York: Holt, 1929).
26. See especially F. Thistlethwaite, *The Anglo-American Connection in the Early Nineteenth Century* (Philadelphia: University of Pennsylvania Press, 1959).

27. Illustrated in E. C. Rozwenc, ed., *Ideology and Power in the Age of Jackson* (New York: Anchor Books, 1964), pp. 91–183.
28. See C. S. Griffin, Religion benevolence as social control, 1815–1860. *Mississippi Valley Historical Review*, Vol. 44, December 1957, pp. 423–44 and *Their Brothers' Keepers: Moral Stewardship in the United States, 1800–1865* (New Brunswick: Rutgers University Press, 1960); Frank D. Watson, *The Charity Organisation Movement in the United States: A Study in American Philanthropy* (New York: Macmillan, 1922), Chap. 3. The middle-class morality and conservatism of many of the religious reformers are also emphasized by Charles I. Foster, *An Errand of Mercy: The Evangelical United Front, 1790–1837* (Chapel Hill: University of North Carolina Press, 1960). A dissenting note, suggesting that the revivalists were sympathetic to the principles of Jacksonian democracy is sounded in Miller, *op. cit.*, Bk 1, pp. 39–40, and W. G. McLoughlin's foreword to Charles Grandison Finney's *Lectures on Revivals of Religion* (Cambridge, Mass.: Belknap Press of Harvard University Press, 1960), pp. vii–xlix.
29. On the abolitionist leadership, see D. Donald, Toward a reconsideration of abolitionists. In *Lincoln Reconsidered: Essays on the Civil War Era* (New York: Vintage Books, 1956); and the critique by R. Skotheim, A note on historical methods: David Donald's 'Toward a reconsideration of abolitionists,' *Journal of Southern History*, Vol. 25, August 1959, pp. 356–65; on temperance, Joseph R. Gusfield, in *Symbolic Crusade: Status Politics and the American Temperance Movement* (Urbana: University of Illinois Press, 1972), pp. 36–60, stresses the rural-orientated conservative leadership of the movement during its initial phase but seems unduly reliant on the example of New England minister, Lyman Beecher; M. Curti, in *The American Peace Crusade, 1815–1860* (Durham: Duke University Press, 1929), pp. 8–9, 19, 21–3, 34, 217–9 notes the importance of New Englanders to the movement but also points out their prosperity and local prestige. And see Michael B. Katz, *The Irony of Early School Reform: Educational Innovation in Mid-Nineteenth Century Massachusetts* (Cambridge, Mass.: Harvard University Press, 1968).
30. See Wyatt-Brown, Prelude to abolitionism: Sabbatarian politics and the rise of the second party system. *Journal of American History*, Vol. 58(2), September 1971, pp. 316–41, esp. p. 336.
31. These emphases are to be found in John R. Bodo, *The Protestant Clergy and Public Issues, 1812–1848* (Princeton: Princeton University Press, 1954), and Stanley M. Elkins, *Slavery—A Problem in American Institutional and Intellectual Life* (New York: Grossett and Dunlap, 1963). For the view that the lack of institutional restraints was a positive boon to American reformers, consult Arthur M. Schlesinger, Sr., *The American as Reformer* (Cambridge, Mass.: Harvard University Press, 1951).
32. E. W. Emerson and W. E. Forbes, eds, *Journals of Ralph Waldo Emerson* (Boston: Houghton Mifflin, 1911), Vol. 5, p. 474.
33. See A. F. Tyler, *Freedom's Ferment: Phases of American Social History*

from the Colonial Period to the Outbreak of the Civil War (New York: Harper Torchbooks, 1962), pp. 325, 341, 493, 358–95.

34. Although the linked and disruptive issues of prohibition and nativism cut across party lines, in the end they proved at odds with the progressive community favoured by the Republicans; see R. E. Paulson, *Women's Suffrage and Prohibition: A Comparative Study of Equality and Social Control* (Glenview, Ill.: Scott Foresman, 1973), pp. 62–73.
35. M. Curti, *Peace or War: The American Struggle, 1636–1936* (Boston: J. S. Canner, 1959), pp. 40–1.
36. See Alma Lutz, *Crusade for Freedom: Women of the Anti-Slavery Movement* (Boston: Beacon Press, 1968); on women's war work, Katherine Wormeley, *The Cruel Side of War with the Army of the Potomac: Letters from the Headquarters of the United States Sanitary Commission During the Peninsular Campaign in Virginia in 1862* (Boston: Roberts Brothers, 1892); L. P. Brockett and M. C. Vaughan, *Women's Work in the Civil War* (Boston and Philadelphia: Zeigler, McCurdy, 1867); and E. M. Massey, *Bonnet Brigades* (New York: Alfred A. Knopf, 1966).
37. An excellent discussion of the disputes within the anti-slavery movement is found in Aileen Kraditor's *Means and Ends in American Abolitionism: Garrison and his Critics on Strategy and Tactics, 1834–1850* (New York: Pantheon Books, 1969). Kraditor suggests that the tactics of the conservative abolitionists did not pay off because they offered insufficient challenge to the accustomed modes of thought and living of potential converts (p. 107). In more recent works, however, there is a tendency to play down the significance of these schisms; see especially R. G. Walters, *The Antislavery Appeal* (Baltimore: The Johns Hopkins University Press, 1976).
38. See, for example, N. R. Luttbeg and H. Ziegler, Attitude consensus and conflict in an interest group: an assessment of cohesion. In N. R. Luttbeg, ed., *Public Opinion and Public Policy: Models of Political Linkage* (Homewood, Ill.: Dorsey Press, 1968), pp. 80–3.
39. Kraditor, *op. cit*., Chap. 8, esp. p. 244, notes that the abolitionists' emphasis on principle, individuals and the rejection of sin prevented them from allying with labour reformers, who stressed interest, classes and institutional change.
40. See, especially, L. Richards, *Gentlemen of Property and Standing: Anti-Abolition Mobs in Jacksonian America* (New York: Oxford University Press, 1970); on the involvement of 'respectable' elements in anti-black and anti-abolitionist riots.
41. Lorman Ratner, *Powder Keg: Northern Opposition to the Anti-Slavery Movement, 1831–1840* (New York: Basic Books, 1968).
42. See E. Flexner, *Century of Struggle: The Women's Rights Movement in the United States* (Cambridge, Mass.: Belknap Press of Harvard University Press, 1973)), p. 108 and Gusfield, *op. cit*., p. 75, on the marked increase in alcohol consumption by 1870.
43. See G. M. Fredrickson, *The Inner Civil War: Northern Intellectuals and the Crisis of the Union* (New York: Harper and Row, 1965), Chap. 8 on

the growing moderation of leading abolitionists; on their activities after 1861, see J. M. McPherson, *The Struggle for Equality: Abolitionists and the Negro in the Civil War and Reconstruction* (Princeton: Princeton University Press, 1967).

44. Moderate abolitionist, J. M. McKim, quoted in McPherson, *op. cit.*, pp. 397–8.
45. For white attitudes to the Freedmen's Savings Bank, see Carl R. Osthaus, *Freedom, Philanthropy, and Fraud: A History of the Freedmen's Savings Bank* (Urbana: University of Illinois Press, 1976), Chap. 1 and *passim*; William S. McFeely, *Yankee Stepfather: General O. O. Howard and the Freedmen* (New Haven, Conn.: Yale University Press, 1968), Chaps. 5, 10 and *passim*; Fredrickson, *op. cit.*, Chap. 7, on the Sanitary Commission.
46. For an analysis of the deficiencies of Republican policies, see W. R. Brock *An American Crisis: Congress and Reconstruction, 1865–1867* (London: Macmillan, 1963).
47. See Richard Hofstadter, *Social Darwinsim in American Thought* (Boston: Beacon Press, 1966); G. Daniels, ed., *Darwinism Comes to America* (Waltham, Mass.: Blaidsell, 1968); R. W. Wilson, ed., *Darwinsim and the American Intellectual* (Homewood, Ill.: Dorsey Press, 1967).
48. On farm problems and organizations, see F. Shannon, *The Farmers' Last Frontier: Agriculture, 1860–1897* (New York: Holt, Rinehart and Winston, 1945); Murray R. Benedict, *Farm Policies of the United States 1790–1950* (New York: Twentieth Century Fund, 1953); Theodore Saloutos, *Farmer Movements in the South, 1865–1933* (Lincoln: Nebraska University Press, 1964); Theodore Saloutos and John D. Hicks, *Agricultural Discontent in the Middle West, 1900–1939* (Madison: University of Wisconsin Press, 1951); Wesley McCune, *The Farm Bloc* (Garden City: Double Bay, 1943); O. M. Kile, *The Farm Bureau Through Three Decades* (Baltimore: Waverly Press, 1948).
49. See, for instance, Matthew Josephson's *The Politicos* (New York: Harcourt Brace and World, 1938); *The President Makers* (New York: Harcourt Brace, 1940).
50. On the 'Mugwump' wing of the Republican party, which favoured tariff and civil service reform, there is Richard Hofstadter's brilliant *The Age of Reform: From Bryan to F.D.R.* (New York: Alfred A. Knopf, 1956), Chap. 4, though the author tends to underestimate the power and prestige of this group; on the labour reformers, David Montgomery, *Beyond Equality: Labour and the Radical Republicans, 1862–1872* (New York: Vintage Books, 1967).
51. The business element in the highly diverse Progressive movement is analysed by Robert H. Wiebe in *Businessmen and Reform: A Study of the Progressive Movement* (Cambridge, Mass.: Harvard University Press, 1962).
52. C. E. Bonnett, *Employers' Associations in the United States: A Study of Typical Associations* (New York: Macmillan, 1922); Norman Ware *The Labour Movement in the United States, 1860–1895. The Reaction*

of American Industrial Society to the Advance of the Industrial Revolution (Gloucester, Mass.: P. Smith, 1959); Philip Taft, *The A.F. of L. in the Time of Gompers* (New York: Harper, 1957); Herbert G. Gutman, *Work, Culture, and Society in Industrializing America* (New York: Alfred A. Knopf, 1976).

53. See Fredrickson, *op. cit.*, pp. 18–21.
54. Two of the best introductions to Progressive reform and its context are Robert H. Wiebe, *The Search for Order, 1877–1920* (New York: Hill and Wang, 1968) and S. P. Hays, *The Response to Industrialism, 1885–1914* (Chicago: University of Chicago Press, 1963).
55. On the more muted religious developments of this era, see Charles H. Hopkins, *The Rise of the Social Gospel in American Protestantism, 1860–1915* (New Haven, Conn.: Yale University Press, 1940); Henry F. May, *Protestant Churches and Industrial America* (New York: Harper 1949); A. I. Abell, *The Urban Impact on American Protestantism, 1865–1900* (Cambridge, Mass.: Harvard University Press, 1943); though it is clear that not all Protestant clergy succumbed to the conservatism of the Gilded Age, and that the Christian message was still capable of inspiring radical dissent: see H. G. Gutman, Protestantism and the American labour movement: The Christian spirit in the gilded age. *American Historical Review*, Vol. 62(1), October 1966, pp. 74–101.
56. See C. Lasch, *The New Radicalism in America, 1889–1963: The Intellectual as a Social Type* (London: Chatto and Windus, 1966), which emphasized intellectuals' belief in the need for cultural as much as political reform, and also Charles Forcey, *The Crossroads of Liberalism: Croly Weyl, Lippmann and the Progressive Era, 1900–1925* (New York: Oxford University Press, 1961) on the *New Republic* group. Morton G. White's *Social Thought in America: The Revolt Against Formalism* (Boston: Beacon Press, 1963) and Eric Goldman, *Rendezvous with Destiny: A History of Modern American Reform* (New York: Alfred A. Knopf, 1952), emphasize the moral relativism of the reformers; David W. Noble, *The Paradox of Progressive Thought* (Minneapolis: University of Minnesota Press, 1958), stresses the Utopian element in their thinking.
57. See A. S. Link, What happened to the progressive movement in the 1920s? *American Historical Review*, Vol. 64, July 1959, pp. 833–51; Herbert Margulies, Recent opinion on the decline of the progressive movement. *Mid-America*, Vol. 45, October 1963, pp. 250–68; Otis L. Graham, *An Encore for Reform: The Old Progressives and the New Deal* (New York: Oxford University Press, 1968).

Chapter 3

1. See Nathan Glazer, The universalization of ethnicity: peoples in the boiling pot. *Encounter*, Vol. 44(2), February 1975, pp. 8–17, esp. p. 9; Blacks and ethnic groups: the difference, and the political differ-

ence it makes. In N. Huggins, M. Kilson and D. M. Fox, eds, *Key Issues in the Afro-American Experience*, 2 Vols, (New York: Harcourt Brace Jovanovich, 1971), Vol. II, pp. 193–211; and O. Handlin, *The Newcomers* (Cambridge, Mass.: Harvard University Press, 1959), for an older study which plays down the differences between black and white ethnic groups in the urban environment.

2. See Ivan H. Light, *Ethnic Enterprise in America: Business and Welfare Among Chinese, Japanese and Blacks* (Berkeley: University of California Press, 1972); for recent works emphasizing the differences between black and white ethnic groups, see R. Daniels and H. H. L. Kitano, *American Racism: Exploration of the Nature of Prejudice* (Englewood Cliffs, N.J.: Prentice-Hall, 1970), p. 121; and *Report of the National Advisory Commission on Civil Disorders* (Washington, D.C.: Government Printing Office, 1968), p. 144.
3. See Daniel Bell, *The Coming of the Post-Industrial Society: A Venture in Social Forecasting* (Harmondsworth: Peregrine Books, 1976), pp. 309–13.
4. See M. Kilson, Political change in the Negro ghetto, 1900–1940s. In Huggins *et al.*, *op. cit.*, p. 191.
5. Bell, *op. cit.*, pp. 415–9; for a discussion of the Bakke decision concerning reverse discrimination, see below, pp. 286, 296–7.
6. See, for instance, Indian claim on Maine. *Financial Times*, 1 March 1977; and for a further discussion of this development, see below, pp. 157, 299.
7. For a discussion of the colonial and revolutionary background, see above, pp. 25–35.
8. Although the term was popularized as the title of a 1908 play written by a Jewish immigrant, Israel Zangwill, the ideas it embodied gained currency from colonial times.
9. J. Higham, *Strangers in the Land: Patterns of American Nativism, 1860–1925* (New York: Atheneum, 1969), pp. 19–23, 106–25.
10. *Ibid.*, Chap. 1, pp. 23–34 and *passim*.
11. See W. Jordan, *White Over Black: American Attitudes Toward the Negro, 1550–1812* (Chapel Hill: University of North Carolina Press, 1968).
12. See D. J. MacLeod, *Slavery, Race and the American Revolution* (Cambridge: Cambridge University Press, 1974), Chaps. 4 and 5; B. Bailyn, *The Ideological Origins of the American Revolution* (Cambridge, Mass.: Harvard University Press, 1967).
13. A. Zilversmit, *The First Emancipation: The Abolition of Slavery in the North* (Chicago: University of Chicago Press, 1967).
14. A. Lauber, *Indian Slavery in Colonial Times Within the Present Limits of the United States* (New York: Columbia University Press, 1913).
15. That hostility towards slavery which sprang from race prejudice was nonetheless unpleasantly marked in those areas where whites enjoyed absolute dominance. As Tocqueville wrote, 'The prejudice of race appears to be stronger in the states that have abolished slavery than in those where it still exists; and nowhere is it so intolerant as in those states where servitude has never been known.' See Alexis de Toc-

queville, *Democracy in America* (New York: Alfred A. Knopf, 1945), Vol. 1, p. 373. See also J. Kovel, *White Racism: A Psychohistory* (London: Penguin Press, 1970), on such antipathies.

16. See my Red, black and white in nineteenth-century America. In A. Hepburn, ed., *Minorities in History* (London: Edward Arnold, 1978), Chap. 8.
17. See William S. Willis, Divide and rule: red, white and black in the South East. In B. A. Glasrud and A. M. Smith, eds, *Promises to Keep: A Portrayal of Nonwhites in the United States* (Chicago: Rand McNally, 1972), pp. 62–75; Kenneth W. Porter, Relations between Negroes and Indians within the present limits of the United States. *J.N.H.*, Vol. 18, July 1932; Negroes on the Southern Frontier. *J.N.H.*, Vol. 33 January 1948; Negroes and the Seminole War, 1817–1818, *J.N.H.*, Vol. 36, July 1951; Negroes and the Seminole War, 1835–1842, *J.S.H.*, Vol. 30, November 1964; James H. Johnston, Documentary evidence of the relations of Negroes and Indians. *J.N.H.*, Vol. 14, January 1929.
18. See, for instance, Frances Trollope, *Domestic Manners of the Americans*, 5th edn, (London: Richard Bentley, 1839), pp. 175–6.
19. See V. G. Kiernan, *The Lords of Human Kind* (London: Weidenfeld and Nicolson, 1969).
20. See my review article, Return of the native: some reflexions on the history of American Indians. *J.A.S.*, Vol. 8(2), pp. 254–5; and for abolitionist attitudes, my article, The antislavery origins of concern for the American Indians. In C. Bolt and S. Drescher, eds, *Anti-Slavery, Religion and Reform: Essays in Memory of Roger Anstey* (Folkestone: William Dawson and Hamden: Archon, 1980).
21. K. G. Goode, *From Africa to the United States and Then . . . A Concise Afro-American History* (Glenview, Ill.: Scott, Foresman, 1969), p. 40, and Kilson, *op. cit.*, pp. 168–9.
22. See L. F. Litwack, *North of Slavery: The Negro in the Free States, 1790–1860* (Chicago: University of Chicago Press, 1965), Chap. 3, pp. 231–2, 238, 240, 241–2 and *passim*; Howard H. Bell, *A Survey of the Negro Convention Movement, 1830–61* (New York: Arno Press, 1970); B. Quarles, *Black Abolitionists* (New York: Oxford University Press, 1969), Chaps. 4, 5 and 8; A. Pinkney, *Red Black and Green: Black Nationalism in the United States* (Cambridge: Cambridge University Press, 1976), Chap. 2.
23. See L. H. Fishel, Jr, and B. Quarles, eds, *The Black American: A Documentary History* (Glenview, Ill.: Scott, Foresman, 1970), pp. 160–1.
24. See M. Stedman, *Religion and Politics in America* (New York: Harcourt, Brace and World, 1964); Carter G. Woodson, *The History of the Negro Church* (Washington, D.C.: Associated Publishers, 1921).
25. See Litwack, *op. cit.*; J. H. Bracey, Jr, A. Meier and E. Rudwick, eds, *Free Blacks in America, 1800–1860* (Belmont, Calif.: Wadsworth, 1971); Ira Berlin, *Slaves Without Masters: The Free Negro in the Antebellum South* (New York: Pantheon Books, 1974), esp. Chaps. 7, 9–11; E. D. Genovese on free blacks, The slave states of North America. In D. W. Cohen and J. P. Greene, eds, *Neither Slave Nor*

Free: The Freedman of African Descent in the Slave Societies of the New World (Baltimore and London: Johns Hopkins University Press, 1972), pp. 258–77; Howard H. Bell, National Negro conventions of the middle 1840s: moral suasion vs. political action. *J.N.H.*, Vol. 42, October 1957, pp. 247–60; and B. Quarles, *op. cit.*, Chap. 8.

26. Litwack, *op. cit.*, p. 75. Rhode Island removed racial restrictions on the suffrage in 1842—*ibid.*, p. 80; R. W. Shugg, Negro voting in the ante-bellum South. *J.N.H.*, Vol. 22, October 1963.
27. R. C. Dick, *Black Protest: Issues and Tactics* (Westport, Conn.: Greenwood Press, 1974); Chap. 3, esp. p. 121; Litwack, *op. cit.*, pp. 88–9; Quarles, *op. cit.*, Chap. 8.
28. Berlin quoted in Genovese, *Roll, Jordan, Roll* (New York: Vintage Books, 1976), p. 410.
29. 'Declaration of sentiment' of the Fifth Annual Convention for the Improvement of the Free People of Colour in the United States, meeting in Philadelphia in June 1835, reproduced in Fishel and Quarles *op. cit.*, pp. 162–3; and Bell, *National Negro Conventions, op. cit.*, p. 317.
30. See Dick, *op. cit.*, pp. 242–3.
31. See below, pp. 174–5.
32. See Goode, *op. cit.*, p. 43.
33. See R. Bardolph, *The Negro Vanguard* (New York: Random House, Vintage Books, 1961), pp. 57, 62–3, 64–5.
34. See M. L. Dillon, The abolitionists as a dissenting minority. In A. F. Young, ed., *Dissent: Explorations in the History of American Radicalism* (Dekalb, Ill.: Northern Illinois University Press, 1968), pp. 85–6.
35. Quoted in E. B. Reuter, *The Mulatto in the United States* (Boston: Richard G. Badger, Gorham Press, 1918), p. 342.
36. See J. P. Staudenraus, *The American Colonization Movement, 1816–1865* (New York: Columbia University Press, 1961); L. R. Mehlinger, The attitude of the free Negro toward African colonization. *J.N.H.*, Vol. 1, July 1916.
37. See Dick, *op. cit.*, Chap. 4; Litwack, *op. cit.*, Chap. 7; Quarles, *op. cit.*, pp. 47–54; W. H. and J. H. Pease, Antislavery ambivalence: immediatism, expediency, race. In J. H. Bracey, Jr., A. Meier and E. Rudwick, eds, *Blacks in the Abolitionist Movement* (Belmont, Calif.: Wadsworth, 1971), pp. 95–107; L. F. Litwack, The emancipation of the Negro abolitionist. *ibid.*, pp. 67–78.
38. See A. Meier and E. Rudwick, The role of the Blacks in the abolitionist movement. *ibid.*, esp. pp. 114, 118 on black organizations; C. H. Wesley, The Negro in the organization of abolition. *ibid.*, pp. 54–66; Dick, *op. cit.*, pp. 170–7, 194. The quotation is from Quarles, *op. cit.*, p. 55.
39. See Quarles, *op. cit.*, pp. 56–8, 179–86. For a re-evaluation of black escapes from slavery, see L. Gara, *The Liberty Line: The Legend of the Underground Railroad* (Lexington: University of Kentucky Press, 1961).
40. On white feelings that treaties with the Indians were outmoded, see F. P. Prucha, Andrew Jackson's Indian policy: A reassessment. *J.A.H.*,

Vol. 56, 1969, pp. 527–39; for a condemnation of white disregard for Indian treaties, see J. Evarts, *Essays on the Present Crisis* (Philadelphia: Thomas Kite, 1830), p. 99.

41. See K. Turner, *Red Men Calling on the Great White Father* (Norman, Oklahoma: University of Oklahoma Press, 1951).
42. On Jefferson's ability to deceive himself about Indian reactions, see R. Horseman, American Indian policy in the Old Northwest, 1873–1812. *W.M.Q.*, Vol. 18, January 1961, pp. 35–53; on Jefferson, see also F. M. Binder, *The Color Problem in Early National America as Viewed by John Adams, Jefferson and Jackson* (The Hague, Paris: Mouton, 1968), pp. 48–81; N. O. Lurie, Indian cultural adjustment to European civilization. In J. M. Smith, ed., *Seventeenth-Century America: Essays in Colonial History* (Chapel Hill: University of North Carolina Press, 1959), pp. 44–5.
43. Although mixed-blood or light-skinned individuals have always been active in militant black movements, including abolitionism—see for example, Bardolph, *op. cit.*, p. 67, and Litwack, *op. cit.*, p. 182—their importance may have been exaggerated; on Indian half-breeds among the Five Civilized Tribes, see Mary E. Young, Indian removal and land allotment: the civilized tribes and Jacksonian justice. *A.H.R.*, Vol. 64, October 1958, pp. 31–45.
44. For an account of some Indian leaders eventually admired by whites and Indians alike, see A. M. Josephy, Jr, *The Patriot Chiefs: A Chronicle of American Indian Resistance* (New York: Viking, 1969); for the problems of presenting early tribal politics and factionalism in white terms, see R. Berkhofer, Jr, Native Americans. In J. Higham, ed., *Ethnic Leadership in America* (Baltimore, Maryland: Johns Hopkins University, 1978), pp. 121–2.
45. *The Autobiography of Black Hawk*,1833; section reproduced in M. Astrov, ed., *American Indian Prose and Poetry* (New York: Capricorn, 1962), p. 139.
46. See W. T. Hagan, *The Sac and Fox Indians* (Norman, Oklahoma: University of Oklamoma Press, 1958), pp. 57–9 and *passim*.
47. On King Philip, see A. T. Vaughan, *The New England Frontier: Puritans and Indians, 1620–1675* (Boston: Little, Brown, 1965), pp. 310–23; D. E. Leach, *Flintlock and Tomahawk: New England in King Philip's War* (New York: Norton, 1958); Glen Tucker, *Tecumseh* (Indianapolis: Bobbs-Merrill, 1956); N. A. Lurie, *op. cit.*, pp. 43–6, on Powhatan; and on the Iroquois, W. R. Fenton, Problems arising from the historic Northeastern position of the Iroquois. In *Essays in the Historical Anthropology of North America* (Smithsonian Miscellaneous Collections, Vol. 100, 1940).
48. See Marion Starkey, *The Cherokee Nation* (New York: Alfred A. Knopf, 1946); Wilson Lumpkin, *The Removal of the Cherokee Indians from Georgia*, 2 Vols. (New York: Dodd and Mead, 1907); Grant Foreman, *Indian Removal: The Emigration of the Five Civilized Tribes of Indians*, 2nd edn (Norman, Oklahoma: University of Oklahoma Press, 1953).

49. See Mary E. Young, The Creek frauds: a study in conscience and corruption. *M.V.H.R.*, Vol. 47, December 1955, pp. 411–37; A. Debo, *The Road to Disappearance* (Norman, Oklahoma: University of Oklahoma Press, 1941).
50. See M. H. Wright, *A Guide to the Indian Tribes of Oklahoma* (Norman: University of Oklahoma Press, 1971), *passim*; Berkhofer, Native Americans. *op. cit.*, pp. 120, 145–6.
51. See F. P. Prucha, Andrew Jackson's Indian policy. *op. cit.*; see also, by the same author, *American Indian Policy in the Formative Years, 1790–1834* (Lincoln: University of Nebraska Press, 1962), pp. 225–6, 229–31, 233, 238, 243; D. F. Littlefield, *Africans and Seminoles: From Removal to Emancipation* (Westport, Conn.: Greenwood Press, 1977), Chap. 1; W. E. Washburn, Indian removal policy: administrative, historical and moral criteria for judging its success or failure. *Ethnohistory*, Vol. 12, Summer 1965, pp. 274–8.
52. See E. E. Dale, *The Indians of the Southwest: A Century of Development Under the United States* (Norman, Oklahoma: University of Oklahoma Press, 1971).
53. See comments of the New York *Evening Post* and Senator J. C. Calhoun, quoted in M. Steinfield, *Cracks in the Melting Pot: Racism and Discrimination in American History* (Beverly Hills, Calif.: Glencoe Press, 1970), pp. 74–6; and for the attitudes of early American writers to the Mexicans, see C. Robinson, *With the Ears of Strangers: The Mexican in American Literature* (Tucson: University of Arizona Press, 1963), pp. 69–93. For a brief account of the historical background to Mexican-American relations in the United States, see C. McWilliams, *North from Mexico: The Spanish Speaking People of the United States* (New York: Greenwood Press, 1968), pp. 98–108.
54. Of the South-Western tribes, the Apache, Navajo, Shoshone, Ute and Comanche were clearly warlike; the United States, however, proved no more successful in its conduct of relations with peaceful tribes like the Pueblos or the Mission Indians of California, though it recognized their claim to 'civilization'.
55. See below, pp. 180–1, 187.
56. The preceding paragraphs have drawn on: R. F. Heizer and A. F. Almquist, *The Other Californians: Prejudice and Discrimination under Spain, Mexico and the United States to 1920* (Berkeley, Los Angeles and London: University of California Press, 1971), pp. 138–52; L. Pitt, *The Decline of the Californios: A Social History of the Spanish-Speaking Californians, 1846–1890* (Berkeley, Los Angeles and London: University of California Press, 1966), pp. 246, 250, 254–62; R. Landes, *Latin-Americans of the Southwest* (St. Louis: Webster Division, McGraw-Hill, 1965), pp. 10–17; W. R. Kenny, Mexican-American conflict on the mining frontier, *Journal of the West*, Vol. 6(4), October 1967; C. McWilliams, *California: The Great Exception* (New York: Current Books, 1949) and *Brothers Under the Skin* (Boston: Little, Brown, 1964); R. Olmsted and C. Wollenberg,

Neither Separate Nor Equal (San Francisco: California Historical Society, 1971).

57. The Works of Hubert Howe Bancroft, Vol. XXIV, *The History of California, Vol. VII; 1860–1890* (San Francisco: The History Co., 1890), p. 336; see also Rodman W. Paul, The origin of the Chinese issue in California. *M.V.H.R.*, Vol. 25, pp. 181–96.
58. See Light, *op. cit.*, pp. 89, Chap. 9 and *passim*.
59. For a further discussion of the Six Companies, see below pp. 107–8. On the nature of the clans and the origins of the Companies, see W. Hoy, *The Chinese Six Companies: A short, general historical resumé of its origin, function, and importance in the life of the California Chinese* (San Francisco: Chinese Consolidated Benevolent Association, 1942), pp. 6–9; Fong Kum Ngon, The Chinese six companies. *Overland Monthly*, Vol. 23, 2nd ser. January–June 1894, pp. 522–6; Betty Lee Sung, *Mountains of Gold: The Story of the Chinese in America* (New York: Macmillan, 1967), pp. 134–6; C. Wollenberg, ed., *Ethnic Conflict in Californian History* (Los Angeles: Tinnon-Brown, 1970), pp. 79–80.
60. See L. G. Brown: *Immigration: Cultural Conflicts and Social Adjustments* (New York: Arno Press, 1969); R. A. Billington, *The Protestant Crusade, 1800–1860: A Study of the Origins of American Nativism* (New York: Macmillan, 1938); on the notion of a WASP 'core culture', see M. Gordon, *Assimilation in American Life: The Role of Race, Religion and National Origins* (New York: Oxford University Press, 1964); and E. Litt, *Beyond Pluralism: Ethnic Politics in America* (Glenview, Ill.: Scott, Foresman, 1970).
61. For details of early immigrant welfare and fraternal associations, see O. Handlin, *The Uprooted* (New York: Grosset and Dunlap, 1951), Chap. VII.
62. For a survey of some of the recent literature on the persistence of ethnic voting, see R. P. Swierenga, Ethnocultural political analysis: a new approach to American ethnic studies. *J.A.S.*, Vol. 5(1), pp. 59–79, and esp. p. 67, quoting S. P. Hays.
63. See, for instance, R. R. Dykstra and H. Hahn, Northern voters and Negro suffrage: the case of Iowa, 1868. *Public Opinion Quarterly*, Vol. 32, Summer 1968, pp. 202–15; and J. L. Stanley, Majority tyranny in Tocqueville's America: the failure of Negro suffrage in 1843. *Political Science Quarterly*, Vol. 34, September 1967, pp. 412–35.
64. See M. A. Jones, *American Immigration* (Chicago: University of Chicago Press, 1961), pp. 161–9.
65. On Reconstruction, see J. H. Franklin, *Reconstruction After the Civil War* (Chicago: University of Chicago Press, 1961); F. G. Wood, *The Black Scare: The Racist Response to Emancipation and Reconstruction* (Berkeley: University of California Press, 1969); R. Cruden, *The Negro in Reconstruction* (Englewood Cliffs, N.J.: Prentice-Hall, 1969); E. M. Coulter, *The South During Reconstruction, 1865–1877* (Baton Rouge: Louisiana State University Press, 1947); Brock, *op. cit.*

66. See M. L. Calcott, *The Negro in Maryland Politics, 1870–1912* (Baltimore: Johns Hopkins Press, 1969), pp. 61, 63, 79–81 and *passim*.
67. See S. D. Smith, *The Negro in Congress, 1870–1901* (Port Washington, N.Y.: Kennikat Press, 1966), pp. 136, 144; J. Williamson, *After Slavery: The Negro in South Carolina During Reconstruction, 1861–1877* (Chapel Hill: University of North Carolina Press, 1965), pp. 343, 362; V. L. Wharton, *The Negro in Mississippi, 1865–1890* (New York: Harper Torchbooks, 1965), pp. 145–6, 157.
68. For a sample of black petitions and details of the NNLU, see H. Aptheker, *A Documentary History of the Negro People in the United States*, 2 Vols, (Secaunus, N.J.: Citadel Press, 1972), Vol. II, pp. 534–47, 551, 560–1, 562–3, 594–5, 600–6, 615–7, 624–5, 629–41, and on colonization pp. 550–1, 567–8; on the NNLU and black conventions, see Cruden *op. cit.*, pp. 33, 48–51, 58, 65; W. E. B. DuBois, *Black Reconstruction in America, 1860–1880* (New York: Atheneum, 1969), pp. 230–5, 285, 361–7, 416, 456, 495–7, 508, 527, 537, 569, 574; see also Fishel and Quarles, *op. cit.*, pp. 274–80.
69. See, for instance, Wharton, *op. cit.*, pp. 95–9.
70. See Cruden, *op. cit.*, pp. 88–9, 96–8, 104–107, 159; also Smith *op. cit.*, pp. 7, 100; Williamson, *op. cit.*, pp. 313–17, 356, and Chap. 10.
71. See Williamson, *op. cit.*, pp. 368–9, 372–3, 376; Wharton, *op. cit.*, pp. 164–6, 264–5, Chap. 20; J. H. Franklin, *From Slavery to Freedom: A History of Negro Americans*, 4th edn (New York: Alfred A. Knopf, 1974), Chap. 16; R. D. Logan, *The Betrayal of the Negro* (New York: Collier Books, 1967), Chap. 15; A. Harris, *The Negro as Capitalist: A Study of Banking and Business among American Negroes* (Philadelphia: American Academy of Politics and Social Sciences, 1936); L. J. Friedman, *The White Savage: Racial Fantasies in the Postbellum South* (Englewood Cliffs, N.J.: Prentice-Hall, 1970), pp. 131–6. For the economic gains made after emancipation, as well as the huge problems facing blacks, see R. Higgs, *Competition and Coercion* (Cambridge: Cambridge University Press, 1977).
72 For their activities, see J. M. McPherson, *The Struggle for Equality, op. cit.*, G. R. Bentley, *A History of the Freedmen's Bureau* (Philadelphia: University of Pennsylvania Press, 1955); H. L. Swint, *The Northern Teacher in the South, 1862–1870* (Nashville: Vanderbilt University Press, Tennessee, 1941).
73. On the Peace Policy, see E. M. Rushmore, *The Indian Policy During Grant's Administration* (Jamaica, New York: Marion Press, 1914); P. J. Rahill, *Catholic Indian Missions and Grant's Peace Policy, 1870–1884* (Washington, DC: Catholic University of America Press, 1953); L. Tatum, *Our Red Brothers and the Peace Policy of President Ulysses S. Grant* (Philadelphia: J. C. Winston, 1899).
74. See R. W. Mardock, *The Reformers and the American Indian* (Columbia, Mo.: University of Missouri Press, 1971), pp. 36, 83, 110, 217; L. B. Priest, *Uncle Sam's Stepchildren: The Reformation of United States Indian Policy, 1865–1887* (New Brunswick, N.J.: Rutgers University Press, 1942), pp. 174–6; F. P. Prucha, *American Indian Policy*

in Crisis: Christian Reformers and the Indian, 1865–1900 (Norman: University of Oklahoma Press, 1976).

75. See L. E. Burgess, *The Lake Mohonk Conferences on the Indian, 1883–1916* (unpublished Ph.D. dissertation, Claremont Graduate School, 1972), pp. 299–300; see Burgess, pp. 442–7, for a breakdown of the Mohonk Conference membership; for an indication of the regional spread of friends of the Indian, see, for instance, *Annual Report of the Women's National Indian Association, November 17, 1885* (Philadelphia, 1885)—to be referred to henceforth as WNIA, followed by date—pp. 42–7, and of the IRA in its early stages, see list in *Fifth Annual Report of the Executive Committee of the Indian Rights Association, for the Year Ending December 20th 1887* (Philadelphia: IRA, 1888)—henceforth IRA, followed by date.
76. See references to Indian visitors at Mohonk in Burgess, *op. cit.*, pp. 91, 97–8, 102–3, 123–4, 146–7, 157, 172, 198, 224–5, 246, 263, 266, 298, 274, 335, 337–9, 343, 372.
77. Burgess, *op. cit.*, pp. 142, 256, 296.
78. *Ibid.*, pp. 71–2, 21, 17, 323, 310, 83–4, 131–2, 160–3, 184, 189, 215–16 and appendices. For a tribute to the work of Mohonk in harmonizing the activities of other Indian reform groups, see *Proceedings of the Seventh Annual Meeting of the Lake Mohonk Conference 1889* (LMC, 1888), p. 11—henceforth LMC, followed by date.
79. See IRA, 1883, pp. 5, 9, 19; 1884, pp. 7, 9–10, 12–13, 20–2, 37–42; 1892, pp. 4, 9; for a typical account of field work, see IRA, 1913, pp. 6–40; see also *Brief Statement of the Nature and Purpose of the Indian Rights Association with a Summary of its Work for the Year 1892* (IRA Tracts, 2nd series, no. 6), pp. 1–2; *Why the Work of the Indian Rights Association should be Supported* (IRA, Tracts, 2nd ser. no. 24, 1895) on the work of the Washington agent.

    On the Mohonk discussion and objection to proposals for a full-time lobbyist, see LMC, 1888, pp. 97–9, but also pp. 44–8 for an indication of how carefully its envoys to Washington looked after the progress of desired legislation. The Mohonk assembly of 1890 established a standing committee of seven to pursue its objectives between the sessions of the Conference: see LMC, 1890, pp. 110–1.
80. See WNIA, 1883, p. 5; 1884, pp. 3–6, 8, 57–8, 60; 1885, pp. 6, 12; *Address of the President of the Women's National Indian Association* (Philadelphia, 1885), p. 2; A. S. Quinton, *Indians and Their Helpers* (no details), p. 6.
81. See Burgess, *op. cit.*, pp. 57–9, 73, 186–7, 270, on favourable response to female involvement in Indian reform at Mohonk; see tribute to Women's National Indian Association in IRA, 1885, p. 13; to Mohonk in *ibid.*, 1891, pp. 9–10; add to the Indian Rights Association in WNIA, 1884, p. 8.
82. On the dangers of seeming to be merely negative critics, see LMC, 1912, p. 48; for a tribute to the sensitivity of Congressmen to public opinion and those who represented it, IRA, 1884, p. 23, and LMC, 1909, p. 86; and for praise of the responsiveness of Indian Commissioner W. A.

Jones, see IRA, 1900, p. 7. For the polite approach favoured by Mohonk and the tributes it sometimes drew from Indian administrators, see LMC, 1892, pp. 15–6, and LMC, 1913, p. 195.

83. Mardock, *op. cit.*, Introduction, pp. 1–6 and *passim*; F. P. Prucha, ed., *Americanizing the American Indians: Writings by the 'Friends of the Indian', 1880–1900* (Cambridge, Mass.: Harvard University Press, 1973), Introduction. On the sectarian education issue, see Burgess, *op. cit.*, pp. 23–4, 65–7, 78–9, 269; *A Response to Senator Pettigrew* (Indian Rights Association Tracts, 2nd Ser. No. 4, 1897); IRA, 1912, pp. 14–19; and *Shall Public Funds be Expended for the Support of Sectarian Indian Schools?* (IRA Tracts, 2nd Ser. No. 99, 1915). For the official statements of aims for the Indian groups under review see *Brief Statement of the Nature and Purpose of the Indian Rights Association*, *op. cit.*, p. 1; front cover of WNIA, 1884, and LMC, 1883.

84. For a good account of abolitionist ambiguities on race questions, see R. G. Walters, *The Antislavery Appeal: Abolitionism After 1830* (Baltimore: Johns Hopkins University Press, 1976), Chap. 4. Indian reformers usually preferred to think of assimilation in the political and social sense, but there is division on this question. On the willingness of visitors to Mohonk to admit Indians to social equality with whites, see Burgess, *op. cit.*, p. 136; see also LMC, 1886, pp. 9–10, for a suggestion that intermarriage might not be regarded with dismay. For an assessment of 'The Advantages of Mingling Indians with Whites' by Richard H. Pratt, see Prucha, *Americanizing*, pp. 260–71. See Priest, *op. cit.*, p. 147, for the view that urging close contacts between the races did not mean reformer support for miscegenation; see also LMC, 1906, pp. 75–6.

85. For efforts to improve medical and temperance programmes among Indians, see Burgess, *op. cit.*, pp. 311, 246; IRA, 1912, p. 80; *The Alaska Situation* (IRA Tracts, 2nd ser. no. 93, 1914); *Address of the President of the* WNIA, *op. cit.*, pp. 6–7.

86. See LMC, 1911, p. 230, for a view regretting the separation between Indian administrators and anthropologists; for a condemnation of anthropological support for tribalism and a defence of the work of anthropologist Alice Fletcher and others, see LMC, 1903, pp. 51, 60, 73, 79–80, 105.

87. On the debate over peyote at Mohonk, see Burgess, *op. cit.*, pp. 346, 348–52, 333–7; for IRA denunciations of peyote, see IRA, 1917, pp. 67–8 and *Peyote—An Insidious Evil* (IRA Tracts, 2nd ser. no. 114, 1918).

88. On the Indian Homestead Act, see Mardock, *op. cit.*, p. 133; for the experiences of the freedmen, Cruden, *op. cit.*, p. 44.

89. See LMC, 1892, pp. 96–7.

90. On the crusade to take politics out of the Indian service and its partial success, see Burgess, *op. cit.*, pp. 309, 16, 23, 80–1, 138–9, 201; IRA, 1886, *passim*; 1887, pp. 8–13; 1888, pp. 32–8; 1890, pp. 27–30; and IRA Tracts, 2nd ser. no. 9 (1893). On the possibilities of an independent commission to replace the Indian Office, see Burgess, *op. cit.*, p. 357.

91. For the debate about the value of Indian education, see pamphlet by C. C. Painter in Indian Rights Association Papers, ser. I, no. 11 (1892); Herbert Welsh, *How to Bring the Indian Citizenship, and Citizenship to the Indian*, in *ibid*., no. 12 (1892), pp. 7–8, 10–11; Francis E. Leupp, *A Summer Tour among the Indians of the Southwest*, in *ibid*., no. 43 (1897), pp. 24–6; M. K. Sniffen and T. S. Carrington, *The Indians of the Yukon and Tanana Valleys, Alaska* (Philadelphia: IRA, 1914), p. 35, on salvation through education, with a school in every village. On Mohonk aims in Indian education, see Burgess, *op. cit*., pp. 86–7; LMC, 1916, pp. 50–1. The priority given to education by the Women's National Indian Association is indicated in WNIA, 1885, p. 26. For the views of one of the most consistent advocates of Indian assimilation, in education as all else, see R. H. Pratt (ed. R. M. Utley), *Battlefield and Classroom: Four Decades with the American Indian, 1867–1904* (New Haven and London: Yale University Press, 1964), pp. 10, 214 and *passim*. For an IRA denunciation of tribalism, see IRA, 1896, p. 12, and for approval of vocational training, IRA, 1915, pp. 34–5. For Indian attacks on the tribal structure, see Burgess, *op cit*., pp. 121, 287–8, 373.
92. Comment on public opinion in 1867 from G. W. Manypenny, *Our Indian Wards* (Cincinnati: Robert Clarke and Company, 1880) p. xi, and later claim from LMC, 1907, p. 183. For tributes to the value of the reform groups as information agencies and opinion formers, see Burgess, *op. cit*., pp. 21–3, 360, 364, 367–8. For a comparison of the financial and membership status of the Indian and anti-slavery movements, see E. A. Gilcreast, *Richard Henry Pratt and American Indian Policy, 1877–1906: A Study of the Assimilation Movement* (unpublished Ph.D. dissertation, Yale University, 1967), p. 180.
93. See Mardock, *op. cit*., pp. 226–8; LMC, 1907, pp. 181–98 (quotations in text drawn from here, pp. 181 and 195, speech by Merrill E. Gates of the Board of Indian Commissioners). For activities in aid of particular tribes and charitable institutions, see Burgess, *op. cit*., pp. 127–8, 140–2, 191–5, 309; LMC, 1891, pp. 109–11; LMC, 1910, pp. 28–32; LMC, 1908, pp. 8, 76; For the concern of the IRA for certain specific Indian groups, see IRA, 1891, pp. 11–23; IRA Tracts, 2nd ser. no. 55 (1901); no. 58 (1901); no. 61 (1902); no. 68 (1904); 1903, pp. 4–16; 1904, pp. 21–2; 1905, p. 29; 1906, p. 16. On the special contribution of Mohonk reformers to the passage of the Dawes Act, see Burgess, *op. cit*., pp. 23, 50, 74.
94. For a general discussion of missionary endeavour in this period, see Henry E. Fritz, *The Movement for Indian Assimilation, 1860–90* (Philadelphia: University of Pennsylvania Press, 1963); and for the efforts of the reformers in support of missions, and their success, see LMC, 1907, p. 194; WNIA, 1884, pp. 8, 54; 1885, pp. 13, 32. Missionary work is defended against charges that it distracts attention from political questions in WNIA, 1883, pp. 10–13; see also *Sketches of Delightful Work* (WNIA pamphlet on the work of its missionary department, 1892).
95. See F. Svensson, *The Ethnics in American Politics: American Indians* (Minneapolis: Burgess, 1973), pp. 23–4.

96. On the complicated allotment legislation, see W. E. Washburn, *The Assault on Indian Tribalism: The General Allotment Law (Dawes Act) of 1887* (Philadelphia: J. B. Lippincott, 1975).
97. See *The Red Man*, Vol. 3(8), April 1911, pp. 323–32; Vol. 5(1), September 1912, p. 35; for a denunciation of the annuity/rations system, see IRA, 1899, pp. 28–31, and *Report of Hon. Theodore Roosevelt Made to the United States Civil Service Commission, Upon a Visit to Certain Indian Reservations and Indian Schools in South Dakota, Nebraska, and Kansas* (IRA Tracts, 2nd Ser. No. 4, 1893), pp. 13–14.
98. See pamphlets and annual reports of the Indian Industries League, on microfilm in Newberry Library, Chicago, esp. for 1907, 1909/10 and 1915; quotation is from the 1909/10 report, p. 4; for the interest of Mohonk in safeguarding Indian industries, see Burgess, *op. cit.*, pp. 185, 202–4, 244.
99. *The Indian Craftsman*, Vol. 2(5), January 1910, pp. 9–16; quotation from p. 10.
100. For suggestions that reformers were running out of steam and that the work of reform was nearly complete (or the white public thought it was), see *The Red Man*, Vol. 5(5), January 1913, pp. 209–10; Burgess, *op. cit.*, pp. 254, 268, 293, 296, 311, 321, 331; F. E. Partington, *The Story of Mohonk* (Mohonk Salesrooms, 1911), p. 29.
101. See LMC, 1907, p. 184, and Burgess, *op. cit.*, p. 175.
102. See Priest, *op. cit.*, pp. 174–6; Pratt, *op. cit.*, pp. 213–14; LMC, 1886, pp. 9–10, 42; E. G. Eastman, *Pratt: The Red Man's Moses* (Norman: University of Oklahoma Press, 1935), pp. 66, 69–70. On the contemporary inability, even among men of science, to escape evolutionary teaching and the confusion of race and culture, see M. Harris, *The Rise of Anthropological Theory: A History of Theories of Culture* (London: Routledge and Kegan Paul, 1968), pp. 37–8, 138; H. R. Hays, *From Ape to Angel: An Informal History of Social Anthropology* (London: Methuen, 1951), p. 276; G. W. Stocking, *Race, Culture and Evolution: Essays in the History of Anthropology* (New York: Free Press, 1968), pp. 123–4; and J. S. Haller, *Outcasts from Evolution: Scientific Attitudes of Racial Inferiority, 1859–1900* (Urbana: University of Illinois Press, 1971), pp. 35, 98–120, 140–4, 148, 162. And for arguments that both red and black races might both be doomed to extinction, see F. L. Hoffman, *Race Traits and Tendencies of the American Negro* (New York: Macmillan, 1896), pp. 323–4, 328–9.
103. See Reuter, *op. cit.*, pp. 360–1, 366–7, 369–70, 372–3.
104. Argument about an inevitable progression by minorities through stages of adjustment was, of course, developed in part as a rejection of the view that some races and groups were unassimilable; for the classic formulation of the former hypothesis, see R. E. Park, *Race and Culture* (New York: Free Press, 1950).
105. See G. Wootton, *Interest-Groups* (Englewood Cliffs, N.J.: Prentice-Hall, 1970), pp. 25–6.
106. See Fiona Spiers, *The Leadership of the Talented Tenth Among*

Afro-Americans, 1895–1919 (unpublished Ph.D. Thesis, University of Edinburgh, 1974), pp. 104–27.

107. See Reuter, *op. cit.*, pp. 372–3; I. G. Penn, *The Afro-American Press and its Editors* (Springfield, Mass.: John Wiley, 1891); M. Brooks, *The Negro Press Re-examined* (Boston: Cristopher Publishing House, 1959); Spiers, *op. cit.*, pp. 14–15, 19–20, 34, 42, 43–4, 50, 53–5, 101–2, 127, 196, 353–8; Friedman, *op. cit.*, pp. 137–40, 143–9.
108. See F. G. Castles, Towards a theoretical analysis of pressure politics. In E. S. Malecki and H. R. Mahood, eds, *Group Politics: A New Emphasis* (New York: Charles Scribner's Sons, 1972), p. 287.
109. See M. Lipsky, Protest as a political resource. In *ibid*, pp. 170–2; Spiers, *op. cit.*, p. 320.
110. Spiers, *op. cit.*, pp. 288–9, 356–7; H. Bloch, Labor and the Negro, 1866–1910. *J.N.H.*, Vol. 6, July 1965; B. Mandel, Samuel Gompers and the Negro workers, 1886–1914. *Ibid.*, Vol 40, January 1955; G. N. Grob, Organized labor and the Negro worker, 1865–1900. *Labour History*, Vol. 1, Spring 1960; J. D. Hicks, *The Populist Revolt: A History of the Farmers' Alliance and the People's Party* (Minneapolis: University of Minnesota Press, 1931); I. Kipnis and R. L. Moore, 'Flawed Fraternity: The American socialist response to the Negro, 1901–1912. *The Historian*, Vol. 32, November 1969, pp. 1–18; and A. Meier, *Negro Thought in America, 1800–1915* (Ann Arbor: University of Michigan Press, 1963), pp. 184–9.
111. See Light, *op. cit.*, pp. 127–9, 136–9.
112. On the efforts of the Afro-American Council to reconcile militancy and accommodation, see A. Meier, *op. cit.*, pp. 172–4, 176; on Niagara, see *ibid.*, pp. 178–9; E. Rudwick, The Niagara movement. *J.N.H.*, Vol. 42, July 1957; Aptheker, *op. cit.*, pp. 897–915; Fishel and Quarles, *op. cit.*, pp. 357–8, 372–4. For a reappraisal of Washington's conservativism, see August Meier, Toward a reinterpretation of Booker T. Washington. *J.S.H.*, Vol. 23, May 1957, pp. 220–7.
113. See Meier, *op. cit.*, pp. 182–4; L. Hughes, *Fight for Freedom: The Story of the N.A.A.C.P.* (New York: W. W. Norton, 1962), pp. 20–8; Fishel and Quarles, *op. cit.*, pp. 382–5; Aptheker, *op. cit.*, pp. 915–28; B. Joyce Ross, *J. E. Spingarn and the Rise of the N.A.A.C.P., 1911–1939* (New York: Atheneum, 1972), pp. 13–15, 18–20, 20–5; C. F. Kellogg, *N.A.A.C.P.: A History of the National Association of Colored People, 1909–1920*, Vol. I, (Baltimore: Johns Hopkins Press, 1967), Chaps I–III, V–VII and W. D. St. James, *The National Association for the Advancement of Colored People: A Case Study in Pressure Groups* (New York: Exposition Press, 1958), pp. 39–43; and on DuBois's debate about the officially integrationist programme of the NAACP, see F. L. Broderick, The gnawing dilema: separatism and integration, 1865–1925. In Huggins, Kilson and Fox, *op. cit.*, Vol. II, pp. 101–2.
114. See Nancy J. Weiss, *The National Urban League, 1910–1940* (New York: Oxford University Press, 1974), Chaps. 2–6; Fishel and Quarles, *op. cit.*, pp. 385–7.

115. See Weiss, *op. cit.*, pp. 54–5.
116. See below, p. 85.
117. See Friedman, *op. cit.*, pp. 140–3 on the deification of black women.
118. See Spiers, *op. cit.*, Chaps. 4, 6 and 7.
119. For this fundamental change in American social thought, see above pp. 52, 55, 58.
120. Weiss, *op. cit.*, pp. 86–8; and T. L. Philpott, *The Slum and the Ghetto. Neighborhood Deterioration and Middle-Class Reform, Chicago, 1880–1930* (New York: Oxford University Press, 1978), *passim*.
121. See above, p. 61.
122. See Higham, *Strangers in the Land*, *op. cit.*, pp. 86, 169, 173; and below, p. 183.
123. Apart from Kallen probably the best known advocate of cultural pluralism was Randolph Bourne; see his Trans-National America. In R. Bourne, *War and the Intellectuals: Collected Essays, 1915–1919* (New York and London: Harper Torchbooks, 1964), pp. 107–23. Also Higham, *op. cit.*, pp. 123–4, 188, 303–4; Weiss, *op. cit.*, pp. 53–4; Handlin, *op. cit.*, pp. 186–9, 193–4; Jones, *op. cit.*, pp. 225, 261–2; and J. Higham's Introduction in *Ethnic Leadership in America*, *op. cit.*, as well as the subsequent articles on Jewish, German, Eastern and Southern European and Irish leaders.
124. See H. M. Blalock, *Towards a Theory of Minority–Group Relations* (New York: John Wiley, 1967), pp. 93, 118–25, 134–42, 169, 177–8; P. S. Taylor, *An American–Mexican Frontier: Nueces County, Texas* (Chapel Hill: University of North Carolina Press, 1934), pp. 173–5; and N. L. Gonzalez, *The Spanish Americans of New Mexico: A Distinctive Heritage* (University of California: Mexican–American Study Project, Advance Report 9, 1967), pp. 63–6.
125. See Alexander Saxton, *The Indispensable Enemy: Labor and the Anti-Chinese Movement in California* (Berkeley and Los Angeles: University of California Press, 1971); and A. Hinton, Justice for the Chinese. *The West Coast Magazine*, Vol. 11(2), November 1911, pp. 155–60, on the disreputable character of the labour opposition to the Chinese.
126. See Roger Daniels, *The Anti-Japanese Movement in California and the Struggle for Japanese Exclusion* (Berkeley and Los Angeles: University of California Press, 1962).
127. See Light, *op. cit.*, Chaps. 1–6, esp. Chap. 4 on the Kenjinkai, and pp. 98–100 on the differences between the Chinese and Japanese organizations. On the extended black family, see H. Gutman, *The Black Family in Slavery and Freedom, 1750–1925* (Oxford: Oxford University Press, 1976), Chap. 10. See also Bradford Smith, *Americans From Japan* (Philadelphia and New York: J. B. Lippincott, 1948), pp. 226–7, 337; Forrest E. LaViolette, *A Study of Assimilation in the American Community* (Toronto: Canadian Institute of International Affairs, 1945), pp. 42–4, 69.
128. See Yoshi Saburo Kuno, *The Japanese Situation in California* (Tribune

Publishing Company, 1920), pp. 6–7, 11–13, 15; Smith, *op. cit.*, p. 226.

129. See Tamato Ichihashi, *Japanese in the United States: A Critical Study of the Problems of the Japanese Immigrants and their Children* (Stanford, Calif.: Stanford University Press, 1932), pp. 224–6; W. Petersen, *Japanese Americans: Oppression and Success* (New York: Random House, 1971), pp. 50, 57–8; M. Fujita, The Japanese Associations in America, in *Sociology and Social Research*, Vol. 13, January–February 1929, pp. 211–28; 1919 petition from the Association stressing its loyalty, in *California and the Oriental: Japanese, Chinese and Hindus. Report of the State Board of Control of California to Governor William D. Stephens, June 19, 1920. Revised to January 1, 1922* (Sacramento: California State Printing Office, 1922), pp. 221–33; E. M. Boddy, *The Japanese in America* (Los Angeles: E. M. Boddy, 1921), pp. 70–7; and Roger Daniels, The Japanese, in Higham, *Ethnic Leadership in America*, *op. cit.*, pp. 41–4.

130. On Japanese–Chinese hostility, see article by Foo Pan Key, The Yellow Peril. *The West Coast Magazine*, Vol. 20(3), June 1911, p. 326; and on Japanese hostility to Negro migrants, see Petersen, *op. cit.*, pp. 226–7.

131. See Hoy, *op. cit.*, pp. 10, 21–2, 28–9, 33; Fong Kum Ngon, *op. cit.*, p. 525; a defence of Six Company democracy combined with a fear of potential Chinese power in an article by the Rev. William Speer in *Harper's New Monthly Magazine*, Vol. 37, June–November 1868 (New York: Harper and Brothers, 1868), pp. 847–8; Rev. Otis Gibson in *The Chinese in America* (Cincinnati: Hitchcock and Walden, 1877), pp. 339, 341, 345, 399, notes Company waste of funds but admits their moderate political activities and limited powers; on Chinese docility and deference, see A. W. Loomis, The Six Chinese Companies. *The Overland Monthly*, Vol. 1(1), July 1868, p. 226; and for complaints about the independence of Chinese institutions and Company activities, see C. F. Holder, The Chinaman in American politics. *North American Review*, Vol. 166, January–June 1898, pp. 226–30, 232–3; G. B. Densmore, *The Chinese in California* (San Francisco: Pettit and Russ, 1880), pp. 16, 18; T. H. Hittell, *History of California*, Vol. IV (San Francisco: N. J. Stone, 1898), p. 100; and for arguments on both sides, see *Chinese Immigration; Its Social, Moral and Political Effect. Report to the California State Senate of the Special Committee on Chinese Immigration* (Sacramento: California State Printing Office, 1876), pp. 60, 82, 91–2, 122, 186, 188, 194, 205, 208–9 and *passim*; Richard H. Dillon, *The Hatchet Men: The Story of the Tong Wars in San Francisco's Chinatown* (New York: Coward-McCann, 1962), pp. 78, 87–90; Charles C. Dobie, *San Francisco's Chinatown* (New York: D. Appleton Century, 1936), pp. 120–3, 127, 134–5.

132. See *Chinese Equal Rights League of America. Memorial in Support of the Bill to Permit the Naturalization of Americanized Chinese* (no details, Huntington Library), pp. 1–5; Dillon, *op. cit.*, pp. 78–9, 91; Dobie, *op. cit.*, p. 134–5; and F. L. K. Hsu, *The Challenge of the*

American Dream: The Chinese in the United States (Belmont, Calif.: Wadsworth, Minorities in American Life series, 1971), p. 46.

133. See E. S. Redkey, *Black Exodus* (New Haven, Conn.: Yale University Press, 1969), and A. Pinckney, *op. cit.*, Chaps. 1 and 2.

Chapter 4

1. See A. Marwick, *War and Social Change in the Twentieth Century* (London: Macmillan, 1974); N. A. Wynn, *The Afro-American and the Second World War* (London: Paul Elek, 1976), Chap. 1.
2. See above, pp. 51 and 79.
3. Higham, *Strangers in the Land, op. cit.*, p. 214.
4. See A. Spear, The origins of the urban ghetto, 1870–1915. In Huggins, Kilson and Fox, *Key Issues in the Afro-American Experience, op. cit.*, pp. 153–66.
5. See Emmett J. Scott, *The American Negro in the World War* (Chicago: Homewood Press, 1919).
6. See Higham, *Strangers in the Land, op. cit.*, Chap. 8; also H. G. Petersen and G. C. Fite, *Opponents of War, 1917–1918* (Madison, Wis.: University of Wisconsin Press, 1957), and W. Preston, Jr., *Aliens and Dissenters* (New York: Harper and Row, 1963).
7. See Weiss, *The National Urban League, op. cit.*, Chap. 8, esp. pp. 112 and 123.
8. See Nancy J. Weiss, The Negro and the new freedom: fighting Wilsonian segregation. *P.S.Q.*, Vol. 84, March 1968, pp. 61–79; and S. Coben, The failure of the melting pot. In G. B. Nash and R. Weiss, eds, *The Great Fear: Race in the Mind of America* (New York: Holt, Rinehart and Winston, 1970), pp. 144–64.
9. See Ross, *J. E. Spingarn, op. cit.*, Chaps. 2 and 3; Hughes, *Fight for Freedom, op. cit.*, pp. 28–37; Franklin, *From Slavery to Freedom, op. cit.*, Chap. 18.
10. See Burgess, *The Lake Mohonk Conferences, op. cit.*, pp. 354–5, 361–4.
11. See IRA, 1918, pp. 7–8, 66–72.
12. *Thirty-Eighth Annual Report of the Massachusetts Indian Association, November 1920* (Boston, 1920), p. 10.
13. See Hazel W. Hertzberg, *The Search for an American Indian Identity: Modern Pan-Indian Movements* (Syracuse, N.Y.: Syracuse University Press, 1971), pp. 18–19, 57–8, 74, 96, 103, 111, 133; for defences of the off-reservation policy, see *The Quarterly Journal* (henceforth *Q.J.*), Vol. 1(2), 1913, pp. 141–2; and *The American Indian Magazine* (henceforth *A.I.M.*), Vol. 4(3), 1916, pp. 214–15; on the pleasant appearance and intelligence of SAI delegates, see *ibid.*, p. 213.
14. See Hertzberg, *op. cit.*, pp. 75, 96–7, 109, 126, 132.
15. For indications of money difficulties, see *Q.J.*, Vol. 1(4), 1913, p. 342; *Q.J.*, Vol. 2(1), 1914, p. 93, Treasurer's Report; *A.I.M.*, Vol. 4(2), 1916, p. 166; *A.I.M.*, Vol. 4(3), 1916, pp. 227, 230–1. For member-

ship details see Hertzberg, *op. cit.*, pp. 111–12, 146; and for dues, the Society's Constitution, By-Laws, Article 1, *Q.J.*, Vol. 1(2), 1913, p. 224.

16. See Hertzberg, *op. cit.*, p. 153.
17. The Secretary at first received only office expenses and the occasional use of a stenographer—see *Q.J.*, Vol. 1(2), 1913, p. 239; for details of the Secretary's salary, see the Society's Constitution, By-Laws, Article 5, *ibid.*, p. 225. See appeal for voluntary workers in *ibid.*, (3), p. 277.
18. Quotation from SAI Constitution, Article II, Statement of purposes, Section 1, third clause, *ibid.*, (2), p. 223; the circulation figure for SAI propaganda is from *A.I.M.*, Vol. 4(2), 1916, pp. 167–8; on the Society's concern to develop race leadership, see *Q.J.*, Vol. 1(1), 1913, p. 69; *A.I.M.*, Vol. 4(1), 1916, p. 12.
19. For an indication of some grievances of specific Indian groups noted at SAI conferences, see *Q.J.*, Vol. 1(1), 1913, pp. 73–4; their importance was urged in *Q.J.*, Vol. 3(3), 1915, pp. 216–7; (4) p. 287; and for evidence that some of these claims were taken up, Vol. 1(4), p. 409, and *A.I.M.*, Vol. 4(3), 1916, p. 220; for suggestions that the Society should devote more of its time to such matters and its response, see Hertzberg, *op. cit.*, pp. 133, 135, 136, 138, 139, 151.
20. See P. Drucker, *The Native Brotherhoods* (Washington, D.C.: Bureau of American Ethnology, Bulletin 168, 1958), pp. 16ff.
21. For praise of white reform organizations by the Society, see *Q.J.*, Vol. 1(4), 1913, pp. 338–9, 343; *Q.J.*, Vol. 2(3), 1914, pp. 173–4; *Q.J.*, Vol. 2(4), 1914, p. 302; *A.I.M.*, Vol. 4(1), 1916, p. 6; *A.I.M.*, Vol. 6(2), 1918, p. 64.
22. See comments on the need for codification of Indian law, Indian civil rights and action before the Court of Claims in *Q.J.*, Vol. 1(2), 1913, pp. 233, 238; *Q.J.*, Vol. 1(3), 1913, pp. 261–2; *Q.J.*, Vol. 1(4), 1913, pp. 351–2; *Q.J.*, Vol. 2(3), 1914, p. 231; *Q.J.*, Vol. 3(3), 1915, pp. 220–3; *A.I.M.*, Vol. 4(4), 1916, pp. 282–4; *A.I.M.*, Vol. 5(1), 1917, p. 16. The need for action against peyote and for temperance work, as well as Indian interest in this, is stressed in *Q.J.*, Vol. 3(3), 1915, p. 177; *Q.J.*, Vol. 3(4), 1915, pp. 286–7; *A.I.M.*, Vol. 4(3), 1916, pp. 223–4; *A.I.M.*, Vol. 4(4), 1916, pp. 311–4; *A.I.M.*, Vol. 5(1), 1917, p. 207. Allotment is urged in *Q.J.*, Vol. 3(4), 1915, p. 252, though there is a defence of the reservation as a home for the old, poor and ill in *A.I.M.*, Vol. 7(3), 1919, pp. 169–71. On educational needs, see *Q.J.*, Vol. 1(1), 1913, p. 46; *A.I.M.*, Vol. 4(3), 1916, pp. 223–4. For exhortations to pride of race and faith in progress, the Society's Constitution (Article II, first clause) urged that Indians be free to develop as individuals 'according to the natural laws of social evolution'—see *Q.J.*, Vol. 1(1), 1913, pp. 69, 91. On the necessity for self-help, see *Q.J.*, Vol. 1(3), 1913, p. 268; *Q.J.*, Vol. 3(3), 1915, p. 149. Wild West shows are denounced in *Q.J.*, Vol. 2(3), 1914, pp. 224–8. Pratt's comment is quoted in *Q.J.*, Vol. 1(1), 1913, p. 64. For the debate on the value of the Indian Bureau, see *Q.J.*, Vol. 1(2), 1913, p. 106; *A.I.M.*, Vol. 4(3), 1916, pp. 223–4; *A.I.M.*, Vol. 5(4), 1917,

pp. 213–15; *A.I.M.*, Vol. 7(3), 1919, pp. 127, 140, 151, 153. And on all these matters, see Hertzberg, *op. cit.*, pp. 71, 73–4, 97–8, 100, 117, 126, 128, 134, 137, 143–4, 147–9, 152.

23. For the argument that a race organization was not reactionary, see *Q.J.*, Vol. 1(3), 1913, p. 273; on the national Indian day, see *A.I.M.*, Vol. 4(2), 1916, p. 118, and Hertzberg, *op. cit.*, pp. 141–2.
24. See Hertzberg, *op. cit.*, pp. 75, 98–9.
25. See above, p. 88, also *Q.J.*, Vol. 2(1), 1914, p. 67, and below, p. 326.
26. See *Q.J.*, Vol. 2(1), 1914, p. 71; *Q.J.*, Vol. 2(2), 1914, article by F. A. McKenzie; *Q.J.*, Vol. 3(3), 1915, pp. 190, 193–4, 205; *A.I.M.*, Vol. 3(2), 1919, p. 94; and Hertzberg *op. cit.*, p. 126.
27. See *A.I.M.*, Vol. 5(1), 1917, pp. 5–6; *ibid.* (2), p. 69; *ibid.* (3), pp. 13–18, 146–53, 203–4.
28. *A.I.M.*, Vol. 6(3), 1918, pp. 113–4.
29. See Svensson, *The Ethnics in American Politics, op. cit.*, pp. 24–5.
30. See *Q.J.*, Vol. 1(2), 1913, pp. 101, 184–5; *Q.J.*, Vol. 2(1), 1914, pp. 27–8.
31. See *Q.J.*, Vol. 1(1), 1913, pp. 3–4.
32. See below, pp. 156–8.
33. See *Wassaja*, Vol. 1, 1916–17: (1), pp. 1, 3, 4; (2), pp. 2–4; (3), pp. 3–4; (4), pp. 1–4; (5), pp. 1–4; (6), pp. 2–3; (7), p. 3; (8), p. 2; (10), pp. 3–4; (12), p. 3.
34. For the Society and the Press, see *A.I.M.*, Vol. 4(2), 1916, pp. 110–11; Hertzberg, *op. cit.*, p. 137. For tributes to the SAI in other reform-group publications, see IRA, 1912, pp. 40–3; IRA, 1913, pp. 46–9; IRA, 1915, pp. 71–4; IRA, 1916, pp. 64–6; LMC, 1911, p. 88.
35. This was the objective attributed to the Council by the Indian Rights Association publication *Indian Truth*, Vol. 3(3), 1926, p. 3; details of the Council in Hertzberg, *op. cit.*, p. 207.
36. For its activities, see *Indian Truth*, Vol. 3(2), 1926, p. 2; *ibid.*, Vol. 4(2), 1927, pp. 3–4; *ibid.*, Vol. 6(9), 1929.
37. On the Society of Oklahoma Indians, see *The American Indian*, Vol. 1(9), 1927, p. 2; on the Tushkahoma League, *ibid.*, Vol. 2(1), 1927, p. 6, and Vol. 2(3), 1927, p. 4.
38. See *The American Indian*, Vol. 1(5), 1927, p. 7; *ibid.*, Vol. 3(7), 1929, p. 4.
39. See *Indian Truth*, Vol. 4(1), 1927, p. 2. The Indian Welfare Committee of the General Federation of Women's Clubs agitated in the twenties for increased appropriations for the Indian service; see *ibid.*, Vol. 6(1), 1929, p. 1.
40. See Drucker, *op. cit.*, pp. 44–59, 131–4, 159–60. Drucker estimated that many Brotherhood aims had not been achieved but that the movement had developed organizational skills and race pride.
41. For an indication of the tension between the two, see *Indian Truth*: Vol. 1(3), 1924, p. 3; Vol. 1(7), 1924, p. 3; Vol. 2(1), 1925, p. 3; Vol. 2(2), 1925, p. 4; Vol. 2(3), 1925, p. 3; Vol. 2(4), 1925, p. 2. For attacks on the reservation and isolation from whites in *The American Indian*, see Vol.1(5), 1927, p. 8; Vol. 4(2), 1929, pp. 14–15; Vol. 5(1), 1930, p. 4.

42. See *The American Indian*, Vol. 4(2), 1929, pp. 2–3; *ibid.*, Vol. 4(8), 1930, p. 4.
43. See W. E. Washburn, *The Indian in America* (New York: Harper and Row, Colophon Books, 1975), pp. 255–7.
44. See Hertzberg, *op. cit.*, p. 289; *Tenth Annual Report. National Association on Indian Affairs* (New York, 1934), pp. 3–6, 10–12; *Eleventh Annual Report. National Association on Indian Affairs* (New York, 1935), pp. 5–6, 11, 14; *Indian Affairs*, Vol. 2(1), 1934; *ibid.*, Vol. 3(3), 1935; and *Indian Truth*, Vol. 5(10), 1928, p. 1.
45. See Svensson, *op. cit.*, p. 26; *The American Indian*, Vol. 2(2), 1927, p. 4; *ibid.*, Vol. 4(6), 1930, p. 4; *ibid.*, Vol. 4(7), 1930, p. 4; and on Indian diversity, Berkhofer, *Native Americans, op. cit.*, p. 131f.
46. The immigrants increased from 49,000 in 1901–10 to 459,000 in 1921–30. The term 'wetback' derives from the inference that the immigrants had swum across the Rio Grande to avoid legal points of entry. See W. Fogel, *Mexican Americans in Southwest Labor Markets* (University of California, Mexican–American Study Project, Advance Report No. 10, 1967), pp. 191–3; Jones, *op. cit.*, pp. 290–2; and Manuel P. Servin, The pre-World War II Mexican American: an interpretation, *California Historical Society Quarterly*, Vol. 45, 1966, pp. 325–38.
47. C. Robinson, *With the Ears of Strangers*, *op. cit.*, pp. 135, 171, 174.
48. These points are made by most writers on the subject: see especially R. J. Flores, *The Socio-Economic Trends of the Mexican People Residing in Arizona* (San Francisco and Saratoga, Calif.: R. & E. Research Associates, 1973, reprint of 1951 edn), pp. iv, 39, 46; J. Samora and R. A. Lamanna, *Mexican Americans in a Midwest Metropolis: A study of East Chicago* (University of California, Mexican–American Study Project, Advance Report No. 8, 1967), pp. 92–3; Fogel, *op. cit.*, pp. 188, 197; E. G. Shelton, Jr, *Political Conditions Among Texas Mexicans Along the Rio Grande* (San Francisco and Saratoga, Calif.: R. & E. Research Associates, 1974, reprint of 1946 University of Texas thesis), pp. 7, 9–10, 12, 110; Sister Frances Jerome Woods, *Mexican Ethnic Leadership in San Antonio, Texas* (Washington, DC: Catholic University of America Press, 1949), pp. 29, 37, 42, 56, 62.
49. L. Grebler, et al., *The Mexican-American People: The Nation's Second Largest Minority* (New York: Free Press, 1970), p. 559. See also, R. Landes, *Latin-Americans of the Southwest, op. cit.*, p. 12, on the relatively benign policies of New Mexico.
50. Grebler et al., *op. cit.*, p. 561; Landes, *op. cit.*, pp. 62, 66.
51. Gonzales, *op. cit.*, pp. 55–8, 78, 80; Woods, *op. cit.*, pp. 37, 47, 117, 120.
52. Shelton, *op. cit.*, pp. 11, 104–9.
53. Grebler *et al.*, *op. cit.*, p. 546.
54. Gonzales, *op. cit.*, pp. 43–5, 47–8.
55. Woods, *op. cit.*, pp. 69–72; Ruth D. Tuck, *Not With the Fist: Mexican-Americans in a Southwest City* (New York: Harcourt, Brace, 1946), pp. 146–7.

56. See C. Wollenberg, ed., *Ethnic Conflict in California History* (Los Angeles: Tinnon-Brown, 1970), pp. 141–4; Gonzales, *op. cit.*, p. 77.
57. For some general observation on this negative approach, see Tuck, *op. cit.*, pp. 90–2.
58. See Petersen, *Japanese Americans, op. cit.*, pp. 51–3; and Masakazu Iwata, The Japanese immigrants in California agriculture. *Agricultural History*, Vol. 36, 1962, pp. 25–37.
59. See Bradford Smith, *Americans from Japan*, *op. cit.*, pp. 257–8; LaViolette, *A Study of Assimilation in the American Community*, *op. cit.*, pp. 154–7.
60. See Smith, *op. cit.*, pp. 226–7; LaViolette, *op. cit.*, pp. 148–51, 155; Light, *Ethnic Enterprise in America*, *op. cit.*, pp. 175, 178.
61. LaViolette, *op. cit.*, pp. 157–9; Light, *op. cit.*, pp. 173–5; Petersen, *op. cit.*, pp. 59, 186, 199, 203, 225–6, 231–2.
62. See Betty Lee Sung, *Mountains of Gold*, *op. cit.*, p. 136, 139–40; Light, *op. cit.*, pp. 177–8; Daniels, The Japanese, *op. cit.*, p. 46.
63. See Dillon, *The Hatchetmen*, *op. cit.*, pp. 36–7; Hsu, *The Challenge of the American Dream*, *op. cit.*, pp. 48–50; also H. B. Melendy, *Asians in America: Filipinos, Koreans and East Asians* (Boston: G. K. Hall, 1977), Chaps. II–V on white discrimination against Filipinos, their economic problems and attempts to organize; citizenship was granted in 1946.
64. See above, p. 68; E. Rudwick and A. Meier, Black Violence in the Twentieth Century: A Study in Rhetoric and Retaliation, in their *Along the Color Line: Explorations in the Black Experience* (Urbana, Chicago and London: University of Illinois Press, 1977), pp. 224–7, 232–6.
65. See, in *ibid.*, Attorneys black and white: a case study of race relations within the NAACP, pp. 129–73; and The rise of the black secretariat in the NAACP, 1909–35, pp. 94–127. See also the evaluation of the Association in St. James, *The National Association for Colored People*, *op. cit.*, Chap. IX.
66. B. Joyce Ross, *op. cit.*, pp. 48–59.
67. For cautious NAACP praise for The Roosevelt Record, see *The Crisis*, Vol. 47, November 1940, p. 343.
68. See Meier and Rudwick, *op. cit.*, Integration vs. separatism: the NAACP and CORE face challenge from within, pp. 242, 244; and Ross, *op. cit.*, Chaps. 6 and 8. St. James, *op. cit.*, p. 163, cites the fact that the Association has won thirty-four victories out of thirty-eight cases presented before the Supreme Court as 'evidence that it is one of America's most successful pressure groups'.
69. See Goode, *From Africa to the United States, op. cit.*, p. 128; and R. Wolters, *Negroes and the Great Depression: The Problem of Economic Recovery* (Westport, Conn.: Greenwood Press, 1970), esp. pt. 3, on the deficiencies of the NAACP.
70. On the failure of black capitalism, see Patrick Renshaw, The black ghetto, 1890–1940. *J.A.S.*, Vol. 8(1), April 1974, pp. 43–9.
71. See Weiss, *op. cit.*, pp. 282–97, 303–6.
72. On Garvey, see A. J. Garvey, ed., *Philosophy and Opinions of Marcus*

Garvey (New York: Arno Press, 1969); E. D. Cronon, *Black Moses* (Madison: University of Wisconsin Press, 1964); Pinkney, *op. cit.*, Chap. 3; T. G. Vincent, *Black Power and the Garvey Movement* (Berkeley, Calif.: Ramparts Press, 1971); E. C. Fox, *Garvey: The Story of a Pioneer Black Nationalist* (New York: Dodd, Mead, 1972); Tony Martin, *Race First: The Ideological and Organizational Struggles of Marcus Garvey and the Universal Negro Improvement Association* (Westport, Conn.: Greenwood Press, 1976).

73. See W. Record, *The Negro and the Communist Party* (Chapel Hill: University of North Carolina Press, 1951); I. Howe and L. Coser, *The American Communist Party* (New York: Praeger, 1962), pp. 175–273; The origins of nonviolent direct action in Afro-American protest: a note on historical dimensions. In Meier and Rudwick, *op. cit.*, pp. 332–41.
74. See D. A. Shannon, *The Socialist Party of America* (New York: Macmillan, 1955), pp. 150–3, 232, 246.
75. See Meier and Rudwick, The origins of nonviolent direct action, *op. cit.*, pp. 307–32.
76. See N. A. Wynn, *op. cit.*, Chap. 1, esp. pp. 16–20.
77. See H. Garfinkel, *When Negroes March: The March on Washington Movement in the Organizational Politics for F.E.P.C.* (New York: Athenaeum, 1969); Jervis Anderson, *A. Philip Randolph: A Biographical Portrait* (New York: Harcourt Brace Jovanovich, 1973).
78. See L. Ruchames, *Race, Jobs and Politics: The Story of F.E.P.C.* (Westport, Conn.: Negro Universities Press, 1971).
79. See Hughes, *op. cit.*, pp. 99–100.
80. See Wynn, *op. cit.*, Chap. 6; R. M. Dalfiume, The 'forgotten' years of the Negro revolution. *J.A.H.*, Vol. 55(1) 1968, pp. 90–106.
81. See Meier and Rudwick, The origins of nonviolent direct action, *op. cit.*, pp. 347–53; M. Rich, The Congress of Racial Equality and its strategy. In Mahood, *Pressure Groups in American Politics*, *op. cit.*, pp. 197–8.
82. See Roger Daniels, *Concentration Camps U.S.A.: Japanese Americans and World War II* (New York: Holt, Rinehart & Winston, 1971); Petersen, *op. cit.*, Chaps.4 and 5; Smith, *op. cit.*, p. 302; E. H. Spicer *et al.*, *Impounded People: Japanese Americans in the Relocation Centres* (Tucson: University of Arizona Press, 1969).
83. Gonzalez, *op. cit.*, p. 67; Taylor, *An American-Mexican Frontier*, *op. cit.*, pp. 245–6; J. Samora (ed.), *La Raza: Forgotten Americans* (Notre Dame, Ind.: University of Notre Dame Press, 1966), pp. 139, 141–2; Landes, *op. cit.*, p. 74. On the conservatism of servicemen's groups, see M. R. Remond, quoted in and queried by G. Wootton in *Pressure Groups in Britain*, *op. cit.*, pp. 94–5.
84. Dorothy Joan Laxon, *Aspects of Acculturation Among American Indians: Emphasis on Contemporary Pan-Indianism* (unpublished Ph.D. dissertation, University of California, Berkeley, 1972), pp. 168–9, 180; M. L. Wax, *American Indians: Unity and Diversity* (Englewood Cliffs, N.J.: Prentice-Hall, 1971), p. 146; see appeal for better financial support from the tribes at the twelfth convention of the

NCAI reported in *The Christian Century*, 21 September 1955; by 1956 the individual membership fee was $3, tribal membership, according to the size of the tribe, ranged from $25 plus 5 cents per member to $250 plus half a cent per member; individual associate members were charged $10 and organizations $25: see Constitution and By-Laws of the NCAI as amended 2 September 1955 and 1 November 1957.

85. Quotation from NCAI Constitution in *Indian Truth*, Vol. 21(5), 1944, p. 6; see also Svensson, *op. cit.*, pp. 30–1.
86. *Indian Truth*, Vol. 21(3), 1944, pp. 3–4.
87. See, for instance, E. Y. Essien-Udom, *Black Nationalism* (Chicago: University of Chicago Press, 1962); C. E. Silberman, *Crisis in Black and White* (New York: Random House, 1964); F. Barbour, ed., *The Black Power Revolt* (Boston: Porter Sargent, 1968); L. Lomax, *The Black Revolt* (New York: Signet, 1962); F. Broderick and A. Meier, eds, *Negro Protest Thought in the Twentieth Century* (Indianapolis: Bobbs-Merrill, 1965); M. L. King, Jr, *Why We Can't Wait* (New York: Harper and Row, 1964); A. I. Waskow, *From Race Riot to Sit-In, 1919 and the 1960s* (New York: Doubleday, 1966).
88. J. Q. Wilson, *Negro Politics: The Search for Leadership* (New York and London: Free Press, 1960), p. 4.
89. See Rudwick and Meier, Black violence in the twentieth century, *op. cit.*, pp. 230–1 and *passim*.
90. Quoted in Steven F. Lawson, *Black Ballots: Voting Rights in the South, 1944–1969* (New York: Columbia University Press, 1976), pp. 175–6.
91. On the problems involved in defining the various components of black protest as a social movement, see M. Lewis, The Negro protest in urban America. In J. R. Gusfield, *A Reader in Social Movements, op. cit.*, pp. 149–53; on white expectations of how black organizations should act, and reaction to departure from type, see Wilson, *op. cit.*, pp. 114, 138, 140–2.
92. On the differences between NAACP and CORE see Rudwick and Meier, Integration vs. separatism. *op. cit.*, pp. 238–63.
93. See *ibid.*, p. 239; A. J. Matusow, From civil rights to black power: the case of SNCC, 1960–1966. In B. J. Bernstein and A. J. Matusow, *Twentieth-Century America: Recent Interpretations* (New York: Harcourt, Brace and World, 1969), pp. 533–57; Howard Zinn, *SNCC: The New Abolitionists* (Boston: Beacon Press, 1965); Pinkney, *Red, Black and Green, op. cit.*, Chap. 6; for an account of the disillusioning white opposition, see Numan V. Bartley, *The Rise of Massive Resistance: Race and Politics in the South during the 1950s* (Baton Rouge: Louisiana State University Press, 1969); Lawson, *op. cit.*, Chaps. 4, 5, 9 and 10.
94. See below, pp. 299, 340.
95. See Pinkney, *op. cit.*, pp. 117–18, 142, 147–50 and *passim*.
96. See *PUSH*, Vol. 2(1), 1978, pp. 6–8; *Chicago Tribune*, 25 September 1975.

97. See Pinkney, *op. cit.*, pp. 137–40.
98. See Lawson, *op. cit.*, p. 345; Litt, *Beyond Pluralism*, *op. cit.*, pp. 165–6.
99. See below, pp. 296–8.
100. See Pinkney, *op. cit.*, pp. 132–7, 142, 216.
101. See D. P. Moynihan, The professionalization of reform. In Gusfield, *op. cit.*, pp. 245–58; also Lawson, *op. cit.*, pp. 338–9, 344–50 and *passim*; W. R. Keech, *The Impact of Negro Voting* (Chicago: Rand McNally, 1970); Wilson, *op. cit.*, pp. 38–9, 90, 100, 112–13, 164–5.
102. For a typical summary of black progress, drawn from the eighth annual Census Bureau report on the black population, see *Star-News*, Pasadena, 28 July, 1975; see also article, Black success story?, *Economist*, 11 August, 1973; and S. Levitan, *et al.*, *Still a Dream: The Changing Status of Blacks Since 1960* (Cambridge, Mass.: Harvard University Press, 1975).
103. See Renshaw, *op. cit.*, pp. 52–9.
104. The cities particularly involved were Chicago, Cleveland, Oklahoma City, Denver, Oakland, San Francisco, Los Angeles; see Joan Ablon, American Indian relocation: problems of dependency and management in the city. *Phylon*, Vol. 24, 1965, pp. 362–71.
105. See, for instance, S. Hood, Termination of the Klamath tribe in Oregon. *Ethnohistory*, Vol. 19, Fall 1972, pp. 379–92; N. O. Lurie, Menominee termination: from reservation to colony. *Human Organization*, Vol. 31, Fall 1972, pp. 257–70.
106. See below, p. 159.
107. See, in the Newberry Library microfilm collection, NCAI circular *To the People Who Have Settled These United States* (no details): Report of the Field Foundation, Inc.—National Congress of American Indians Workshop Project, *A New Frontier in American Indian History* (1951), pp. 1, 4, 9–10, 15–27; *Proposal for Elements to be Included in a 'Point Four Program for American Indians'* (1951); *Circular of the Executive Council of the N.C.A.I. . . . December 14, 1955*, p. 2; What Indians Want, article in *The Christian Century*, 21 September 1955; NCAI Thirteenth Annual Convention, September 24–28, 1958; NCAI Minutes of the Annual Meeting, Executive Council, 1 November 1957; *Declaration of Trust Establishing the N.C.A.I. Fund* (1957); NCAI Financial Statements, 31 December 1958; Release of 23 March 1959, *Official American Indian Leaders Wind Up Week-Long Session: Denounce White House Picketing by Unrepresentative Tribe*; 13 September 1963, Grand Pacific Hotel, Bismark, North Dakota, *Remarks by Attorney General Robert F. Kennedy Before the N.C.A.I.*, pp. 3–6; McNickle's comments are from his address at the 78th annual meeting of the IRA, 1961, in *Indian Truth*, Vol. 38(1), pp. 4–5.
108. See Robert Burnette and John Koster, *The Road to Wounded Knee* (New York: Bantam Books, 1974), *passim.* See also, Pine Ridge report, NCAI *Bulletin*, August 1975, pp. 1, 6, for an account of the BIA and Interior Department Investigation.

109. *National Indian Youth Council Policy Statement to the American Indian People*, Adopted Annual Meeting, Stewart, Nevada (NIYC, Inc., 11 August 1973); Laxon, *op. cit.*, p. 178; National Indian Youth Council's *Annual Report, 1977*; and Berkhofer, Native Americans, *op. cit.*, pp. 134–6.
110. Board Report of the NIYC, August 1975.
111. NCAI pamphlet of 1966; NCAI pamplet entitled *The Indians of the United States Seek Together to Attain in Their Own Plans and Action the Full Promise of Citizenship* (NCAI, Washington, n.d.); Laxon, *op. cit.*, pp. 172–3.
112. See Svensson, *op. cit.*, pp. 42–3; Laxon, *op. cit.*, pp. 173–4, 184–5; membership claim in NTCA letter, *To: The President of the United States the Honorable Gerald Ford The White House*; see also James Wilson, *The Original Americans: U.S. Indians* (London: Minority Rights Group, Report No. 31, 1976), p. 24. On the National Indian Education Association, see *What You Should Know About N.I.E.A. in 1975*, information leaflet in the Newberry Library's Indian Center.
113. See Laxon, *op. cit.*, pp. 50–100.
114. See the NAC's *Red Letter*, August 1975, copy in the Newberry Library's Indian Center.
115. For an indication of similar material goals compare NCAI policy statements with NIYC Policy Statement, *op. cit.*, and *A Program of Action for Executive, Legislative, and Judicial Branches of United States Government. Presented by the Board of Directors of National Tribal Chairmen's Association. Wendell Chino, President. March 1975.*
116. NCAI *Bulletin*, July 1975, pp. 17–20; NIYC Policy Statement, *op. cit.*, p. 3.
117. For a statement on the distinctive Indian status by a prominent spokesman, see Vine Deloria, Jr, *We Talk, You Listen* (New York: Macmillan, 1970). Among the most important recent legal victories for the Indian should be included the partial recognition of the fishing rights of Washington tribes and the settlement of the Alaskan land claims.
118. NCAI Bulletin, *op. cit.*, pp. 1, 2, 6–7, 14–15; Wilson, *op. cit.*, pp. 6–9, 23–5; NTCA address to President Ford, *op. cit.*, pp. 2, 3, 5; NIYC Policy Statement, *op. cit.*, p. 3. The Commission's task forces were concerned with trust responsibilities and treaties; tribal government; federal administration and the structure of Indian affairs; federal, state and tribal jurisdiction; Indian education; Indian wealth; reservation resource development and protection; urban and rural non-reservation Indians; Indian law revision: consolidation and codification; terminated and non-federally recognized Indians; and alcohol and drug abuse. Quotation about the task forces from Vine Deloria in *Los Angeles Times*, 17 August 1975, pt. IV, p. 5. For a convenient summary of the voluminous Commission findings, see *Summary Task Force Reports. American Indian Policy Review Commission* (ed. A. T. Anderson; courtesy Union Carbide Corporation, December 1976).

119. See Laxon, *op. cit.*, pp. 189, 199ff. for a discussion of Indian political problems at the beginning of the 1970s; and Svensson, *op. cit.*, pp. 39–45. The current Indian Education Act encourages Indians to develop their own programmes in the public schools and to run their own schools, but being administered by the Department of Health, Education and Welfare, it is not subject to BIA control or delays.
120. See Vine Deloria, *Custer Died For Your Sins: An Indian Manifesto* (New York: Macmillan and Collier-Macmillan, 1969), Chap. 4; for a discussion of some the issues raised by Deloria, see Laxon, *op. cit.*, pp. 182–3, 217; Bernard L. Fontana, Savage Anthropologists and Unvanishing Indians of the American Southwest, in *The Indian Historian*, Vol. 6(1), Winter 1973; Mario D. Zamora, Moral, immoral science: the case for cultural anthropology. *Ibid.*, Vol. 6(2), Spring 1973; and Wendell H. Oswalt. *This Land Was Theirs: A Study of North American Indians* (New York: John Wiley, 1973), pp. 592–5.
121. See Karen C. Wong, *Chinese History in the Pacific Northwest* (no details, USA, 1972), pp. 103–5, 110–11, 116–17, 119–20; D. Y. Yuan, Voluntary Segregation: A Study of New York Chinatown, in M. L. Barron, *Minorities in a Changing World* (New York: Alfred A. Knopf, 1967), pp. 263–76; F. W. Riggs, *Pressures on Congress: A Study of the Repeal of Chinese Exclusion* (New York: King's Crown Press, 1950), esp. Chaps 7, 9 and pp. 194–6.
122. See Petersen, *op. cit.*, pp. 126, 138–43, 221–32; Daniels, Japanese Americans. *op. cit.*, pp. 59–61.
123. L. and M. Shannon, *Minority Migrants in the Urban Community. Mexican and Negro Adjustment to Industrial Society* (Beverly Hills, Calif.: Sage Publications, 1973), pp. 19–21; Wollenberg, *op. cit.*, pp. 144–5; Joseph L. Love, La Raza: Mexican-Americans in rebellion. In Glasrud and Smith, *Promises to Keep*, *op. cit.*, p. 358; Pitt, *The Decline of the Californios*, *op. cit.*, pp. 293–4.
124. See Fogel, *op. cit.*, pp. 174, 176–7, 182, 184–5, 191.
125. See Jennifer Hursfield, The educational experiences of Mexican Americans: 'cultural pluralism' or internal colonialism? *Oxford Review of Education*, Vol. 1(2), 1975, p. 137.
126. See Hurstfield, *op. cit.*, pp. 138–49, espec. p. 146; Landes, *op. cit.*, pp. 66–7, 85; J. Samora, ed., *La Raza: Forgotten Americans, op. cit.*, pp. 51, 55, 138–42; Woods, *op. cit.*, pp. 39, 101–4, 107–9; Gonzalez, *op. cit.*, p. 67; Tuck, *op. cit.*, pp. 162–3; Taylor, *op. cit.*, pp. 244–245.
127. See Gonzalez, *op. cit.*, pp. 58–77; Love, *op. cit.*, pp. 355–63; and articles by Antonio Camejo, A report from Aztlan: Texas Chicanos forge own political power, and Herring, Reies Lopez Tijerina: Don Quixote in New Mexico. In E. Simmen, ed., *Pain and Promise: The Chicano Today* (New York and London: New American Library, Mentor Books, 1972), pp. 240–8, 286–96.
128. For information on recent pressure groups and their problems, see Samora, *op. cit.*, pp. 51, 55–8, 138–46; Grebler *et al.*, pp. 545–58, 566–70; Samora and Lamanna, *op. cit.*, pp. 85–9, 92–9; Gonzalez,

op. cit., pp. 64–79, 81; Woods, *op. cit.*, pp. 37, 39, 56, 62, 63–4, 81, 104–12, 119–21; Heizer and Almquist, *The Other Californians*, *op. cit.*, p. 153; Pitt, *op. cit.*, p. 296; Tuck, *op. cit.*, pp. 149–50, 160–1; Taylor, *op. cit.*, pp. 245–9, 263–6; Landes, *op. cit.*, pp. 65–6, 72, 74–5, 83–4, 94.

129. See Pinkney, *op. cit.*, pp. 121–2, 211–12, 230; also *PUSH*, *op. cit.*, p. 7, for support for coalitions among ethnic groups at the local political level.
130. See Landes, *op. cit.*, p. 72; Grebler *et al.*, pp. 568–9; Samora, *op. cit.*, pp. 139, 142–3; Samora, *op. cit.*, pp. 49, 58, 146; Gonzalez, *op. cit.*, p. 80; Samora and Lamanna, *op. cit.*, p. 99 (source of quotation from the *Latin Times*); Taylor, *op. cit.*, pp. 268–9; Fogel, *op. cit.*, pp. 174, 181, 183–5, 189, 197; Hertzberg, *op. cit.*, *passim*; V. Deloria, *Custer*, *op. cit.*, Chap. 8; J. O. Waddell and J. M. Watson, *The American Indian in Urban Society* (Boston: Little, Brown, 1971), pp. 175, 239; Laxon, *op. cit.*, pp. 179–80; Petersen, *op. cit.*, pp. 226–7.
131. See, on bureacratization, M. N. Zald and R. Ash, Social movement organizations: growth, decay, and change. In Gusfield, *op. cit.*, pp. 516–37. See also Jeffrey M. Berry, *Lobbying for the People: The Political Behavior of Public Interest Groups* (Princeton, N.J.: Princeton University Press, 1977), pp. 176, 269, 280–4.
132. See, for instance, John Bodnar, *Immigration and Industrialization: Ethnicity in an American Mill Town, 1870–1940* (Pittsburgh: University of Pittsburgh Press, 1977), pp. 154–5.
133. See J. R. Pole, *The Pursuit of Equality in American History* (Berkeley and Los Angeles: University of California Press, 1978), esp. Chap. 9; also R. Jeffreys-Jones, *Violence and Reform in American History* (New York: New Viewpoints, 1978).

Chapter 5

1. I am indebted to Dr P. Haffenden for the New England references here and in Note 2. See William Wood, *New-England's Prospect, etc.* (Boston, Prince Society, 1865; orig. publ. 1635), pp. 108–9.
2. Essex Result, quoted in R. J. Taylor, *Massachusetts, Colony to Commonwealth* (Chapel Hill: University of North Carolina Press, 1961), p. 81.
3. See Kraditor, *Means and Ends in American Abolitionism*, *op. cit.*, Chap. 3; Lutz, *Crusade for Freedom*, *op. cit.*, pp. 104, 112–13, 117–19, 121, 124–5; and B. G. Hersh, *The Slavery of Sex: Feminist Abolitionists in America* (Urbana: University of Illinois Press, 1978), Chap. 1.
4. Lutz, *op. cit.*, pp. 233–7.
5. See Curti, *Peace or War*, *op. cit.*, p. 114, on initial discrimination against women in the peace movement; Tyler, *Freedom's Ferment*, *op. cit.*, pp. 448–50, on similar problems in the temperance crusade.
6. For a discussion of part of their output—the 'domestic novels'—see H. W. Papashvily, *All The Happy Endings* (New York: Harper and

Brothers, 1956), and James D. Hart, *The Popular Book: A History of America's Literary Taste* (New York: Oxford University Press, 1950). Indeed, the sentiments they expressed should have won male approval, had they really believed their own propaganda about women's role.

7. See Flexner, *Century of Struggle*, *op. cit.*, pp. 73, 81; Hersh, *op. cit.*, Chap. 6; *Proceedings of the Woman's Rights Conventions Held at Seneca Falls and Rochester, N.Y., July and August, 1848* (reprinted New York: Arno Press, 1969); and N. F. Cott, *The Bonds of Womanhood. Women's Sphere in New England, 1780–1835* (New Haven: Yale University Press, 1977), esp. Introduction, Chaps. 1, 2 and Conclusion.
8. Augustus Longstreet, quoted in A. F. Scott, *The Southern Lady: From Pedestal to Politics, 1830–1930* (Chicago and London: University of Chicago Press, 1970), p. 5. And see Barbara Welter, The cult of true womanhood: 1820–1860. *American Quarterly*, Vol. 18, Summer 1966, pp. 151–74, for a general account of this ideal.
9. Scott, *op. cit.*, Chaps. 1–3.
10. Flexner, *op. cit.*, p. 82; Hersh, *op. cit.*, Chap. 2, esp. pp. 74–5; and E. C. DuBois, *Feminism and Suffrage: The Emergence of an Independent Women's Movement in America, 1848–1869* (Ithaca and London: Cornell University Press, 1978), Chap. 1.
11. For contrasting views about the motives and risks involved in the Fifteenth Amendment, see J. H. and La Wanda Cox, Negro suffrage and Republican politics: the problem of motivation in reconstruction historiography. *J.S.H.*, Vol. 33, 1967, pp. 303–30, and W. Gillette, *The Right to Vote: Politics and the Passage of the Fifteenth Amendment* (Baltimore: Johns Hopkins University Press, 1965).
12. On attitudes to women's suffrage during the debates, see Pole, *The Pursuit of Equality in American History*, *op. cit.*, pp. 174–5, 304–5. On the general impact of war and postwar developments, see Hersh, *op. cit.*, pp. 67–74; DuBois, *op. cit.*, pp. 54–5, 61–2, 75–6, 85–9.
13. See postwar testimony of anti-slavery lecturer, Frances Harper, in E. C. Stanton *et al.*, *The History of Woman Suffrage*, Vol. II (New York: Fowler and Wells, 1881–1922, henceforth *H.W.S.*), pp. 391–2: see also pp. 193–4; on the later enforced conservatism of black women see above, pp. 101–2. And see DuBois, *op. cit.*, pp. 70–71.
14. See A. P. Grimes, *The Puritan Ethic and Woman Suffrage* (New York: Oxford University Press, 1967), Chaps. 2 and 3; it was assumed that women would be a conservative political element, at this stage.
15. A. Kraditor, *The Ideas of the Woman Suffrage Movement, 1890—1920* (New York: and London: Columbia University Press, 1965), p. 5.
16. I. H. Harper, *Life and Work of Susan B. Anthony* (Indianapolis and Kansas City: Bowen-Merrill, 1898), Vol. I, pp. 390–4; L. Eaves, *A History of California Labor Legislation, With an Introductory Sketch of the San Francisco Labor Movement* (Berkeley: Berkeley University Press, 1910), p. 313. Clearly, female apathy was a great obstacle in California, as elsewhere, at this time: see fragment of letter from Clara

Foltz in Ida Husted Harper Collection, HM 10621, Henry E. Huntingdon Library, San Marino, California.

17. *Woman's Journal*, Vol. 27, 23 May 1896, p. 164.
18. See information in Harper, *op. cit.*, Vol. 2, pp. 863–74.
19. See, for instance, *Woman's Journal*, Vol. 27, 5 December 1896, article by Harriet May Mills.
20. See Grimes, *op. cit.*, Chap. 4; Gusfield, *Symbolic Crusade*, *op. cit.*, Chap. 4; A. Sinclair, *The Better Half* (New York: Harper and Row, 1965), Chap. 19; D. Morgan, *Suffragists and Democrats* (Lansing: Michigan State University Press, 1972), pp. 21–2; M. Rogin and J. Shover, *Political Change in California* (Westport: Greenwood, 1970), Chap. 1.
21. *Woman's Journal*, Vol. 27, 23 May 1896, p. 164.
22. *Women's Journal*, Vol. 27, 11 July 1896, p. 218, and Harper, *op. cit.*, Vol. 2, pp. 873–4.
23. *H.W.S.*, 1883–1900, Vol. 4, pp. 492; Harper, *op. cit.*, Vol. 2, pp. 883–884; *Woman's Journal*, Vol. 27, 21 November 1896, p. 373.
24. D. J. Spencer, *A History of the Woman's Christian Temperance Union of Northern and Central California. Written by Request of the State Convention of 1911* (Oakland, Calif.: West Coast Printing Company, 1911), pp. 26–7, 29, 126; M. A. Garbutt, *Victories of Four Decades: A History of Woman's Christian Temperance Union of Southern California, 1883–1924* (no details, 1924), pp. 128–9; G. M. Ostrander, *The Prohibition Movement in California, 1848–1933* (Berkeley and Los Angeles: University of California Press, 1957), p. 58. Nationally the WCTU commitment to women's suffrage was marked by the creation of a committee and then a department of franchise, 1881–2, after some opposition to it in the 1870s. The Union was founded in 1874. See E. P. Gordon, *Women Torch-Bearers: The Story of the Woman's Christian Temperance Union* (Evanston, Ill.: WCTU Publishing House, 1924), pp. 194, 196.
25. On the general feminist-temperance link, see Hersh, *op. cit.*, pp. 167–70; Ostrander, *op. cit.*, p. 53, on its dangers; and Gusfield, *op. cit.*, pp. 88–91.
26. Ostrander, *op. cit.*, pp. 78–83.
27. For a general statement of liquor-interest opposition to women's suffrage, see Gordon, *op. cit.*, pp. 192–3, 201, 204.
28. Anthony to Elizabeth Boynton Harbert, Tenafly, New Jersey, 19 March 1882, in Harbert Collection Miscellaneous 'A' File, Box 2, Huntington Library.
29. Quoted in Harper, *op. cit.*, Vol. 2, pp. 881–2.
30. Quoted in *Woman's Journal*, Vol. 27, 21 November 1896, p. 376; see testimony of Abigail Scott Dunaway, *Path Breaking: An Autobiographical History of the Equal Suffrage Movement in the Pacific Coast States*, 2nd edn (Portland, Oregon: James Kerns and Abbott, 1914), p. 205, that Anthony kept the two issues apart in the 1896 California campaign.
31. *Woman's Journal*, Vol. 27, 7 November 1896, p. 356.
32. *H.W.S.*, 1883–1900, Vol. 4, p. 492.

33. *Ibid.*, p. 273. The Union set great store by organization as, in Frances Willard's words, 'the sun glass which brings to a focus scattered influence and effort'; by 1883 'every state and territory had been organized with regularly elected officers', and by 1886 the Union had available 'eleven field workers, eight organizers and three lecturers', apart from the state workers. See pamphlet *What is the W.C.T.U.?* (no details), p. 3, and A. D. Hays, *Heritage of Dedication. One Hundred Years of the National Woman's Temperance Union, 1874–1974* (Evanston, Ill.: Signal Press, 1973), p. 41.
34. *Woman's Journal*, Vol. 27, 7 November 1896, p. 356.
35. *Ibid.*, 23 May 1896, pp. 164; Harper, *op. cit.*, Vol. 2, p. 868; and *H.W.S.* 1883–1900, Vol. 4, pp. 491–2, 499; their figures differ slightly.
36. *Woman's Journal*, Vol. 27, 7 November 1896, p. 360.
37. *Ibid.*, 15 August 1896, p. 264; 5 September 1896, p. 287; 3 October 1896, p. 320.
38. *Ibid.*, Vol. 27, 21 November 1896, p. 372.
39. See biographical sketches of the leading suffragists in Reda Davis, *California Women: A Guide to Their Politics, 1885–1911* (San Francisco: California Scene, 1967), pp. 137–84.
40. Eaves, *op. cit.*, pp. 311, 314–15, and Davis, *op. cit.*, pp. 147, 158, 161, 183–4.
41. E. G. Ruddy, ed., *The Mother of Clubs. Caroline M. Seymour Severance: An Estimate and Appreciation* (Los Angeles: Baumgardt, 1906), pp. 24, 34, 45, 49; and J. M. Jensen, After slavery: Caroline Severance in Los Angeles. *Southern California Quarterly*, Vol. 48(2), June 1966, pp. 179, 181.
42. Undated pamphlet entitled, An open letter to women's clubs. An essential step forward, Harbert Collection, File 136, Box 9.
43. Quoted in article on the club movement by Sidona V. J. McIsaac, pp. 3–4, 24 January 1908, in Caroline Severance Collection, Box 29, Huntington Library.
44. Letter by S.S.D. about the purpose of the General Federation of Women's Clubs in Severance Collection, Box 15.
45. See M. W. Wells, *Unity in Diversity: The History of the General Federation of Women's Clubs* (Washington: General Federation of Women's Clubs, 1953), on the movement; letters to Mrs Severance disapproving of this caution, 18 August 1912, 16 July 1913, in Severance Collection, Box 14; Ruddy *op. cit.*, on race questions, pp. 72–5; and Jensen, *op. cit.*, p. 184.
46. See statements of aims in *The Club Woman*, journal of the General Federation, Vol. 11(5), January 1904, pp. 3–4; Vol. 11(8), April 1904, pp. 5–6; Vol. 11(12), August 1904, pp. 3, 5.
47. H. E. Bandini to I. H. Harper, 20 September 1909, Pasadena, in Harbert Collection, File 28, B (Miscellaneous).
48. See, for instance, *H.W.S.*, Vol. 4, p. 273, 493–4; Harper, *op. cit.*, Vol. 2, p. 890; *Woman's Journal*, Vol. 27, 7 November 1896, p. 356.
49. See Harper, *op. cit.*, Vol. 2, p. 890; *Woman's Journal*, Vol. 27, 5 September 1896, p. 288.
50. See, for instance, S. Solomons, *How We Won the Vote in California: A*

True Story of the Campaign of 1911 (San Francisco: New Woman Publishing Company, 1911), pp. 3–4.

51. Kraditor, *The Ideas of the Woman Suffrage Movement*, *op. cit.*, p. 5.
52. See *Winning Equal Suffrage in California. Reports of Committees of the College Equal Suffrage League of Northern California in the Campaign of 1911* (National College Equal Suffrage League of Northern California, 1913), p. 9.
53. Details reported in *Woman's Journal*, Vol. 27, 28 November 1896, pp. 382–3.
54. Solomons, *op. cit.*, pp. 4–13; Rogin and Shover, Chaps. 2–3.
55. For this hope, see letter from F. J. Garrison to Mrs Severance, 15 October 1911, in Severance Collection, Box 17.
56. Solomons, *op. cit.*, pp. 16, 17, 25–33; *Woman's Journal*, Vol. 42, 16 September 1911, p. 291.
57. J. H. Braly, *Memory Pictures: An Autobiography* (Los Angeles: Meuner, 1912), pp. 225–7.
58. Braly, *op. cit.*, pp. 227–8, 237–48; Harbert Collection, Box 10, File 143, for various reports on Braly's activities.
59. See tributes to Braly in Severance Collection, Box 24, Elizabeth Lowe Watson to Severance, 18 December 1910; in Harbert Collection, Box 9, File 137, ms. entitled, 'How California Won Suffrage for Women'; and at the back of his autobiography, pp. 250–63. For a complaint about Braly's high-handedness, see Harbert Collection, Box 10, File 143, Letter from Grace C. Simons, Los Angeles, to Mrs C. W. McCulloch. Also on Braly, H.W.S., 1900–20, Vol. 6, pp. 40–2.
60. Harbert Collection, Box 9, File 137.
61. On Mrs Stanton, see Harbert Collection, Box 10, File 138, 'Susan B. Anthony. An Address Delivered Before the Friday Morning Club on the Anniversary of the Birth of Susan B. Anthony, February 15, 1911', p. 3; on the role of men in the two national societies, see Harbert Collection, Box 2, letter from Susan B. Anthony to Mrs Herbert, from Rochester, New York, 7 July 1880.
62. For testimony to the efforts of her husband and other men, see Mrs Harbert, Harbert Collection, Box 9, File 137, 'How California Won Suffrage for Women', and letters from Mrs Harbert to Mrs Severance of 22 September and 16 October 1911 in Box 18 of Severance Collection; see also letter from Mrs Watson to Mrs Severance, August 1910, in Severance Collection, Box 24; and for complaint about male caution see letter, 11 February 1909, in Alice Locke Park Collection, PK 208, Huntington Library.
63. See 'Another Own Story' by Mrs Severance in collaboration with E. G. Ruddy in Severance Collection, Box 29, and correspondence in Box 11.
64. See letters from Foltz to Clara Bewick Colby 1904–9, in Colby Collection, CC23 (1–4), Huntington Library. After the death of her husband, a Republican, it is surely no accident that Mrs Severance felt able to move steadily to the left: see Jensen, *op. cit.*, p. 183.
65. *Winning Equal Suffrage in California*, pp. 17–18, 21, 23, 32, 51–2, 61–2, 68, 78–82, 119; incomplete letter from 1671 North Raymond

Avenue in Harbert Collection, Box 10; letter of February 1911 of the California Equal Suffrage Association in Park Collection, PK 208 (1–13); Solomons, *op. cit.*, pp. 38, 53, 57; *Woman's Journal*, Vol. 42, 25 March 1911, p. 93; H.W.S., Vol. 6, pp. 42–9.

66. *Winning Equal Suffrage in California*, p. 94; Clara Foltz to Clara Colby, 26 June 1908, Los Angeles, Colby Collection, CC 23.
67. *Winning Equal Suffrage in California*, pp. 76–7, 101.
68. Mrs Sargent's husband, a businessman and politician, agitated for women's suffrage while he was in Washington; Mrs Goodrich married first a successful businessman and California legislator, sympathetic to women's interests, and then a prosperous architect; Mrs Sperry ran her husband's lucrative flour mills in Stockton after his death: see Reda Davis, *op. cit.*, pp. 159–60, 170, 173–4; the testimony of Susan Anthony in letters to Clara Colby, 26 July 1896, from San Francisco, and 19 December 1903, from Rochester, in Colby Collection, C3; Clara Foltz to Clara Colby in *ibid.*, CC23, 6 June 1904, 8 April 1909 from San Francisco and Los Angeles respectively. Other key California contributors were Mrs Foltz, Mrs Mary J. Gamage, Mrs Mary McHenry Keith and Mrs Elizabeth Lowe Watson. See Solomons, *op. cit.*, p. 53. On Britain, see B. Harrison, *Separate Spheres: The Opposition to Women's Suffrage in Britain* (London: Croom Helm, 1978), pp. 27–31, Chaps. 4, 5, pp. 127, 137–42, 193.
69. *Winning Equal Suffrage in California*, p. 102.
70. Solomons, *op cit.*, p. 38.
71. *Woman's Journal*, Vol. 42, 16 September 1911, p. 292; *Winning Equal Suffrage in California*, pp. 86–7.
72. *Woman's Journal*, Vol. 42, 3 June 1911, p. 175; 17 June 1911, p. 189; Solomons, *op. cit.*, pp. 42–3; and a Political Equality League pamphlet in Folder 7 of the Harbert Collection.
73. Spencer, *op. cit.*, pp. 95–6.
74. *Ibid.*, p. 142.
75. See, for example, Vol. 4(22), 30 May 1889; and P. H. Odegard, *Pressure Politics: The Story of the Anti-Saloon League*, *op. cit.*, pp. 85–7. In fact, eight years elapsed—and a considerable period in other states conferring the suffrage—between granting the women the vote in California and the adoption of prohibition.
76. Ostrander, *op. cit.*, pp. 65–7. For a modern association of settlers from Europe with the 'drinking customs learned in their days across the ocean', see G. C. Howard, *The Woman's Crusade: Forerunner of the W.C.T.U.* (WCTU pamphlet, no details), p. 4.
77. Vol. 14(43), 31 October 1889; see also Vol. 14(39), 3 October 1889.
78. See *California Voice* reprinting a pro-suffrage article from the *Modesto News*, Vol. 38(36), 3 September 1908, p. 12; also *Winning Equal Suffrage in California*, p. 102.
79. Alice Park to Mrs Severance on the insensitivity of club-women she knew towards the club janitor, a Socialist—'if they had thought of him, a man who couldn't speak plain English, they would have scorned him. While he is far more advanced than they are, and knows it!', 29 May 1908, in Box 22, Severance Collection. Among California suf-

fragists Mrs Park, Mrs Severance, Charlotte Whitney, Maud Younger, Gail Laughlin, Laura de Force Gordon and Elizabeth Geberding were all progressive in their politics. See also *Winning Equal Suffrage in California*, p. 102. On contemporary fears of Socialism advancing as a result of women's suffrage, see article of 13 October 1911, in *Pasadena Daily News*, Harbert Collection, Folder 3. Also in Harbert Collection, Box 10, File 143, see note of 1 September 1911 to the effect that the Socialist Party was campaigning actively for women's suffrage.

80. *Winning Equal Suffrage in California*, p. 101, and Los Angeles *Tribune*, October 1911, pp. 1–2, in Harbert Collection, Folder 7; see, in same folder pamphlet by Maud Younger on 'Why Wage-Earning Women should Vote', which suggests that these women had to look after their own interests, and, unlike the rich, had to rely on their votes, not their influence; this applied even to the labour movement, 'where women are probably treated with greater courtesy than elsewhere'. Unsigned letter of 17 October 1911 in Harbert Collection, Box 10, file 143, also emphasizes the support of 'the working men'.
81. For a summary of the failings of the late nineteenth-century women's movement, see Paulson, *Women's Suffrage and Prohibition*, *op. cit.*, pp. 140–1.
82. Mrs Severance's opposition to militancy is alluded to and supported in letters to her from S. L. Avery, 21 February (no other date), Box 14 and Georgia Ferguson, 16 February 1912, Box 16, Severance Collection; in her biography (see Park Collection, Box 8, PK 7, pp. 25–6 and 102) Mrs Park recalled that California newspaper editors disapproved of militant tactics, but noted that the vote would not have been won without 'parades and soap-boxing and publicity demonstrations'. Unsigned letter of 17 October 1911 in Harbert Collection, Box 10, File 143, emphasizes the decision to 'act like *ladies* and to modestly ask the voters to vote for Woman Suffrage'. Curiously, many American feminists seem to have accepted the exaggerated male view of British suffragette behaviour, in which violent tactics were held to be the norm rather than the exception.
83. For a statement of the city problem, see Severance Collection, Box 17, letter from F. J. Garrison to Mrs Severance, 15 October 1911.
84. For the belief that this was the effect of women's efforts on their own behalf, see *Winning Equal Suffrage in California*, p. 106.
85. Solomons, *op. cit.*, pp. 12–13.
86. On this sympathy, see Alice Locke Park biography, pp. 23–4, in Park Collection, Box 8, PK 7. For the British situation, see B. Harrison, *op. cit.*, Chaps. 6–8; in Britain, however, despite their shortcomings, the 'antis' gained sympathy when some suffragettes resorted to violent tactics—see p. 147.
87. See articles by W. H. Wright in *The West-Coast Magazine*, Vol. 9(1), October 1910, pp. 591–2; George S. Patton, *ibid.*, Vol. 10(6), September 1911, pp. 689–701; and Patton *ibid.*, Vol. 11(1), October 1911, pp. 51–6. See also pamphlet by 'Veritas Vincit', entitled 'Don't Vote to Ruin California. Vote Against the Female Suffrage Amend-

ment. No One Can Exaggerate the Evils and Perils to the Nation of Female Franchise and Office Holding', in Folder 7, Harbert Collection; and summary of the arguments of the 'antis' in Solomons, *op. cit.*, pp. 44–51.

88. See testimony to the good effects of women's suffrage quoted in the *Pasadena Star*, 5 June 1911, extract in Folder 3 of Harbert Collection; Clifford Howard, 'Why Women Should be Given the Vote', pamphlet written for the Political Equality League, Folder 7 in *ibid.*: ex-judge Waldo M. York, 'Political Equality for Women', 1910 pamphlet in *ibid.*; Mrs S. A. Simons, president of the Political Equality League, 'Why Women Should Have the Privilege and Responsibility of the Ballot', 1911 pamphlet in *ibid.*; comments on the 'antis' in *Winning Equal Suffrage in California*, pp. 11, 23; *Woman's Journal*, Vol. 42, 26 August 1911, p. 256; Dunaway, *op. cit.*, pp. 124–5, 158, 160–2, 164, 177–8; testimony about the impact of the vote in Wyoming in Park Collection, PK 82; File 142, Box 10 of Harbert Collection, article on the reasons for the ballot, pp. 1–4; Mrs Harbert to Mrs Severance in Severance Collection, 3 March 1907, Box 18, and Mrs Severance to Mrs M. E. Hart, 7 March 1895, Box 26 in *ibid.*; fragment in Harbert Collection, Box 10, on military duty and the vote; and replies to the arguments of the 'antis' alluded to in Harbert Collection, File 43, Box 3.
89. Solomons, *op. cit.*, p. 58.
90. *Ibid.*, pp. 66–7.
91. Reda Davis, *op. cit.*, p. 146 especially, but also pp. 140–84; Alice Locke Park biography, 'The Influence of Women Voters in California' (1916), pp. 97–8, Park Collection, PK7.
92. For a discussion of the League see below, pp. 208–22.
93. The territory was Alaska; the nine states were Wyoming, Utah, Colorado, Idaho, Washington, California, Arizona, Kansas and Oregon. See article by David Morgan, Woman suffrage in Britain and America in the early twentieth century, in H. C. Allen and R. Thompson, eds, *Contrast and Connection, Bicentennial Essays in Anglo-American History* (London: G. Bell and Sons, 1976), pp. 275–6; Kraditor, *The Ideas of the Woman Suffrage Movement, op. cit.*, pp. 8–10 and Chap. 8; Flexner, *op. cit.*, Chaps. 19–21.
94. See Alice Park to K. Boyles, 18 June 1917, from Washington, DC, Anthony Family Collection, AF 54, Huntington Library; and Alice Locke Park biography, pp. 46–8, 51, PK7, Park Collection.
95. Theodore Roosevelt expressed the enlightened male view when he wrote to Ida Husted Harper: 'Winning the War is the great issue—and all patriotic women will put it far ahead of woman suffrage, just as I do, and I speak as an ardent suffragist.' 16 September 1918, HM 10727, in Harper Collection.
96. Alice Locke Parke biography, 'The influence of Women Voters in California', pp. 95–7, PK7, Park Collection.
97. Foltz to Park, 18 December 1923, PK33, Park Collection. See also Malecki and Mahood, *op. cit.*, p. 29.
98. See A. F. Scott, *op. cit.*, Chaps. 8 and 9.

99. See J. S. Lemons, *The Woman Citizen: Social Feminism in the 1920s* (Urbana: University of Illinois Press, 1973).
100. See Odegard, *op. cit.*, Chaps. 6 and 8; Paulson, *Women's Suffrage and Prohibition*, *op. cit.*, pp. 157–61, 165–8, 173.
101. See Gusfield, *op. cit.*, Chap. 5, and Social structure and moral reform: a study of the Woman's Christian Temperance Union. *American Journal of Sociology*, Vol. 61(2), 1955, pp. 221–32; and current WCTU *Catechism and Principles* (Evanston, Ill.: Signal Press, n.d.), p. 6.
102. See Hays, *op. cit.*, *passim*; WCTU Annual Convention, Los Angeles, California. September 4–*8, 1970*, pp. 48–50; H. E. Tyler, *Where Prayer and Purpose Meet: The W.C.T.U. Story, 1874–1949* (Evanston, Ill.: Signal Press, 1949), pp. 251–67; *What is the W.C.T.U.?, op. cit.*, pp. 10–11; WCTU pamphlet, *A Line or Two about the W.C.T.U.*; and article by the current president of the Union, Mrs Herman Stanley, in *The Union Signal*, Vol. 101(9), September 1975, pp. 7–12. By this time the Union claimed some 10,000 local branches throughout the states, territories and insular possessions of the United States.
103. See Hays, *op. cit.*, pp. 112–13.
104. See *What is the W.C.T.U.? op. cit.*, p. 9; Hays, *op. cit.*, p. 60.
105. 2 June 1923, p. 124, leader.
106. *Equal Rights*, 20 September 1922 and 20 October 1923, p. 286.
107. See *ibid.*, 28 July 1923, p. 188, and 1 September 1923.
108. *Equal Rights*, 19 May 1923, p. 109; 6 October 1923, leader; 20 October 1923, p. 285; and 22 December 1923, pp. 358–9.
109. Carrie Chapman Catt to K. Boyles, 3 May 1925, New York, AF 35, Anthony Family Collection.
110. See Lemons, *op. cit.*, p. 199ff.
111. For a discussion of this movement and other key developments relevant to the inter-war years, see, in addition to Lemons, K. A. Yellis, Prosperity's child: some thoughts on the flapper. *American Quarterly*, 21, Spring 1969, pp. 44–64; W. L. O'Neill, *Everyone Was Brave: The Rise and Fall of Feminism in America* (Chicago: Quadrangle, 1969), Chaps. 7–9; W. H. Chafe, *The American Woman: Her Changing Social, Economic, and Political Roles, 1920–1970* (New York: Oxford University Press, 1972), Part One; June Sochen, ed., *The New Feminism in Twentieth Century America* (Lexington, Mass.: D. C. Heath, 1971); A. Kraditor, ed., *Up From the Pedestal: Selected Writings in the History of American Feminism* (Chicago: Quadrangle, 1968); J. C. Burnham, The progressive era revolution in American attitudes toward sex. *J.A.H.*, Vol. 59(4), 1973, pp. 885–908; E. B. Freedman, The new woman: changing views of women in the 1920s. *Ibid.*, Vol. 61(2), 1974, pp. 372–93; A. F. Scott, After suffrage: southern women in the twenties. *J.S.H.*, Vol. 30(3), 1964, pp. 298–318; W. H. Chafe, Sex and Race: The Analogy of Social Control, *The Massachusetts Review*, Vol. 18(1), 1972, pp. 147–76; and D. J. Pivar, *Purity Crusade: Sexual Morality and Social Control, 1868–1900* (Westport, Conn.: Greenwood Press, 1973).
112. *The Home* (New York: McClure Phillips, 1903).

113. For a typical expression of feminist faith in the Republican party, combined with impatience about what it was actually doing, see Ida Husted Harper to Theodore Roosevelt, 11 September 1918, HM 10726, in Harper Collection; and on 22 October 1918, HM 10728, and 31 October 1918, HM 10729, in *ibid*.
114. See M. Gruberg, *Women in American Politics: An Assessment and Source Book* (Oshkosh, Wis.: Academia Press, 1968).

Chapter 6

1. See above, pp. 195–204.
2. See, for example, the articles quoted in Freedom for the second sex. In George Mowry, ed., *The Twenties: Fords, Flappers and Fanatics* (Englewood Cliffs, N.J.: Prentice-Hall, 1963), pp. 173.
3. F. L. Allen, *Only Yesterday* (Harmondsworth: Penguin, 1938), pp. 132–3.
4. Quoted in *Forty Years of a Great Idea* (League of Women Voters of the United States, Washington, n.d.), p. 11.
5. *Ibid*., p. 11.
6. *Ibid*., p. 11. By this time Mrs Catt felt that the League must be forward-looking, i.e., in advance of the thinking in the political parties on these issues.
7. *Ibid*., p. 27.
8. Cf. J. Stanley Lemons, *The Woman Citizen: Social Feminism in the 1920s*, *op. cit*., *passim*.
9. Lois W. Banner, *Women in Modern America: a Brief History* (New York: Harcourt Brace Jovanovich, 1974), p. 134.
10. See H. S. Commager, *Documents of American History* (New York: Appleton Century Crofts, 1958), pp. 788–9.
11. *Forty Years of a Great Idea*, *op. cit*., pp. 46–7.
12. Interview material.
13. See, for example, Alec Barbrook, *God Save the Commonwealth: An Electoral History of Massachusetts op. cit*., Chap. 7.
14. *The Proposed Reduction in the Size of the Massachusetts House: A Factual Analysis Prepared by the Office of Speaker John T. X. Davoren* (duplicated by the Massachusetts League, n.d.).
15. *Statement of the League of Women Voters of Massachusetts in support of Bill H3766 presented before the Joint Judiciary Committee of the Great and General Court, March 11th, 1968* (duplicated).
16. *Christian Science Monitor*, 7 November 1974.
17. From a leaflet entitled 'Illinois Needs a Constitutional Convention' (League of Women Voters of Illinois, n.d.).
18. *Sixth Illinois Constitutional Convention, Address to the People adopted by the Convention, September 7, 1970*, p. 1.
19. League of Women Voters of Illinois, 'Organizing a Community Committee in Support of the Proposed Illinois Constitution' (LWV pamphlet, September 1970).

20. From Tax Pack No. 1, a leaflet entitled 'Does Business Pay its Fair Share of Florida Taxes?' (May 1971).
21. Interview material, July 1972.
22. James Ryan, *St Petersburg Times*, 15 July 1970.
23. *League of Women Voters of California, 1973–75 State Program* (San Francisco, August 1974), p. 2.
24. Air Quality/Transportation Action Kit (San Francisco: League of Women Voters of California, August 1974), p. 3.
25. Interview material, June 1975.
26. *The Report of the Findings of the League Self-Study* (Washington: League of Women Voters, 1974), p. iii. In 1976 the total membership of the League was 140,000 (*including 4000 men*); from 'Facts', published by the League of Women Voters, n.d.).
27. *Ibid*., p. 12.
28. *Ibid*., p. iii.
29. Banner, *op. cit*., p. 234. See Jo Freeman, *The Politics of Women's Liberation* (N.Y. and London: Longman, 1975), Chap. 3, for a detailed history of the early years of NOW.
30. This figure was that claimed by a NOW spokesman. Other sources put the figure lower, perhaps as low as 40,000 in 1975. On the other hand, by 1979, NOW was claiming a membership close to 100,000.
31. Quoted in a 1975 United States Information Services pamphlet, 'Focus on Women: the New Awakening'.
32. Bernice Sandler, 'The Day WEAL Opened Pandora's Box,' reprinted by WEAL from the *Chronicle of Higher Education*, VII (16), 22 January 1973.
33. *Christian Science Monitor*, November 1974.
34. *Women's Political Times*, Vol. 2(1), Winter 1977, p. 6. Comment by Audrey Rower Colom, Chairperson, NWPC.
35. NWPC *Newsletter*, Vol. 4(3), April 1975, p. 4.
36. Mancur Olson, *The Logic of Collective Action, op. cit., passim.*
37. At random the list includes such groups as: American Association of University Women; American Nurses Association; Federally Employed Women; National Association of Women Deans and Counselors; National Federation of Business and Professional Women; Women United.

Chapter 7

1. David Loth, *Public Plunder: A History of Graft in America* (New York: Carrick and Evans, 1938), p. 12.
2. *Ibid*., p. 215.
3. Frank Mason Stewart, *A Half Century of Municipal Reform* (Berkeley and Los Angeles: University of California Press1950), p. 10.
4. For example, see Leo Hershkowitz, *Tweed's New York* (New York: Doubleday, 1977).
5. Lincoln Steffens, *The Shame of the Cities* (New York: McClure, Phillips, 1904), p. 195.

6. Stewart, *op. cit.*, p. 50.
7. Melvin G. Holli, *Reform in Detroit; Hazen S. Pingree and Urban Politics* (New York: Oxford University Press, 1969).
8. Robert K. Merton, *Social Theory and Social Structure* (New York: Free Press, 1949, 1957), pp. 71–2.
9. Richard Hofstadter, Introduction to *The Progressive Movement 1900–1915* (Englewood Cliffs, N.J.: Prentice-Hall, 1963), p. 9.
10. Richard Hofstadter, *The Age of Reform*, *op. cit.*, p. 185.
11. Arthur A. Ekirch Jr, *Progressivism in America* (New York: New Viewpoints, 1974), p. 260.
12. Stuart Chase, *Democracy Under Pressure* (New York: Twentieth Century Fund, 1945), pp. 16–17.
13. *Ibid.*, p. 24.
14. Wm. E. Leuchtenburg, *Franklin D. Roosevelt and the New Deal, 1932–1940* (New York: Evanston; London: Harper and Row, 1963), p. 88.
15. *New York Times*, 27 November 1944, p. 24.
16. Colston E. Warne, Consumer action Programs of the Consumers Union of the US. In R. M. Gaedeke and W. W. Etcheson, eds, *Consumerism* (San Francisco: Canfield Press, 1972), p. 99.
17. See Grant S. McLellan, ed., *The Consuming Public* (New York: H. H. Wilson, 1968), pp. 198–9.
18. For example, see James Reichley, *States in Crisis* (Chapel Hill: University of N. Carolina Press, 1964); Robert S. Allen, ed., *Our Sovereign State* (New York: Vanguard Press, 1949).
19. Mark V. Nadel, *The Politics of Consumer Protection* (Indianapolis, New York: Bobbs-Merrill,), p. 32.
20. *Ibid.*, pp. 36–43.
21. Nader was not the first person to advocate this approach to highway safety. Daniel Patrick Moynihan (who employed Nader briefly to research into the subject when Moynihan was Assistant Secretary for Labor), Dr William Huddon and others were also writing along the same lines in the early sixties. See Charles McCarry, *Citizen Nader* (London: Jonathan Cape, 1972), Chap. 4.
22. Ralph Nader, *Unsafe at Any Speed* (New York: Grossman Publishers, 1965), pp. 332–3.
23. See Thomas Whiteside, *The Investigation of Ralph Nader* (New York: Arbor House, 1972), *passim*.
24. Thomas Whiteside, Profiles: a countervailing force, I. *New Yorker*, 8 October 1973.
25. From Meet Ralph Nader: everyman's lobbyist and his consumer crusade. *Newsweek*, 22 January 1968.
26. Ralph Nader, 'A Citizen's Guide to the American Economy' in *New York Review of Books*, 2 September 1971.
27. Ralph Nader, The great American gyp. In David A. Aaker and George S. Day, *Consumerism: Search for the Consumer Interest* (New York: Free Press, 1971), p. 58 (reprinted from the *New York Review of Books*).
28. Whiteside, Profiles: a countervailing force. *op. cit.*, pp. 66–7.

29. M. Barone, G. Ugifusa and D. Matthews, *The Almanac of American Politics 1976* (New York: E. P. Dutton, 1975), p. 891.
30. Statement of Senator Abe Ribicoff (D., Conn.), introducing the CPA, 1977 (duplicated sheet, Washington, April, 1977).
31. *Public Citizen*, Issue 3, 1976, p. 3.
32. Susan Gross, The Nader network. *Business and Society Review*, Issue 13, Spring 1975, p. 5.
33. Charles McCarry, *Citizen Nader* (London: Jonathan Cape, 1972), p. 184.
34. See, for example, *The Chemical Feast* (1970); *The Closed Enterprise System* (1972); *The Interstate Commerce Commission* (1970); *The Water Lords* (1971); *Vanishing Air* (1970); all published by Grossman Publishers and Bantam Books.
35. See Fred Riggs, *Administration in Developing Countries* (Boston: Houghton Mifflin, 1964), *passim*.
36. From a leaflet entitled 'Nuclear Power: Silent Dangers, Hidden Costs' (Critical Mass 75, Washington, DC, 1976).
37. See Jack Anderson, Student activism: idealism is not dead. *Washington Post*, 22 September 1974; also Peter Reich, Success on a shoestring. *Juris Doctor*, (MBA Communications Inc., N.Y.), July/August 1975,
38. Samuel M. Loescher, Student public interest groups: educational internships for responsible, active citizenship. (PIRG reprint: originally in *Indiana Business Review*, August/September. 1972).
39. Mark J. Green, James M. Fallows, David R. Zwick, *Who Runs Congress?* (New York: Bantam Books, 1972). Additional information obtained from interviews in Washington, April 1977. Also see Paul L. Leventhal, Nader's study of Congress sparks controversy on hill. *National Journal*, Vol. 4(39), 23 September 1972, pp. 1483–95.
40. Joe Klein and Ralph Nader, The man in the class action suit. *Rolling Stone*, 20 November 1975, reprinted pp. 1–11.
41. Letter to the writer dated 25 May 1977, written by Ruth C. Fort, Centre for Study of Responsive Law.
42. From Ralph Nader faces the nation's business, an address to the National Consumber Assembly, Washington, DC, November 1967, given by Ralph Nader. In McLellan *op. cit*.
43. John W. Gardner, in Helen Rowan, ed., *No Easy Victories*, (New York, Evanston, London: Harper and Row, 1968), p. 145.
44. John W. Gardner, *The Recovery of Confidence* (New York: W. W. Norton, 1970), p. 69.
45. John W. Gardner, *In Common Cause* (New York: W. W. Norton, 1972), p. 73.
46. *Ibid*., p. 15.
47. For example, the Urban Coalition was such an organization under 501(c)(3) of the I.R. Code, while Common Cause, as a lobby, came under 501(c)(4).
48. John Gardner, Pre-history of common cause (duplicated memorandum, August 1976).
49. Gardner, *In Common Cause*, *op. cit*., p. 17.

50. *Common Cause Report from Washington*, Vol. 4(4), March 1974.
51. *Common Cause Report from Washington*, Vol. 5(4), March 1975.
52. Thomas B. Edsall, Ethics-code advocates gain new status *Sun*, 13 March 1977.
53. Interview material, Washington, April 1977.
54. From a Common Cause pamphlet, 1977.
55. Allen H. Center, *Public Relations Practices—Case Study 24: Organizing a Citizens' Lobby* (Englewood Cliffs, N.J.: Prentice-Hall, 1975).
56. David S. Broder, Elitist people's lobby *Boston Sunday Globe*, 24 April 1977, p. A7.
57. There are four full-time lobbyists and seventy-five other 'professionals' in Washington, *New York Times*, 16 February 1977.
58. Norman C. Miller, Common Cause's growing muscle. *Wall Street Journal*, 10 April 1974,
59. *Common Cause Report from Washington*, Vol. 6(4), March 1976.
60. From interviews and literature obtained in the states cited, 1975 and 1977.
61. John Gardner, quoted by Elizabeth Drew in *New Yorker*, 23 July 1973,
62. *New York Times*, 16 February 1977,
63. *Consumer Federation of America News*, Washington, DC, February–March 1977.
64. *New Directions Special Report* (Washington DC, January 1977).
65. J. M. Berry, *Lobbying for the People: The Political Behaviour of Public Interest Groups op. cit.*, pp. 13–16.

Chapter 8

1. Oscar Handlin, *The Uprooted op. cit.*, p. 217.
2. Yates v. United States, 1957. See, for example, Leo Pfeffer, *This Honorable Court* (Boston: Beacon Press, 1965), pp. 396–7. The Court, by now under Chief Justice Earl Warren, argued that the Smith Act did not prohibit the teaching and advocacy of the forcible overthrow of government as an *abstract principle* but only prohibited the support of *concrete action* for this end. This was possible in 1957 because of the relatively liberal attitudes of the Warren Court and also because the anti-communist hysteria of the early fifties had subsided.
3. Christopher Lasch, *The Agony of the American Left* (London: Pelican Books, 1973), pp. 18–19.
4. A. J. Beitzinger, *A History of American Political Thought* (New York: Dodd, Mead, 1972), Chap. 25, *passim*.
5. *Ibid.*, p. 596. As a further irony, it should be pointed out that much of the American pragmatic tradition in political science draws on the inspiration of Max Weber and on the Central European Positivist school of thought.
6. Daniel Bell, *The End of Ideology: On the Exhaustion of Political Ideas in The Fifties* (New York: Free Press, 1960), p. 402.
7. *Ibid.*, p. 404.

8. Michael Novak, An end of ideology. In Chaim J. Waxman, *The end of Ideology Debate* (New York: Simon and Schuster, 1968), p. 389.
9. Frederick W. Obear, 'Student Activism in the Sixties', in Julian Foster and Durwood Long, eds, *Protest: Student Activism in America* (New York: William Morrow, 1970), p. 17.
10. Alexander Werth, *America in Doubt* (London: Robert Hale, 1959), pp. 8–9.
11. Shoben, Werdell and Long, Radical student organizations. In Foster and Long, *op. cit.*, p. 217.
12. Stokely Carmichael and Charles V. Hamilton, *Black Power* (Harmondsworth: Penguin, 1967, 1968), p. 61.
13. Howard Zinn, *SNCC: The New Abolitionists op. cit.*, *passim*. Also see above, esp. pp. 146–7.
14. William R. O'Neill, *Coming Apart; An Informal History of America in the 1960s* (Chicago: Quadrangle, 1971), p. 337.
15. See, for example, Sheldon Wolin and John Schaar, Berkeley: the battle of the people's park. *New York Review of Books*, 19 June 1969,
16. George Kennan, *Democracy and the Student Left* (Boston: Little, Brown, 1968), p. 193.
17. Alan Adelson, *SDS* (New York: Charles Scribner's Sons, 1972), pp. 203–5. Some authorities date the emergence of SDS as 1960–1.
18. Adelson, *op. cit.*, p. 203.
19. E. Joseph Shoben, Philip Wardell, Durwood Long, Radical student organizations. In Foster and Long, *op. cit.*, pp. 208–10. The techniques involved in ERAP included the settlement of a group of field workers in a slum community (Newark, NJ, was one such), the study by them of the major social problems and an attempt to press programmes of reform on the city authorities. Although short-lived, the programme did have some success in these communities.
20. Adelson, *op. cit.*, p. 221.
21. Daniel Bell, Columbia and the new left. In Daniel Bell and Irving Kristol, *Confrontation: The Student Rebellion and the Universities* (New York: Basic Books, 1968), p. 101.
22. Norman Mailer, *Miami and the Siege of Chicago* (New York: Signet Books, 1968), p. 134.
23. David English, *Divided They Stand*, (London: Michael Joseph, 1969), p. 322.
24. Stuart Daniels, The Weathermen. *Government and Opposition*, Vol. 9(4), Autumn 1974, pp. 430–59.
25. Daniels, *op. cit.*, *passim*. As is well known, the organization took its name from Bob Dylan's line You don't need a weatherman to know which way the wind blows ('Subterranean Homesick Blues').
26. Seymour Martin Lipset and Earl Raab, *The Politics of Unreason*, *op. cit.*, p. 3.
27. *Ibid.*, p. 3.
28. Oscar Glantz, New left radicalism and punitive moralism. *Polity*, Vol. 8(3), Spring 1975, pp. 281–303.

29. Joseph R. Starobin, *American Communism in Crisis, 1943–1957* (Cambridge, Mass.: Harvard University Press, 1972), p. xiii.
30. It has been argued that prosperity fuelled the radicalism and 'counter culture' of the 1960s. To many, it seemed that the 'end of scarcity' had been reached in the West and that 'with the resources of technology, absolute equality had ceased to be an impossible goal or a utopian value.' Cf. David Bouchier, *Idealism and Revolution* (London: Edward Arnold, 1978), p. 7. With the onset of the energy crisis, the 'end of scarcity' now seems almost a pipe-dream.

Chapter 9

1. See Lyndon B. Johnson, *The Vantage Point: Perspectives of the Presidency, 1963–1969* (New York: Popular Library, 1971), Chap. 18, *passim*, and Bouchier, *Idealism and Revolution, op. cit.*, pp. 6, 79–80, 175–8; Bouchier notes, however, the mushrooming of the radical press.
2. Quoted in *New Society*, 29 June 1978, p. 699. See also article on the Panthers in *Sunday Times*, 30 July 1978.
3. Brian Barry, *Sociologists, Economists and Democracy* (London: Collier-Macmillan, 1970), p. 47; see also Mancur Olson Jr, *The Logic of Collective Action*, *op. cit.*, *passim*.
4. Matthew A. Crenson, *The Un-Politics of Air Pollution: A Study of Non-Decisionmaking in the Cities* (Baltimore and London: Johns Hopkins Press, 1971), esp. p. 165.
5. Berry, *Lobbying for the People, op. cit., passim.*
6. *See T. R. Reid*, Public trust, private money. *Washington Post Magazine*, 26 November 1978, pp. 12–20, 25, 28–31.
7. Arthur Woodstone, The consumer army: rebels with a cause. *Washington Post Parade*, 12 November 1978, pp. 10–12; also Reid, *op. cit.*, p. 15.
8. *The Washington Lobby* (Washington, Congressional Quarterly Inc., 1974, 2nd edn), p. 10.
9. *Congressional Quarterly Guide to Current American Government* (Washington, Congressional Quarterly Inc., Fall 1977), pp. 90–1.
10. See The swarming lobbyists. *Time*, Vol. 112(6), 7 August 1978, pp. 19, 21–3.
11. *Ibid.*, pp. 19–20.
12. *The Washington Lobby*, *op. cit.*, p. 37.
13. *Ibid.*, p. 38
14. *Congressional Quarterly Weekly Report*, Vol. 36(17), 29 April 1973, pp. 1027–8.
15. Virginia Held, *The Public Interest and Individual Interest* (New York: Basic Books, 1970), p. 176.
16. James Q. Wilson, *Political Organizations* (New York: Basic Books, 1973), p. 345.
17. *Ibid.*

18. Robert Dahl, *A Preface to Democratic Theory, op. cit.*, and other writings by this author.
19. See, for example, David S. Broder, *The Party's Over* (New York: Harper and Row, 1971); Abbott and Rogowsky, eds, *Political Parties* (Chicago: Rand McNally, 1978); Chambers and Burham, eds, *The American Party System* (New York: Oxford University Press, 1975); Wootton, *Pressure Groups in Britain, op. cit.*, pp. 101–4.
20. Todd Gitlin, Local pluralism as theory and ideology. In C. A. McCoy and J. Playfoot, eds, *Apolitical Politics* (New York: T. Y. Crowell, 1967), pp. 124–45.
21. Quoted in Fishel and Quarles, *The Black American, op. cit.*, pp. 287–9; for a complaint about the power of special interests in Washington, see Carter's major energy speech of July 1979, quoted in *The Guardian*, 25 July 1979, p. 19.
22. See *PUSH*, January 1978, article on Minorities and the media, pp. 85–7; and D. G. Garrow, *Protest at Selma, Martin Luther King Jr., and the Voting Rights Act of 1965* (New Haven: Yale University Press, 1978), on the crucial need for media and public support.
23. See National Indian Youth Council Statement on 'Congressional Legislation', April 1978.
24. See article entitled, Bakke bomb. PUSH, *op. cit.*, p. 38 and *passim*.
25. See Parren Mitchell, The economic crisis. *PUSH*, *op. cit.*, p. 31.
26. See Warren Brown, Black, Hispanic Groups to Cooperate on Goals, in *Washington Post*, 14 November 1978, Section A, p. 9; John A. Morsell, Ethnic Relations of the Future, in *The Annals of the American Academy*, Vol. 408, July 1973, pp. 83–93; and J. Higham, in *Ethnic Leadership in America, op. cit.*, pp. 11–12.
27. For a discussion of these texts which argues for a three-dimensional view of power, see Steven Lukes, *Power. A Radical View* (London: Macmillan, 1974); for earlier important work, see R. Dahl, *Who Governs?* (New Haven: Yale University Press, 1961); N. Polsby, *Community Power and Political Theory* (New Haven: Yale University Press, 1963); P. Bachrach and M. S. Baratz, The two faces of power. *A.P.S.R.*, Vol. 56, 1962, pp. 947–52; and *ibid.*, Decisions and non-decisions: an analytical framework. *A.P.S.R.*, Vol. 57, 1963, pp. 641–51.
28. See comments of Cal Noel, NCAI spokesman, in *C.Q.*, 2 December 1978, p. 3388.
29. See Meier and Rudwick, eds, *Along the Color Line, op. cit.*, p. 5.
30. See article on Baraka by Hollie I. West in *Rochester Democrat and Chronicle*, 12 July 1978, Section C, pp. 1–2: I am indebted for this reference to Professor Stanley Engerman; and *Hustler*, January 1978, p. 87.
31. See Arthur T. Hadley's article, The Rich, Happy, Educated Non-voter, in *Washington Post*, 12 November 1978, Section B, pp. 1, 4; see also R. Dahl, *Who Governs?, op. cit.*, Chap. 25; B. R. Berelson, P. F. Lazarsfeld and W. M. McPhee, *Voting* (Chicago: University of Chicago Press, 1954).
32. On the organization of behaviour in one slum community, see William

F. Whyte's classic, *Street-Corner Society* (Chicago: University of Chicago Press, 1943). The discussion of the problems of community organizations has been influenced by Michael Parenti's article Power and pluralism: a view from the bottom. In M. Surkin and A. Wolfe, eds, *The End to Political Science: The Caucus Papers* (New York: Basic Books, 1970), pp. 111–43; and by P. Bachrach and M. S. Baratz, *Power and Poverty: Theory and Practice* (New York: Oxford University Press, 1970).

33. See E. Banfield, *The Unheavenly City: The Nature and Future of our Urban Crisis* (Boston: Little, Brown, 1970).
34. See article in *PUSH*, *op. cit.*, pp. 6, 12 and *passim*.
35. See The State of the Indian Nation, a special report by Charles Raisch for *Hustler, op. cit.*, pp. 85–6.
36. See Wootton, *Pressure Groups in Britain*, *op. cit.*, General introduction, Interpretation, and pp. 75–98, for points about the British situation influencing this section; P. Hollis, ed., *Pressure from Without, op. cit.*, An introduction.
37. See The swarming lobbyists. *Op. cit.*, pp. 19–24.
38. See Pole, *The Search for Equality in American History, op. cit.*, esp. Chaps. 2 and 3.
39. See D. Truman, *The Governmental Process, op. cit.*, and R. Salisbury, An exchange theory of interest groups. *Midwest Journal of Political Science*, Vol. 13, February 1969, pp. 1–32.
40. See Samuel P. Huntington, Post industrial politics: how benign will it be? *Comparative Politics*, Vol. 6(2), January 1974, pp. 163–91; and Bouchier, *op. cit.*, Chap. 1.
41. Irving Louis Horowitz in I. L. Horowitz and S. M. Lipset, *Dialogues on American Politics* (New York: Oxford University Press, 1978), p. 42.

Index